Bangladesh

The Next Afghanistan?

aph beg
..', the
e are fe
a c   .' has be
credit   a Bhasha
re ac   a by Fazl
en he   ited Fro

pertai   text on
e), refe   n Das'
'engal   Delhi:
iversity ess, 199

ons

Bangladesh

The Next Afghanistan?

Hiranmay Karlekar

SAGE Publications
New Delhi • Thousand Oaks • London

First published in 2005 by

Sage Publications India Pvt Ltd
B-42, Panchsheel Enclave
New Delhi 110 017
www.indiasage.com

Sage Publications Inc **Sage Publications Ltd**
2455 Teller Road   1 Oliver's Yard, 55 City Road
Thousand Oaks, California 91320   London EC1Y 1SP

Published by Tejeshwar Singh for Sage Publications India Pvt Ltd, photo-typeset in 10/12 pt Calisto MT by Star Compugraphics Private Limited, Delhi and printed at Chaman Enterprises, New Delhi.

Library of Congress Cataloging-in-Publication Data

Karlekar, Hiranmay, 1938–
    Bangladesh, the next Afghanistan?/Hiranmay Karlekar.
        p. cm.
    Includes index.
    1. Islamic fundamentalism—Bangladesh. 2. Islam and politics—Bangladesh. 3. Religion and politics—Bangladesh. 4. Bangladesh—Politics and government. I. Title.

BP63.B3K37   320.5'57095492—dc22   2005   2005028035

ISBN: 0–7619–3401–4 (Pb)   81–7829–552–0 (India–Pb)

Sage Production Team: Rrishi Raote, Sanjeev Sharma, Girish Sharma and Santosh Rawat

In memory of my mother Kalyani Karlekar
and my adoptive father, Govind Vinayak Karlekar,
the finest man I have known

Contents

Acknowledgements

Every book requires a certain environment to be written, one in which the author can concentrate on his work without too many distractions. I had such an environment at home thanks to my wife Malavika who, despite her own writing and numerous professional commitments, saw to it that I could sit undisturbed in front of the computer as long as I needed to. My son Indraneel and daughter Kamini contributed with words of encouragement across the oceans and, from time to time, with reminders that I did not have a decade to complete the book. And of course, the three tail-wagging quadruped members of the family—Senior Dog Zorba, now in his 14th year; the prima donna, Bijli; and the perennially effusive Lara—provided relief and affectionate interludes whenever my fatigued brain could no longer churn out arguments and sentences.

I am also grateful to Chandan Mitra, editor of the *Pioneer* for being unfailingly supportive of all my ventures, ranging from efforts to ensure humane treatment to India's stray dogs to attending meetings of the Press Council of India and seminars, photography expeditions and, of course, the writing of this book. I am also thankful to several of my other colleagues for their courtesy and cooperation and, particularly, to Colvin Massey of the *Pioneer* library, for providing me with a wide range of clippings, often at very short notice.

Shahriar Kabir, well-known author and journalist, who fought in Bangladesh's liberation war in 1971 and has since then striven tirelessly to uphold its secular and democratic values, despite relentless persecution, imprisonment and torture, has given me blanket permission to quote from his works. I am grateful to him not only for this but also for his insights into—and comments on—developments in Bangladesh since liberation. I am also grateful to him for ensuring my participation in the 'European Human Rights Conference on Bangladesh: Extremism, Intolerance and Violence', held at the School of Oriental and African Studies, London, on 17 June 2005, and to Lord Eric Avebury for inviting me to the conference. I must also thank Sujit Sen and Ansar Ahmed Ullah for making arrangements for my travel to London.

Thanks are due to Mr K.P.S. Gill and Dr Ajai Sahni of the Institute of Conflict Management for not only sending issues of *Faultlines* which I needed to read literally within hours' notice but also for providing urgently-needed references without fail.

My friend Wg Cdr (Retd) Mohammad Yusuf Khan kindly agreed to have a look at parts of Chapter One to make sure that my references to the teachings of Islam did not contain bloomers. I thank him for this and for generally helping me to understand India's Islamic tradition. On several occasions, Dipanjan Roy Chaudhury, Delhi correspondent of Bangladesh's widely-circulated Bengali language daily, *Prothom Alo*, provided me with useful information and comments on current events in that country. Thanks are due to him as well as to Priya Viswanath for constant support.

I must thank Omita Goyal for initiating the process of publishing this book when she was Acquisitions Editor for Sage; Rrishi Raote, for painstakingly going through the manuscript, correcting literals and suggesting changes; Mimi Choudhury, the present Commissioning Editor at Sage for being patient and long-suffering while I laboured to ensure that the book, though on current affairs, did have a reasonably long shelf life and contained the latest information that was possible to incorporate. I must also thank Tejeshwar Singh, Sunanda Ghosh and Ritu Vajpeyi-Mohan for bringing out the book a remarkably short time after I finished writing it.

Three Bangladeshi friends of mine have provided valuable references for this book but have requested anonymity as they already face serious threats to their lives from Islamist extremists. I hope to thank them publicly some day when terror does not stalk the lives of Bangladeshi writers, intellectuals, secular politicians and journalists. Meanwhile, I must put on record my profound admiration for the courage and resolution with which institutions of Bangladesh's civil society, intelligentsia, journalists and newspapers are resisting the violent onslaught of religious fundamentalism and standing up for secular, humanist and democratic values. It has few parallels in recent history.

In conclusion, I must confess that I and I alone am responsible for all translations from Bengali to English, whether from books or newspapers, used in this book. While translating, particularly complex polemical pieces and ideological expositions, it is most difficult to convey subtle nuances and shades of meaning. In my effort to retain the sense of the original Bengali as faithfully as possible, I have given precedence to authenticity over linguistic elegance and idiomatic correctness. As a result there are sentences that do not read too well. For this, and for some of the errors that may have crept in despite my best efforts, I apologize in advance. The fault in respect of these would be mine and mine alone.

List of Organizations

AASU	All-Assam Students Union
AGP	Asom Gana Parishad
AHAB	Ahle Hadith Andolan Bangladesh
AHIF	Al-Haramain Islamic Foundation
AHJS	Ahle Hadith Juba Sangha
AIAPC	Anti-Islamic Activities Prevention Committee
ARNO	Arakan Rohingya National Organisation
ASC	Afghan Support Committee
ATTF	All-Tripura Tiger Force
BAC	Bureau of Anti-Corruption
BCL	Bangladesh Chhatra League
BDB	Bikalpa Dhara Bangladesh
BDR	Bangladesh Rifles
BMTA	Bangladesh Madrassa Teachers' Association
BNP	Bangladesh Nationalist Party
BPC	Constitutional Basic Principles Committee
Brac	Bangladesh Rural Advancement Committee
BRO	Border Roads Organisation
BSF	Border Security Force
BSS	Bangladesh Sangbad Sanstha
CAD	Covert Action Division
CCC	Chittagong City Corporation
CIA	Central Intelligence Agency
CID	Criminal Investigation Department
CMP	Chittagong Metropolitan Police
CPI(M)	Communist Party of India (Marxist)
CPJ	Committee to Protect Journalists
CPWD	Central Public Works Department
DGFI	Directorate General of Forces Intelligence
DRU	Dhaka Reporters' Unity
DUTA	Dhaka University Teachers' Association

EOKA	Ethniki Organosis Kyrion Agoniston
FBI	Federal Bureau of Investigation
FCB	Film Censor Board
HI	Hayatul Igachha
HM	Hizbul Mujahideen
HUJIB	Harkat-ul-Jihad-al-Islami Bangladesh
HuM	Harkat-ul Mujahideen
IIFS	International Islamic Federation of Students
IIFSO	International Islamic Federation of Student Organisations
IIRO	Islamic International Relief Organisation
IKNMB	International Khatme Nabuwat Movement Bangladesh
IOJ	Islami Oikya Jote
IRCON	Indian Railways Construction Corporation
ISI	Inter-Services Intelligence Bureau
Jamaat	Jamaat-e-Islami Bangladesh
JeM	Jaish-e-Mohammad
JCD	Jatiyatabadi Chhatra Dal
JJD	Jatiyatabadi Jubo Dal
JKLF	Jammu and Kashmir Liberation Front
JMJB	Jagrata Muslim Janata Bangladesh
JOM	Jatiya Oikya Mancha
KPP	Krishak Praja Party
LeT	Lashkar-e-Toiba
MULTA	Muslim United Liberation Tigers of Assam
NBCC	National Building Construction Corporation
NBR	National Board of Revenue
NDA	National Democratic Alliance
NDFB	National Democratic Front of Bodoland
NLFT	National Liberation Front of Tripura
NSCN(I-M)	National Socialist Council of Nagalim (Isak–Muivah)
NSI	National Security Intelligence
PBCP	Purba Banglar Communist Party
PCJSS	Parbatya Chattargam Jana Sanhati Samiti
PFLP	Popular Front for the Liberation of Palestine
PLA	People's Liberation Army
PLO	Palestine Liberation Organization

PMO	Prime Minister's Office
RAB	Rapid Action Battalion
Rabita	Rabita Al-Alam Al-Islami
RIHS	Revival of Islamic Heritage Society
RSO	Rohingya Solidarity Organisation
SAH	Shahadat al-Hiqma
Shangha	Islami Chhatra Shangha
SCBA	Bangladesh Supreme Court Bar Association
Shibir	Islami Chhatra Shibir
SIMI	Students' Islamic Movement of India
ULFA	United Liberation Front of Asom
UNLF	United National Liberation Front
UPA	United Progressive Alliance
WAMY	World Assembly of Muslim Youth
World Islamic Front	World Islamic Front for Jihad against Jews and Crusaders

One
Setting the Perspective

The question mark against the title of this book—*Bangladesh: The Next Afghanistan?*—emphasizes the fact that Bangladesh is by no means irrevocably set to become a country like Afghanistan under Taliban rule. There is, however, a serious danger of its becoming not only that but also a global exporter of terrorism, as Afghanistan had become. This book seeks to analyse the why and how of Bangladesh's drift towards fundamentalist Islam. To get a perspective on the discourse, one needs to understand what the term 'terrorism', which has many interpretations, precisely means and whether Islam, as a religion, inexorably leads to it. One must recognize the difference between Islam as the religion that the Prophet preached and its fundamentalist Talibanized version. One also needs to examine the causes of the Taliban's emergence, and see whether these exist in Bangladesh today.

Of the many different definitions of terrorism, I prefer the one by Bruce Hoffman, according to which

> terrorism is the deliberate creation and exploitation of fear through violence or the threat of violence in the pursuit of political change. All terrorist acts involve violence or the threat of violence. Terrorism is specifically designed to have far-reaching psychological effects beyond the immediate victim(s) or object of the terrorist attack. It is meant to instill fear within, and thereby intimidate, a wider 'target audience' that might include a rival ethnic or religious group, an entire country, a national government or political party, or public opinion in general. Terrorism is designed to create power where there is none or to consolidate power where there is very little. Through the publicity generated by their violence, terrorists seeks to obtain the leverage, influence and power they otherwise lack to effect political change on either a local or international scale.[1]

Islam is not more prone to terrorism than any other religion. Terrorism, as Walter Laqueur points out in his exhaustive work, *The Age of Terrorism*, is 'not an ideology but an insurrectionary strategy that can be used by people of various political convictions'.[2] As Laqueur shows, one of the earliest known terrorist movements was that of the Sicarii, active in Palestine between A.D. 66 and 73. Their favourite weapon was the short sword (*sica*), which they carried hidden under their coats. Extremist, nationalist and anti-Roman, they also constituted a movement of social protest.[3] 'Assassins', who combined messianic hopes with terrorism, were an offshoot of the Ismailis who appeared in the 11th century and were suppressed by the Mongols in the 13th. They displayed features very similar to those of contemporary terrorist groups. Spreading out from Persia to Syria, they operated in complete secrecy, with their terrorist fighters (*fidayeen*) disguised as strangers, or even as Christians. According to Laqueur, they courted death and martyrdom and used only daggers to kill because murder was to them a sacramental act.[4]

There have been many terrorist groups since then. Irish terrorism began in the late 18th century, was active in the 1870s and 1880s and raised its head again in the 20th century.[5] Systematic terrorism, however, Laqueur points out, began in the second half of the 19th century. Radical nationalist groups in Macedonia, Serbia and Armenia used terrorism as a weapon. Anarchists unleashed terror on France, Italy and Spain.[6] In the United States, violence by the Molly Maguires, and later, the Western Union of Mineworkers, provided examples of working-class terrorism. The most significant terrorist group of the 19th century was perhaps the Narodnaya Volya of Russia. Though its operations lasted only from January 1878 to March 1881, it was responsible for the killing of Tsar Alexander II of Russia on 1 March 1881.[7] In Russia, again, the Social Revolutionary Party launched two waves of terrorism. The first, marked by the assassination of the Interior Minister, Sipyagin, in 1902, petered out in 1911; the second, which followed the Russian Revolution of 1917, was mainly directed against Communist leaders. Uritsky, the head of the secret police, was killed and Lenin wounded before the Bolsheviks suppressed the Social Revolutionaries.[8]

Both communist and nationalist ideologies spawned terrorism in the 20th century. In Palestine, two Jewish groups, Irgun Zvai Le'umi (Nationalist Military Organization) and Lohamel Herut Yisrael (Freedom Fighters for Israel) were active against the British in the 1940s.[9]

Ethniki Organosis Kyrion Agoniston (EOKA), or the Nationalist
Organization of Cypriot Fighters, fought for Cyprus' independence
from the British. Later, the Palestinian struggle against Israeli occupation produced several terrorist organizations like the Popular Front
for the Liberation of Palestine (PFLP) and the Palestine Liberation
Organization (PLO).

These are just a few of numerous examples. Islam had nothing to
do with any of these. As Karen Armstrong points out, terrorism is repugnant to the Quranic view of warfare which, she says, is very similar
to the West's view of a 'just' war.[10] She points out that Islam regards
war as always an 'awesome evil' which Muslims sometimes have to
undertake to prevent persecution. 'They may never initiate hostilities,
however, and aggressive warfare is always forbidden. The only
permissible war, therefore, is the war of self-defence, but the moment
the enemy sues for peace, hostilities must cease. Retaliation is permitted to avenge an attack, but it must be proportionate, and patience
is the best option; it is best to refrain from any retaliation at all.'[11]

Islam is by no means the violently proselytizing, intolerant, obscurantist and socially reactionary religion that turns women into virtual
slaves that its contemporary fanatical adherents make it. While some
passages in the Quran and the words of Muhammad suggest sanction
for violence and intolerance and appear socially repressive, the Tenth
Sura (chapter), Ayat 100, of the Quran clearly states,

> And if thy Lord had willed, whoever
> is in the earth would have believed,
> all of them, all together. Wouldst thou
> then constrain the people, until
> they are believers?
> It is not for any soul to believe
> save for the leave of God . . .[12]

The Quran also rules out hate and prescribes piety and mutual help
among people. Thus the Fifth Sura, Ayat 2, states,

> Let not detestation for a people who
> barred you from the Holy Mosque move you
> to commit aggression. Help one another to
> piety and godfearing, do not help each other
> to sin and enmity. And fear God; surely God is
> terrible in retribution.[13]

Until the advent of Islam, the Arabian desert was inhabited by 'a number of tribes perpetually engaged in feuds and warfare'.[14] Islam united them into one state under the Khalifs.[15] This and the expansion that followed involved military conquests which in turn involved inspiring the 'Army of God' with religious fervour and zeal for conversion. Yet, as M.N. Roy points out, there 'is no end of testimonies to prove that even in the predominantly martial period of their history, the Saracens were far from being barbaric bands of fanatical marauders, spreading pillage and rapine, death and destruction in the name of religion'.[16] The legendary First Commander of the Faithful, Abu Bakr, in his famous injunction to his troops, said:

> Be just; the unjust never prosper. Be valiant; die rather than yield. Be merciful; slay neither old men, nor women, nor children. Destroy neither fruit trees, nor grains nor cattle. Keep your word even to your enemy. Molest not those men who have retired from the world.[17]

Very different is the conduct of current-day fundamentalist Islamist terrorists who kill indiscriminately and whose victims are mostly ordinary human beings who only want to live peacefully.

In the early days of Islam, conquered people were treated generously and left free to practice their religion. M.N. Roy points out that the inhabitants of Jerusalem were left in possession of their worldly goods and allowed freedom of worship after the city had capitulated to Khalif Umar. For a nominal tax of two pieces of gold, the entire Christian community, along with their patriarch and clergy, were granted a special quarter of the city to live in. Muslim conquerors stimulated pilgrimage to the holy city of Jerusalem mainly for the commercial returns it brought.[18] It is hardly surprising, then, that 'everywhere the Saracen invaders were welcomed as deliverers by people oppressed and tyrannized by Byzantine corruption, Persian despotism and Christian superstition'.[19]

Makhan Lal Roy Choudhury, the great scholar of Islam in India, says that the early history of the Khalifs provides examples of tolerance of which any religion should be proud. Umar ordered the payment of compensation for damages done to the people of the country through which he passed during his Syrian expedition.[20] When Muhammad ibn Qasim informed Khalif Walid that he had destroyed temples, converted Hindus to Islam and successfully waged war against them, the Khalif reprimanded him because his actions were contrary to the sanctions and usages of Islamic law and asked ibn Qasim to provide compensation for the damage he had done.[21]

Roy Choudhury's testimony is all the more valuable because he never shies away from citing acts of savagery and intolerance that many Muslim rulers perpetrated. He quotes the historian Utbi's description in the *Tarikh-i-Yamini* of how Mahmud of Ghazna 'demolished idol temples and established Islam in them. He captured cities, killed the polluted wretches, destroying the idolatrous and gratifying Muslims'.[22] He also cites Hasan Nizami writing of how Muhammad of Ghor 'purged by his own sword the land of the Hind from the filth of infidelity and vice, and freed the whole of that country from the thorn of God-plurality and the impurity of idol worship, and by his royal vigour and intrepidity, left not one temple standing'.[23] Sultan Iltutmish, he further pointed out, built the crest of the Arhai-din-ka Jhopra mosque with the fragments of destroyed Hindu and Jain temples.[24]

The military victories of Islam, however, were not the religion's principal and distinctive achievement. The Goths, Visigoths, Huns, Vandals, Mongols and others had done as well in warfare. In the case of Islam, military might brought about political unity, which led to the rise of a new social order, economic prosperity and intellectual activity. These became the hallmarks of a civilization which played a critical role in ushering modernity in to Europe.

The policies of the Islamic state, 'determined and directed'[25] by Arab traders, encouraged industry, agriculture and trade. The result was a marked quickening of economic activity. The ruling classes in the 'Roman world' as well as all the other 'lands of antique civilisation' detested productive labour. The noble professions were war and worship. It was different with the Arabs. 'Nomadic life in a desert had taught them to appreciate labour as the source of freedom. With them trade was an honourable as well as a lucrative occupation of the free man. Thus the Islamic state rested on social relations entirely different from those of the old. Religion extolled industry, and encouraged a normal indulgence of nature. Trade was free, and as noble a profession as statecraft, war, letters and science.'[26]

Intellectual life flourished. The Abbasid Khalif, Al-Mansur, who built Baghdad in 762,

> invited religious scholars and intellectuals to come from far and near, and encouraged the rendering of books in various languages into Arabic. This work started under the patronage of the state. In 830 Al Mamun

established in Baghdad his famous Bayt al Hikmah, a combination [of]
library, academy and translation bureau, and an astronomical obser-
vatory. The work of translation continued with such speed and on such
a vast scale that, within eighty years after the establishment of Baghdad,
most of the books in Greek had already been rendered into Arabic.[27]

As Maulana Wahiduddin Khan shows, both the Holy Roman Empire
and the Persian empire suppressed freedom of thought. By destroying
both, Islam enabled people to pursue scientific and metaphysical
explorations as well as life and religion without the fear of persecution.
Islam's severe monotheism helped: pre-Islamic polytheistic cultures
that existed at that time in the Arabian peninsula and adjoining regions
had created an intellectual climate in which the veneration of a multiplicity of deities, and the fear of offending them, had created a diffident
mindset that hampered free and enthusiastic exploration of natural
and human phenomena in search of knowledge. Maulana Wahiduddin
Khan writes,

> Through the Arabs, monotheism, and a civilization born under its
> influence, spread everywhere. Its impact was felt in the major parts of
> the inhabited world of the time. Thus an atmosphere and an
> environment was produced in which scientific research, leading to the
> conquest of nature's phenomena, could be freely and independently
> undertaken.[28]

Scholarship and scientific experimentation flourished. The large-
scale manufacture of paper in the Abbasid era greatly facilitated the
writing of books.

> There were more than 400,000 books in the library at Cordova (Spain)
> in the tenth century, whereas in Europe at that time, according to the
> Catholic Encyclopaedia, the library at Canterbury was at the top of
> the list of European libraries with 1800 books in the thirteenth century.[29]

The Arabs made tremendous progress in medicine. They not only
learnt from the Greeks but also made their own contribution. They
established medical colleges and hospitals, building the first hospital
in Baghdad in A.D. 800 at the initiative of Khalif Harun al-Rashid.[30]
The Muslims of Spain put agriculture on a scientific basis. The system
of numerals in use now, including the zero which has a critical function, was invented in India. It was introduced in Baghdad at the time

of Khalif Al-Mansur by an Indian traveller whose works were translated into Arabic and adopted for general use after the great Arab mathematician Al-Khawarizmi certified its usefulness.[31] Introduced to Europe by Leonardo of Pisa,[32] it revolutionized mathematics there by liberating it from the cumbersome straitjacket of Roman numerals. Also significant was the Arabic contribution to astronomy and physics.

A number of complex historical forces—social, economic, religious and cultural—brought about the European Renaissance that stretched from the 14th to the 16th centuries, revolutionized the history of the world and inaugurated the modern age. One of these was the rediscovery of the art, knowledge, humanist philosophy and rationalism of classical Greece. While the medieval European scholastics had played an important role in preserving the classics, the contribution of the Arabs cannot be underestimated.

The question of women

An issue that invariably comes up in any discussion on Islam's historical role as a facilitator of modernization is the status it prescribes for women. The social policies of the Taliban, who consigned women to virtual domestic slavery in Afghanistan, comes to mind whenever the subject is mentioned. Even in Islamic countries that have not adopted the extreme policies of the Taliban, women labour under restrictions from which their counterparts in modern democracies are free. The phenomenon of women in the *burqa* or the *hijab* is an anachronism in the modern world, where gender justice and equality is a critical element in social, political, economic and cultural discourse.

One has here another example of how contemporary practices in some Islamic countries go against the revolutionary thrust toward gender justice and equality which the Prophet had generated in his time, when women had few rights in the feudal societies of the West. Muhammad stridently proclaimed the equality of men and women and their equal rights to the fruits of their labour. The Third Sura of the Quran, entitled 'The House of Imran', Ayats 193 and 194, says, 'And their Lord answers them: "I waste not/the labour of any that labours among you/be you male or female—the one of you/is as the other."'[33] The Quran says in the Fourth Sura, entitled 'Women', Ayats 36 and 37: 'To the men a share of what they have earned/and to the women a share of what they/have earned. And ask God of his bounty./God knows everything.'[34]

Islam also provides women with a share of the parental inheritance. The Quran says, also in the Fourth Sura, Ayat 7 and 8,

> To the men a share of what parents and kinsmen
> leave, and to the women a share of what
> parents and kinsmen leave, whether it be
> little or much, a share apportioned;
> and when the division is attended by
> kinsmen, orphans and the poor,
> make provision for them out of it
> and speak to them honourable words.[35]

Not only that, in the same Sura, the Quran apportioned the exact share of the inheritance to which each relative was entitled. Of course, men were given a larger share, but the very fact that women received a precisely defined share was a major advance in the context of the times. In fact, Muhammad did much more. According to the principles of Islam he enunciated, a woman had the same capacity for freedom as a man. She could propose marriage to a man, freely chose her husband, reject a suitor, get a divorce from an estranged husband against his will; she could not be forcibly married. Islamic jurisprudence held women to be competent to own and dispose of property in any manner.

Women were also present on battle fields, providing water to the wounded, carrying them to safety and treating their wounds—thus anticipating the remarkable work done by Florence Nightingale during the Crimean War (1854–60) by more than 12 centuries. Several eminent ladies, including the Prophet's own wife, Syeda Ayesha, rendered such services at the battle of Uhud. Muhammad no doubt prescribed a severe dress code for women, prohibiting the display of any part of the body other than the hands and face in public. Islam permits only close relatives of women to see them wearing ornaments. Women are also unequal to men as witnesses; rape laws are severely tilted against them. Proving adultery by them, however, is as difficult as proving rape. Muhammad prohibited women wearing perfume from passing close to men. There were strict limits to intermingling, and a woman could not meet any man alone in the absence of her husband.

Viewed in their entirety and in the context of the times, Muhammad conferred on women a status which was almost revolutionary. Islam is a religion that governs every aspect of a person's life in great detail. Muhammad, therefore, took existing realities into account before formulating rules of conduct; too radical a departure might have led to rejection or breaches in practice. Given, however, the direction of his thoughts, Islam should have led the way in the evolution of women's rights. Unfortunately, the opposite is often true today.

The fundamentalist deviation

What explains the rise of fundamentalist Islam, that robbed the religion of the spirit of tolerance and intellectual vibrancy that had made it a vehicle of modernization, scholarship, science, equality, democratization and gender justice in its early days? Makhan Lal Roy Choudhury traces the beginning of the process to the conversion of the Turks and Central Asian tribes to Islam. To these violent people 'Islam offered two worlds—power in this world and pleasure in the next. Consequently, in their hands the true precepts of Islam underwent distortion, as was the case with Christianity in the hands of the barbarian conquerors of Europe.'[36]

The rise of a violent, intolerant and socially reactionary stream in Islam followed the Mongol conquest of the domains of the Omayyad (660–750) and Abbasid (750–1258) Khalifs. It was in many respects a reaction to the humiliation of defeat at the hands of the Mongols and the atrocities that ensued—which were attributed to the Arabs abandoning the pristine and austere ways they followed during the Prophet's lifetime and for a century thereafter. An important proponent of this view was a Hanbali jurist, Taqi Al-Din Ahmad Ibn Taimiyya, who was born in 1263, five years after the Mongol ruler Hulagu captured Baghdad in 1258 and killed the last Abbasid Khalif. He wanted a return to the Sunni orthodoxy as Ibn Hanbali had left it.[37]

Ibn Taimiyya condemned as 'un-Islamic' both Shiism and Sufism and attributed the decline of Islam particularly to the latter.[38] He severely condemned dancing and playing of music at khanqas[39] as un-Islamic and the worshipping of the mazars (tombs) of Sufi saints as idolatrous.[40] Taimiyya was severely critical of the dilution of the rigorous punishments provided for crime under Sharia law through the grant of remissions and imposition of fines. He was the first to revolt against the uncritical acceptance of the tenets of Islam as interpreted by the *ulama* who always bowed to the will of the ruler.[41] The *ulama*, however, proved too strong for him. He was thrown into prison, where he died.

Taimiyya, however, had a popular following in Baghdad, and views like his continued to appeal to a substantial section of Muslims. The fundamentalist element in Islam was strengthened when the Ottoman Turks established their sway over the Arabian peninsula, Persia, Asia Minor and large parts of Europe, including Greece and Eastern Europe. In the 18th century, it found a powerful exponent in the cleric Muhammad ibn Abd al-Wahhab (1703–87), who also belonged to the Hanbali school. A native of what is now Saudi Arabia, he conducted an aggressive campaign against Sufism and worship at *mazars*, and declared that all knowledge not based on the Quran and the Sunnah was outside the pale of Islamic belief.[42] Al-Wahhab stood for compulsory performance of the obligatory prayers, a puritanical life, and legal penalties for smoking and drinking.[43] He built up a large army of followers, which included Abdul Rahman Al Saud and the latter's son Abdul Aziz, known as Ibn Saud, who were involved in a 28-year war with the Sheikh of Riyad. In the first decade of the 19th century, Abdul Aziz won a series of remarkable victories and set up a Wahhabi kingdom in what is now Saudi Arabia. Ever since then Saudi Arabia has remained the principal bastion and exporter of the Wahhabi version of Islam, which has been militant from the beginning.

Shah Waliullah Dehlavi of Delhi (1703–64), an eminent Naqshbandi Shaikh educated in Mecca and Madina, was a contemporary of al-Wahhab in India. He felt that only a revival of pure Islam could save the Mughal empire, which appeared to be in terminal decline after Emperor Aurangzeb's death in 1707. For this, Islam had to be cleansed of the influence of the Hindus and converts, who had made Muslims forget their own ethics and links with the Islamic world.[44] Muslims in India, he felt, should consider themselves a part of the greater Islamic world and seek not only to resurrect the power and glory of the Mughal empire but also to unite under a Khilafat (Caliphate) to provide perpetual spiritual and temporal guidance to Muslims and keep their rulers under control.[45]

Since no Muslim ruler in India was willing to undertake such a massive venture or seemed capable of succeeding in it, Waliullah invited Ahmad Shah Abdali, who had become the ruler of Afghanistan, to invade India. Almost simultaneously, he wrote to various Muslim nobles to help Abdali who, he said, was coming to deliver Muslims.[46] Unfortunately for him, Abdali came, defeated the Marathas at the third battle of Panipat in 1761 but, instead of establishing Muslim power in India on a strong footing, left after plundering.

The Mughal empire continued to disintegrate. Ahmed Barelvi, a disciple of Waliullah's son Abdul Aziz, launched a movement called Tariq-e-Muhammadiya (The Way of Muhammad), an order 'which coupled sufi discipline with sharia orthodoxy'.[47] He proclaimed a jihad against the Sikhs and led his followers to the Indo-Afghan border to establish a truly Islamic state. The Sikhs defeated and executed him in 1831. Tariq-e-Muhammadiya, however, survived as a militant movement and played an important role in the great uprising triggered by the sepoys of the East India Company's army in 1857,[48] which has been described as the 'most dramatic instance of traditional India's struggle against foreign rule'.[49]

This is hardly surprising. A significant section of Muslims in India, particularly the *ulama*, belonged to the fundamentalist and intolerant stream of Islam. Even Sufi saints could be bigoted. Sayyid Nuruddin Mubarak Ghaznavi, a Shaikh of the Suhrawardy order who had been appointed Shaikh-ul Islam by Iltutmish, led an *ulama* deputation to the latter, requesting that Hindus be asked to choose between conversion and death because, not being Christians and Jews, they could not be treated as 'dhimmies'.[50] Instructed by Iltutmish, the Wazir told the assembled *ulama* that Muslims constituted so small a part of the population that such a misadventure would mean the end of the Sultanate. The delegation dispersed, but not before telling the Wazir that kings should 'at least strive to disgrace, dishonour and defame the idol-worshipping Hindus who are the worst enemies of God and the Prophet'.[51]

While most Muslim rulers in India tried to avoid extreme action that would drive the Hindus, who constituted the overwhelming majority of the country's population, to desperation and revolt, the *ulama* often urged them to convert or slaughter the Hindus, impose the *jizya*[52] and destroy temples. Some rulers gave them short shrift, others yielded. Among the latter was Firuz Shah Tughlak. The son of a Hindu mother, he imposed the *jizya*, destroyed temples and converted them into mosques. He killed Shias, burned their books and banned visits by Muslim women to the shrines of Sufi saints.[53] Sikandar Lodhi literally followed in Firuz Shah Tughlak's footsteps.[54]

The Great Mughals

Though Akbar (r. 1556–1605), one of the greatest emperors ever to rule India, abolished the *jizya* in 1564 and pursued a tolerant and enlightened course, the tyranny of the orthodox Sunni *ulama* continued for the first 21 years of his reign. At the head of the *ulama* were Abu-n Nabi, a bigoted Sunni whom Akbar had appointed Sadr-us-Sudur,[55] and Abdullah Sultanpuri, the Makhdum-ul-Mulk.[56] They severely persecuted the Shias and Sufis. Angered by the Emperor's liberalism, they conspired in 1580 to oust him by inciting a half-brother of his to rebel; they even tried to get the Emperor of Persia to help them. Their efforts failed. After his victory, Akbar took important measures to reform the *ulama* and regulated the establishment of mosques and madrasas.[57] Finally, he abolished the post of Sadr-us-Sudur in November 1581, and set up instead six provincial Sadrs in different parts of the country.[58] At the beginning of 1582, Akbar promulgated a new Sufi creed, the Din-i-Ilahi, which he had largely shaped.

Though a powerful force, the *ulama* could not dominate in the reign of Akbar's son and successor Jahangir (r. 1605–27), who believed in God but was not a devout follower of Islam. He loved conversing with Hindu and Muslim saints and Christian preachers, and valued religious pictures, particularly those of the Christians. He, however, remained a Muslim and did not accept the practices and rituals of Hindus, Christians or Zoroastrians. Shah Jahan (r. 1627–58), his son and successor, was not quite as liberal. It was, however, only in the reign of his son Aurangzeb that the *ulama* had reason to be pleased with the religious conduct of the emperor.

Aurangzeb (r. 1658–1707) was a champion of Sunni orthodoxy, as opposed to the liberal and scholarly ways of his brother Dara Shukoh. A fanatical believer in the strict implementation of the Quranic law as interpreted by the most orthodox *ulama*, he, like the Taliban three-and-a-half centuries later, appointed Censors of Public Morals to regulate the lives of people in strict conformity with Islamic law. He forbade music at court, dismissed the musicians and singers, and stopped patronizing art and literature. He prohibited the production and public consumption of wine and *bhang*, ordered dancing girls and sex workers to marry or leave the kingdom, and reimposed the *jizya* in 1679.

Even his bleak and intolerant regime, however, could not choke the liberal and creative stream in Islam which has been flowing in India ever since the beginning of Muslim conquest. In fact, by the time Akbar had become emperor, military and political compulsions and economic interests had brought Hindus and Muslims increasingly together and the Hindu element had become a permanent factor in Muslim administration.[59] Apart from this, the mere fact of social living, involving daily interaction, brought the two communities together without their even being conscious of it.

Roy Choudhury identifies several factors that facilitated the process. The Turks, Afghans and Pathans were satisfied with the Hindus reciting the Kalima[60] and changing their names, and tended to leave them to their own devices thereafter. Conversions often cut across families, with one branch becoming Muslim and another remaining Hindu. Finally, the appeal of tribal and local allegiances and customs was strong and often transcended religious barriers. Thus, one finds many instances of Muslims worshipping Hindu deities and vice versa. Roy Choudhury gives a long list of these.[61] The teachings of great saints like Ramanand and his first disciple Kabir, who later came to personify Hindu–Muslim fusion, reinforced the process. Dadu, like Kabir, made a conscious effort to unite Hindus and Muslims.[62] It was no different in Bengal. Referring to the developments there between the 12th and the 18th centuries, the noted scholar Qazi Abdul Wadud has written, 'the separateness of Hindu–Muslim societies had not disappeared at any time, yet the fact that the flow of the best thoughts and reflections of both communities had gradually come to be moving in the same direction, is proved by Baul literature and the works of the Muslim Vaishnavite poets'.[63]

Enter the British

The process of Hindus and Muslims moving closer to one another as friends and colleagues, was, however, interrupted following the arrival of the British in India, which gave a fillip to the Wahhabi movement in the country. This clearly owed much to the feeling of grievance that Muslims of India began harbouring against the British. Wadud cites three lines of development, elaborated by W.W. Hunter in his book, *Our Indian Mussalmans: Are They Bound to Owe Allegiance to the Queen?*, that hit the Muslims of Bengal very hard in the late 18th and early 19th centuries.[64] The first was the series of changes introduced by

Lord Cornwallis and Sir John Shore that ended with the Permanent Settlement of 1793. The latter not only created large landed estates, but also replaced the Muslim revenue farmers with 'their army of troopers and spearmen' by the 'English collector and his unarmed fiscal police'.

Second, the larger estates went to the Hindus, 'For the whole tendency of the [Permanent] Settlement was to acknowledge as the land-lords the subordinate Hindu officers who dealt directly with the husbandmen. It not only gave them a proprietary right in land but allowed them to accumulate wealth which would have gone to the Mussalmans under their rule.' Third, the resumption of rent-free land grants between 1828 and 1846, which generated an additional revenue of £300,000 sterling every year against an initial outlay of £800,000 sterling, hit Muslims hard. A large part of the revenue was derived from lands held free by Muslims and Muslim foundations which had been careless about preserving title deeds and other records.

During the same period when rent-free land grants were resumed, English replaced Persian as the language of the courts. Muslims did not take to English for two reasons—the fear that it would lead to conversions to Christianity and resentment toward British rule.[65] In a great measure, this resentment was a result of the economic distress of Muslim peasants caused by exploitation by landlords (mostly Hindu), British indigo planters and the British administration. An early manifestation of this in Bengal was the revolt by Titumir (1782–1831) whose other name was Mir Nissar Ali.[66] Trained in the use of the *lathi* and the sword and employed as a muscleman (*palwan*) by a *zamindar* (landlord) in his early life, he was imprisoned for participation in a riot. Visiting Mecca after his release, he returned converted to the Wahhabi creed. Using the Barasat (a subdivision in the current North 24-Parganas District of West Bengal in India) area as base, he started propagating reform of Islam in accordance with the Wahhabi creed in 24 Parganas, Nadia (a district in West Bengal) and Jessore and Faridpur (now in Bangladesh). Gradually, a large number of poor peasants and members of the weaver community became his followers as he sought to protect them from unjust taxation by *zamindar*s and the depredations of indigo planters. This brought him into conflict with local *zamindar*s and the British. He won and lost some of the skirmishes that took place between his followers and forces of the British, and was finally killed in 1831 in one such clash.

Other militant protagonists of the Wahhabi creed in Bengal were Haji Shariatullah (1781–1840) of Faridpur and his son Mohsinuddin Ahmed, known as Dudu Mian (1819–60). Born into a family of weavers, Shariatullah went to Mecca in 1799 and returned in 1818 as a convert to the Wahhabi faith. Launching a movement called Fariadi (Complainant), he tried to protect his followers from exploitation by mullahs and *maulvi*s by revoking the exploitative regulations of the brand of Islam then in vogue. Simultaneously, he carried on propaganda against exploitation by *zamindar*s and indigo farmers. Innumerable peasants of Dhaka and Faridpur Districts became his enthusiastic followers. He, however, fell foul of the *zamindar*s and conservative rich Muslims, who forced him out of Dhaka District.[67]

Dudu Mian went to Mecca early in his life and, returning, devoted himself to teaching his father's Fariadi creed and organizing support for it. The principal leader of the Fariadi revolt in Faridpur, he too believed in the precepts of the Wahhabi creed. Arrested on charges of looting in 1838, 1844 and 1847, and released on each occasion for lack of evidence, he was interned as a precautionary measure during the great uprising of 1857. His health ruined by lifelong struggle and repeated imprisonment, he died in 1860.

Adversity and religion

The British government finally put down the Wahhabi revolt in 1868. Wadud points out that the crushing of the sepoy and Wahhabi revolts greatly weakened the Muslims, or rather, their weakness became manifest. They had no alternative to seeking the ruling class' favour.[68] In this period of adversity, they began thinking anew about religion. Resistance became a matter of the past. Their mainstay became the observance of untroubled religiosity in their daily life.[69]

Wadud stated that confusion about the secular world and excessive anxiety about the hereafter could be described as having largely been the hallmark of Muslim life till this age.[70] Yet developments in wider human society such as the victorious march of science, humankind's success in worldly affairs, the rise of the depressed and downtrodden, and the march of the deprived were 'knocking on the door of their heart'. These had not yielded the desired response but, in the ultra-modern times (*ati-adhunik*, as he puts it), had created the feeling that Muslims should not remain inactive. And the strong feeling had arisen in them that Hindus, their companions at all times, were responsible for all their various adversities.[71]

An important reason for this was exploitation by Hindu landlords. Like their Hindu counterparts, Muslim peasants had no security of tenure and lived at the mercy of the Hindu *zamindars*. Besides regular rent they had to pay *abwabs* (cesses) 'for services or events ranging from remuneration of *amlas* (*zamindari* officials), to the performance of *pujas* (worship) and the opening of additional classes in schools to special occasions such as marriages or births in the *zamindars'* families'.[72] A tenant could not even dig tanks, build houses or cut trees without the *zamindar's* permission, which generally came for a fee.[73] Sometimes they had also to agree not to slaughter cattle on religious or social occasions and to pledge loyalty to the *zamindars* from generation to generation.[74]

As exploitative were Hindu *mahajans* (moneylenders)—mainly Bengalis of the Shaha caste and Marwaris—who dominated the credit business. 'Their rates of interest varied from 24 per cent to 50 per cent, and sometimes was even as high as 100 per cent.'[75] Moneylenders

> also imposed additional subscriptions such as *Ishwar Britti* for the maintenance of Hindu idols. Most of the Muslim ryots were thus permanently in debt to Hindu money-lenders, to whom they had sold their crops at 60 per cent or 50 per cent below current prices to repay the money borrowed in times of distress.[76]

Joya Chatterji, however, rightly cautions against holding that 'the *jotedar–zamindar* contest was directly translated into communal terms as a conflict essentially between Hindus and Muslims'.[77] Nor does she agree with the contention by Rajat and Ratna Ray that 'it was the conflict between Zamindars and Jotedars in East Bengal which constantly fed the Muslim separatist movement in the province and led ultimately to the partition of Bengal in 1947'.[78] Chatterji argues,

> Admittedly, the vast majority of landlords were high caste Hindus and most peasants and many jotedars were Muslims. However, there was not an insignificant number of Muslim landlords, particularly in East Bengal. Men such as the Nawab of Dhaka and Khwaja Mohiuddin Faroqui owned vast estates spread over several districts.

Zamindars made an important contribution to efforts by the Muslim upper classes to make sure that Bengali Muslims, despite their poverty, maintained, in J.H. Broomfield's words, 'their separate communal identity with remarkable vigour'.[79] The efforts of the upper classes, he writes, to preserve the study of Islamic history and literature was matched in the 19th century by work among the peasantry of revivalist mullahs, who developed a vernacular religious literature in East Bengal dialects and founded 'puritan sects which gained widespread support by their attack on rural injustice. Efforts to popularize the pilgrimage to Mecca provided a common ground for cooperation between the rural zamindars and mullahs, the former supplying the funds and the latter publicity and organisation.'[80]

A strong anti-Hindu message was inherent in the preachings by the mullahs because, as Suranjan Das points out, 'The Islamic reform movement of the late nineteenth and early twentieth centuries sought to restore the "purity" of the faith by purging it of "idolatrous practices".'[81] According to Das, Bengali Muslims responded enthusiastically when revivalist organizations initiated a new movement for purifying Islamic practices. Its chief message was dissociation from Hindu festivals and banning of music near mosques. Muslims were also encouraged to violate the sanctity of the caste system by touching Hindu wells and water-pots.[82] Das further points out that such developments led to the growth of a new Islamic idenity among Bengali Muslims, which in turn led to the social alienation of Muslim villagers from their Hindu neighbours with whom they shared a common pattern of rural life. The heightening of the consciousness of a separate cultural identity 'made the Bengali Muslims feel that as Muslims they are required to be distinct from Hindus and to orient their manners, customs, personal and family names in accordance with pan-Islamic norms'.[83]

The preaching of the mullahs had a powerful influence on Muslims, a very large section of whom were peasants, for two reasons. First, they

commanded a traditional authority within the subordinate social groups in the community and whenever they addressed congregations, the local Muslims listened to their discourse as a matter of custom. Regular congregations in the village mosques were well-attended; the average Muslim ryot of eastern Bengal offered prayers punctiliously and taught his/her children to do so.[84]

Hindu–Muslim tensions developed not only in rural but also in urban areas, where the poverty of the Muslims played an important role in making them receptive to propaganda by mullahs. Since an

English-language education was a pre-requisite for government employment, the Hindus, who had taken to it enthusiastically, forged ahead of the Muslims, who had kept away from it for a long time. 'There was only one Muslim to every seven Hindus in government jobs and professional occupations; the situation changed only marginally in the 1940s.'[85]

In Kolkata (then Calcutta), Muslims mainly worked as day labourers butchers, carpenters, coachmen, stable-boys, tailors, boatmen, lascars, book-binders and petty traders.[86] Some Muslims had doubtless established 'considerable mercantile networks',[87] but their position declined substantially by 1918, 'when the Marwari monopoly over the internal trade of north and east India had become "virtually complete"'.[88] Meanwhile, Hindu domination of the bureaucracy, the professions and trade alarmed the Muslims—particularly the community's upper strata—who, deprived of their status as rulers, were feeling insecure and were apprehensive of losing their religious and cultural identity. The character of India's slowly-crystallizing national consciousness and the symbols used to express it and mobilize people were predominantly Hindu. This aggravated Muslim apprehensions. Simultaneously, exploitation gave disprivileged Muslims a common feeling of victimhood, which not only reinforced religion-based solidarity but also gave it a militant anti-Hindu character. Thus, both industrial action and peasant unrest invariably tended to assume a communal character.

The first communal riots in Calcutta occurred in an industrial suburb of the city in 1891; the Bakr-Id disturbances of 1896 and the Tala riots of 1897 also occurred in working-class areas. These were examples of embryonic labour protests taking a communal rather than a class character.[89] The communal riots of 1906–1907 in Mymensingh District, however, had a much more complex origin. To exploitation by zamindars was added a steep rise in the prices of food items because of speculative hoarding by British companies, which benefited the Hindu traders who acted as middlemen, and hit the Muslims hard. The latter also suffered more from the cholera and malaria epidemics that visited the area several months before the riots.[90]

The partition of Bengal and after

The immediate cause of the violence was the attempt by Hindus to enforce the boycott of British goods under the Swadeshi movement that was a part of the massive agitation against the partition of Bengal (1905–11). The partition, enforced by the Viceroy, Lord Curzon, involved the detachment of the Divisions of Dhaka, Chittagong and Rajshahi from Bengal—which then included Bihar and Orissa—and their incorporation into a new province called East Bengal and Assam, with Dhaka as its capital.

While Bengali Hindus bitterly opposed the partition, which they saw as an attempt to undermine their culture, language and political salience by making them minorities in both provinces, Muslims welcomed it enthusiastically as the British had convinced them that they would benefit immensely in terms of jobs and political power. They actually did; and, as a result of the pro-Muslim tilt of British policy, the Muslim elites switched to a pro-British line. They followed the lead taken by Sir Syed Ahmed Khan, the founder of the Aligarh movement, while the Hindus led the fledgling national movement which was crystallizing around the Indian National Congress, formed in 1885.

The partition worsened Hindu–Muslim relations as the bulk of the two communities took diametrically opposite stands on it. In addition, the Swadeshi and boycott movements were opposed by a large majority of Muslims who, being poor, preferred imported goods, particularly clothing, which were cheaper than those produced in India. The massive struggle that the Hindu *bhadralok*[91] spearheaded against the partition of Bengal saw, for the first time in Indian history, the large-scale use of direct political action in the form of general strikes and enforcement of the call to boycott foreign goods which the Swadeshi movement involved. It also saw the emergence of a terrorist strand of the freedom movement that resulted in the assassination of several British officers. The outcome of the movement, which forced the government to annul the partition in 1911, was a qualitative change in the character of the national struggle—away from the pre-partition days of petitioning and towards mass action. It was this mass action which convulsed the entire nation during the Non-Cooperation Movement of 1920–22 and the Civil Disobedience Movement of 1930–31.

The events during the partition of Bengal and its aftermath also saw Muslim politics in India and Bengal acquire its distinct contours. The Muslim League, formed in Dhaka in 1906, emerged as a cohesive political force. The annulment of the partition left the Muslims furious. The British, they felt, had sold them down the river to pander to Hindu extremists. The traditional leadership of the Muslim League, which had Nawab Salimullah of Dhaka at its centre, however, thought it wiser to lump it and, instead, obtain from the British as many concessions as possible as compensation for the loss they suffered on account of the annulment.

Muslim *bhadralok*

A new element, however, soon emerged in Muslim politics, in the form of younger professional men who insisted that the community must adopt a more aggressive stance towards the British to improve its fortunes.[92] The most prominent among them was A.K. Fazlul Huq, who came from a family of Barisal lawyers, had studied at Calcutta's famous Presidency College, earned a law degree and, after a stint of teaching at the local college in his home district, returned to Calcutta to become an articled clerk in the chamber of the famous Sir Asutosh Mookherjee.[93] Unlike the traditional Muslim leaders, whose influence was local and based on landholding and who usually came from one of the great Muslim families, Huq was a professional who rose because of his ability. In his education and his experience in teaching, law, administration and political organization, he had everything in common with the Hindu *bhadralok* except religion. He emerged as an important figure in Calcutta while retaining contact with his home district in East Bengal.[94]

A year or so after Nawab Salimullah's death in January 1915, Huq and Muslim *bhadralok* like him began to control the Bengal Presidency Muslim League. Huq, who was now the organization's secretary, responded to appeals by Bengal Congressmen for a Hindu–Muslim alliance against the British to wrest constitutional concessions—and later power—on the basis of a pre-arranged scheme that would give Muslims their fair share of the benefits. For the first time, the possibility of a national struggle that would unite both Hindus and Muslims seemed to materialize, when the Congress and the Muslim League signed the Lucknow Pact in December 1916. This agreement conceded the principle of separate communal electorates and representation of minorities in provinces in excess of their numerical strength.

Unfortunately, neither the Lucknow Pact nor Mahatma Gandhi's move to combine the Non-Cooperation Movement with the Khilafat Movement, which Muslims in India had launched in protest against the abolition of the Khilafat (Caliphate) in Turkey after the First World War, could unite Hindus and Muslims. In Bengal, the Lucknow Pact was unpopular with the Muslims from the very beginning because it gave them 40 per cent of seats in the legislature when their population formed 52.6 per cent of the total. The fact that it gave Muslims in other provinces more seats than they would have received on the basis of population was ignored, and communalist elements launched a fierce attack on Fazlul Huq and his associates. At the all-India level, Mahatma Gandhi's unilateral suspension of the Non-Cooperation Movement following the murder of 22 policemen in Chauri Chaura in Uttar Pradesh in 1922 alienated the Muslims.

Several factors were driving Hindus and Muslims increasingly apart—the rise in Calcutta of fanatical and mainly non-Bengali Muslim leaders who commanded an increasing influence over the community's poor, many of whom were from outside Bengal and whose grievances they exploited; Muslim anger over the previous year's riots in Shahabad, Bihar, in which their co-religionists had suffered seriously; apprehensions about the abolition of the Khilafat; and the price rise caused by the First World War, which hit them hard. They held malpractices by the Marwaris—the city's dominant trading community, whom they also hated for their opposition to cow slaughter and construction of houses on land from which Muslim slums had been cleared by the Calcutta Improvement Trust—responsible.

The immediate cause of the riots of September that year was the publication in the 27 July 1918 issue of an Anglo-Indian newspaper, the *Indian Daily News*, of an item considered derogatory to Prophet Muhammad. Non-Bengali Muslim leaders and Calcutta's Urdu publications called for severe action against the paper; public rallies in Calcutta, Burdwan and Dhaka called for a jihad against the government for its unwillingness to act. An all-India protest rally was planned on 8, 9 and 10 September. Muslim leaders from all parts of the country began arriving in Calcutta from early in the month. The government banned the rally on 8 September. Violence erupted on 9 September with Muslim mobs taking to the streets.[95]

The riot, which was finally put down on 11 September, was in many ways a landmark in Bengal politics. As Suranjan Das points out, the September 1918 riots

anticipated many of the trends in future Muslim rioting in Calcutta— the mosque as an important rallying point, the upcountrymen as the main component of the violent crowd, the Marwari merchant as a favourite target of attack, and the vernacular press as the main forum for expressing communal animosities.[96]

The riots, according to Broomfield, showed Muslim politicians that violence could be an effective political expression of their anger and frustration. Also, 'it was apparent that the mere threat of violence could force the British and the Hindu *bhadralok* to pay more serious attention to Muslim demands'. Besides, 'the techniques of promoting [violence] had been well noted. Future Muslim agitators appreciated all too well the response which could be evoked with the watchcry "Islam in danger", and they valued the agency of the molla in sounding the alarm.'[97]

The pattern of mobilization and violence was repeated in the subsequent riots. In all these, the economic plight of the bulk of the Muslims and their exploitation by Bengali and Marwari moneylenders and traders, was a factor in sharpening communal animosities. The main targets of the Muslim rioters in 1918 were Britishers, Anglo-Indians and Marwaris and their properties. Bengali Hindus were generally left alone, and Bengali Muslims generally stayed away from violence. (Although there was some participation by them in the 1926 riots in Calcutta.) It was, however, only in the 1940s that the feelings of Hindu and Muslim communal solidarity respectively and their expression in adversarial terms swamped cultural, ethnic and class identities and loyalties, and became a factor in shaping the course of politics. The instrument used was violence.

With the Government of India Acts of 1919 and 1935 perpetuating the communal electorates set up by the Indian Councils Act of 1909, elections to the limited representative institutions established by the British were marked by increasingly aggressive communal campaigns in a situation of worsening Hindu–Muslim relations. The moderation that would inevitably have come if candidates had to address both Hindu and Muslim voters was absent. Of course, this was not always the case. Joya Chatterji points out that

Krishak Praja[98] leaders were usually keen to play down their communal leanings, and in the campaign for Assembly elections purposely chose prominent Muslim zamindars as targets to demonstrate their impartiality.... The programme and style of the Krishak Praja movement was not couched in religious terms, and even though the Party contested only Muslim seats in the elections it tried to maintain a non-communal stance. It was not the Krishak Praja Party but the traditional Muslim ashraf leaders, both urban and rural, who made much of Muslim solidarity in an effort to win the new Muslim vote.[99]

Growing communalism among Hindu *bhadralok*, largely stemming from their determination to maintain their political, economic and social dominance prevented the emergence of a truly secular main-stream politics in Bengal. Leaders like Deshbandhu Chittaranjan Das, Subhas Chandra Bose and Sarat Chandra Bose no doubt sought to achieve Hindu–Muslim unity against the British by accommodating the legitimate aspirations of the Muslims. It was at Das' initiative that the Swaraj Party[100] entered with the Muslim leaders in December 1923 what has come to be known as the Bengal Pact. Under its terms, representation in the Legislative Council was to be through separate electorates and in proportion to population. In local bodies, the major-ity and minority communities would have 60 and 40 per cent of the seats respectively in each district. Fifty-five per cent of government jobs were to be reserved for Muslims and, until that was achieved, candidates from the community could fill as many as 80 per cent of the vacancies. No resolution affecting the religion of any community could be passed without the consent of the elected representatives of that community. There was to be no playing of music near mosques and no interference with cow killing.[101]

The pact, which produced a vicious reaction in the Hindu communal press and the bulk of the Hindu *bhadralok*, was rejected by the Congress and subsequently repudiated by the Swaraj Party itself. The dispute over franchise and representation in legislatures and local bodies con-tinued—with Muslims favouring expansion to make their superior numbers count and Hindus opposing it—and led to further bitterness. So did the Hindu *bhadralok*'s determined opposition to any law meant to benefit the poor at the cost of some of their privileges. Thus, all sections of the Congress and the Swaraj Party opposed the Bengal Tenancy Bill of 1928, aimed at strengthening the position of tenants against *zamindars*. The younger and radical Muslims were deeply disappointed and saw the Congress as representing merely the rich, the landed gentry and the educated minority.[102] They were equally disillusioned by the Hindu *bhadralok*'s bitter opposition to the Rural Primary Education Bill, 1929, which sought to provide compulsory and free primary education throughout Bengal. Administered by District School Boards and meant mainly to benefit the peasantry, the expansion of the primary education system was to be financed by an education cess to be paid mainly by the *bhadralok*.[103] The bill finally became an act in 1930 in the teeth of bitter opposition by the *bhadralok*, who refused to pay the cess as their children were already provided for and they were apprehensive about the results of the spread of education among peasants.

The Fazlul Huq–led ministry that assumed office after the 1937 elections under the Government of India Act of 1935 pushed ahead with its pro-peasant agenda. It appointed a commission to examine the land revenue system and made sure that it recommended the abolition of the Permanent Settlement. It severely curbed *zamindars'* power to enhance rents and recover arrears, and further restricted moneylending. The ministry amended the Calcutta Municipal Act, giving greater representation to Muslims through separate electorates, and giving seven Hindu *bhadralok* seats to the Scheduled Castes.[104] Not surprisingly, the Hindu *bhadralok* were incensed and Hindu–Muslim relations, worsened by the loss of the Hindu *bhadralok*'s political hegemony in the province and the increasing savagery of the communal riots in Calcutta, Dhaka and Pabna in 1926, the Dhaka and Kishorganj riots of 1930 and the Chittagong riots of 1931, seemed increasingly beyond repair. The two communities were now irrevocably set on the path to their separate subcontinental destinies. The Pakistan resolution of the Muslim League in May 1940, the Dhaka riots of 1941, the Great Calcutta Killing of 1946, the Noakhali and Bihar riots of 1946–47 and violence in Punjab and elsewhere in India led inexorably to the Partition of India.

New exploiters

At independence in 1947 East Bengal, which was rechristened East Pakistan in 1955, and which is now Bangladesh, had a strongly entrenched tradition of Islamist fundamentalism cast in the Wahhabi mould, a fledgling Muslim *bhadralok* elite steeped in Bengali culture— whose secular instincts could not achieve their potential due to circumstances that included the vested interests of the Hindu *bhadralok*— and a tradition of participation in electoral politics. Thanks to the developments leading to Partition, however, the bulk of the people was more conscious of its identity as Muslims rather than anything else. Finally, there were great expectations. As Badruddin Umar points out,

> The Muslim peasants, workers and middle class people were taught to visualize Pakistan as a dreamland, where milk and honey would flow, everyone would get education and suitable job [sic], healthcare would be a routine matter, and there would be a flowering of the culture espoused during the Pakistan movement. What really happened was that the Muslims of East Bengal, who constituted the vast majority of the population were quite confused by the dreamland called Pakistan, where they had to go hungry and die of famine, where no surplus land was distributed among the poor peasants and sharecroppers, where very little new opportunities were opened up for the working masses and educated sections of people, and life in all aspects remained as tortuous as before.[105]

The central leadership of the Muslim League treated East Bengal almost as a colony. As it is, there was a basic inequality in the relationship between the eastern and western wings. The bureaucracy and the armed forces were overwhelmingly dominated by West Pakistanis. 'In 1947, the Civil Service of Pakistan was composed mostly of West Pakistanis, optees and refugees from India, who were mainly Urdu-speaking.'[106] This made a major difference as officers in Pakistan enjoyed much greater power than their counterparts elsewhere, including India, because of the Muslim League's lack of competent men and organizational weaknesses. In the initial stages, 'civil servants were not only executive officers but very influential as policy-makers as well. They never abandoned this role, and thus in major policy-making decisions, or in actual execution of policies, East Pakistan did not have any effective say.'[107]

Army officers in Pakistan were drawn almost entirely from West Pakistan—Punjab, the North-West Frontier Province, Sindh and Baluchistan. The armed forces, a major source of employment and contracts from the very beginning, ruled the country from 1957 to 1968 and then again from 1979 to 1988. The Army, in particular, called the shots even when a civilian government was in power. The armed forces invariably sought to promote the interests of West at the expense of East Pakistan, and looked down on the Bengalis as 'non-martial'—very much like the British, who recruited to the British Indian Army mainly from those sections of undivided India's population they classified as 'martial', as opposed to certain other sections, mainly Bengalis, which they labelled 'non-martial' and, by implication, cowardly and effeminate.

From the very beginning, the central government's policies ensured that the entire foreign exchange earned by East Bengal by exporting jute flowed into West Pakistan. Even the proceeds of the sales tax realized in East Bengal went to the western wing. In the words of Umar, 'the industrial development of Pakistan became a central government concern, which was virtually in the hands of West Pakistanis, who advocated the oneness of Pakistan's economy and diverted available resources to the West as far as it was politically practicable'.[108]

Such partisan policies aggravated the impact of certain developments which followed from Partition. The overwhelming majority of Muslim businessmen and their capital flowed into West Pakistan. Mostly from Mumbai, Gujarat, Kathiawar and Central India, they had more in common with the people of West Pakistan than with those of the eastern wing. Also, West Pakistan developed faster because the country's capital, Karachi, was situated there and it was easier for people in the western wing not only to get licenses for starting business and industrial units but also utilize various types of banking facilities and services that institutions like the State Bank of Pakistan and the National Bank, both located in Karachi, provided. On the other hand, people from East Pakistan had to come all the way to West Pakistan for licenses and loans. 'The situation in the later period was not much different.'[109]

The bias against East Bengal affected the Centre's response to specific situations in the province, like the famine that began to set in from the first quarter of 1947. The East Pakistan government's efforts to procure rice and paddy from the eight surplus districts out of a total of 17 and dispatch them to the deficit districts, and to build up government stocks to sustain rationing in some urban areas, including Dhaka, did not work because of corruption and administrative efficiency. On the other hand, forcible confiscation of grain from peasants without surplus, and problems created for migrant agricultural workers carrying home rice and paddy earned as wages created widespread discontent. The crisis deepened in 1948.[110] Yet the central government did not import grain to cope with the situation, and used export earnings from East Pakistan's jute in West Pakistan's interest. Worse, grain from West Pakistan, instead of being sent to East Pakistan, was exported to India.[111]

The assistance of 70,000 tons of grain that the central government provided was hardly adequate and the famine continued till 1951. This and the steep rise in the price of salt, from that year—thanks to faulty government policies—affected millions in East Pakistan.[112] The political impact of this was first felt in the 1949 by-election in Tangail in which Shamsul Huq, who later became the first general secretary of the Awami Muslim League, badly defeated the Muslim League candidate, Khurram Khan Panni.[113] Pakistan's central government, however, failed to get the message. This was because its conscious or subconscious objective was to dominate East Pakistan. It was manifested at one level in its attempt to completely dominate the affairs of the East Bengal Muslim League and, at another, to impose their own politics and culture on the eastern wing.

Their attitude was a result both of feudal arrogance and the vested interests of West Pakistani businessmen and industrialists. Referring to the situation at the time of partition, Umar writes, 'The central leadership of the Muslim League was composed mainly of the representatives of the feudal landlord class and the business community.' Jinnah, though himself a member of the bourgeoisie and a lawyer, 'as the supreme leader of the Muslim League ... was tied to the feudal aristocracy and the leaders of business'.[114] Besides, inside the Muslim League he was a dictator who tolerated no dissent. Resigning from the Muslim League in 1941 following serious differences with him, Fazlul Huq wrote to the party's high command saying that it was not possible for him to submit to the arbitrary wishes of a single individual.[115] In his arrogance, Jinnah, obediently supported by Prime Minister Liaquat Ali Khan, sought to run the East Bengal Muslim League as his personal fiefdom. Even after the League's victory in Bengal in the 1946 general elections, Jinnah nominated neither Huseyn Shaheed Suhrawardy nor Abul Hashim, the two most important men in the Bengal Muslim League, to the Muslim League's Working Committee. Instead, he nominated Khwaja Nazimuddin and Mirza A. Ispahani, both of whom were then in the political wilderness. Besides, he and Liaquat Ali Khan denied Huseyn Shaheed Suhrawardy, who had been elected unanimously as leader of the Muslim League Parliamentary Party, the post of the Prime Minister of East Bengal and got Khwaja Nazimuddin elected to it.[116] Nazimuddin and the new party president, Akram Khan, made sure that supporters of Suhrawardy and Abul Hashim, particularly those with Leftist leanings, were denied even admission forms. The resulting absence of young and experienced workers and intense internal dissension reduced the organization of the East Bengal Muslim League to a shambles by 1949.[117]

The decline of the Muslim League and the growing discontent among the masses led to the formation of several new parties. Two of these deserve mention. The Awami Muslim League emerged from a conference in Dhaka on 23 and 24 June 1949 with Maulana Bhashani as President, Shamsul Huq as general secretary, and Khandakar Mushtaq Ahmed and Sheikh Mujibur Rahman as Joint Secretaries.[118] On 23 August 1953, Fazlul Huq revived the Krishak Praja Party as the Krishak Shramik Party.

The language movement

If Jinnah's arrogance led to the language movement—which perhaps did more than anything else to put East Pakistan on the path of liberation as Bangladesh—that of his successor triggered a massive unrest in the eastern wing on the issue of Pakistan's constitution. The incipient stirrings of the language movement followed statements by Pakistan's central education minister, Fazlur Rahman, in late 1947, that Urdu would be the only state language of Pakistan.[119] Strong opposition by Liaquat Ali Khan and others led to the rejection of a resolution moved to make Bengali a language of the Constituent Assembly along with Urdu and English, on the first day of its session on 23 February 1948.[120] This sparked a massive burst of anger in the East. Jinnah's visit to East Pakistan from 19 to 28 March 1948, during which he reiterated his stand that Urdu would be Pakistan's sole state language and warned Bengalis about the activities of 'subversive elements' out to destroy Pakistan, caused further anger.

After a lull, resentment flared up again when the interim report of the Constitutional Basic Principles Committee (BPC), submitted on 28 September 1950, stated that Urdu would be the state language of Pakistan.[121] The movement reached its peak after Nazimuddin (who had become Prime Minister after the assassination of Liaquat Ali Khan on 16 October 1951), read out from Jinnah's speech in Dhaka saying that Urdu would be Pakistan's sole state language. Not only that, he denounced those who demanded Bengali as a state language as 'provincialists' and, as such, enemies of the Pakistani state.[122] A series of meetings and demonstrations that followed culminated in a general strike throughout East Bengal on 21 February 1952. Police firing on students of Dhaka University, who were at the forefront of the language movement, killed four. The four—Rafiq, Barkat, Jabbar and Salam—are now remembered as the martyrs of the language movement. Dhaka and many parts of East Bengal were paralysed on the 22nd, when two persons were killed in firing—and 45 wounded in *lathi* charges and teargassing—by policemen. The next few days saw the movement intensify throughout East Bengal, with shops and offices closed, train and bus services paralysed over wide areas and Dhaka simmering in anger. The government responded with severe repression, which caused the general strike in Dhaka on 5 March 1952 to fail; but by then the movement had spread to even remote corners of East Bengal and it became a matter of time before the central government had to admit Bengali as a state language. This it did on 19 April 1954 when Pakistan's Constituent Assembly decided that both Urdu and Bengali would be Pakistan's state languages.

The language movement remains a landmark in the history of East Bengal and Bangladesh. A mass movement involving almost every part of the province and every section of the people, it sharpened the self-perception of the overwhelming majority of people of East Bengal as Bengalis as well as Muslims—and not, as immediately after Partition, as Muslims over everything else. It also prompted the province's rising middle class to identify itself passionately with Bengal's rich, eclectic, liberal humanist culture which acted as a powerful countervailing force against the spread of Islamist fundamentalism in its ranks.

The language movement came on top of the famine, the rise in the price of salt and the publication of the report of the Constitutional Basic Principles Committee—appointed on 12 March 1949—on 28 September 1950. The latter provided for a constitution which would have, if implemented, not only neutralized the numerical superiority of East Bengal in the area of administration and governance and put it completely under the domination of West Pakistan but also created a presidency whose incumbent, by virtue of the arbitrary powers vested in the office, could easily proclaim himself dictator. Following widespread agitation, a resolution moved by Prime Minister Liaquat Ali Khan announced on 21 November 1950 that further discussion on the Committee's report was being postponed to give an opportunity to those who wanted to make specific recommendations to amend it.[123] Much damage, however, had already been done. The committee's report and the language movement inclined the people of East Bengal to think of Pakistan's central government as being intent on dominating and exploiting them. This again deeply eroded the influence of the Muslim League which ruled Pakistan and whose provincial organization invariably endorsed what its central leadership did.

The rout and after

The result was the rout of the Muslim League in the elections of March 1954, which were swept by the United Front formed by Fazlul Huq's Krishak Shramik Party and the Awami Muslim League. The Front won 228 of the 237 seats reserved for Muslims in East Bengal, while the Muslim League won only 10.[124] The result marked much more than the replacement of one set of rulers by another. It marked the emergence of regional autonomy and the cultural identity of Bengalis as the two issues that defined political discourse and praxis in East Bengal and East Pakistan until the latter's emergence into freedom as Bangladesh in 1971. This was because the most important elements in the 21-point declaration read out by Maulana Bhashani after the formation of the United Front on 4 December 1953 were— full autonomy for East Bengal with Pakistan's central government being responsible for only defence, foreign affairs and currency regulation; recognition of Bengali as a state language; and the declaration of 21 February as a national holiday to commemorate the martyrdom of the four students killed in police firing on that day.

Pakistan's central government dismissed the United Front government on 30 May, following two developments. The first was a speech earlier that month in Calcutta during which Maulana Bhashani reportedly said, 'We are fellow workers in a common cause. If we have the common cause in view it is idle to say that I am a Bengali, someone is a Bihari, someone is a Pakistani, and someone is a something else.' Stating that India existed as a whole, he added 'I shall dedicate my services to the cause of the motherland and work with those who will try to win for India—Hindustan and Pakistan—a place among the countries of the world.'[125] The second was rioting between Bengali and non-Bengali workers in Karnafuli in Chittagong which led to several hundred deaths. Dismissing the Huq ministry, the governor general imposed 'governor's rule' under Section 92A of the Government of India Act of 1935, appointed Defence Secretary Iskander Mirza Governor and despatched 10,000 troops to maintain order.

All this further alienated East Bengal and intensified the struggle for autonomy spearheaded by Bangladesh's rising middle class. With the departure of Hindu landlords and moneylenders, Muslims took their places. This eroded the identification of Hindus with exploiters. On the other hand, East Bengal's middle class saw 'non-Bengali Muslims running the bureaucratic governmental machine, controlling business and whatever industry there was. They saw that the Bengali politicians of the ruling party were nothing but servitors of West-Pakistan based Muslim League and the central government.'[126] This transformed their entire political perspective. The communal contradiction which partitioned India was 'replaced by contradictions between the two regions and the ethnically and linguistically different people who belonged to the Muslim community'.[127]

This basic contradiction continued to widen even though the Constitution of Pakistan, promulgated in 1956, recognized Bengali as a state language along with Urdu. Much of the responsibility for this must rest with the military dictatorship of Ayub Khan (1958–68), whose real character could not be disguised by the fraudulent representative rule introduced on 23 March 1962. Political repression and economic exploitation of East Pakistan was compounded by cultural imperialism. Monaem Khan, Governor of East Pakistan from 1962 to 1968, banned public meetings, censored the press, controlled radio programmes, banned the import of books and films from West Bengal and the broadcast of Tagore songs from Dhaka radio. Such measures, and the perceived neglect of East Pakistan's defence during the India–Pakistan war of 1965, only strengthened East Pakistan's demand for autonomy, which found a dramatic expression on 12 February 1966 when Sheikh Mujibur Rahman announced his famous Six-Point Programme at an all-party meeting in Lahore.

The six-point volley

Reduced to a skeletal outline, the Six-Point Programme provided for the following:

1. The Federation of Pakistan should have a parliamentary form of government based on the supremacy of a legislature directly elected on the basis of universal adult franchise. Representation in the federal legislature should be on the basis of population.

2. The federal government should be responsible only for defence and foreign affairs.

3. There should be two separate currencies mutually and freely convertible in each wing for each region. Alternatively, there should be a single currency in a federal reserve system with regional federal reserve banks to prevent the transfer or resources and flight of capital from one part of the country to another.

4. The federating units will decide fiscal policy and provide the federal government, in a manner laid down in the constitution, with revenue to meet the requirements of its functions relating to defence and the conduct of foreign policy.

5. The constitution should provide for the maintenance of separate accounts for the foreign exchange earnings of each federating unit under the control of their respective governments which should meet the foreign exchange requirements of the federal government according to the procedure laid down in the constitution. The regional governments should have the power to negotiate foreign trade and aid within the framework of the country's foreign policy.

6. The governments of the federating units should be empowered to maintain a militia or paramilitary force to contribute effectively to national security.[128]

The central government's response to the demand for autonomy and the restoration of democracy was intensified repression. In May 1967, Sheikh Mujibur Rahman was arrested under the Public Safety Act. There were general strikes in several cities and police firing which killed 10 persons. In June 1968, the government initiated the Agartala Conspiracy Case against 35 persons, including Sheikh Mujibur Rahman, for conspiring to engineer East Pakistan's secession from Pakistan with India's help.

Meanwhile, growing discontent against the Ayub regime was leading to a massive surge of protest throughout Pakistan. A wave of strikes and protest demonstrations swept East Pakistan in November 1968. At a meeting in Dhaka on 8 January 1969, leaders of eight opposition parties formed a Democratic Action Committee to fight Ayub's one-man rule. Events moved swiftly. On 21 February 1969, Ayub Khan announced that he would not seek re-election as President. On the following day, the government withdrew all charges against

Sheikh Mujibur Rahman and all other accused in the Agartala Conspiracy Case. On 17 March 1969, the government announced that ships loaded with troops, tanks and armament had sailed for East Pakistan. Ayub Khan resigned as President on 25 March and Yahya Khan became President on the 31st of the same month. Preparations for holding elections on the basis of adult franchise began with the appointment of an Election Commission headed by a Bengali Supreme Court judge.

Finally, elections to the National Parliament were held on 7 December 1970. The Awami League—as the Awami Muslim League had been rechristened in 1955—emerged triumphant, winning 160 of the 162 seats to which elections had been held, giving it an absolute majority in the 300-seat national parliament.[129] Zulfikar Ali Bhutto's Pakistan People's Party won 81 of the 138 seats in West Pakistan.[130] From the elections to liberation was a chronologically short—little more than a year—but politically and militarily tumultuous period. As Sheikh Mujibur Rahman stood firm on the demand for autonomy and his right to form the government because of the absolute majority the Awami League had won in the elections, Pakistan's ruling junta, in alliance with Bhutto, prepared for a crackdown. Launched on the night of 25 March 1971, its savagery—which has few parallels in history—led to resistance, which turned into a liberation war with India's assistance and, finally, Pakistan's attack on India on 3 December 1971, which triggered a full-scale war between the two countries. It ended with the ceasefire ordered by Islamabad and the surrender of the Pakistani Army in East Pakistan to the Indian Army and Bangladesh's Mukti Bahini (Liberation Army), on 16 December 1971.

The new nation

On 16 December 1971, a day celebrated in Bangladesh as Bijoy Dibash or Victory Day, a new nation was born. It had been a terribly painful birth. In the effort to abort it, Pakistan's military junta, scripting a new and chilling chronicle of savagery in history, 'had killed three million people, raped 425,000 women, destroyed hundreds and thousands of habitations and forced 10 million people to leave their homes and lead the unfortunate lives of refugees in India'.[131] Events had come full circle since the birth of Pakistan in 1947. Religion had been proved to be an insufficient basis for national identity. In Bangladesh, the Bengali identity had prevailed over the Islamic identity. The Constitution of the new nation, adopted by its Constituent Assembly on 4 November 1972, and promulgated on 16 December of the same year, stated in its preamble that the country accepted 'nationalism', 'socialism', 'democracy' and 'secularism' as principles of state policy.[132] Article 12 provided that the principle of secularism would be realized through the elimination of 'communalism in all forms, the granting by the state of political stature to any religion, the abuse of religion for political purposes' and of 'any discrimination against or persecution of persons practising any particular religion'. Further, Article 38 laid down that no 'person shall have the right to form or be a member or otherwise take part in the activities of, any communal or other association or union, which in the name or on the basis of any religion has for its object or pursues a political purpose'.

These provisions are absent in the present Constitution of Bangladesh, thanks to amendments following political changes since the Constitution was promulgated. The most visible and important of these changes are the revival of religious fundamentalism and ascent to political power of those who had collaborated with—or participated in—the Pakistani army's savage onslaught in 1971 and who had either fled Bangladesh or crawled into the woodwork after the country's liberation. How did this happen?

Efforts to reunite Bangladesh with Pakistan began almost immediately after the former's liberation. While most leaders of the Jamaat-e-Islami who had collaborated with the Pakistanis were arrested after 16 December 1972, some went underground.[133] A few, like Golam Azam[134] and Maulana Abdur Rahim, who had managed to flee the country before that day, first met in Pakistan where an 'East Pakistan Recovery Week' was observed under Golam Azam's leadership.[135] Soon, however, there was a strong groundswell of resentment against them for their complicity in the implementation of the policies and mass slaughter that led to the creation of Bangladesh. They were, therefore, sent off to Saudi Arabia along with the country's Haj delegation. From there, Golam Azam and some of his followers appealed for donations for defending Islam in Bangladesh, where, they said in advertisements in various publications in the Middle East, mosques were being torched and Hindus were killing Muslims and burning their homes. They raised a huge amount of money.[136] Even today committees exist in various countries of the Middle East to raise funds for the Jamaat's activities.

After visiting Dubai, Abu Dhabi, Kuwait and Beirut, they reached London in April 1972, where they set up an office of an 'Islamic Movement' and resumed the publication of *Sangbad*. Incidentally, the sudden publication of *Dainik Sangbad* (Daily News) as the mouthpiece of the Jamaat during Yahya Khan's rule had raised many questions, which were quickly answered when 'its anti-people and anti-liberation of Bangladesh role became clear'.[137]

From London, Golam Azam started rebuilding the Jamaat in Bangladesh. Maulana Abdur Rahim, who had returned to Bangladesh after performing Haj, took up the responsibility for carrying out the task. The work continued in secret.[138] The Jamaat has continued to grow since then, for which a part of the blame must surely be borne by Sheikh Mujibur Rahman. Despite his promises to ensure exemplary punishment for the collaborators involved in murder, rape and torture, the Bangladesh Collaborators (Special Tribunals) Order 1972, issued on 24 January of that year, had several huge loopholes. As a result, out of the 37,471 cases instituted under the Order, only 2,848 were decided by 31 October 1973. Of the accused, only 752 were punished. The remaining 2,096 were proclaimed not guilty.[139] Besides, the punishments were ridiculously light. A member of the Al-Badr militia, convicted for abducting the famous writer/journalist Shahidullah Kaisar, who was murdered, was sentenced to only seven years' imprisonment.[140]

In the midst of growing public discontent over what was widely perceived as unwarranted softness towards the collaborators, Sheikh Mujibur Rahman suddenly proclaimed on 30 November 1973, a general amnesty that covered all who were under trial and all who had been convicted, under the Bangladesh Collaborators (Special Tribunals) Order 1972. Not only that, he ordered their release within a week so that they could participate in the third Victory Day Celebrations on 16 December 1973, and called upon them to participate in the rebuilding of the country.[141]

While there have been many interpretations, some charitable to Sheikh Mujibur Rahman and some harshly critical, the fact is that the amnesty made it possible for the collaborators to return to Bangladesh's political life. They became increasingly, albeit surreptitiously, active following the devastating floods of 1974 during which there was widespread criticism of the government's relief operations, and three unpopular and authoritarian steps by Sheikh Mujibur Rahman—the declaration of a State of Emergency on 28 December 1974, making himself President for five years on 25 January 1975, and the setting up of the Bangladesh Krishak Shramik Awami League as the country's only political party.

Assassination and return of the collaborators

The ground for the collaborators' open return to politics was prepared by the civilian figureheads and military dictators who assumed power after Sheikh Mujibur Rahman's assassination on 15 August 1975. In the upheaval that followed, Khandkar Mushtaq Ahmed, a Minister in Sheikh Mujibur Rahman's government, became President on 20 August and, on 25 August 1975, Maj. Gen. Ziaur Rahman became Chief of the Army Staff. It was during Ahmed's presidency that, on the night of 3 November 1975, the entire top leadership of the Awami League was killed inside Dhaka Central Jail by a group of military officers. Significantly, all those killed had led the liberation struggle and held important positions in the Bangladesh government-in-exile— Syed Nazrul Islam having been the Acting President, Tajuddin Ahmed the Prime Minister, M. Mansur Ali the Finance Minister and A.H.M. Qamaruzzaman the Minister for Home Affairs and Relief and Rehabilitation.

The aim was clearly to cripple the Awami League and make it impossible for it to ever return to power. That the dastardly act was the handiwork of the post-assassination regime is clear from the fact that Khandkar Mushtaq Ahmed, almost immediately after the murders, proclaimed the infamous Indemnity Ordinance which gave the jail killers as well as Sheikh Mujibur Rahman's murderers immunity from punishment and blocked investigation into both crimes. Significantly, another attempt to wipe out the entire leadership of the Awami League was made on 21 August 2004 when a number of grenades were hurled at an Awami League rally in Dhaka. Prime Minister from 1996 to 2001 and currently Leader of the Opposition, Sheikh Hasina escaped by a whisker, while several important leaders were injured. Equally significantly, the attackers remain undetected and unpunished.

Khandkar Mushtaq Ahmed, however, did not last long as President. A coup and counter-coup led to his replacement on 6 November 1975 by Justice Abu Sadat Mohammad Sayem. On 8 November, Sayem was appointed Chief Martial Law Administrator, and Maj. Gen. Ziaur Rahman and the Air Force and Navy Chiefs as Deputy Chief Martial Law Administrators. On 29 November Maj. Gen. Ziaur Rahman became the Chief Martial Law Administrator when Sayem relinquished the post. The process of enabling the fundamentalist war criminals and Islamist fundamentalist collaborators to participate openly in politics began almost immediately. On 31 December 1975, President Sayem revoked the Bangladesh Collaborators (Special Tribunals) Order of 1972. Another proclamation order—III of 1976—issued on 4 May 1976 revoked Article 38 of the Constitution prohibiting the formation of communal parties or associations.

Soon, the Islamization of Bangladesh began. Maj. Gen. Ziaur Rahman, who made himself President on 21 April 1977, not only inserted (by Proclamation Order I of 1977, issued on 23 April) the invocation 'Bismillah-ir-Rahman-ir-Rahim' (In the name of Allah, the Beneficent, the Merciful), above the preamble to the Constitution but also, by amending Article 8(1), removed secularism from among the principles of state policy. The amended part read, 'the principle of absolute trust and faith in the almighty Allah, nationalism, democracy and socialism meaning economic and social justice, together with the principles derived from them . . . shall constitute the fundamental principles of state policy'. It repealed Article 12, which defined what secularism meant in practice. A new clause was added to Article 25 declaring the intention of the state to stabilize, preserve and strengthen fraternal ties with Muslim states on the basis of Islamic solidarity.

All of these changes were ratified by the Sixth Constitution Amendment Act passed by Bangladesh's Jatiya Sansad (National Parliament) on 6 April 1979. There were numerous other changes besides, which made for Islamization by giving Islam primacy and relegating other religions to the background. Thus, the second session of the Jatiya Sansad opened on 21 May 1979 with recitation only from the Quran; the earlier sessions had opened with readings from the sacred texts of all religions. Rehabilitation of collaborators gained momentum. President Ziaur Rahman appointed as his Prime Minister Shah Azizur

Rahman, who had gone as a member of a Pakistani delegation to the United Nations to conduct anti-Bangladesh propaganda and had said, on 4 May 1971:

> With great eagerness, President Yahya Khan sought to establish unhindered democracy in the country by giving [political] parties greater freedom. And wrongly interpreting this opportunity, one of East Pakistan's main political parties, the now defunct Awami League, emerged from the election as the majority party through beheading people and using force, and demanded the right to rule the country unchallenged and according to its own whims. In this manner, it allowed itself to be washed away as a result of its own pride, impatience and arrogance.
>
> I am appealing to the people to help the patriotic armed forces to wreck this evil design by imperialist India.[142]

Golam Azam's return

The process of rehabilitation was dramatically underlined when Golam Azam was allowed to return to Bangladesh on 11 July 1978 on a Pakistani passport and a two-week visa that he had been granted on the basis of his plea that he wanted to see his ailing mother. Not only was he not tried for the serious accusations levelled against him, but he was allowed to stay on at his residence in Mogbazar, Dhaka, even after the expiry of his visa. He continues to flourish in Bangladesh.

The work of rebuilding the Jamaat continued apace following Golam Azam's return. It formally re-emerged as a political party at a convention in Dhaka on 25–27 May 1979. Golam Azam was secretly made Ameer of the Jamaat while Abbas Ali Khan was made the officiating Ameer. Jamaat held its first public meeting at Baitul Mukarram.[143] Addressing the Jamaat's first press conference, Abbas Ali Khan said on 7 December that year, 'What I did for the country and the race was right in 1971 and was meant to defend Bangladesh from the Indian aggressor.[144]

According to several Bangladeshi journalists, President Zia, who launched the Bangladesh Nationalist Party (BNP) on 1 September 1978, cultivated the fundamentalists and Jamaat leaders for political support. Whatever his reasons, his rule gave a major boost to the Jamaat and other fundamentalist Islamist organizations in Bangladesh. His assassination on 30 May 1981 did not change the situation. He was succeeded as President by Abdul Sattar, a former Supreme Court judge whom he had made Vice-President in June 1977. Lt. Gen. H.M. Ershad, who had become the Chief of Army Staff, however, ousted Sattar in a military coup on 24 March 1982. Ershad, who became President on 11 December 1983, replacing A.F.M. Ahsanuddin Chowdhury, who had been placed in the position on 24 March 1982, accelerated the process of Islamization. In early 1983, he declared that the painting of *alpana* (designs on the ground) on the premises of the Shaheed Minar (Martyrs' Monument) was un-Islamic and should be substituted by recitations from the Quran. In 1986, he called for the building of a mosque-based society in Bangladesh. He encouraged both the grant of funds for mosques and the receipt of foreign assistance for their development. Finally, on 7 June 1988, he enacted the Constitution (Eighth Amendment) Act and made Islam Bangladesh's state religion with the proviso that other religions might be practised in peace and harmony in the republic.

A massive popular upheaval forced Ershad to resign as President on 6 December 1990. By then, however, the Jamaat and the cluster of allied fundamentalist organizations were well on their way to becoming a formidable political force. Flush with funds from Pakistan and Saudi Arabia, they had spread their tentacles deep into Bangladesh's countryside by setting up madrasas for children and Shariat courts. They had been particularly harsh on women, driving many to suicide by issuing arbitrary and inhuman *fatwas*.[145] They had launched in many parts of Bangladesh a campaign of violence and intimidation against non-governmental organizations educating women and helping them to become economically independent. They had been harassing secular intellectuals and issuing death threats against them.

The birth of the Nirmul Committee

Alarmed by these developments, the Awami League and the secular Leftist forces as well as elements in Bangladesh's civil society had started organizing resistance to the fundamentalist Islamist onslaught. Things moved towards open confrontation after the return of democracy. Winning a majority in a free and fair election held under a caretaker government on 25 February 1991, the BNP formed a government with Begum Khaleda Zia as Prime Minister. Begum Zia was President Ziaur Rahman's widow, and had became the party's

President on 10 May 1984. The first shot, so to speak, was fired by the Jamaat when it elected Golam Azam as its Ameer on 29 December 1991.[146] On 19 January 1992, 101 widely respected citizens of Bangladesh set up the Ekattorer Ghatak Dalal Nirmul Committee (Committee to Uproot the Killers and Collaborators of Seventy-one) to build up public opinion for Azam's trial. The Nirmul Committee, as it has come to be called generally, said in its first declaration that it would try Azam, war criminal and violator of the Constitution, at a People's Court if the government did not try him.[147] While the movement for his trial drew a massive response, the leaders of the Nirmul Committee sought the cooperation of all political, social and cultural organizations that had supported the liberation war, as it could not ensure a massive public presence at the people's court without the support and participation of political parties. Thirteen political parties including the Awami League, Communist Party, Workers' Party, Jatiya Samajtantrik Dal (National Socialist Party), National Awami Party and the Ganatantri Dal (Democratic Party) supported the programme of trying Azam at a People's Court.[148] On 11 February 1992, the Muktijuddher Chetana Bastabayan o Ekattorer Ghatak Dalal Nirmul Jatiya Samanyay Committee[149] (National Coordination Committee to Realise the Consciousness of the Liberation War and Uproot the Killers Collaborators of Seventy-one) was formed to bring the political parties, mass organizations and professional and social-cultural bodies supporting the movement on a single platform. Jahanara Imam, a respected public figure, one of whose sons had become a martyr during the liberation war, was its convenor.

The BNP government was from the beginning hostile to the movement. Despite its vigorous opposition, and steps like the stoppage of all long distance train, bus and launch services and the imposition of orders under Section 144 of the Criminal Procedure Code forbidding the gathering of five or more persons, and the erection of barricades on all major approach roads to the venue, nearly 500,000 people were present at the people's court on 26 March 1992 at Dhaka's Suhrawardy Udyan (Suhrawardy Garden). It was a massive success despite the BNP government's all-out opposition.[150]

Failing to disrupt the holding of the People's Court, the BNP government, led by Begum Khaleda Zia, filed sedition charges against 24 respected citizens who were its convenors. All this only steeled the people's determination to participate in the movement. At a huge rally at the southern gate of Baitul Mukarram, attended by over 100,000

people, speakers raised four demands—constitute a special tribunal
to try Golam Azam, ban the fundamentalist and communalist politics
of the Jamaat–Shibir[151] group, withdraw the false cases of sedition
filed against 24 respected citizens who were among the organizers of
the movement for a people's court, and stop the countrywide persecution of leaders and activists of the movement, including the filing
of false cases against them by the police.[152]

Faced with a mass movement and the pressure of opposition parties
within the National Parliament, Begum Zia had to conclude a four-
point pact with the opposition parties. Its first two points were that
the government would try Golam Azam and withdraw the false cases
against the 24 organizers of the people's court movement. Instead,
of being prosecuted, however, Golam Azam received citizenship of
Bangladesh. Not only were the cases not withdrawn but Shahriar
Kabir, a leading member of the Nirmul Committee, was removed
without notice from the post of Executive Editor of *Bichitra*, a weekly
published by a government-controlled trust.[153] In spite of all this and
attacks on the leaders of the movement by activists of the Jamaat, the
Nirmul Committee had collected, by December 1992, 1 million sig-
natures for Golam Azam's trial.

The movement, however, seemed to lose some of its steam after
Jahanara Imam's death on 26 June 1994. To a large extent this
happened because in that year the Jamaat became a partner in the
Awami League's campaign for holding the next general elections under
a caretaker government.[154] It was now the Awami League's turn to
sup with the Jamaat!

In many ways, 1994 is an important year in Bangladesh's contemporary history. It saw the fundamentalists launch a campaign
against the writer Taslima Nasreen who they wanted tried for blasphemy for an interview she gave an Indian newspaper in which she
was quoted as calling for a revision of the Quran. Nasreen surrendered
to the court on 3 August 1994 and was given bail. She, however, left
the country for Sweden because fundamentalist organizations, backed
by the Jamaat, had openly threatened to kill her. In fact she was not
left alone even after she left the country. On 12 August 1994 there
were demonstrations in Dhaka and elsewhere demanding that
Muslims in Sweden ensure her return to Bangladesh. 'We want the
infidel back in our country. . . . Our Muslim brothers in Sweden must
help us,' said Zairul Islam, a leader of the Committee to Resist Anti-
Islamic Activity.[155] He added, 'Taslima Nasreen has insulted our

religion and she is safe nowhere in the world.'[156] Earlier, on 29 July 1994, nearly 70,000 heavily-armed fundamentalists had staged a march through Dhaka, organized by the then newly-constituted Sammilita Sangram Parishad (United Struggle Council) of 13 fundamentalist organizations.[157]

Addressing a mass gathering from a podium in front of the National Parliament on Manik Mia Avenue in Dhaka, leaders of the 13 fundamentalist organizations demanded the death not only of Taslima but also of Bangladesh's leading poet, Shamsur Rahman, National Professor Kabir Chowdhury and intellectual Ahmed Sharif, on the grounds that they were against Islam.[158] In this first open show of strength by Islamist fundamentalists in Bangladesh after liberation, the speakers at Manik Mia Avenue also demanded the banning of several publications including the leading Bengali daily *Janakantha*.[159] Earlier, on 30 June, Bangladesh's religion-based parties, backed by the Jamaat, had called for a nationwide half-day strike demanding Nasreen's trial, the banning of NGO activities, the enactment of a blasphemy law and the banning of several 'identified' national dailies.[160] On the same day, the Anti-Communal Students' Society, backed by the Awami League, Left-leaning parties and a number of social and cultural organizations had called for a dawn-to-dusk *hartal* demanding Golam Azam's trial and a ban on religion-based political parties.[161] One person was killed and hundreds, including a number of policemen, were injured in clashes throughout the country between supporters of the rival *hartals*.[162]

Show of force and after

The show-of-force march on 29 July and the *hartal* on 30 June underlined the increasingly aggressive posture Islamist fundamentalists were beginning to assume in Bangladesh. The BNP government not only did not respond strongly enough but often sided with the Islamists. Thus, on 8 June 1994, Toab Khan and Borhan Ahmed, Advisory Editor and Executive Editor respectively of *Janakantha*, were arrested under Section 295(A) of the Bangladesh Penal Code for having allegedly offended religious sentiments of the people. The paper's editor, Atiquallah Khan Masud, and an Assistant Editor, A.T.M. Shamsuddin, were reportedly marked for arrest.[163] Taken into custody on the basis of a complaint filed by Nurul Alam, Officer-in-Charge of Dhaka's

Motijheel police station, for the publication of a post-editorial article on 12 May 1994 which allegedly hurt the religious sentiments of Muslims, Toab Khan and Borhan Ahmed were denied bail by the Chief Metropolitan Magistrate, Dhaka, and sent to jail.[164]

Reacting strongly, Kazi Shahed Ahmed and Enayetullah Khan, President and General Secretary respectively of the Bangladesh Sangbadpatra Parishad (Bangladesh Newspaper Council) condemned the arrests as having been made at the instigation of the forces opposed to national liberation, religion and humanism.[165]

Also charged under Section 295(A) of the Penal Code was Ahmed Sharif, a prominent Left-leaning intellectual and a former professor of Bengali at Dhaka University, on the complaint of a local leader of Gopalganj, Maulana Mohammad Yusuf, that his public comments on *azaan*[166] had offended the religious sentiments of Muslims. Sharif moved the High Court, which shifted his case from Gopalganj and directed him to appear before the Chief Metropolitan Magistrate, Dhaka, who gave him bail on 8 August 1994.[167] Earlier, on 17 June 1994, fundamentalists had thrown at least 10 bombs at his residence in Dhanmondi, Dhaka, in the dead of night. Fortunately, neither he nor any of his family members was hurt.[168]

The BNP government's submissiveness towards fundamentalist forces became clear when Begum Zia cancelled, on 27 August 1994, her plan to visit Cairo to attend the UN-sponsored World Population Conference beginning on 5 September 1994. Her decision followed harsh criticism of the conference by some Muslim religious leaders and groups holding birth control to be against Islam and alleging that the conference was aimed at 'exterminating Muslims'.[169] Needless to say, actions like Begum Zia's further emboldened fundamentalist Islamist clerics and politicians trying to forcibly recast Bangladesh's society according to their views.

The persecution of women, NGOs and social workers increased. Thus, on 11 May 1994, an illegal village court, presided over by a local Muslim cleric in Dhamsar village in Brahmanbaria District, ordered that a 13-year-old girl who had been raped the previous year and had delivered a child, had to be struck a thousand times by a broom. Acquitting the accused for want of witnesses, it pronounced the girl, Sapnahar, guilty of having had illicit sex.[170] Another girl, 19-year-old Rina, committed suicide on 16 December 1994 in Hasanpur Village in Feni District, after she had been hit 101 times with a broom on 13 December following a *fatwa* by an illegal village court headed by a cleric, which had pronounced her guilty of having illicit relations with a man. Not only that, two days later, she was compelled to host, as a part of her 'penance', a feast for those who had issued the *fatwa* and decreed her punishment. And all this despite the fact that the chief of the local Union Parishad and the village administration had found her not guilty of the charges![171]

According to reports in Dhaka newspapers on 26 March 1994, Abdul Rashid, a young man, had been hit with shoes, thrown to the ground and whipped, and had his head shorn at the instance of a clerical court at Hairpur village in the Manikganj area near Dhaka. A resident of the same village, he had also been ordered to leave. His father had been asked to pay a fine of Tk 25,000. His crime? He had been leading a movement for women's education regardless of threats and opposition by clerics who wanted him to stop. The police had not arrested anyone.[172]

The tragic story of Sapnahar and Rina, the brutal treatment meted out to Abdul Rashid, and the thrust of the state's policies in Bangladesh since the installation of President Ziaur Rahman's regime clearly indicate that the present surge of violent Islamist fundamentalism in Bangladesh is not so much a result of neglect in combating it, as of a planned effort.

The bid to revive Islamist fundamentalism, which had been pushed out of the public space in Bangladesh by the liberation war, began abroad. Nevertheless, it had been so thoroughly exposed and discredited that it could not stage a comeback on its own. The process of Islamization of state and society launched by the governments of Presidents Ziaur Rahman and H.M. Ershad, prepared the ground for its revival. The huge flow of funds from Saudi Arabia and other West Asian countries, as well as Pakistan, coupled with active patronage from the state, enabled the Jamaat and the cluster of fundamentalist organizations allied with it or spawned by it, to grow to a point where, by 1994, they could not only take on the secular and modernist forces in the streets but also issue death threats to writers and intellectuals, impose their anti-woman and obscurantist social and judicial codes in the countryside, and brutally assault social workers and the staff of NGOs with impunity.

As the subsequent chapters would show, today the state in Bangladesh protects Islamist fundamentalists not from the wrath of the people for their role in 1971 but from the legal consequences of their actions, like the grenade attack on 21 August 2004 in Dhaka, the killing of Prof. Mohammad Yunus in Rajshahi and the murderous attacks on Prof. Humayun Azad in Dhaka. While the BNP is not a fundamentalist party itself and its ranks include not only secular elements but many who had participated in the liberation war, its top leadership seems to be working in tandem with the Jamaat, Islami Oikya Jote (IOJ) and other fundamentalist Islamist parties. Hence the question: Can the march of the Taliban brand of Islamist fundamentalism be halted in Bangladesh?

Notes

1. Bruce Hoffman, *Inside Terrorism* (New York: Columbia University Press, 1999), pp. 43–44.
2. Walter Laqueur, *The Age of Terrorism* (Boston and Toronto: Little Brown and Company, 1987), p. 4.
3. Ibid., p. 12.
4. Ibid., p. 13.
5. See Ibid., p. 15, 17.
6. Ibid., p. 15.
7. Ibid., p. 16.
8. Ibid.
9. Ibid., p. 21.
10. Karen Armstrong, 'Was this Inevitable? Islam Through History', in James F. Hoge, Jr, and Gideon Rose (eds), *How Did This Happen? Terrorism and the New War* (Public Affairs Reports) (New York: The Perseus Press, 2001), p. 60. Mr Hoje and Mr Rose are editor and managing editor, respectively, of *Foreign Affairs*.
11. Ibid., pp. 60–61.
12. Arthur J. Arberry, *The Koran Interpreted* (Oxford: Oxford University Press, 1979), p. 208.
13. Ibid., p. 99.
14. M.N. Roy, *The Historical Role of Islam* (Delhi: Ajanta Publications, 1981), p. 22.
15. A Khalif (Caliph) is the civil and religious head of a Muslim state who is regarded as a representative of Allah.
16. Ibid., p. 14.
17. Quoted in ibid., p. 11.
18. Ibid., pp. 35–36.
19. Ibid., pp. 11–12.
20. Makhan Lal Roy Choudhury, *The Din-i-Ilahi or the Religion of Akbar*, 2nd ed. (Calcutta: Das Gupta & Co, 1952), p. 2.
21. Ibid., p. 2.
22. Ibid., p. 3. From Elliot and Dowson's translation of the *Tarikh-i-Yamini*.
23. Ibid., p. 3.
24. Ibid., pp. 3–4.

25. Ibid., p. 16.
26. Ibid., p. 17.
27. Maulana Wahiduddin Khan, *Islam: Creator of the Modern Age*, trans. Dr Farida Khanum (New Delhi: The Islamic Centre, 1995), pp. 35–36.
28. Ibid., p. 32.
29. Ibid., p. 36.
30. Ibid., p. 44.
31. Ibid., p. 88.
32. Ibid., pp. 88–89.
33. Arthur J. Arberry, *The Koran Interpreted*, p. 70.
34. Ibid., p. 77.
35. Ibid., p. 73.
36. Ibid., p. 3.
37. M.A. Karandikar, *Islam in India s Transition to Modernity* (New Delhi: Orient Longman, 1968), p. 100.
38. Ibid., p. 99.
39. A *khanqa* is an abode of Sufi saints and holy men.
40. Ibid.
41. Ibid., p. 100.
42. Ibid., p. 101.
43. Ibid.
44. Ibid., p. 127.
45. Ibid.
46. Ibid., p. 129.
47. Dilip Hiro, *War Without End: The Rise of Islamist Terror and Global Response* (London: Routledge and New Delhi: Roli Books, 2002), p. 37.
48. Ibid.
49. Bipan Chandra, in Bipan Chandra, Mridula Mukherjee, Aditya Mukherjee, K.N. Panikkar and Sucheta Mahajan, *India s Struggle for Indpendence* (New Delhi: Penguin, 1989), p. 41.
50. Karandikar, *Islam in India s Transition to Modernity*, p. 105. A *dhimmi* is an inhabitant of a Muslim state who belongs to an officially protected non-Muslim religion.
51. Ibid., p. 106.
52. *Jizya*, or poll tax, is a personal tax levied on non-Muslims in a Muslim state. Those who pay it have to be supported, protected, granted freedom of faith and treated on a footing of justice and equality with Muslims.
53. Ibid., p. 107.
54. Ibid.
55. Chief Religious Officer in Akbar's reign. Sadr is the head of religion in court.
56. Literally, Makhdum-ul-Mulk means 'beloved of the country'. Abdullah Sultanpuri, whose official title it was, held a high religious office.
57. Roy Choudhury, *The Din-i-Ilahi or the Religion of Akbar*, p. 57.
58. Ibid.
59. Ibid., pp. 30–31.
60. To become a Muslim, a person must believe in and recite the Kalima, which reads: 'There is only one God and Muhammad is His Prophet.'
61. Ibid., pp. 5–7.
62. Ibid., pp. 8–9.

63. Qazi Abdul Wadud, *Banglar Mushalmaner Katha* (The Story of the Mussalmans of Bengal) (Kolkata: Mreettika: Swadesh Samakal Granthamala, 2003), p. 28.

64. Ibid., pp. 34–36 for the Bengali translation and pp. 45–48 for relevant extracts from the original English carried in the book.

65. Ibid., p. 37.

66. For a short but remarkably comprehensive account of Titumir's life, see Subodh Chandra Sengupta and Anjali Basu (eds), *Sansad Bangali Charitrabhidan: Pratham Khanda* (Sansad Dictionary of Biographies of Bengalis, First Part), 3rd rev. ed. (Kolkata: Sahitya Sansad, 1994), p. 196.

67. Muin-ud-Din Ahmed Khan, 'Religious Reform Movement of the Muslims', in Sirajul Islam (ed.), *History of Bangladesh 1704–1971*, vol. 3 (Dhaka: Asiatic Society of Bangladesh, 1992), p. 272, 285 and 287. See also Sengupta and Basu, *Sansad Bangali Charitrabhidan*, pp. 210, 513.

68. Ibid., p. 40.

69. Ibid., p. 41.

70. Ibid., pp. 40–41. 'This age' refers to Wadud's time.

71. Ibid., p. 41–42.

72. Ibid., p. 18.

73. Ibid.

74. Ibid.

75. Ibid.

76. Ibid., p. 19.

77. Joya Chatterji, *Bengal Divided: Hindu Communalism and Partition, 1932–1947* (Cambridge University Press, Cambridge, and Foundation Books and the Book Review Trust, New Delhi, 1995), p. 78.

78. Rajat Ray and Ratna Ray, 'Zamindars and Jotedars: A Study of the Rural Politics of Bengal', *Modern Asian Studies* 9(1), 1975, p. 101.

79. J.H. Broomfield, *Elite Conflict in a Plural Society: Twentieth Century Bengal* (Berkeley and Los Angeles, CA: University of California Press, 1968), p. 44.

80. Ibid., pp. 44–45.

81. Suranjan Das, *Communal Riots in Bengal 1905–1947* (Delhi: Oxford University Press, 1993), p. 23.

82. Ibid., p. 24.

83. Ibid.

84. Ibid.

85. Ibid., p. 20.

86. Ibid.

87. Ibid.

88. Ibid., p. 21.

89. Ibid., pp. 2–3.

90. Ibid., p. 40.

91. J.H. Broomfield describes the *bhadralok* (literally, 'gentle folk') as a 'socially privileged and consciously superior group, economically dependent on landed rents and professional and clerical employment'. He carefully distinguished between the *bhadralok* and the middle class. According to him the *bhadralok* were upper—and not middle-class, if class was taken as a status group. Nor could *bhadralok* be considered as a middle class in the Marxian sense of the latter as an economic group. For the *bhadralok* did not include many middle class elements

like merchants and prosperous peasants, while encompassing some persons from both higher and lower classes. See Broomfield, *Elite Conflict in a Plural Society*, p. 14.

92. Broomfield, *Elite Conflict in a Plural Society*, pp. 63–64.
93. Ibid., p. 64.
94. Ibid., p. 65.
95. For details of the riots, their causes, aftermath and implications, see Suranjan Das, *Communal Riots in Bengal 1905–1947*, pp. 60–75, and J.H. Broomfield, *Elite Conflict in a Plural Society*, pp. 119–25.
96. Das, *Communal Riots in Bengal 1905–1947*, pp. 74–75.
97. Broomfield, *Elite Conflict in a Plural Society*, p. 123.
98. Krishak Praja Party (Peasant Tenant Party) was established in 1936 under the leadership of A.K. Fazlul Huq and others to fight the elections due in Bengal in 1937 under the provisions of the Government of India Act of 1935. It grew out of the Bengal Praja Party (Bengal Tenants Party) which was established by Huq and others in 1929—and which become the Nikhil Banga Praja Samiti (All-Bengal Tenants' Association) by the end of the year—to defend and restore the rights of peasants and make tenants the owners of their land by abolishing the *zamindari* system.
99. Chatterji, *Bengal Divided*, pp. 78–79.
100. The Swaraj Party was formed on 1 January 1923 by Deshbandhu Chittaranjan Das and Pandit Motilal Nehru, with the former as President, to contest elections to the legislative councils established under the Government of India Act of 1919. Its declared aim was to 'wreck the Councils from within', which, however, Mahatma Gandhi was opposed to. According to the Mahatma, the lure of ministerial office would prove too strong for Congressmen elected to a majority in the Councils. Offered such posts, they would drop all pretence at non-cooperation. Motilal Nehru and Chittaranjan Das set up a separate party as their strategy was rejected by the Congress at its Gaya session in December 1922. For circumstances leading to the formation of the Swaraj Party, see Leonard A. Gordon, *Brothers Against the Raj: A Biography of Indian Nationalists Sarat and Subhas Chandra Bose* (Penguin Books, New Delhi, and Columbia University Press, New York and London, 1990), pp. 97–98. For a broader idea about the role and ethos of the party, see Chapter Four, 'Swarajists in Calcutta and Mandalay, 1923–27', pp. 96–150.
101. Broomfield, *Elite Conflict in a Plural Society*, p. 246.
102. Chatterji, *Bengal Divided*, pp. 29–30.
103. See Broomfield, *Elite Conflict in a Plural Society*, pp. 285–86.
104. Ibid., p. 293.
105. Badruddin Umar, *The Emergence of Bangladesh: Class Struggles in East Pakistan (1947–58)* (Karachi: Oxford University Press, 2004), pp. 15–16.
106. Ibid., p. 11.
107. Ibid., p. 12.
108. Ibid., p. 13.
109. Ibid., p. 12.
110. Ibid., pp. 18–21.
111. Ibid., p. 22.
112. Ibid., pp. 24–25.

113. Ibid., p. 26.
114. Ibid., p. 8.
115. Ibid., p. 9.
116. Ibid.
117. Ibid., p. 10.
118. Ibid., pp. 108–10.
119. Ibid., p. 31.
120. Ibid., p. 32.
121. Ibid., p. 161.
122. Ibid., p. 190.
123. Ibid., p. 172.
124. Richard Sisson and Leo E. Rose, *War and Secession: Pakistan, India and the Creation of Bangladesh* (Berkeley and Los Angeles, CA: University of California Press, 1990), p. 14.
125. Ibid., p. 13. Cited from *The Hindu*, 10 March 1954.
126. Umar, *The Emergence of Bangladesh*, p. 15.
127. Ibid.
128. Ibid., p. 20. Summarized from the full text of the programme reproduced by Umar.
129. Ibid., p. 32.
130. Ibid.
131. Shahriar Kabir, *Bangladeshe Amraa ebong Ora* (We and They in Bangladesh) (Dhaka: Ananya, 2005), p. 2 of the Introduction.
132. *The Constitution of the Republic of Bangladesh* (Dhaka: Government of Bangladesh, Ministry of Law, 1972), p. 5.
133. For atrocities perpetrated during the liberation war by leaders of the Jamaat-e-Islami and allied organizations, see Chapter Five of this book.
134. Golam Azam was a leading collaborator who has been accused of participating in genocide and mass rape.
135. Shahriar Kabir, *Ekattorer Ghatak o Dalalra Ke Kothaye* (Killers and Collaborators of Seventy-one: Who is Where?), 2nd ed. (Dhaka: Muktijuddhere Chetana Bikash Kendra [Centre for Spreading the Consciousness of the Liberation War], 1987), p. 20.
136. Ibid., pp. 69–70.
137. Ibid.
138. Ibid., pp. 70–71.
139. Ibid., p. 69.
140. Ibid., p. 21.
141. Ibid., p. 22.
142. Ibid., p. 91.
143. Baitul Mukarram is Bangladesh's national mosque.
144. Kabir, *Ekattorer Ghatak o Dalalra Ke Kothaye*, pp. 71–72.
145. A *fatwa* is a religious directive by Islamic clergy.
146. Kabir, *Bangladeshe Amraa ebong Ora*, p. 11.
147. Ibid., p. 11.
148. Ibid., p. 12.
149. Ibid.
150. Ibid.

151. Shibir here refers to the Jamaat's front organization among students, Islami Chhatra Shibir, details of which appear later in the book.
152. Kabir, *Ekattorer Ghatak o Dalalra Ke Kothaye*, p. 13.
153. Ibid., p. 14.
154. Ibid., p. 16.
155. News item, 'Fundamentalists Demand Taslima's Return', *The Asian Age* (New Delhi), 13 August 1994.
156. Ibid.
157. Zahirul Huq, 'Bangladesh: 70 Hajar Moulabadi Long Marche' (Bangladesh: 70,000 Fundamentalists in a Long March), *Aajkaal* (Kolkata), 1 July 1995.
158. Ibid.
159. Ibid.
160. News item, 'Sporadic Clashes Mark Hartal: One Killed, Hundreds Hurt', *The Daily Star* (Dhaka), 1 July 1994.
161. Ibid.
162. Ibid.
163. News report, 'Police Case Against Janakantha, Toab Khan, Another Sent to Jail', *The Daily Star* (Dhaka), 9 June 1994.
164. Ibid.
165. Ibid.
166. The call for prayer given from mosques.
167. Zaglul A. Chowdhury, 'Bangla Leftist Gets Bail for Blasphemy', *The Times of India* (New Delhi), 9 August 1994.
168. Zahirul Huq, 'Dharmaghate Rastaye Berolayi Shasti: Jamaat: Ahmed Sharifer Badite Boma' (Punishment for Stepping Out into the Road during Hartal: Jamaat: Bombs [Thrown] at the House of Ahmed Sharif), *Aajkaal* (Kolkata), 18 June 1994.
169. News report, 'Khaleda Gives in to Radicals, Avoids Population Meet', *The Asian Age* (New Delhi), 28 August 1994.
170. News report, 'Fatwa Against 13-year-old Girl', *The Hindu* (New Delhi), 30 June 1994.
171. Pallab Bhattacharya (Press Trust of India), 'Fatwa Pushes Bangladesh Teenager to Suicide', *The Asian Age* (New Delhi), 6 January 1995.
172. Zahirul Huq, 'Bangladeshe Moulabadi Kirti: Matha Mudiye, Jooto Mere Narishikshar Shaja' (Fundamentalist Feat in Bangladesh: Shorn Head, Beating by Shoes Punishment for [Promoting] Women's Education), *Aajkaal* (Kolkata), 27 March 1994.

Two

The Troubling Question

On the evening of 21 August 2004, an attack on a rally in the heart of Dhaka, Bangladesh's capital, shook the country and the world. The attack, in the course of which between nine and 13 grenades were hurled, according to divergent accounts, was on a rally by the Awami League, the main opposition party, which had spear-headed Bangladesh's liberation struggle from its embryonic stage and had ruled the country from 1971 to 1975 and again from 1996 to 2001. Sixteen people died on the spot and over 200 were wounded. In the days that followed, the death toll rose to 22. While this caused deep and widespread shock and anger, the implications of the attack and what it indicated about the possible motives, disturbed many. Had the attack succeeded, the entire top leadership of the Awami League, including Sheikh Hasina Wajed, its President, who had been Prime Minister of Bangladesh from 1996 to 2001, would have been killed. This, in turn, would have crippled the party and prevented it from playing an effective role in Bangladesh's politics for a long time.

The result would have been the destruction of Bangladesh's political balance, which would have enabled the coalition government—comprising its mainstay, the Bangladesh Nationalist Party (BNP), along with the Jamaat-e-Islami (or Jamaat), the Islami Oikya Jote (IOJ) and the Jatiya Party (Naziur) or JP(N)—to remain in power for the foreseeable future. As the enormity of the crime and its implications registered in the public mind, a question that I had been asking myself for some time[1] suddenly seemed to require careful examination—was Bangladesh on its way to becoming a country like Afghanistan under Taliban rule?

Prior to 21 August 2004, most people tended to dismiss such a possibility. Bangladesh did not feature in the United States Central Intelligence Agency's annual *Patterns of Global Terrorism* reports, and had proclaimed its enthusiastic support for the US-led global war on terrorism. Until the attack, US officials had repeatedly praised it as a moderate Islamic country. Besides, since 1991 Begum Khaleda Zia and Sheikh Hasina had alternated as Prime Minister. Neither of them could be unaware of the fact that fundamentalist Islam had no place for women in politics, to say nothing of a woman becoming Prime Minister of a country.

In any case, the fundamentalist Islamist parties in Bangladesh had rather limited support. The Jamaat won only 18 of the 300 elected seats in the country's Jatiya Sansad or National Parliament in the general elections held on 1 October 2001. It subsequently got two of the 30 seats reserved for women who are elected by members of parliament allotted to it by Bangladesh's ruling four-party alliance.[2] The other fundamentalist Islamist party, the Islami Oikya Jote, won only two seats. Given the limited electoral support the fundamentalist Islamist parties enjoyed, it seemed inconceivable to most that they would ever be able to win an absolute majority and form in Bangladesh a government that would Talibanize the country.

The prospect seemed all the more remote considering that the secular ethos of Bangladesh's liberation struggle still powerfully influenced a large section of the people. Although the secular and left-of-centre Bangladesh Awami League lost the October 2001 elections, winning only 62 of the 300 directly elected seats in the National Parliament, it nevertheless secured over 40 per cent of the votes polled, a clear indication of the support it commanded. Also, Bangladesh had a vibrant, strongly secular and politically active civil society and intelligentsia, a lively NGO sector playing a major role in empowering women, and a strong women's movement.

What many people failed to recognize, however, was the fact that fundamentalist Islamist elements did not need to capture power electorally in Bangladesh to take hold of its government and turn it into a second Afghanistan. All they needed was a government they could bend to their will. After all, Al Qaeda did not rule Afghanistan, the Taliban did. Nor did the majority of Afghans approve of the reductionist Islam the Taliban and Al Qaeda imposed on their country. Yet Al Qaeda called all the shots. In this context, it would be instructive to read what Maj. Gen. (Retd) Vinod Saighal has to say with regard to Afghanistan in *Dealing with Global Terrorism: The Way Forward*:

The outrage [9/11] had been perpetrated by elements who had imposed themselves on a hapless nation [Afghanistan] and who did not enjoy the support of the people. The people were first terrorized for several years by forces sponsored by a neighbouring State. Thereafter they were again terrorized on account of the massive retaliation that followed. The precedent has been set. Technically, it becomes possible then for a terrorist group to impose itself on a weak state and leverage that state as a base to carry out terrorist attacks on a foe far away. This can invite response that would cause untold damage and suffering on the leveraged state and very little, in comparison, on the shadowy figures who carry out the outrage and, thereafter, melt away, as was the case in Afghanistan.[3]

Maj. Gen. (Retd) Saighal's observation has a poignant relevance to Bangladesh that would be clear to all those who recall a bit of the country's history. The steady revival of fundamentalist Islamist politics, which had suffered a severe setback following Bangladesh's liberation from Pakistani rule on 16 December 1971, was made possible by Sheikh Mujibur Rahman's assassination on 15 August 1975 and the slaughter of the top layer of the Awami League's leadership on the night of 3–4 November 1975, by the same group of military officers that had killed him. While this and the repression that was unleashed upon its followers hobbled the Awami League, the military men who ruled the country between 1975 and the restoration of democracy in 1991 needed allies. They cultivated the fundamentalists and launched Bangladesh, which had been a secular state under Sheikh Mujibur Rahman (henceforth, Sheikh Mujib), on a course of Islamization.

Eliminating Awami League leaders?

The process was described in some detail in Chapter One. Meanwhile, it is difficult to ignore the possibility that the attack on the Awami League's rally on 21 August 2004 was designed to eliminate the party's leadership, destroy the party permanently, extend the rule of the present ruling coalition indefinitely and, under its supportive cover, terrorize Bangladesh's secular politicians and intelligentsia, and establish a fundamentalist Islamist order in the country.

Speaking of such a possibility, it is significant that Bangladesh has been in Al Qaeda's sights since the early 1990s. As will be seen in greater detail in Chapter Five, Osama bin Laden helped in the setting up of the Harkat-ul-Jihad-al-Islami Bangladesh (HUJIB) in 1992. One of the six signatories to the *fatwa* issued by the World Islamic Front for Jihad Against Jews and Crusaders on 23 February 1998 was Sheikh Abdul Salam Mohammad, 'Emir of the Jihad Movement in Bangladesh'.[4]

Further, it is no secret that Pakistan's Inter-Services Intelligence Directorate (ISI, as it is commonly known) has close links with Al Qaeda. According to Yossef Bodansky, bin Laden had finalized a deal with the ISI in the spring of 1998 under which his men were to carry out 'spectacular terrorist strikes at the heart of India' in the name of anti-Israel and anti-US 'campaigns' and 'organisations'. In return, Pakistan was to provide Al Qaeda with support, protection and sponsorship.[5] Bodansky further states that the ISI actively helped bin Laden in the expansion of an Islamist infrastructure in India. He writes, 'Very effective are the propaganda cassettes distributed throughout India's Muslim population. In these cassettes, bin Laden and other Islamist authorities describe India, along with the United States and Israel, as the great enemy of Islam.' He adds that institutions run by the Ahle Hadith religious charity, which is closely associated with the Pakistan-spornsored terrorist group Lashkar-e-Toiba, are the primary venues for the distribution of Islamist propaganda and incitement material.[6] We shall see in Chapter Six how the Ahle Hadith Andolan Bangladesh (AHAB), which has been promoting Islamist militancy in its own country, has links with and bases in India and is supplied with funds from across the India–Bangladesh border.

In this context, it is important to remember that the ISI, established in 1948 after the Pakistani government felt that its military intelligence had performed poorly during the first India–Pakistan war in Kashmir in 1947–48[7], has a long record of targeting India. In the 1950s, General-turned-President Mohammad Ayub Khan created within it a Covert Action Division (CAD) for assisting secessionist insurgents in northeastern India.[8] In particular, CAD trained and armed Naga and Mizo hostiles as a part of Pakistan's proxy war against India which, as B. Raman points out, had begun as early as the 1950s and 1960s. Such assistance, in turn, followed from the Pakistani intelligence community's assessment in the early 1950s that 'keeping India destabilized and its military pre-occupied with internal security duties would be one way of neutralizing, at little cost, the superiority of the Indian armed forces over their Pakistani counterpart'.[9]

The strategic doctrine of which this perception is the core remains. The motivation for 'bleeding' India this provides has been reinforced by Pakistan's desire to get even with it for its role in the liberation of

Bangladesh in 1971. Nor has there been any difference even after Pakistan's achievement of 'a psychological parity with India' following its acquisition of military nuclear and missile capabilities. Its target is not merely to neutralize India's military advantage but also to prevent the latter 'from emerging as the paramount military and economic power of the region', by keeping its army bleeding'.[10] Pakistan's defeat in its war with India in December 1971, the consequent liberation of Bangladesh, and Sheikh Mujib's assumption of office on 12 January 1972 under the Provisional Constitution of Bangladesh Order passed on the previous day, ended the ISI's activities in what is now Bangladesh.

As it turned out, it was only for the time being. The ISI gradually resumed its efforts after Sheikh Mujib's assassination on 15 August 1975. The military rulers who exercised power after the crime, and who ruled the country either directly or through civilian dummies until the restoration of democracy in 1991, needed at least some political support. Since they did not expect this from the Awami League and its followers, they not only courted the Islamist fundamentalists who had sided with Pakistan and were guilty of savage war crimes in 1971, but also allowed the ISI to resume its operations in Bangladesh.

During the 1980s the ISI's principal business was organizing and directing, with funds and arms provided by the US Central Intelligence Agency (CIA), the jihad in Afghanistan against Soviet occupation. It was also, however, actively assisting the secessionist movement in Punjab for an 'independent' Sikh state of 'Khalistan', and training Kashmiri terrorists in camps meant for *jihadis* fighting in Afghanistan. Bodansky points out that by the mid-1980s Islamabad already had proof of the strategic value of subversion from its long experience of sponsoring terrorism in Punjab, India. He adds,

In 1985 and 1986, as the quantity and quality of weapons provided by the ISI improved, Sikh terrorism and subversion in the Punjab and throughout India showed greater militarization and radicalization. Among the novelties of the revived terrorist campaign were sophisticated bomb-making techniques identical to those being used by the Afghan Mujahideen.[11]

Bodansky quotes the founder of the Jammu and Kashmir Liberation Front (JKLF), Hashim Qureshi, as saying that in 1984, the ISI asked him to send 'young people for training from the Valley so that they could fight India on return'. He further quotes Qureshi as saying that when he refused, the ISI took over 'the struggle' and installed Amanullah Khan in his place.[12] Bodansky also says that Pakistan used the massive financial and arms assistance it received from the US to further the Afghan jihad as a 'cover for expanded sponsorship of and support for other insurgent groups dedicated to subversive activities in India'[13] and prevented Washington from finding out about this. He writes that 'the main reason the ISI decided to keep the US Central Intelligence Agency out of the training camps for Afghan Mujahideen was 'the extent of training and support non-Afghan "volunteers" and others were getting in these camps. Most numerous were the thousands of Islamist trainees from Indian Kashmir and to a lesser extent the Sikhs from the Punjab.'[14]

The ISI's new playground

Things began to change with the completion of the Soviet withdrawal from Afghanistan on 15 February 1989. While continuing to assist the Punjab secessionists, the ISI concentrated on widening and intensifying its campaign of cross-border terrorism in India, for which it had been training volunteers from the mid-1980s, to compel India to yield Kashmir to Pakistan. The collapse of the secessionist movement in Punjab in the early 1990s administered a major setback to the implementation of Pakistan's designs. It, however, also enabled the latter to concentrate on escalating its campaign of cross-border terrorism in Kashmir and extend it to other parts of India as well—a development that was strikingly underlined by the ISI's staging, with the help of the underworld czar Dawood Ibrahim's criminal network, the devastating serial explosions in Mumbai on 12 March 1993 which left 257 persons dead and about 1,400 wounded.

As we have seen, the ISI formalized a deal with Osama bin Laden in the spring of 1998, for carrying out terrorist strikes at the heart of India. Bodansky states that it was under this arrangement that a daring plan to stage devastating car-bomb explosions in front of the US embassy in Delhi and the US consulates-general in Chennai and Kolkata on 26 January 1999 was hatched.[15] Fortunately, it was foiled by Delhi Police when it arrested a 27-year-old Bangladeshi national, Syed Abu Nasir, in Delhi in January 1999. Nasir, who had earlier worked for the Islamic International Relief Organisation (IIRO), an international Islamist charity outfit established by Osama bin Laden, had been picked up by the ISI and posted in Dhaka, from where the intelligence agency, in cooperation with Bangladesh's Directorate General of Forces Intelligence (DGFI), coordinated its assistance to north-eastern India's several secessionist militias and its project of sending Indians to training camps in Pakistan and infiltrating terrorists, funds, arms and explosives into India.

According to Bodansky, who gives a detailed account of the entire episode[16], Nasir attended a high-level planning meeting at the office of the Al-Haramain Islamic Foundation, an Islamic charity organization linked to Bin Laden, on 17–18 September 1998. Among those who attended were Sheikh Ahmed Al-Gamdi, President of IIRO, Professor Hafeez Mohammad Sayeed, head of Lashkar-e-Toiba (LeT), Sheikh Ahmed Heddeshi, President of Al-Haramain Islamic Foundation (AHIF), Dr Saleh Saud Al-Ansari and Muhammad Tahir, both of the International Islamic Federation of Students Organisations (IIFSO), and Azam Chima, a leading LeT commander. At the meeting, Nasir and several others were told that they had been selected to bomb US diplomatic installations in India and Bangladesh in the near future. Nasir and some of his associates crossed over to India from Bangladesh on 2 October 1998 and reconnoitred the US consulate-general in Chennai to draw up an operational plan. Returning to Dhaka, he took back with him his entire team—three Indians, four Egyptians, one Sudanese and one person from Arakan in Myanmar. Despatching the three Indians to the important north-Bengal city of Siliguri, where they established contact with the existing ISI and IIRO networks and set up a forward support base, he took the other six to Chennai, where they were to stay in a safe house until the day of the strike. From there he came to Delhi, where the police arrested him shortly after he received 4 kgs of RDX explosive and five detonators.

One should not miss the incident's significance. According to Bodansky, the 'structure of the network exposed—Abu Nasir's—confirmed the close relationship and cooperation existing between the intelligence services of sponsoring states—Pakistan's ISI in this case—and the ostensibly "independent" terrorists such as Osama bin Laden'.[17] It also showed that Bangladesh, which had earlier been a staging ground for the ISI's efforts to foment trouble in north-eastern India, had now become one of Al Qaeda's launching pads for operations against the US. It was, therefore, only natural that, ousted from

Afghanistan by the US and its allies and the Northern Alliance, the Taliban and Al Qaeda would choose Bangladesh as one of their new bases, if not the main one.

The choice would seem all the more logical for two reasons. First, Al Qaeda, as we have seen, had already been active in Bangladesh and the ISI had close links with the DGFI. Second, the ISI is virtually the Taliban's creator. To quote Raman again, 'The idea behind the creation of the Taliban for using it to achieve Pakistan's strategic objective in Afghanistan was the brain-wave of Maj. Gen. (Retd) Nasirullah Babar, the Interior Minister in the Cabinet (1993–96) of Benazir Bhutto, General Pervez Musharraf who was then the Director General of Military Operations (DGMO) under her, and General Mohammad Aziz, who was the then Deputy Director-General of the Inter-Services Intelligence (ISI) and in charge of ISI's operations in India and Afghanistan.[18] As Raman points out, ISI's Joint Intelligence North (JIN) division is 'responsible for the proxy war in Jammu & Kashmir and the control of Afghanistan through Taliban'.[19] It controls the Army of Islam, consisting of organizations like Al Qaeda, Harkat-ul Mujahideen (HuM), LeT, Al Badr and Maulana Masood Azhar's Jaish-e-Mohammad (JeM), besides all opium cultivation and heroin refining and smuggling in Pakistani and Afghan territory.[20]

People may argue that the ISI's links with Al Qaeda and the Taliban had snapped in the aftermath of 9/11. It is, however, difficult to tell, given the strict secrecy that characterizes the ISI's functioning. Though Pakistan has handed over to the US a number of important Al Qaeda leaders and fighters, Mullah Omar, the head of the erstwhile Taliban regime in Afghanistan, remains at large, along with most of his close associates. Second, though organizations like the LeT and JeM have been officially banned, they still seem to be operating without any great difficulty in Pakistan. Finally, if at any stage, Pakistan does really want to get rid of them under American pressure, to what better place can they shift their bases than Bangladesh, which has a number of well-organized, well-armed and lavishly funded fundamentalist militias and parties and a government that yields to their pressure on almost all important matters?

Understandably, therefore, there has been a growing concern over the possibility of Bangladesh becoming a country like Afghanistan under Taliban rule and emerging as a base for terrorist violence in other countries. Addressing a press conference in Dhaka on 5 September

2004, Joseph Cofer Black, the US State Department's Coordinator for Counter-Terrorism, who was visiting the country in the wake of the attack on the Awami League's rally on 21 August that year, affirmed that his country was looking at Bangladesh's role as a terrorist platform. According to Bangladesh's English-language newspaper, the *Daily Star*, asked about an interview Black gave to an Indian magazine where he had said the US would look closely at the potential of Bangladesh being used as a platform to launch terrorism internationally, he replied, 'It is not a condition specific or unique to Bangladesh.' He added. 'We are looking at all countries,' he said, adding that Bangladesh's potential as a terrorist platform was also being looked at from the perspective of the global threat of terrorism.[21]

Shifting nurseries

Of course, the mere fact that a question is being asked does not validate it. In the present instance, it begs three others: Can nurseries and headquarters of terrorism shift? Why should Islamist terrorist groups want Bangladesh to become another Afghanistan? Would they succeed?

Spawning grounds of terrorism have shifted before. Rohan Gunaratna writes, 'As many as three dozen Middle Eastern, Asian and European terrorist groups trained in Syrian-controlled Bekaa Valley in Lebanon in the 1970s and 1980s. In the early 1990s Afghanistan replaced Lebanon as the major centre of international terrorist training, and by 2001, forty foreign terrorist groups were operating there.'[22]

Yossef Bodansky has a different view. He writes,

By the late 1980s the world of international terrorism was changing. The camps of Afghan resistance in Pakistan actually became the centre of radical Islamist terrorism, with Sunni Islamists constituting the majority of the fighters. . . . The emergence of a new generation of Islamist terrorists from the mujahideen camps in Afghanistan and Pakistan coincided with the decline of other major terrorist movements in the Muslim world. In the 1980s radical Arab terrorism was slowly collapsing. Although the refugee camps and slums of the Middle-East were still a source of radicalized youth. . . . The failure of the Palestinian Revolution and the absence of a new generation of charismatic leaders meant that radicalized and frustrated youth were diverted from socialist-nationalist movements into the fold of traditionalist radical Islam.[23]

Despite the slight difference in their views as to whether Afghanistan or Pakistan had become the new centre of international terrorism, both Gunaratna and Bodansky agree that the centre has shifted, which is the material issue here. Many would, however, scoff at the suggestion that a further shift might be underway from Afghanistan and Pakistan to Bangladesh, arguing that the situation in Bangladesh today is very different from Afghanistan in 1994 when the Taliban emerged as a major force in that country. Bangladesh is a far more developed country than Afghanistan. It has tasted democracy, has an organized system of political parties and a vocal and assertive civil society supported by an active and secular intelligentsia. More important, it is a moderate Muslim country with a significant degree of religious tolerance, where women play important roles in the country's political, intellectual, cultural, social and economic lives.

When regimes collapse

The positive features attributed above to Bangladesh also applied to Italy and Germany when these countries went under Fascist and National Socialist (Nazi) control respectively. Specific circumstances enabled this to happen. Referring to these, Eric Hobsbawm writes,

> What gave them [the Fascists and Nazis] their chance after the First World War was the collapse of the old regimes and, with them, of the old ruling classes and their machinery of power, influence and hegemony. Where these remained in good working order, there was no need for fascism.[24]

In Italy, Fascism grew rapidly between 1920 and 1922—'two years of economic distress amid periodic scares of a communist revolution'.[25] It was the collapse of the Weimar Republic, weighed down by the burden of reparations to be paid under the Treaty of Versailles (1919) and staggering under the impact of the Great Depression of 1929–32, that made Adolf Hitler's rise to power possible. Unemployment figures in Germany rose from 1,320,000 in September 1929 to 3,000,000 in September 1930, 4,350,000 in September 1931 and 5,102,000 in September 1932.[26] In the Reichstag elections in September 1930, the Nazi party's number of seats rose to 107 from the 12 it had won in the elections held in 1928.[27] From 18.7 per cent in

November 1930, its share of the votes cast in the elections rose to 37.3 per cent in July 1932 and the number of seats to 230 out of a total of 608 seats.[28]

Explaining the increase in Hitler's mass support, Alan Bullock writes in his enduring work, *Hitler: A Study in Tyranny*,

> The argument that things must change, and the promise that, if the Nazis came to power, they would, proved a powerful attraction in a country driven to the limit of its endurance by two years of economic depression and mass unemployment, made worse by the inability of the Government to relieve the nation's ills.[29] Yet, the Nazi tally of seats and share of the votes polled in terms of percentage was still much short of an absolute majority. Worse, there was a decline in Nazi fortunes in the Reichstag elections of November, 1932. Their share of the popular votes cast declined from 37.3 per cent to 33.1 per cent and share of seats to 196 out of 584.[30]

As Bullock points out, despite the mass support he had won,

> Hitler came to office in 1933 as a result, not of any irresistible revolutionary or national movement sweeping him to power, nor even of a popular victory at the polls, but as part of a shoddy political deal with the 'old gang' whom he had been attacking for months past. Hitler did not seize power; he was jobbed into office by backstairs intrigue.[31]

In Afghanistan too, there was chaos on the eve of the rise of the Taliban. Lt Gen. Kamal Matinuddin writes,

> There was mismanagement everywhere and the existing mujahideen were either unwilling or unable to curb the rising tide of anarchy in Afghanistan. Chaotic conditions prevailed throughout the country at that time, with the sole exception of the six northern provinces 'governed' by the Uzbek General, Abdul Rashid Dostum.
>
> Afghanistan had become a failed state, like Somalia, Rwanda and Burundi. Although physical boundaries still existed and the country did indeed still have a flag, a national anthem, a government of sorts, membership of the United Nations, and embassies abroad, the writ of the Government was not running even inside the capital. Warlords and petty chieftains had taken over the country. There was an economic collapse. . . . It did not take much effort, therefore, by the Taliban to garner support for ending the fratricidal war and the anarchy which was prevailing in their land.[32]

Ahmed Rashid writes, in a similar vein,

> Afghanistan was in a state of virtual disintegration just before the
> Taliban emerged at the end of 1994. The country was divided into war-
> lord fiefdoms and all the warlords had fought, switched sides and fought
> again in a bewildering array of alliances, betrayals and bloodshed.

And what was warlord rule like? Rashid writes,

> The warlords seized homes and farms, threw out their occupants and
> handed them over to their supporters. The commanders abused the
> population at will, kidnapping young girls and boys for their sexual
> pleasure, robbing merchants in the bazaars and fighting and brawling
> in the streets.[33]

The question of whether law and order and other conditions in
Bangladesh can deteriorate to the point where a fundamentalist
Islamist takeover is possible will be discussed in Chapter Eight, which
will deal with the chances of such a venture succeeding. It will also
deal with the possibility of fundamentalist Islamist forces being able
to dictate to the current or any future government of Bangladesh on
all matters important to them. Meanwhile, it is important to note that
there are other reasons why the Taliban, Al Qaeda and their allied
organizations in Bangladesh, like the Jamaat and HUJIB, might want
to turn the latter into a seedbed, an important base if not the headquarters, and a staging centre of their globalized activities.

The reasons why

One reason that makes Bangladesh an ideal base for their operations
is that it has a soft state with ineffective governance and an inefficient
police force, which fundamentalist Islamist organizations like the
Jamaat, IOJ and HUJIB, with their highly organized, trained and
armed cadres, can dominate without much trouble since they already
have a foot in the government. These organizations enjoy a great deal
of latitude and often seem to be above the law. They have already made
considerable progress towards bending the government to their will
in their bid to destroy the country's civil society, infiltrate its institutions

of governance and put its vibrant social, cultural and intellectual life
into the straitjacket of Islamist orthodoxy. Significantly, little progress
has been made in bringing to justice the culprits of even the more
widely noted acts of violence like the near-fatal knife attack on the
celebrated writer, critic and scholar Prof. Humayun Azad, on 27
February 2004, and the grenade attack on the *mazar* of Hazrat
Shahjalal, which wounded the British High Commissioner to
Bangladesh and killed three others, on 21 May 2004. The same applies
to those behind the grenade attack on the Awami League rally in
Dhaka on 21 August 2004.

In the case of the murder of Bangladesh's highly respected and
scholarly former Finance Minister, Shah A.M.S. Kibria on 27 January
2005, the police submitted a chargesheet in a city court in Habiganj
naming ten accused. All ten were linked to the BNP, including the
alleged mastermind of the crime, BNP district Vice-President A.K.M
Abdul Quaiyum.[34] Asma Kibria, widow of the slain leader, however,
rejected the chargesheet saying that the investigation was incomplete.
The nation, she said, wanted to know the names of the people who
had ordered Kibria's killing. The investigation, she said, did not reach
the level at which it could do that because the investigators did not
have a free hand. Demanding an international probe into the murder,
she said that no investigation except one by the US Federal Bureau of
Investigation (FBI), was acceptable to her.[35]

It is only in the case of the murder of Ahsanullah Master, the
Awami League MP and President of the party's labour front organization, the Shramik League, on 7 May 2004, that a verdict has been
given, and that too a stunning one. In a judgement on 16 April 2005
that awarded the highest number of death sentences ever in a single
case in Bangladesh, the judge at the Speedy Trial Tribunal No. 1 in
Dhaka prescribed the gallows for 22 persons and life imprisonment
for six. Of the 22 given the death penalty, 17 were BNP leaders and
activists, three were from the Awami League and two from the JP(N).
The alleged mastermind of the killing was a leader of the BNP's youth
wing, the Jatiyatabadi Jubo Dal (JJD), Nurul Islam Sarker, brother
of the party's leader in Tongi, Hasan Sarker.[36]

The soft and ineffective nature of the state in Bangladesh will be
discussed in Chapter Eight. We will examine the circumstances,
implications and message of the 21 August 2004 grenade attack in

Chapter Three. Chapter Four will examine, among other things, the attacks on Professor Azad, who subsequently died in Germany on 7 August 2004, and on the *mazar* of Hazrat Shahjalal. Meanwhile, it is important to note some of the observations the German Ambassador to Bangladesh, Dietrich Andreas, made on 10 October 2004, the first day of a four-day seminar on 'Religious Militancy and Security in South Asia' organized by the Bangladesh Institute of International and Strategic Study and the German Embassy in Dhaka. He said that the victims of bomb and grenade attacks were parties and groups holding views different from the conservative Islamist worldview and that possible links between these attacks and fundamentalists or extremists should be probed. Among other things, he cited the threats held out to and attacks on the Ahmadiyyas, and the movement to stop women from participating in sports as examples of the presence of religion-based militancy in Bangladesh.[37]

Apart from the fact that their allies in Bangladesh function with impunity, the other factor that makes the country an ideal base and launching pad for terrorism for Al Qaeda, the Taliban and the ISI, is its geo-strategic location. From their bases in that country, Al Qaeda and Taliban elements and their Bangladeshi associates can coordinate terrorist activities in countries as far apart as Spain and Indonesia—a threat which should weigh considerably with a number of governments, given the growth of organizations affiliated with Al Qaeda in countries like Thailand, Malaysia, Singapore and Indonesia. Second, continued influx across extremely porous borders has created sizeable pockets of illegal Bangladeshi migrants in India, not only in cities like Delhi and Bombay but, even more, in areas adjacent to the Bangladesh border. Bases can be set up in both these areas for harbouring terrorists on the run and planning terrorist outrages in India and elsewhere. Bangladesh's fundamentalist Islamist organization AHAB has support bases among enclaves of illegal Bangladeshi immigrants in West Bengal's border districts.

Cross-border bases: In India

Many of these enclaves are large enough to permit such activity. While precise figures are not available, a report in the *Hindustan Times* of 7 November 2003 quoted a document by India's Intelligence Bureau, meant for presentation at the 38th Conference of State Directors-General of Police held in Delhi on 4–5 November, as estimating the number of illegal immigrants from Bangladesh settled in India to be over 15 million. Of these, eight million were in West Bengal and five million in Assam. According to the same document, over 475,000 illegal immigrants had settled in Katihar, Sahebganj, Kishenganj and Purnia Districts of Bihar, while the figure for Nagaland had shot up from 20,000 in 1991 to 80,000 at the time the report was written.[38]

The *Pioneer* of 6 November 2003 carried a report[39], datelined Silchar, by Surajit Talukdar and Swapan Kumar Paul of *Newsfile*, listing 15 Islamist terrorist/fundamentalist organizations active in Assam. These included the Islamic Liberation Front of Assam, Islamic Sevak Sangh, Muslim Security Force of Assam, Muslim Liberation Army, Muslim Liberation Front, Muslim Liberation Tigers of Assam, Muslim Security Council of Assam, Muslim Security Force, Muslim Tiger Force, Muslim United Liberation Tigers of Assam, Muslim Volunteer Force, United Reformation Protest of Assam, Adam Sena and HUJIB.

The report further stated that the administration of Cachar District in south Assam had, for a period of two months, banned trade, movement of people and the plying of fishing boats along the India–Bangladesh border from 8 P.M. to 5 A.M. every day. Besides, the Border Security Force (BSF) had been asked to intensify patrolling not only in Cachar but also the districts of Karimganj and Hailakandi in the state, that shared the porous international border between India and Bangladesh. The heightened security measures, according to the report, were meant to neutralize a plan for subversion in the three districts drawn up at a meeting organized in Bangladesh's Sylhet District by the DGFI in the presence of a 'high-ranking' operative of Pakistan's ISI and leaders of two fundamentalist Islamist organizations of Bangladesh and the Muslim United Liberation Tigers of Assam (MULTA). The report stated that the continued growth of Islamist fundamentalism in Assam was widely attributed to the continuing influx of Bangladeshis into the state, where Muslims accounted for 33 per cent of the population in 2003 against 12 per cent in 1947. They were believed to be in a position to influence the outcome of elections in 30 of the state's 126 Assembly seats. According to the report, Muslims were believed to constitute 49.17 per cent, 54.19 per cent, and 34.49 per cent of the population of Karimganj, Hailakandi and Cachar Districts respectively.

Schooling *jihadis*

A development that has followed the growing illegal influx is the mush-rooming of madrasas in the border districts of West Bengal and Assam. Many of them, particularly those recognized by the government, stick to the legitimate business of providing Islamic education to their students, who are often from deprived backgrounds. They thereby serve an important social purpose. Many of them are, however, unauthorized, and teach a Talibanized version of *jihadi* Islam, and engage in planning and carrying out violent anti-state activities that undermine social cohesion and national security and integrity. According to a report in the *Pioneer* of 25 January 2002[40], as a result of investigations into the role of madrasas after the terrorist attack in front of the American Centre in Kolkata on 22 January 2002 which left four policemen dead (another died later in hospital) and over 20 people injured, the West Bengal government had identified unauthorized madrasas across the state and was poised to act against at least 125 of them. The report also stated that the government's decision in 2001 to revive an old law which made it mandatory to secure the district administration's permission and police clearance before building any shrine, followed intelligence reports, a series of arrests of Pakistani spies and recovery of arms and explosives from places of worship. The government, it said, was surprised to find that 1,050 mosques of all sizes had come up in the districts bordering Bangladesh in the preceding few years. The contrast with urban centres in the interior was striking. The report stated, quoting a BSF survey, that while Kolkata, the state capital and a city of 14 million, had only 131 seminaries (read madrasas) and 67 mosques, the small border town of Krishnanagar in Nadia District had 404 seminaries and 368 mosques.

The report quoted the Chief Minister of West Bengal, Buddhadeb Bhattacharjee, as stating that some of the unauthorized seminaries were being used to provide sanctuary to terrorists at the behest of the ISI, and that some of them had been receiving huge donations from abroad. Referring to unauthorized madrasas, Bhattacharjee, according to the report, said that these 'should be affiliated with the State Madrasa Board. They should join the mainstream. But some people are deliberately refusing to get affiliated to the Madrasa Board and are teaching only Arabic and theology. Some anti-national elements are operating from these madrasas. This must be stopped.'

A report in Kolkata's Bengali daily *Aajkaal*, which too was published on 25 January 2000[41], also described the Chief Minister talking in the same vein. According to the report, Mr Bhattacharjee said at the Writers Building[42] that pupils in many of the unrecognized madrasas were learning only theology, Arabic and Persian, which did not constitute education suited to the age. They would not be able to carry on in the days ahead on the basis of this education alone. He also said, 'We have specific information that anti-national education is being imparted in many unrecognized madrasas.'

Al Qaeda elements, to say nothing of Bangladeshi terrorists belonging to organizations like HUJIB, can cross over and hide in madrasas and mosques in West Bengal's border areas—which, as will be seen in Chapter Six, is already happening—in the same way that Al Qaeda and Taliban elements are hiding in the tribal areas of Pakistan bordering Afghanistan. Indeed, it has been reported on several occasions that Osama bin Laden and some of his top lieutenants are in these areas. Thus bin Laden and Al Qaeda are continuing, albeit under different circumstances, a process that began during the war in Afghanistan against Soviet occupation. In *The Bear Trap: Afghanistan's Untold Story*, a book that he co-authored with Maj. Mark Adkin, Brig. Mohammad Yousaf writes, 'The guerrillas in Vietnam could obtain reinforcements, supplies and sanctuary across the border in Laos and Cambodia, while the Mujahideen sought the same in Pakistan'.[43] Describing the conditions necessary for an armed resistance movement to succeed, he mentions 'a safe haven—a secure base area to which the guerrilla could withdraw to refit and rest without fear of attack. Pakistan provided the Mujahideen with such a sanctuary.'[44] Despite protestations to the contrary, Pakistan provides both sanctuary, bases and assistance to terrorist militias like the JeM, LeT and the Hizbul Mujahideen (HM), engaged in cross-border terrorism in India.

The importance of bases

Emphasizing the importance of such bases, Mao Zedong wrote in his famous treatise on guerrilla warfare, 'A guerrilla base may be defined as an area, strategically located, in which the guerrillas can carry out their duties of training, self-preservation and development. Ability to fight a war without a rear is a fundamental characteristic of guerrilla action, but this does not mean that guerrillas can exist and function over a long period of time without the development of base areas.'[45] In his introduction, in the same book, to Che Guevara's booklet on guerrilla warfare, Maj. Harries-Clichy Peterson writes, 'A sanctuary is an indispensable element in guerrilla warfare. Mao operated in a vast and populous country. He evaded extermination by long marches of withdrawal and by disappearing into the populace.'[46]

It is important to note the reference to 'disappearance into the populace'. Bases and sanctuaries where guerrillas can easily pass themselves off as visitors, professionals, mechanics or even residents, enable members of guerrilla bands to do precisely that. They did it in China and Vietnam, and are doing it in Pakistan's tribal areas bordering Afghanistan and even in its cities in the interior. In the case of Al Qaeda and Taliban elements or Bangladeshi Islamist terrorists using Muslim concentrations in areas of India bordering Bangladesh as sanctuaries, it will be the reverse of what is happening in the case of terrorist outfits like the United Liberation Front of Asom (ULFA), National Democratic Front of Bodoland (NDFB), All-Tripura Tiger Force (ATTF), National Liberation Front of Tripura (NLFT), People's Liberation Army (PLA) and United National Liberation Front (UNLF) of Manipur and the National Socialist Council of Nagalim (Isak–Muivah)—NSCN(I-M)—which are being sheltered and actively assisted by Bangladesh in its territory. In the case of Al Qaeda and Taliban elements and Bangladeshi militants, however, it will not be the Government of India and its intelligence agencies but the fundamentalist Islamists active in India's Bangladeshi majority areas along the India–Bangladesh border who will provide them with sanctuary and assistance in terms of arms, equipment and training.

While the thoroughly porous nature of the India–Bangladesh border makes clandestine illegal crossings quite safe, arrivals and departures through airports, seaports or railway stations, which are bound to be under close surveillance by Indian intelligence agencies, hold a greater risk of detection and arrest. Apart from mounting terrorist strikes within India, sanctuaries on Indian soil can be used by fundamentalist Islamist leaders—whether Bangladeshi, Afghan or Chechen—or organizations in Bangladesh under pressure in that country, for staging terrorist attacks in any country, or just lying low. (We will see in Chapter Six instances of this actually happening.)

Growing influx

Some, of course, would scoff at the idea and assert that Indian authorities would never allow terrorists crossing over from Bangladesh to
hide in, and plan strikes from, the country's border districts. They
would be ignoring the possibility that neither the central government
in Delhi nor the governments of the states adjoining Bangladesh
would be able to do anything of the sort, given the compulsions of
India's electoral politics. That this is not an exaggeration is clear from
the fact that very little has been done to stem the influx of illegal
immigrants from Bangladesh or to identify and expel those who have
come in. For one thing, there are only rough assessments of the magni-
tude of the influx. I have cited, above, a report in the *Hindustan Times*
of 7 November 2003 giving the Indian Intelligence Bureau's estimated
figures of the total number of illegal Bangladeshi immigrants in the
country and in the districts bordering Bangladesh. India's Union
Minister of State for Home, Sriprakash Jaiswal, however, presented
somewhat different figures before Parliament while replying to a
question submitted on 14 July 2004.[47] According to him, the total
number of illegal immigrants in the country was 12 million, and the
statewise break up was: Assam, 5 million; West Bengal, 5.7 million;
Bihar, 479,000; Delhi, 375,000; Tripura, 325,000; Nagaland, 59,500;
Meghalaya, 30,000; and Maharashtra, 20,000. The same report, however, quoted him as saying in the Rajya Sabha on 23 July 2004, 'The
annexure giving the estimated number of illegal immigrants (as 12
million) reported by the field organisations had a clarification which
was inadvertently not seen.' According to the clarification, 'The figures
reported are not based on any comprehensive survey or sample study
but on hearsay and that too from interested parties.' He added, 'No
realistic view can be given of illegal immigrants into Assam . . . [I]n
West Bengal also the figures are based on unrealistic estimates.'

Why present to Parliament figures based on 'hearsay' from 'interested parties' or 'unrealistic estimates'? It is difficult to believe that
Mr Jaiswal had done it inadvertently. He should have been much more
careful and looked at the document very closely before talking about
it in Parliament. Was he not aware that even the Group of Ministers'
report on the national security system, presented in February 2001,
had mentioned 15 million Bangladeshis living illegally in the country?[48]
Had he also not heard of the report on illegal migration submitted to

the President of India on 8 November 1998 by a former Governor of Assam, Lt Gen. (Retd) S.K. Sinha? If he had not, then it was a major lapse on his part, given the thoroughness of the report and its projection of the serious implications of continued illegal migration from Bangladesh, including the loss of several of India's strategically important border districts to the latter.

Not so simple

In this context, what the Union Home Minister, Shivraj Patil, told reporters on 26 May 2004 is significant.[49] He had said, 'You cannot compare the illegal influx from Bangladesh with the infiltration happening across LoC/international border in J&K. The Bangladeshis come here mostly to seek employment and, thus, their deportation should be done with a human face, without causing them unnecessary harassment.' Mr Patil overlooked the fact that what could once have been viewed purely as people crossing over to India in search of jobs cannot now be seen as such because of the rise of Islamist fundamentalist political parties like the Jamaat and IOJ and terrorist militia like HUJIB in Bangladesh, and the promotion of cross-border terrorism in India by them as well as by the Bangladesh government through its intelligence agencies. Not only that, these organizations and the Bangladesh government's DGFI are deeply connected and operate in close cooperation with one another, the ISI and global Islamist 'charity' organizations that fund terrorism.

If one has any doubt on this score, one has only to consider the attempt to blow up the United States embassy in Delhi and consulates-general in Chennai and Kolkata on 26 January 1999, which we have already discussed. The entire episode clearly shows four things. First, that the ISI, its creations (like the LeT) and Saudi 'charitable' entities linked to bin Laden functioned unhindered in Bangladesh. Of these, the Al-Haramain Islamic Foundation has been made to close down its operation and its staff have left Bangladesh. The others, however, remain active. Second, these have been planning terrorist strikes against US establishments in India, from Dhaka. Third, these have support networks operating in Indian cities like Siliguri and Chennai. Fourth, ISI agents—indeed, anyone—can come and go across the India–Bangladesh border at will.

Encouraging influx

Yet, Shivraj Patil, responsible for India's internal security as Union Home Minister, does not seem to recognize the dangers posed by a porous border and continuous illegal immigration from Bangladesh. This, however, should not surprise anyone. The stand of his party, the Indian National Congress, on the issue of illegal immigration from Bangladesh has been a matter of controversy since the 1950s. Since that decade, a section of Assam's Congress leaders has been accused of seeking to increase the number of its communal and ethnic supporters by encouraging illegal immigration from Bangladesh and providing those arriving clandestinely with ration cards, besides getting their names included in voters' lists. It was the massive and sometimes violent agitation in Assam, launched in 1979 by the All-Assam Students Union (AASU) and the Asom Gana Parishad (AGP) against the continuing and unchecked infiltration of illegal Bangladeshi migrants into the state, that prompted the Centre to enact the Illegal Migrants (Determination by Tribunal) Act or IMDT Act which came into force in 1983 and which the Supreme Court of India set aside in a historic judgement in July 2005. Its title was a misnomer. It should really have been called the Illegal Migrants (Protection by Tribunal) Act. For one thing, illegal immigration would have been checked more effectively if, instead of enacting the IMDT Act, the Foreigners Act of 1946, which applied to the whole of the country, was implemented seriously in Assam. The latter is a far more effective instrument for the detection and subsequent deportation of illegal immigrants. For example, it puts on the foreigner accused of being an illegal immigrant the onus of proving that he or she is not so. Under the IMDT Act the onus rested on the complainant. This was bound to—and it did— make determination of illegal status most difficult given the fact that illegal immigration from Bangladesh was actively promoted by important political figures in Assam. Second, there is no provision for appeal against decisions taken by tribunals set up under the Foreigners' Act, while one could appeal against a judgement by the tribunals established under the IMDT Act both to an appellate tribunal and a High Court that has jurisdiction over the area.

As if these were not hurdles tall enough in the way of detection and deportation of illegal immigrants, the task was made more difficult by the fact that complaints against a person for being an illegal immigrant could only be filed by someone who lived within a 3-km radius of the accused's residence and that the complainant's affidavit had to be supported by that of another person who also lived within a range of 3 km from the residence of the accused. If this limited the number of those who could level allegations, the fact that the Act applied only to those arriving in India after 25 March 1971 prevented the deportation of the huge number of people who came to India before that. Not only that, the definition of an illegal immigrant as 'one without being in possession of a valid passport or any other travel document or any other lawful authority' made conviction difficult because one could always claim that one had lost one's passport and the onus of proving one's claim false lay on the complainant!

It is hardly surprising that progress in identifying and deporting illegal immigrants has been pathetic. In a presentation on the working of the IMDT Act, made in mid-1999 in connection with a court case, the Union Home Ministry admitted that inquiries had until then been instituted in 302,514 cases since the Act came into force and 31,264 cases were reported to the tribunals constituted under the Act. The number of those declared illegal immigrants was 9,625, out of whom 1,461 were actually deported![50]

That the Act would not serve any purpose was clear from the very beginning and demand for its repeal were voiced in Assam almost immediately after it came into force. An agreement providing 'a time frame' for a 'clause-by-clause' implementation of the Assam Accord of 15 October 1985, signed by the representatives of the Union Home Ministry and the government of Assam on 27 January 1991, stated that a decision on repealing the IMDT Act would be taken by 28 February 1991. Of course, no decision was taken. Hence one found, in his address to a joint session of both Houses of Parliament on 22 February 1999, the then President K.R. Narayanan saying that the Acts' repeal was under consideration. Indeed, one heard the same refrain from officials of the Union Home Ministry at the various meetings they had with representatives of the Assam government and the All-Assam Students Union (AASU). Since nothing happened, a former AASU President, Sarbananda Sonowal, filed a writ petition in the Supreme Court in March 2000, praying for the striking down of the IMDT Act on the ground that it was against the Constitution's provisions and was discriminatory in that Assam was the only state in the country to which the other and more effective laws did not apply.

The petition came up for hearing several times with the Asom Gana Parishad (AGP) and the AGP-led government of Assam filing an affidavit supporting the PIL and the Congress government of the state, which came into power in 2001, filing an additional affidavit reversing the stand taken in the original affidavit. If this suggested that the Congress government of Assam did not want to deport illegal immigrants from the state, the impression that the Congress as a party did not want to do so followed from the decision of the United Progressive Alliance (UPA) government, taken at a meeting of the Union Cabinet on 27 October 2004[51], not to revoke the IMDT Act which its predecessor, the National Democratic Alliance (NDA) government, had decided to do. Hence, until India's Supreme Court struck down the Act on 12 July 2005, one had the ironical situation in which the IMDT Act applied in Assam, which is being flooded by illegal Bangladeshi immigrants, while the much more rigorous Citizenship Act of 1946 applied in the rest of the country.

Nor has anything significant been done on the Indian side of the border to stanch illegal immigration. Considering the natural porosity of the 4,096-km-long border, characterized by hilly and densely forested terrain in India's North-east and a bewildering multiplicity of creeks and waterways in the Sundarbans area in West Bengal's South 24 Parganas District, the deployment of BSF personnel remains grossly inadequate. Work on erecting barbed wire fences along the border to prevent infiltration, initiated by the NDA government in 2002, is not making adequate progress. A report in the *Indian Express* of 9 January 2004[52], quoted Assam government sources as saying that the target year for completing the fence, which had initially been fixed at 2003, had to be postponed to the end of 2006 for lack of funds. During 2001–2002 and 2002–2003, the Centre had only released Rs 50 million to Assam and the state had to spend Rs 162.9 million to keep the work going. In a statement in the Assam Legislative Assembly in December 2003, the Minister in charge of the state's Public Works Department said that the Centre had, till 2000–2001, sanctioned a total sum of Rs 1,236.1 million for the fence and a road along the India–Bangladesh border. In the financial year 2003–2004, however, it had allocated Rs 1,670 million for the project's second phase, aimed at completely ending illegal trans-border immigration. Rs 150 million had already been released to the Assam government. Besides funds, certain physical difficulties like those encountered in fencing off certain low-lying areas of Assam and West Bengal—pointed out by the BSF— had also slowed down progress.

By June 2004 work had picked up, tenders had been called and closed, and the various public sector undertakings to be entrusted with fencing different stretches of the border—Indian Railways Construction Corporation (IRCON), National Building Construction Corporation (NBCC), Border Roads Organization (BRO), IPEL, the Central Public Works Department (CPWD) and state Public Works Departments (PWDs) in Tripura and Meghalaya, the state PWD in Assam, and the CPWD in West Bengal—had been identified. Suddenly, however, the Union Home Ministry under the UPA government put the work 'on hold for review' in June 2004, a few days after assuming office, despite expressions of reservation by its own Border Management Wing and the forces charged with protecting the border.[53]

The reason reportedly was strong opposition from Bangladesh, which argued that an India–Bangladesh agreement of 1974 prohibited the construction of defensive structures by either country in their respective territories within 150 yards of the border and that a fence was a defensive structure. What the Bangladesh government over-looked or chose not to recognize was the fact that the agreement was not between the two governments but between India's Border Security Force (BSF) and its own Bangladesh Rifles (BDR) and that a fence could hardly be called a 'defensive structure' under conditions of mod-ern warfare. Wisdom, however, finally dawned in Delhi and at its meeting on 14 October 2004, the Cabinet Committee on Security de-cided to resume fencing the border. Needless to say, a great deal of valuable time had been lost.

The seriousness of the situation is clearly reflected in some of the observations made and directions issued by the judiciary over the past few years. While hearing a public interest litigation filed by one O.P. Saxena calling for effective fencing along the porous India–Bangladesh border to end illegal immigration, a bench of the Supreme Court comprising the then Chief Justice A.S. Anand and Justices R.C. Lahoti and Brijesh Kumar expressed the fear, on 26 February 2001, that unchecked illegal immigration by Bangladeshi nationals could pose a serious threat to India's economy and security. It added that the in-flow would continue until the government took steps like deporting some of the illegal immigrants.[54] As seen above, however, work on the fencing remains incomplete and the influx of people from across the border continues. According to the report of the Intelligence Bureau presented to the 38th Conference of Directors General and Inspectors General of Police held in Delhi on 4–5 November 2003, there were 375,000 illegal Bangladeshis even in Delhi, India's capital. One, therefore, finds a division bench of the Delhi High Court, comprising Chief Justice B.C. Patel and Justice A.K. Sikri, directing Delhi Police, on 22 September 2003, to identify and deport 3,000 illegal Bangladeshi immigrants per month.[55] The Delhi government, however, told the court on 8 September 2004 that only 3,147 had been deported since February 2004. Appalled by the information, the court directed the Additional Secretary (Home) of the Delhi government and the Deputy Commissioner (Headquarters) of Delhi Police to explain why the target could not be met.[56] Things, however, did not improve. Taking serious note of the central and Delhi government's lackadaisical approach toward the deportation of illegal Bangladeshi immigrants, the bench, now comprising Chief Justice B.C. Patel and Justice B.D. Ahmed, ordered the Delhi government, on 22 September 2004, to undertake a survey to identify such people and file a compliance report within four weeks. Stating that the Centre 'shall provide' additional funds to the state government if required for undertaking the survey, the bench ruled, 'If the authorities find that the 10 teams formed as per the action plan to deport the illegal migrants are insufficient, they should raise it to 20.[57]

Nor has any progress been made in closing down those unrecognized madrasas in the border areas that had become centres of anti-India propaganda. *Aajkaal* reported on 7 February 2002,

The Chief Minister has ended the misunderstanding over madrasas. He told a meeting of the state Left Front on Wednesday that he had not said that anti-national activities were going on in the unauthorized madrasas. No madrasa in the state will be closed. This is not our policy. Nor is there any law for closing down madrasas. There has been a mistake in understanding what I had said. I had aired my views about the modernization of madrasa education and talked generally about terrorism in the state. Newspaper reports had tied the two issues up. Our party's paper *Ganashakti* had not reported correctly.[58]

About-turn

An important question arises here. How could all sections of the media, including *Ganashakti*, misinterpret what Chief Minister Buddhadeb Bhattacharjee had said, when he is a highly intelligent and articulate person and never at a loss for words? Not surprisingly, many feel that Bhattacharjee and the state government had made an about-turn under pressure. The report in *Aajkaal* referred to in the previous paragraph stated,

> The main issue for discussion at today's meeting of the Left Front was the Chief Minister's recent report about madrasas. All leaders of the constituent parties including Jyoti Basu, Buddhadeb Bhattacharjee, Anil Biswas and Biman Basu were present. A written statement on behalf of the Forward Bloc[59] was distributed among all present at the beginning of the meeting. It was written there that controversy and confusion had been created in the minority community over the Chief Minister's recent statement linking madrasas with anti-national activity. The Chief Minister should come forward and end this controversy and confusion. The Forward Bloc's State Secretary, Mr Ashok Ghose, had said the same thing verbally. The CPI's[60] State Secretary Manjukumar Majumdar and the RSP's[61] State Secretary, Debabrata Bandopadhyaya also expressed concern over the matter.

On the following day, 8 February 2002, *Aajkaal* reported,

> Muslim intellectuals and religious leaders are happy after their discussion with Chief Minister Buddhadeb Bhattacharjee. Twenty-two Muslim intellectuals and religious leaders had come to the secretariat to discuss issues like madrasas and terrorism. The Chief Minister discussed things with them for almost an hour and a half. Buddhadeb is also happy with the discussions. He felt that the misunderstanding with the Muslim community was over. The Government will continue to take measures against the ISI. They [Muslim leaders and intellectuals] told journalists after their meeting with the Chief Minister that there was some misunderstanding over Buddhadeb Bhattacharjee's statement. The Chief Minister has frankly told us what he had to say. The confusion has ended.[62]

According to the report, of the two state Ministers, Mohammad Amin and Mohammad Selim, who were also present at the meeting, the latter said after it was over that no anti-national activity would be tolerated in any religious institution in West Bengal. Also, Buddhadeb Bhattacharjee later said that talks were held with the Muslim leaders on two issues: imparting modern education in madrasas and ensuring that there was no misunderstanding in the Muslim community over the government's statement.

The West Bengal government has doubtless undertaken an impressive programme of modernizing madrasa education. There is, however, no indication that anti-national activity has ended in mosques and madrasas in districts along the border with Bangladesh. In a despatch in the *Pioneer* of 4 December 2003, Sanjay Singh quoted 'a recent classified intelligence report' that said that activists of the Islami Chhatra Shibir or Islamic Students' Camp, the Jamaat's violent student wing, had taken in August of that year seven activists of the banned Students' Islamic Movement of India (SIMI) from Assam and West Bengal to well-known residential madrasas in Chittagong, Rangpur and Dhaka in Bangladesh for higher Islamic studies.

The same report stated that SIMI had held two meetings in West Bengal which were attended by members of the Shibir. The first was held on 27 August 2003 in a madrasa in Malda (a district in West Bengal bordering Bangladesh) under the banner of the Islamic Action Front. The second was held on 31 August and 1 September at a madrasa in Mograhat in North 24-Parganas under the auspices of the Islami Shiksha Shibir or Islamic Education Camp. These meetings, according to the report, decided on a plan to infiltrate madrasas, Muslim clubs, libraries and other cultural bodies for covert mobilization of Islamist forces.[63]

It would, however, be wrong to hold the Communist Party of India (Marxist)[64], or CPI(M), primarily responsible for the continuing increase in illegal immigration from Bangladesh into West Bengal or the failure to squelch anti-India activity in a section of mosques and madrasas. Any attempt to regulate activities in mosques and madrasas or stem illegal immigration raises a storm of protest. It is not only sections of the CPI(M) and its coalition partners in West Bengal's ruling Left Front but also the Congress that stand in the way. On 12 February 2002, almost immediately after the Left Front government ordered madrasas to modernize their curricula, the then West Bengal Pradesh Congress President, Pranab Mukherjee (Defence Minister at the time of writing), said, while addressing a district party convention in Malda, that the Chief Minister had created an 'unnecessary controversy over madrasas'. He added, 'our Constitution has given certain fundamental rights to the minority community to safeguard their culture. Neither a state nor the centre can have anything to say in the matter. Only those who have been running the madrasas can decide whether any change is needed in their education system.' Stepping up the attack on the Chief Minister, he further stated, 'I am surprised that Bhattacharjee, who has been a minister for the past 19 years, could make this announcement. . . . [Despite] being a communist Chief Minister, he has handed over a real issue to the BJP. Now that the issue is being debated all over the country, . . . [the CPI(M) is] talking about provocation and mal-propaganda. But who is responsible for this situation? The Congress and other parties have nothing to do with it. The Marxists themselves are to blame for this.'[65]

The message that Mukherjee's broadside and the events preceding it sends out is clear: any Chief Minister and/or government of West Bengal trying to curb anti-national activity in madrasas or trying to modernize their curriculum will run into strong criticism and will be projected, directly or indirectly, as anti-Muslim. If experience so far is any indication, this is liable to inhibit action because of the genuine fear that it will cost the Chief Minister and his government the electoral support of the state's large number of Muslim voters.

One need hardly be surprised if India's failure to curb illegal immigration as well as anti-national propaganda in a section of mosques and madrasas creates the impression in Bangladesh that it is dealing with a soft, corrupt and inefficient government that can be defied with impunity. This is clearly reflected in the Bangladesh government's changing posture on the issue of illegal immigration. From the beginning, it has done nothing to curb the process—in fact, the BDR and its officers and men in the border districts have actively facilitated the illegal migration—and has even denied its existence. In a way, this is understandable. Illegal migration reduces the burden on Bangladesh's economy, which would otherwise have had to support those who would have left. Besides, a small and weak country often carries a chip on its shoulder vis-à-vis a large and powerful neighbour, a condition that prevents it from admitting that a large section of its population prefers to leave its territory for a better life in the latter. Of late, however, denials are accompanied by a certain cockiness and almost contemptuous references to India. Thus, asked to comment on the issue, Maj. Gen. Mohammad Jahangir Alam Khan Chowdhury, Director General of the BDR, visiting India for talks with the then Director General of the BSF, Ajay Raj Sharma, said in Delhi on 28 September 2004, 'Why should people come from Bangladesh to India? Your economic condition is not better than Bangladesh's. There are 50,000 Indians in Bangladesh who have entered the country illegally.' He added that if India's economy were better than

Bangladesh's, 'You would not have gone for work in Middle East and the Arab countries'.[66]

This brazenness is not confined to the issue of illegal immigration. Referring to the list, supplied by the BSF, of camps in Bangladesh for insurgents from north-eastern India, Maj. Gen. Khan Chowdhury said, on the same occasion, 'There is not a single camp in Bangladesh. We looked for the camps' locations given in the BSF list. Some of the addresses were of our cantonment area and our headquarters. . . . Some addresses even pertained to the Bay of Bengal.'[67] Nor could his barbed sallies be dismissed as an isolated instance. They reflected the general stance of the Bangladesh government, led by Prime Minister Khaleda Zia, towards India. Thus, Bangladesh's Foreign Minister, Mohammad Morshed Khan, lashed out against India in highly minatory language while inaugurating, as chief guest, an 'Indo-Bangladesh Dialogue of Young Journalists' organized in Dhaka by the Bangladesh Enterprise Institute on 7 September 2004. Referring to what he described as restrictions imposed by India on the import of his country's goods, he, according to Bangladesh's highly-respected English daily, the *Daily Star*, said that Dhaka could 'end India's $3 billion dollar [*sic*] trade here by issuing an SRO (Statutory Regulatory Order) on all Indian goods entering Bangladesh'.[68]

Some of Khan's other remarks were even more threatening and were calculated to create tension between the States of north-eastern India and the rest of the country. 'Bangladesh is India-locked. Delhi has also to remember that the seven north-eastern Indian states are Bangladesh-locked.' While an attempt to intimidate is implicit in his reference to the vulnerability of India's north-eastern states vis-à-vis Bangladesh, particularly in the context of India's allegation of Bangladesh's grant of assistance and sanctuary to the secessionist insurgent groups operating in the region, an attempt to sow discord between these states and the rest of India is manifest in his speech as reported in the *Daily Star*. According to the report, '[Mr Khan] blasted the Central Bank of India [the Reserve Bank?] for acting unilaterally against the interests of the common people of the north-eastern states [of India] by imposing non-tariff barriers, such as not allowing individual states to open letters of credit (LCs) without permission from Delhi.'[69]

The outburst, which will be discussed in some detail in Chapter Three, caused shock and anger in India, and was also sharply criticized in Bangladesh. What was India's response? It would be useful to quote from a report in the *Daily Star* of 11 September 2004. It reads,

> India yesterday expressed its 'surprise and dismay' over the remarks by Foreign Minister M. Morshed Khan at a recent seminar of journalists in Dhaka.
>
> Our Delhi Correspondent Pallab Bhattacharya says, Indian Foreign Secretary Shyam Saran summoned Bangladesh High Commissioner to India Hemayetuddin to the External Affairs Ministry and asked him to convey to Dhaka that Morshed's remarks 'could have a negative impact on bilateral relations and on the spirit of goodwill and friendship that has hitherto characterized these relations.
>
> A statement issued by the spokesperson of Indian External Affairs Ministry said Morshed 'made the remarks in the presence of diplomats, including the Indian High Commissioner to Bangladesh Veena Sikri. India has always looked upon Bangladesh as a close friend and valued partner. At recent high-level interactions conducted in a friendly and cordial atmosphere, the two sides reiterated their desire to take the bilateral relationship forward. . . . India, for its part, remains committed to the process.[70]

It is nobody's case that India should have declared war on Bangladesh because of its Foreign Minister's intemperate outburst. It could, however, have found other and stronger ways of conveying its severe displeasure over the matter. It could, for example, have cancelled its then Home Secretary Dhirendra Singh's visit to Bangladesh from 16 to 18 September 2004. It could also have cancelled the visit by the BDR's Director General, Maj. Gen. Khan Chowdhury, later in September. As it is, the visits produced very little. During the Foreign Secretary's visit, Bangladesh and India agreed to coordinate patrols in their own territories by their security forces and Dhaka agreed to grant double-entry and exit visas to Indians transiting through international air and land ports. Dhaka also said it was ready to sign an agreement to enhance cooperation in security issues, if required, and to consider New Delhi's proposal for an extradition treaty and respond to it at a meeting between the two countries likely to be held in January or early February 2005.[71] As seen above, Maj. Gen. Khan Chowdhury's visit did not mark any change in Bangladesh's position of denying the existence of camps for Indian insurgents on its soil. It produced only his barbed remarks about India not being economically better-off than his country and, therefore, there being no cause for illegal immigration from Bangladesh. Nor did Dhaka take long to do a *volte-face* on the issue of coordinated patrolling by the security forces of the two countries.

After this, can the Bangladesh government be blamed for thinking that however serious a provocation that a person like its Foreign Minister (whose words should be considered as expressing its official views) flings at New Delhi, the latter will only make plaintive statements while simultaneously affirming its commitment to continued friendship with Dhaka? Would the Bangladesh government, therefore, be in the least inclined to stop assisting, along with ISI, insurgent groups active in north-eastern India, or wind up the camps it maintains for these? Equally, can it be expected to act against terrorist groups like HUJIB and curb the anti-India activities the ISI conducts from its soil? Will these groups and the ISI not feel that the political compulsions of the governments of Indian states bordering Bangladesh, and the weakness of the country's central government, will prevent any action against such bases and cells as they might set up inside enclaves of illegal Bangladeshi immigrants in India? Will they not take the opportunity to use these cells and bases to harbour hunted terrorists from around the world and conduct terrorist strikes within or even outside India, just as Al Qaeda cells inside Afghanistan were used for planning the 9/11 outrage?

Notes

1. Hiranmay Karlekar, 'Bangladesh: The Next Afghanistan?', *The Pioneer* (New Delhi and Lucknow) 13 December 2002. See also *Newstime* (Hyderabad) on the same date.
2. The Constitution (Fourteenth Amendment) Bill passed by Bangladesh's National Parliament on 16 May 2004 has increased the number of seats reserved for women to 45. While, however, other provisions of the Act have been implemented, this one has not.
3. Vinod Saighal, Maj. Gen. (Retd), *Dealing with Global Terrorism: The Way Forward* (New Delhi: Sterling, 2003), pp. 228–29.
4. Yossef Bodansky, *Bin Laden: The Man Who Declared War on America* (Rocklin, CA: Prima Publishing, 1999), pp. 225–26.
5. Ibid., p. 319.
6. Ibid.
7. B. Raman, *Intelligence: Past, Present and Future* (New Delhi: Lancer Publications, 2002), p. 44.
8. Ibid., p. 45.

9. B. Raman, *A Terrorist State as a Frontline Ally* (New Delhi: Lancer Publications, 2002), p. 5.
10. Ibid., p. 6.
11. Bodansky, *Bin Laden*, p. 16.
12. Ibid.
13. Ibid.
14. Ibid., p. 18.
15. Bodansky, *Bin Laden*, p. 378.
16. Ibid., pp. 377–80.
17. Ibid., p. 380.
18. Raman, *Intelligence*, p. 219.
19. Ibid., p. 49
20. Ibid.
21. News report, 'Counter-terrorism Deal with America Likely: Black Mum on Terrorist Presence in Bangladesh', *The Daily Star* (Internet edition), 6 September 2004.
22. Rohan Gunaratna, *Inside Al Qaeda: Global Network of Terror* (New Delhi: Roli Books), p. 167.
23. Bodansky, *Bin Laden*, p. 26.
24. Eric Hobsbawm, *Age of Extremes: The Short Twentieth Century (1914–1991)*, 10th impr. (London: Michael Joseph, 1995), p. 126.
25. David Thomson, *Europe Since Napoleon* (Harmondsworth: Penguin Books, 1974), p. 594.
26. Alan Bullock, *Hitler: A Study in Tyranny* (Harmondsworth: Penguin Books, 1990), p. 152.
27. Ibid., p. 161.
28. Ibid., pp. 216–18.
29. Ibid., 215.
30. Ibid., p. 230.
31. Ibid., p. 253.
32. Kamal Matinuddin, Lt Gen. (Retd), *The Taliban Phenomenon: Afghanistan 1994–97* (Karachi: Oxford University Press, 1999), p. 24.
33. Ahmed Rashid, *Taliban: Islam, Oil and the New Great Game in Central Asia*, (London and New York: I.B. Taurus Publishers, 2001), p. 21.
34. Julfikar Ali Manik, 'Ten BNP Men Chargesheeted with Killing Kibria', *The Daily Star*, (Internet edition), 17 March 2005.
35. News report, 'Asma Rejects Chargesheet', *The Daily Star* (Internet edition), 21 March 2005.
36. Chaitanya Chandra Halder, Ashraf Shamim and Mahmud Shameem, '22 to Walk Gallows for Killing Ahsanullah: 6 Get Life, Family Demands Quick Execution', *The Daily Star* (Internet edition), 17 April 2005.
37. News report, 'Jongi Bishayak Seminare German Rashtradoot: Hamlar Shikar Hochhe Moulobad Birodhira' (German Ambassador at a seminar on Fundamentalism: The Victims of Attack Are Those Opposed to Fundamentalism), *Prothom Alo* (Internet edition), 11 October 2004; and news report, 'German Ambassador for Probe between Grenade Attacks, Fundamentalist Links', *The Daily Star* (Internet edition), 11 October 2004.

38. Chandan Nandy, 'Bangla Migrants Pose Threat: Over 15 Million Now in India', *The Hindustan Times* (New Delhi), 7 November 2003.

39. Surajit Talukdar and Swapan Kumar Paul, 'High Security on Indo-Bangla Border: Assam Districts Fear Entry of Bangladesh-trained Militants', *The Pioneer* (New Delhi), 6 November 2003.

40. Krittivas Mukherjee (India Abroad News Service), 'Madrasas are being Used to Provide Shelter to Ultras: Muslim Clerics Opposed Action Against Unauthorized Seminaries', *The Pioneer* (New Delhi), 25 January 2002.

41. News report, 'Shwikritiheen Bohu Madrasaye Adhunik Shiksha Nei' (There Is No Modern Education in Many Unrecognized Madrasas), *Aajkaal* (Kolkata), 25 January 2002.

42. The seat of the government of West Bengal.

43. Mohammad Yousaf, Brig. (Retd) and Maj. Mark Adkin, *The Bear Trap: Afghanistans Untold Story*, (Lahore: Jang Publishers, n.d.), p. 63.

44. Ibid., p. 64.

45. *Guerrilla Warfare* (London: Cassell, 1962), by Mao Tse-Tung (trans. Brig. Gen. Samuel B. Griffith II, USMC [Retd]) and Ernesto 'Che' Guevara (introduced by Maj. Harries-Clichy Peterson, Jr), with a foreword by Gp Capt. B.H. Liddell Hart.

46. Ibid., p. 101.

47. News report, 'UPA Clueless about Illegal Influx in East', *The Economic Times* (New Delhi), 24 July 2004.

48. Ibid.

49. News report, 'Humane Approach to Influx: Patil', *The Economic Times* (New Delhi), 27 May 2004.

50. Wasbir Hussain, 'Assam: Demographic Jitters', *South Asia Intelligence Review* 3(10), 20 September 2004. See South Asia Terrorism Portal, www.satp.org/satporgtp/sair/Archives/3_10.htm.

51. News report, 'Cabinet Decides to Retain Illegal Migrants Act', *The Times of India* (New Delhi), 28 October 2004.

52. News report, 'Poor Funds Hold Up Fence along Indo-Bangla Border, *The Indian Express* (New Delhi), 9 January 2004.

53. Rana Ajit, 'CCS Put New OK Stamp on Old Plan', *The Pioneer* (New Delhi), 15 October 2001.

54. News report, 'Illegal Migrants a Security Threat: SC', *The Asian Age* (New Delhi), 27 February 2001.

55. News report, 'High Court Raps Centre on Bangladeshi Migrants' Issue', *The Pioneer* (New Delhi), 23 September 2003.

56. Thomas Abraham, 'HC Indicts Delhi Government for not Evicting Aliens Faster', *The Pioneer* (New Delhi), 9 September 2004.

57. News report, 'Court Orders Full Survey of Bangladeshis', *The Asian Age* (New Delhi), 23 September 2004.

58. News report, 'Bhool Bojhabujhir Aboshan Ghatalen Buddha' (Buddha Brings an End to Misunderstanding), *Aajkaal* (Kolkata), 7 February 2002.

59. A left-of-centre political party that was established by India's nationalist leader Subhas Chandra Bose. It has strong pockets of influence, mainly in West Bengal, and is represented in West Bengal's ruling Left Front government.

60. CPI stands for Communist Party of India which was earlier aligned with the Communist Party of the Soviet Union while the Communist Party of India (Marxist) was ideologically closer to China. The two parties emerged as separate political entities when the original Communist Party of India split in 1964. The CPI retained the old party's name as it was then in control of the party organization, although those who formed the CPI(M) were in a majority.

61. RSP is the abbreviation of the Revolutionary Socialist Party, which is Marxist in its ideology and has strong pockets of influence in West Bengal and Kerala. Like the Forward Bloc, it is represented in West Bengal's Left Front government.

62. News report, 'Buddhar Shange Baithake Khushi Muslim Pratinidhira' (Muslim Representatives Happy over Meeting with Buddha), *Aajkaal* (Kolkata), 8 February 2002.

63. Sanjay Singh, 'SIMI Expanding on the Eastern Horizon: Dhaka Plays Fundamental Facilitator', *The Pioneer* (New Delhi), 4 December 2003.

64. Formed in 1964, the CPI(M) is by far the largest Marxist party in India and is the mainstay of the coalition governments running West Bengal and Tripura at the time of writing. It is also the main opposition party in Kerala where the Left Democratic Front it leads and the United Democratic Front headed by the Congress have been replacing each other in power following every election to the state Legislative Assembly. At the time of writing, it supports—but without participating in—the Congress-led United Progressive Alliance which governs India at the federal level.

65. News report, 'Pranab Fires Madrasa Salvo at Buddha', *The Telegraph* (Kolkata), 13 February 2004.

66. Bhavna Vij-Aurora, 'No Infiltration from Bangla, Says BDR DG', *The Indian Express* (New Delhi), 29 September 2004; and Rana Ajit, 'Indian Economy no Better than Ours: BDR Chief', *The Pioneer* (New Delhi), 29 September 2004.

67. Ajit, *Indian Economy No Better than Ours.*

68. News report, 'Morshed Blasts Delhi for "Unfair Trade": Says Dhaka too Can Retaliate', *The Daily Star* (Internet edition), 8 September 2004.

69. News report, 'Morshed Comments: India Summons Envoy, Expresses Dismay', *The Daily Star* (Internet edition), 11 September 2004.

70. Ibid.

71. News report, 'Dhaka, Delhi Agree to Coordinate Patrols: Bangladesh to Give Indians Double Entry and Exit Visas, Consider Extradition Treaty, *The Daily Star* (Internet edition), 19 September 2004.

Three
August 21: Evening of the Grenades

August is a month of mourning for the Awami League. For, on the morning of 15 August 1975, its inspirational leader and the architect of Bangladesh's liberation movement, Sheikh Mujibur Rahman, was killed, along with all but two members of his family, by a band of young army officers. His daughters—Sheikh Hasina, who went on to become the Prime Minister of Bangladesh from 1996 to 2001, and her sister, Sheikh Rehana—survived because they were abroad at the time.

Twenty-nine years later, August again turned out to be a cruel month for the party. For, on 21 August 2004, a vicious grenade attack led to the deaths of 22 of its supporters and leaders and injuries to over 200. The target was a rally organized by the party in front of its central office on Bangabandhu Avenue in the heart of Dhaka. The purpose was to protest against bomb attacks in Sylhet in north-eastern Bangladesh, the murder of Tushar, a leader of its students' organization, the Bangladesh Chhatra League, at Gopalganj district, and atrocities on its leaders and supporters throughout the country.

As it was the month of mourning, the processions by activists of the party and its associated organizations that began arriving at the venue from the afternoon onwards carried black flags. For the same reason, no dais had been erected. Sheikh Hasina, President of the Awami League and Leader of the Opposition in Bangladesh's Jatiya Sansad or National Parliament, who arrived at the party office at 5 P.M., addressed the vast crowd that had formed, standing on an open truck. With her were members of the Awami League's Presidium and the President and the General Secretary of the Mahanagar (Metropolitan) Awami League. The party's other central leaders sat on the road along with ordinary workers and leaders.[1]

Sheikh Hasina unleashed a strident verbal attack on Bangladesh's ruling coalition headed by Prime Minister Khaleda Zia of the BNP, which had won a landslide majority in elections to the National Parliament. Accusing it of corruption and inefficiency, she said, 'The present Government has established a reign of terror over the whole country. Awami League's popular and competent organizers are being murdered.' Citing the case of the Chhatra League leader, Tushar, she said that prosecution was launched against him after he had been murdered. Describing the government as 'terrorist' and a 'bomb-thrower', she called upon the gathering to save the country by launching a united struggle. 'The days of this Government', she said, 'are over'.[2]

As it turned out, it was most fortunate that her own days were not over. A few seconds later a grenade exploded two yards from the truck-turned-dais, just as she was about to leave after finishing her speech. It was 5.23 P.M. Then, one after another, a number of other grenade explosions followed. Estimates of the total number vary from nine to 13. Within seconds, a stretch of one of Dhaka's main roads in the heart of the city became a scene of carnage and utter confusion, with men and women fleeing in all directions in terror, and cries of agony and pleas for help rending the air.

Almost immediately after the first explosion, one of Hasina's personal security guards covered her, and her supporters formed a protective shield. Others were not so lucky. Sixteen lay dead and 200 wounded, some severely, when the 'rain of grenades', as an eyewitness described it, finally stopped. The critically wounded included several senior Awami League leaders—Abdur Razzak, Amir Hossain Amu, Suranjit Sengupta, Ivy Rahman and Kazi Zafarullah.[3] The death toll rose as the days progressed, finally reaching 22.

One of the victims, Ivy Rahman, was Secretary of the Women's Affairs wing of the Awami League and the wife of the party's general secretary, Zillur Rahman. Both of her legs had to be amputated. She died on 24 August.

By then, two things had become abundantly clear. First, the attack had been carefully pre-planned and carried out by highly-trained people who wanted to kill the maximum number of men and women possible. Second, the targets were Sheikh Hasina and the principal leaders of the Awami League, and the wider objective was the destabilization of the country. In an editorial on 23 August, Bangladesh's widely re-spected Bengali-language daily *Prothom Alo* stated,

We are stunned, perturbed and mortified by the manner in which a grenade attack was carried out on Saturday in a bid to kill the President of the Awami League and the Leader of the Opposition in the National Parliament, Sheikh Hasina. It was unimaginable that such an attack could be mounted on a gathering at the nation's capital, Dhaka, at which Sheikh Hasina was present. . . . It is clear that the assailants had launched the attack with the objective of creating a major disaster like the killing of Sheikh Hasina. The attack occurred just when the Leader of the Opposition, Sheikh Hasina, had finished her speech.[4]

Not just Hasina

The *Daily Star* wrote in an editorial in its issue of 22 August, 'The way the attack was carried out points to a very well-organized, well-planned and profes-sionally executed operation. It would not be wrong to suggest that the timing, the mechanism used and the targets were selected in a manner which would cause the maximum death and destruction.'[5] Returning to the subject, it said in another editorial on the following day,

> The assassination attempt on the main opposition Awami League leader Sheikh Hasina on Saturday that caused widespread death and destruction is not only deplorable but a warning signal to the political parties too. By now it is certain to all of us that the neatly planned and executed, almost to a perfection, bomb attacks on a peaceful rally had the sole objective of destabilizing the country. It is a clear indication of political violence going out of control. The news of setting fire to a passenger train by angry supporters of the Opposition in Bhairab and violent clashes in other parts of the country are an ominous indicator of mounting political tension that must be defused at any cost.[6]

The editorial went on to add,

> The kind of carnage and casualties caused by Saturday's grenade attacks was a rare example of barbarity committed in cold blood. The time has come for the Government to distinguish between routine criminality and terrorism in order to get a clearer view of the situation. All the political parties must keep in mind that the terrorists could only jeopardize the democratic process. And that's why they must close ranks to fight the menace of terrorism that plagues the society as a whole.

Bangladesh, which had seen a steady increase in the incidence of fundamentalist Islamist terrorism, had witnessed nothing like what

happened on Saturday, 21 August 2004. Stating that the attack on the
Awami League's rally was 'qualitatively different' from the previous
ones for several reasons, Brig. Gen. (Retd) Shahedul Anam Khan of
the Bangladesh Army and Editor, Defence and Strategic Affairs, of
the *Daily Star*, wrote in the paper's 26 August issue,

> Never before in Bangladesh were such high value targets made the object
> of militant attack. Never before did we behold a situation where a bomb
> attack was concluded with such precision and professionalism. The
> modus operandi of the perpetrators point to a well-organized group
> trained and committed to carry out a dangerous mission. Never before
> have we seen so many 'bombs' hurled at one gathering and in such
> quick succession.[7]

According to Brig. Gen. (Retd) Khan the target was not just Sheikh
Hasina. Descriptions by eyewitnesses and video clips of the incident
as well as the fact that 'an area weapon was used points to the fact
that no one single individual in particular was the target; the idea was
to take out the Awami League leadership in one go'. Apart from this,
he wrote that a disconcerting aspect of the situation was the gradu-
ation, from the use of indigenous explosive devices (IED), 'to more
sophisticated and lethal devices like hand grenades', and that a cause
for even greater worry was that

> weapons manufactured exclusively for military use, are now in the hands
> of clandestine terrorist groups. Needless to say, it takes some training
> and the self-confidence that comes with it to operate such devices. The
> long and short of the matter is that we are now faced not only with
> the reality of the existence of extremists and militants in our country,
> we are also faced with a disconcerting prospect of having to combat
> this evidently highly trained menace, something that we may not be
> fully prepared for at this moment.[8]

People in Bangladesh and abroad, however, had a good idea of what
the attack signified even before the publication of Brig. Gen. (Retd)
Khan's informed and incisive analysis. On 21 August itself, a statement issued by the Dhaka University Teacher's Association (DUTA),
and signed by 305 academics, termed the blasts as an attack on Sheikh
Hasina that was also aimed at eliminating the Awami League's 'progressive and non-communal political practice'. Expressing concern
over the incident, the signatories said that the coalition government,

led by the BNP and the Jamaat, had to bear the responsibility for the planned attack.[9]

On August 24, the Bangladesh Bar Council said that religious extremists wanted to kill the Opposition leader and Awami League President, Sheikh Hasina, as she stood for the pro-liberation forces. It also called for the immediate resignation of the government for its failure to ensure security to the people.[10]

On the day of the attack itself, the reaction was almost instant and explosive. Sporadic clashes followed in Dhaka and all over the country between supporters of the Awami League on one side and their opponents and the police on the other. Awami League supporters damaged scores of vehicles in Cox's Bazaar and the port city of Chittagong in the extreme south-eastern part of the country. Sylhet in north-eastern, Noakhali in eastern, Rajshahi in north-western, and Pabna and Natore in western Bangladesh, and Manikganj, south of Dhaka, also witnessed clashes.[11]

While the clashes continued and statements condemning the attack poured into newspaper offices, a meeting, chaired by Sheikh Hasina herself, was held at Sudha Sadan, the official residence of the Leader of the Opposition in Bangladesh's National Parliament, which she occupied by virtue of holding that office. In attendance were senior leaders of the 11-party Left alliance[12] and the Jatiya Samajtantrik Dal or the National Socialist Party (which, incidentally, has nothing in common with Adolf Hitler's Nazi party, which had the same official name). Demanding the immediate resignation of the ruling coalition, they endorsed the Awami League's call for the observance of dawn-to-dusk *hartal*s (general strikes) on 24 and 25 August as a part of a combined programme to resist religious fundamentalists.[13]

Anger and concern

The general strike of 24 August, the 37th since the Awami League was voted out of office in October 2001, was the most spontaneous of them all, as a wide cross-section of Bangladesh's society reacted in horror and anger to the events of 21 August. It crippled life throughout the country. Shops, schools, business houses, private offices, stock exchanges, and major seaports remained shut. There was hardly any traffic on the streets. Dhaka's road, rail and steamer links with the rest of the country were snapped. Train services stopped, following attacks on control rooms, trains and stations. Incensed by the news of Ivy Rahman's passing, opposition activists ransacked the Brahmanberia and Akhaura railway stations, the latter an important junction, in north-eastern and eastern Bangladesh. No long-distance bus left or arrived in Dhaka. Launches and steamers lay anchored at Sadarghat, its main ferry station.

Over 100 persons were injured in sporadic clashes between supporters of the strike on the one hand and the activists of the BNP-Jamaat-led coalition and the police on the other. Among the wounded was the General Secretary of the Communist Party of Bangladesh, Mujahidul Islam Selim, who was clubbed and seriously injured by policemen. The Home Minister of Bangladesh in the Awami League government, Mohammad Nasim, was also wounded in a scuffle with the police.[14] On the following day, the duration of the general strike was reduced from 12 to seven hours to enable people to attend the funeral prayers for, and burial of, Ivy Rahman. While the strike continued until the original deadline of 6 P.M. in Chittagong, it concluded in Dhaka at 1 P.M. The day witnessed unprovoked police attacks on peaceful processions, including one with batons to disperse a procession by women Awami League leaders and activists in Dhaka, and widespread arrests of opposition party activists. Twenty-six persons were wounded and 250 arrested. Among the arrested was Nazma Akhter, President of the Awami Jubo Mahila (Youth and Women) League.[15]

As Bangladesh reacted to the grenade attack with horror and mortification, a wave of concern swept the world. India's Prime Minister Manmohan Singh telephoned Sheikh Hasina that very evening to express his grave concern. The German Foreign Minister, Joschka Fischer, strongly condemned the attack in a statement faxed to the Bangladesh Sangbad Sanstha (BSS), the country's government-controlled news agency.[16] The calls spilled over into the next day, with Necmettin Erbakan, the Turkish Prime Minister; L.K. Advani, the Leader of the Opposition in Lok Sabha or the Lower House of India's Parliament; Sonia Gandhi, President of the Indian National Congress, the main constituent of the United Progressive Alliance, the coalition ruling the country; and Christina Rocca, the US Assistant Secretary of State, all expressing concern.[17] So did the United Nations Secretary General, Kofi Annan, whose spokesperson said in a statement, 'The Secretary-General is appalled to learn that the bombing of a rally in Dhaka on Saturday had caused the death reportedly of more than a dozen people and injured a large number of others who had gathered there.' The spokesperson added, 'He strongly condemns the use of violence against the civilian population and reiterates his call for the perpetrators of these acts to be brought to justice.'[18]

Others to express concern were President George Bush and the then Secretary of State, Colin Powell, of the United States. In Dhaka itself, a wave of consternation rippled through the diplomatic community. On 22 August, the Head of the Delegation of the European Commission to Bangladesh, Ambassador Esko Kentrschynskyi, strongly condemned the attack and offered his deepest condolences to the bereaved families. A joint statement by European diplomats in Dhaka on the same day urged the government to thoroughly investigate the attacks and bring those responsible to justice. They also called for the provision of adequate security to opposition leaders.

The strongest and the most forthright, however, was the statement issued by the United States Embassy. Describing the attack as a 'blatant and reckless act of political terrorism', it said that the future of Bangladesh would have suffered a terrible blow if the audacious commando-style assault had succeeded in eliminating the leadership of the main opposition party. It called upon Bangladesh's government to promptly bring to justice the perpetrators of the heinous crime and to demonstrate clearly its commitment to providing a free and secure environment for constitutionally protected political activity. Finally, it stated, 'Yesterday's assault is unfortunately only the latest and the most alarming in a series of incidents in 2004 attacking basic human rights in Bangladesh', and added, 'During this difficult time, we urge all Bangladeshis to exercise maximum restraint and to act only in a peaceful and lawful manner fully consistent with the best traditions of democracy in Bangladesh.'[19]

BNP: Shock and damage control

In Bangladesh, President Iajuddin Ahmed, Prime Minister Khaleda Zia, Speaker of the National Parliament Jamiruddin Sircar, Deputy Speaker Abdul Hamid Siddiqui and BNP Secretary General Abdul Mannan Bhuiyan expressed deep shock on 21 August night itself over the loss of life in the attack. In a statement, the President said, 'Only the enemies of the nation can launch this type of barbaric attack.' Expressing profound shock over the loss of lives, the Prime Minister asked the concerned authorities to ensure proper treatment to the injured and wished their early recovery. She also asked for the identification of the terrorists through proper investigation.[20]

On 22 August, Begum Zia, accompanied by several BNP leaders, visited the Combined Military Hospital, Dhaka, where Awami League leaders, including Ivy Rahman, were being treated. Spending some time by her side, she asked the attending doctors about her condition and instructed them to ensure that she received the best possible treatment.[21] Later, she met Maj. Gen. (Retd) Tareq Ahmed Siddiqui who was also injured on 21 August and was in the same hospital. As she asked how he was and told the doctors to do their best, he gave her a brief account of the attack. On the same day, the government announced the formation of a one-man commission, headed by a senior judge of the High Court division of the Bangladesh Supreme Court, Joynul Abedin, to inquire into the grenade attack and submit a report within three weeks.[22]

In the midst of the worldwide outpouring of concern and nationwide protest, BNP leaders began thinking of ways in which they could counter the backlash generated by the grenade attack. Prime Minister and party chief Begum Khaleda Zia met senior party leaders in the wake of the incident to review the situation. The decision was to revamp the party and launch a massive countrywide campaign through rallies protesting against terrorism, bomb attacks and anarchy.[23] Making clear that the BNP did not want a confrontation with the Awami League, a top leader of the party told the *Daily Star*, 'We will proceed in a peaceful way and we do not want to irritate the Awami League with our programme. We have instructed all units of our party to avoid any provocation and confrontation.' He, however, said on the condition of anonymity that the Awami League did not 'want any dialogue or understanding with the Government to put an end to bomb explosions and attacks'. Rather, it seemed to prefer launching a movement to capitalize on the attack.

While Begum Zia's party prepared to launch its campaign, the charge of complicity with the attack continued to be levelled—or hinted at—against it and her government from the evening of the ghastly event itself. Shortly after the grenade attack, the Communist Party of Bangladesh stated that an attack of the kind mounted could not have been possible without support from high-ups in the government.[24] Talking to reporters at her residence on 24 August, Sheikh Hasina expressed her reservations about the adequacy of the security steps taken by the government to protect the rally and questioned how the attackers could have escaped after such carnage in the presence of a large number of law-enforcers.[25]

Particularly deserving of attention was this statement she made: 'Usually our volunteers stand guard on the rooftops of high-rise buildings around the party headquarters during our meetings and rallies, but on Saturday, the police did not allow our men to get on the rooftops.'[26] It is important in this context to recall yet another point made by Brig. Gen. (Retd) Khan in the article referred to above. The fact that the grenades were aimed at the truck that was acting as the podium, and that 'they all detonated in very close proximity to the truck' suggested, according to him, that they were hurled from a distance of 30 to 35 metres. It also suggested that the attackers had a 'pretty good prior knowledge' of the position of the truck which enabled them to 'pre-position themselves to be within grenade throwing distance from the podium yet at a stand-off range for their own safety'.

Referring to accounts that the grenades were thrown from a recumbent or prone position at the street level, Brig. Gen. (Retd) Khan said it was 'difficult to accept' these 'unless these people were on a suicide mission, which clearly was not the case'. 'The rooftop location from which the grenades were apparently hurled, provided the stand-off distance. . . .' Further, referring to the report by some that there was a large contingent of security and law enforcement agencies in the area, he observed that it was 'difficult to accept the proposition' that several militants slipped through the police cordon, ensconced themselves in close proximity to one another, and threw the

> hand grenades just as soon as Hasina finished her speech with complete freedom of action. One finds it difficult to accept this proposition if the police description of its force deployment was to be taken as accurate. On a secured rooftop, in broad daylight, not only to haul grenades with some degree of accuracy but also fire small arms weapons seems too brazen not to draw attention to oneself.[27]

The question arises: Did the security personnel present deliberately allow the terrorists to position themselves on rooftops for the savage attack? If so, did the government have any role in the attempted assassination? Or did the security personnel act in collusion with some other forces? One would have thought that the one-man judicial commission comprising Justice Joynul Abedin would provide an answer that was credible and acceptable to all. No such thing happened. Even though the fact that the judge chosen had once been a BNP functionary did not draw flak initially, the manner in which the commission was constituted mired it in controversy from the very beginning. In an editorial published on 26 August, the *Daily Star* stated that its reaction to the commission's formation was 'somewhat mixed'. While asserting that 'there could be no question about the need for a thorough investigation into last Saturday's tragedy', it said, 'our doubts stem from the fate of all the previous probe committee reports and the inability to get into the roots of the issue'. It also stated that the time allotted to the Commission to do its job appeared 'unduly optimistic'.[28]

The editorial further asserted that there was 'considerable merit in the suggestion' that to be able to function 'independently and in a neutral manner' the probe should be conducted by 'one or two retired chief justices' and, given the highly sophisticated weapons used, it should 'also comprise weapons experts'. It also held that 'the matter being so grave as to impact on our State security', there was 'considerable merit' in deciding the commission's composition 'through consultation with all concerned'. Stating that 'we are not privy to the terms of reference of the probe body', it argued that the latter 'should be tasked with specific responsibilities, including identifying the perpetrators of this act and their sponsors and cohorts, both inside and outside the country'. The editorial said that the commission should also identify the causes of the lapses in the security arrangements to which the Leader of the Opposition was entitled from the state by virtue of her position. Urging the timely use of the offer of foreign assistance in investigating the attack, it hoped that the government would 'make the report public' and that the probe body 'would deliver' because 'not only was the credibility of the government at stake, most importantly, the safety of the people and the nation' was in jeopardy.

Prompting from the wings?

The editorial had no effect on the government, which persisted with the commission as it was constituted. Worse, while it was still at work, Prime Minister Khaleda Zia and other BNP leaders began airing views that could be regarded as tantamount to trying to influence its conclusions. Addressing a discussion meeting on 2 September 2004 at the Mahanagar Natya Mancha (literally Metropolitan Theatre Stage) in Dhaka to mark the 26th founding anniversary of her party, she claimed that the grenade attack on 21 August was a part of a conspiracy to mar the image of her administration, impede post-flood rehabilitation (a devastating flood had swept several parts of Bangladesh in July) and scare off foreign investors. She added, 'As investigations are on into the incident, I won't name anyone. But I do know for certain that there was a plot, which is still being nursed.'[29] Without mentioning names but making an oblique reference to leaders of the Awami League, she blamed them for the grenade attack which, she alleged, was aimed at diverting the attention of the masses from her government's success that, she said, made them worried about their future. While she widened the ambit of the conspiracy she had alleged by claiming that the recent bomb explosions in different parts of Bangladesh were also set off to scare away foreign investors, the Law Minister in her government, Moudud Ahmed, introduced an entirely new element when he said that the incident on 21 August was a part of a massive anti-Bangladesh campaign a certain quarter had initiated immediately after the 2001 general elections.[30]

Moudud's statement retrospectively acquired a highly controversial character when the Joynul Abedin Commission submitted its report on 2 October. Even earlier, however, Begum Zia's observations had caused widespread disquiet. The *Daily Star* stated in an editorial on 4 September,

> We are constrained to express our reservations on the Prime Minister's remarks made on Thursday not so indirectly pointing her fingers of accusation at the main opposition party, for having carried out the 21 August grenade attack on the Awami League rally.
>
> Coming as it does from the highest executive of the country, it is most regrettable. The PM seems to have all the answers that the investigators so far have no clue about. Given the tendency of our investigative agencies, once they know the mind of the head of the Government they will direct all their energies to prove her claim and NOT to find the truth. This fact makes her remark all the more unfortunate. . . . We had earlier commended the Government for seeking international assistance in the investigation of the incident, which displayed its sincerity in solving the issue. But Thursday's comments of the PM revive public doubts as to how authentic the official investigation will be.[31]

In the event, the apprehensions were justified. Far from unearthing the truth in a manner that left no scope for any reasonable doubt, the report of the one-man commission, submitted on 2 October 2004, ignited a furious controversy. Justice Joynul Abedin said at a press briefing at the Commission's office before submitting his report that local and foreign terrorists and other culprits had launched the attack on 21 August in a pre-planned way to destroy Bangladesh's democracy, independence and sovereignty.[32] According to the Bangladesh Sangbad Sangstha, the country's government-controlled national news agency, the report held that Sheikh Hasina, President of the Awami League, was the apparent target of the attack but the ultimate goal of its planners was to jeopardize the independence of the country to serve the interests of certain external forces. According to the BSS the report further said that the present government, like the previous one, did not serve the terrorists' goal. That was why they were desperately trying to create chaos, even civil war, to project the state as ineffective and make it vulnerable to foreign intervention. The motive was to establish a puppet government that could serve the interest of its masters. According to the Commission the attack was the work neither of the Awami League nor the BNP nor the Jamaat nor any fundamentalist Islamist terrorist group.

The report stated that the Awami League could not have been behind the attack because it was not credible that that party's activists would kill their own senior leaders, including Sheikh Hasina, to regain power. As for the BNP, why should it attract public wrath and dig its own grave by committing such an act? Would a party which had a two-thirds majority in the National Parliament start a process that would destabilize its own government? According to the report, the Jamaat could not have done it because the fundamentalist party could not expect to capture power by killing either Sheikh Hasina or Begum Zia. The report said that fundamentalist Islamist groups existed in Bangladesh but they were marginalized and it was impossible for them to launch such a coordinated attack, which required trained manpower and sophisticated weapons. Hence, pace the Commission, the attackers were foreign agents. It asked the authorities to arrest two suspects who left the meeting venue on a motorcycle immediately after the first or second explosion.[33]

Credibility impaired

The first thing that undermined the credibility of the report was the refusal of either Justice Joynul Abedin or Bangladesh's government to identify the external forces which the former claimed had masterminded the attack. Asked to identify those behind the crime, he said during the press briefing, 'I've mentioned in the report whom I have identified and it is up to the Government whether it would disclose it and implement [the recommendations mentioned in the report]'. When journalists told him that the briefing would make the nation, that was eagerly waiting to know the identity and motives of the perpetrators of the attack, feel frustrated, the judge said, 'People know well about the Commission's jurisdiction and limitations.'[34]

An editorial in the *Prothom Alo* of 4 October 2004, stated:

Since the report has not been placed before the public, the full extent of what it has said is not known. Some of what the report has said, however, has come to be known from the news distributed by the official news agency BSS. Published news has it that in the opinion of the Commission it was the work of foreign agents and that the purpose of the grenade attack was to establish in this country a puppet government, a government that would serve the interests of its masters.

The news that has been circulated does not clearly mention which foreign power it is. One would have known had the full report been placed [before the public]. One, however, had heard of it in a fragmentary way even before that. If there was specific information and proof of the involvement of a foreign power in the grenade attack, then it should have been introduced accordingly. There, however, will be scope for misunderstanding with friendly countries if one talks of an unspecified foreign power. This is not desirable.

Various circles had already hinted at the various things that have featured in the Commission's report. Was it to prepare the ground for their incorporation into its report that the Commission had from time to time publicized these through the BSS? It would undoubtedly be harmful if the Commission's report has been influenced or predetermined by a spin doctor or someone else.

Making a strong plea for the publication of the report, it said,

A judicial inquiry commission's report loses its credibility if it is not made public. People do not get to know whether the Government is properly implementing the inquiry commission's recommendations. The matter of the grenade attack will perhaps be lost if this report is not made public. . . . Hence this report be made public immediately.[35]

The *Daily Star* wrote in an editorial on 4 October 2004, 'There are some very compelling reasons that require the publication of the report.' Apart from the issue of the people's right to know, making the contents public, it said,

> would dispel many reservations, avoid unnecessary speculation and obviate fragmentary reportage in the media. This will also prevent others from embarking on subjective and speculative treatment of the matter. It would, we hope, help to remove the distrust between the major political parties that this incident has unfortunately engendered.
>
> In as much as the Commission has hinted at a foreign linkage with the local elements, it is important that the Government release the whole report to put public misgivings at rest and alley any misperception abroad.
>
> We demand that the contents of the present report should be made public immediately in its entirety.[36]

Sources in a time of speculation

The report was not made public, and the inevitable speculation followed, as did efforts to ferret out the names of the external forces allegedly involved. As always, the proverbial 'sources' and 'informed sources' held out helping hands. The day after the submission of the report to the government, a 'well-placed source' told a Staff Correspondent of the *Daily Star* that considerations of the impact it would have in diplomatic quarters prevented the Commission from mentioning the name of the country involved; nor could the name of the local agents of the latter be mentioned as it was impossible for the judicial commission to identify the perpetrators. The Commission had 'conducted the inquiry at a macro level and hinted only at operatives and masterminds'.[37]

The source's statement, however, ran directly counter to Justice Joynul Abedin's own statement at the press briefing on 2 October. The Dhaka *Independent* had quoted him as saying, 'We have found out the motive and identified the culprits involved in the grenade attack and recommended that necessary action should be taken against them to stop such heinous acts in the future.'[38] Also, the 'sources' raised the question: How could action be taken against the culprits unless they had been specifically identified? Quoting sources, the *Daily Star* report said, 'the Commission conceived the idea of a foreign link after discussions with former officials of the police and intelligence agencies' and 'the officials gave the commission a picture of the operations of foreign intelligence agencies in Bangladesh'. That the sources did not have a multiplicity of foreign agencies but only one of them in mind became clear when the report quoted the source as saying, 'Taking advantage of the confrontationist policies at home, a foreign intelligence agency has been working for long to have a stronghold in Bangladesh.'

What the 'well-placed source' and other sources told the *Daily Star* clearly suggests that the Commission based its conclusion about the involvement of external forces on the basis not of hard evidence but of what former police and intelligence officers—and not serving ones who would have had the latest information and were in touch with events—told it. The report in the *Independent* which incorporated parts of a dispatch filed by the BSS on the briefing, including the portion detailing why the Commission thought that the attack could not be attributed to the Awami League, the Jamaat and the fundamentalist Islamist groups, also suggested that a deductive approach was used, based on a process of elimination. The judge himself tended to confirm the impression when, asked what he meant by saying that the grenade attack was the work of foreign agents, he told Khaled Mohiuddin of *Prothom Alo* on 3 October that he had taken into special consideration Bangladesh's geographical location and the subcontinent's politics while coming to this conclusion.[39] One could perhaps get a faint hint about the foreign forces Justice Abedin had in mind from his response to a telephonic request to say something more about the foreigners involved that *Prothom Alo* made subsequent to the interview on 3 October. He said, 'When foreigners have been mentioned, one has to assume that they are not natives. And it becomes foreign the moment one crosses the geographical boundary of the country.'[40] Asked whether one could assume that the report mentioned the foreign country that was the closest, he said, 'I cannot answer this question of yours now.'

If Justice Abedin had no intention of dropping a hint about the country he had in mind, he could have said that he had nothing to add to what he had said during the interview. Surely, as an experienced judge who had heard many court arguments and who knew how circumstantial evidence was sought to be made clinching, and how messages were conveyed through innuendoes and hints, he must have known the construction that would be put on his statement that 'it' became 'foreign' the moment one crossed the country's geographical boundary!

The question arises as to why one should assume that Justice Abedin was referring to India and no other country. One would do well to recall here that he told Khaled Mohiuddin of *Prothom Alo* on 3 October that he had taken into special consideration Bangladesh's geographical location and the subcontinent's politics while coming to his conclusion about the involvement of a foreign country. Which other country of the Indian subcontinent, apart from India, could have been involved? The suggestion that it might have been Nepal, Myanmar, Sri Lanka, Bhutan or Pakistan would certainly make people laugh. Besides, Begum Khaleda Zia and her party's intense antipathy towards India, to say nothing of the bitter hatred that the Jamaat, their largest partner in Bangladesh's ruling coalition, nurses against it, is no secret in Bangladesh. While she was Leader of Opposition in Bangladesh's National Parliament, Begum Zia had once referred to rebels of the United Liberation Front of Asom and other secessionist rebels groups in north-eastern India as 'freedom fighters'.[41] Equally, the Jamaat, which had actively collaborated with the Pakistani forces' campaign of savage repression to crush the liberation struggle of 1971, has never forgiven India for the help the latter rendered to the liberation struggle. In fact, the Jamaat's basic orientation is bitterly anti-Indian. This is clear from the exposition of its views on Bangladesh's defence by Abbas Ali Khan, who became the Jamaat's officiating Ameer (head) when it was revived in May 1979, after having been banned following Bangladesh's liberation. Khan writes,

Although Bangladesh is the second largest Muslim State in the world, its peculiar geographical position, in which it is hemmed in almost on all sides by India, has cut it off from the Muslim world having no geo-graphical contiguity with it. Fundamental concepts, creeds and phil-osophy of life of the people ruling the state across the borders of Bangladesh are alien and inimical to the fundamental beliefs, concepts and creed that regulate the cultural, social and moral aspects of the overwhelming majority of the people of Bangladesh. As a result such creeds and concepts of the people ruling the neighbour state imbued with the lust for territorial expansion is a threat to the independence and sovereignty of the people of Bangladesh. Uninterrupted stream of cultural propaganda materials flowing down into Bangladesh from across the borders is a step to cultural domination which may be culmin-ated in political domination as well.[42]

The depth and intensity of the Jamaat's hatred for India is further reflected in Khan's essay in the section under the sub-heading, 'National Ideology'. He writes:

> the very word defence raises the pertinent question, 'defence against whom?' Had there been several states around Bangladesh, the answer to this question might not be permanently the same. But as she is almost surrounded by one state, the answer can't be but one. Whenever any kind of aggression comes it shall come from India alone. Consequently the psychology of the defence forces of Bangladesh must be anti-Indian. But only a negative feeling is not sufficient for developing this psychology to the spirit of highest sacrifice for the country. Nobody can deny that the Muslim sentiment or the Islamic spirit is the only positive element necessary for building up the correct and effective psychology of the defence forces. It is the spirit of Jihad which can inspire them to sacrifice their life with the hope that they will be amply rewarded after death. Moreover it is this Muslim sentiment which can effectively inspire both the armed forces and the people to sacrifice their life for the defence of the country with the hope that their posterity will be able to lead real Muslim life only if they remain independent.[43]

Without sense, with innuendo

Given the fact that Justice Abedin had once been a BNP functionary, it is difficult to resist the conclusion that he has, in his report, identified India as the foreign country behind the grenade attack on 21 August. He did not mention it by name presumably for two reasons. First, he had no evidence and hence followed the route of inference and innuendo to reach his conclusion. Second, it would make little sense to the people since the BNP had assiduously carried out a campaign projecting the Awami League as an agent of India. As late as 7 September 2004, the Foreign Minister of Bangladesh, M. Morshed Khan, speaking as the Chief Guest at the inaugural session of the 'India–Bangladesh Dialogue of Young Journalists', organized by the Bangladesh Enterprise Institute at Dhaka, had said with reference to the grenade attack of 21 August, 'Most countries said it was an attack on the country's democracy and phoned to both the prime minister and the opposition leader but', he added in an oblique reference to India, 'some people thought it otherwise'. He went on to say, 'I don't want any more misconception like that arisen from a neighbouring country [read India] conversing with a particular party [read the Awami League] but not the nation', and that 'the responsibility of eradicating that misconception rests with the neighbours themselves'.[44]

Expressing surprise at Khan's 'outburst', the *Daily Star* wondered, in an editorial on 10 September, what

> could have happened in the recent past that could instigate such an outburst by the foreign minister? One, he has perhaps taken umbrage at the fact that while the Indian Prime Minister called up Sheikh Hasina to express his sympathy following the August 21 incident, he did not call the Bangladesh Prime Minister, as was done by the US Secretary of State Colin Powell.
>
> This could have been construed as India's bypassing of the government in Dhaka and siding with the Awami League. The protocol given to Sheikh Hasina, and the level of meetings arranged for her during her visit to India, before any meeting with Prime Minister Khaleda Zia was also not lost on the BNP coalition government.[45]

After Morshed Khan's outburst and the comments that followed in Bangladesh media, the allegation that India was the foreign power behind the 21 August grenade attack would have carried very little conviction. Surely India could gain nothing from wiping out the entire leadership of a party with which, if Mr Khan and others are to be believed, it had a close and special relationship. Besides, why should India seek to destroy democracy in Bangladesh, considering that it was the period of both open and veiled military rule that followed the assassination of Sheikh Mujibur Rahman in 1975 that saw the strengthening of pro-Pakistan and anti-India fundamentalist Islamist elements in that country? And if India had at all wanted to destroy democracy in Bangladesh and put a puppet regime in power—which Justice Abedin had said was the objective behind the 21 August grenade attack—New Delhi's target would have been its opponents rather than its friends.

While the analysis above explains why Justice Abedin did not mention India by name, the claim by a source quoted in the *Daily Star* report, cited earlier, that 'considerations of the impact it would have on diplomatic quarters prevented the Commission from mentioning the name of the country involved', sounds absolutely hollow when one takes into account Morshed Khan's blistering attack on India, which did not seem to have been tempered by any such consideration at all and which was delivered in the presence of the heads of both the Indian and the Pakistani mission in Dhaka. Indeed, Khan had hectored India to 'Stop talking through the media and talk straight to us', adding, 'We don't do politics within the family, and South Asia is our family. It is very important to discuss issues instead of hiding those under the carpet'.[46] Following Mr. Khan's exhortation, one can well ask, why brush under the carpet the name of the foreign forces or country that, according to Justice Abedin's report, was behind the attack on 21 August?

The impression comes through that the idea was to condemn India through deduction and innuendo. This could be the result of two things: first, the BNP and Jamaat's hostility towards India and, second, a desire to divert attention from the real culprit. As to the first, what stood out about Khan's speech was its extreme and minatory tone. It included a sharp attack on what he described as India's maintenance of restrictive measures against the import of Bangladeshi goods so as to keep the balance of trade in its favour. Stating that this was despite Bangladesh's call for an 'equitable bilateral trade', he said menacingly,

> Dhaka too is capable of taking similar restrictive steps against Indian goods to arrive at a win-win situation. . . . If Bangladesh wanted to establish a win-win situation, we could end India's $3 billion trade here by issuing an SRO (Statutory Regulatory Order) on all Indian goods entering Bangladesh.[47]

The threatening tone of Morshed Khan's speech became even more unmistakeable when he reminded Delhi that though Bangladesh was 'India-locked', Delhi had 'also to remember that its north-eastern states' were 'Bangladesh locked'. In what could only be regarded as an attempt to promote discontent in north-eastern India, he added, 'It costs 40 per cent more for north-eastern Indian states to buy most construction goods from Kolkata or other western cities than it would have cost them to buy those from Bangladesh.' In addition, he blasted the 'Central Bank of India' (Reserve Bank of India?) for acting uni-laterally against the interests of the common people of the north-eastern states by imposing non-tariff barriers such as not allowing individual states to open Letters of Credit (LCs) without permission from Delhi.

By all criteria, it was a speech rendered extraordinary by both the spirit of hostility pervading it and the wide-ranging nature of the attack it mounted on India, covering almost all major contentious aspect of

India–Bangladesh relations. Referring to India's allegation that Indian insurgent groups had 195 camps in Bangladesh, he said caustically,

> The list of insurgent camps from their side increases at every meeting between us. But they have not been able to provide a single telephone number or address of these camps.
>
> On the other hand we have given phone numbers, fax numbers and office addresses of Bangladeshi insurgent groups like Bangabhoomi Andolan, who are in India, and criminals who are being hosted by some groups there, but they have not done anything about it.

Dismissing India's allegation of there being terrorist camps in Bangladesh, he said 'No country other than a banana republic would shut its eyes if there were terrorists in its territory.'

Not surprisingly, the speech lent wings to speculation about its purpose. The editorial in the *Daily Star*, mentioned earlier, stated:

> Even if, for the sake of argument, India's prime minister not telephoning our prime minister immediately following August 21 was a breach of protocol, then could it not have been better and more effectively communicated through the normal diplomatic channels? Did it call for such a public outburst?

Wondering whether Bangladesh had 'concluded that our bilateral relations have degraded to such a level that [a] no-holds-barred public denunciation is called for', it asked whether that was indeed the case and added,

> If so, why? We think that the people have a right to know, and the government has a responsibility to tell us, simply because the government needs to carry the people with it, if such a drastic change of policy towards India is to be pursued.
>
> If, on the contrary, the foreign minister's outburst does not reflect the policy of the government, as indicated by other senior ruling party policy-makers, then an immediately damage-control move should be set in motion.[48]

A country's Foreign Minister speaks on behalf of his or her government. It is inconceivable that Khan would have exploded in a vituperative outburst against India without clearance or instruction from Prime Minister Khaleda Zia and her close advisers including other senior members of Bangladesh's Cabinet. If he had, and if what he said did not at least have their approval, then it is reasonable to assume that he would at least have been severely reprimanded if not divested of his portfolio. That nothing of this nature happened indicates that his scorching attack on India had his government's full approval. The BNP government's hostility towards India, which Khan's speech reflected, provides a plausible explanation why Justice Abedin had hinted that India had masterminded the 21 August grenade attack. In this context, it would be instructive to read Justice Abedin's findings along with Bangladesh's Law Minister Moudud Ahmed's statement at the discussion meeting held at the Mahanagar Natya Manch, Dhaka, on 2 September 2004. He, one recalls, had stated then that the grenade attack was a part of a massive anti-Bangladesh campaign that a certain quarter had initiated after the 2001 general elections in Bangladesh. No country was mentioned by name but the reference to India was clear.

There are other indications suggesting not only that this was the intended interpretation, but also that the report was tailored to the wishes of the government. Participating in a press conference on the report addressed by the Awami League General Secretary Abdul Jalil, MP, on 4 October, Tofail Ahmed, an Awami League Presidium member and a former Minister in Sheikh Hasina's government, referred to an issue of September's *Bangla Bazar Patrika,* in which Begum Khaleda Zia had said that India wanted to establish a puppet government in Bangladesh and her party would not allow that to happen.[49] As he pointed out, and as seen above in the BSS' dispatch, Justice Abedin's report also said that motive behind the 21 August attack was to establish a puppet government that would serve the interests of its masters. The coincidence might not have been accidental. As Jalil himself pointed out at the press conference, Justice Abedin had earlier been a vice-President of the BNP, a fact that had made his party conclude that the commission headed by him could never be neutral. The allegation, which remains unrebutted, severely undermines the credibility of the report, which, according to Jalil, 'echoed the instructed and planned report of the government regarding the August 21 carnage'.[50] It also raises serious questions about the Khaleda Zia government's intention—whether it wanted an 'eyewash' or a serious attempt to unearth the truth by a commission whose findings would be nationally and internationally accepted as credible. If the latter had been the case, it would have chosen a person of national standing, and certainly not a former party functionary, to hold the inquiry, as justice has not only to be done but also seen to be done. It seems clear that the desire to have a report that faithfully stated what the government wanted it to made the Commission forget the credibility factor.

Two questions arise at this stage. Was the reference to the involvement of a foreign country meant not only to tarnish India's image but also to divert attention from the real perpetrators of the attack? If the latter was the case, who could the actual perpetrators be?

Notes

1. News report, 'Hamlar Aage Shamabeshe Sheikh Hasina: Shantrashi aar Bomabaaj Sarkarer Biruddhe Oikyabaddha Hone' (Sheikh Hasina at the Gathering Before the Attack: Unite against this Terrorist and Bomb-throwing Government), *Prothom Alo* (Internet edition), 22 August 2004.
2. Ibid.
3. News report, 'Assassination Attempt on Sheikh Hasina', *The Daily Star* (Internet edition), 22 August 2004.
4. Editorial, 'Sheikh Hasinake Hatyar Cheshta: Aatogulo Mrityur Daye Sarkarkei Nite Hobe' (Attempt to Murder Sheikh Hasina: It is the Government that Has to Bear the Responsibility for So Many Deaths), *Prothom Alo* (Internet edition), 23 August 2004.
5. Editorial, 'Attack on AL Rally: We Condemn this Reprehensible Act, *The Daily Star* (Internet edition), 22 August 2004.
6. Editorial, 'Bleeding Politics: Leaders Must Rise to the Occasion', *The Daily Star* (Internet edition), 23 August 2004.
7. Shahedul Anam Khan, NDC, PSC, Brig. Gen. (Retd), 'Saga of Bomb Blasts and Black Saturday', *The Daily Star* (Internet edition), 26 August 2004.
8. Ibid.
9. News report, 'Shock Wave Runs through the Nation's Spine', *The Daily Star* (Internet edition), 22 August 2004.
10. News report, 'Religious Extremism Blamed for the Attack', *The Daily Star*, (Internet edition), 25 August 2004.
11. News report, 'Shock Wave Runs through the Nation's Spine'.
12. The 11-party Left alliance consists of the Communist Party of Bangladesh, Workers' Party, two factions of the Bangladesh Samajtantrik Dal (Socialist Party), two factions of the Bangladesh Krishak Samajbadi Dal (Peasant Socialist Parry), two factions of the Bangladesh Samyabadi (Egalitarian) Party, the Janata Dal (People's Party), the Ganotrantik Dal (Democratic Party), and the Gano Forum (People's Forum).
13. News report, 'Protest *Hartals* on Aug 24, 25', *The Daily Star* (Internet edition), 24 August 2004.
14. News report, 'Country Crippled in *Hartal*', *The Daily Star* (Internet edition), 25 August 2004.

15. News report, 'Arrests, Cop Actions on Pickets Mark *Hartal*', *The Daily Star*, (Internet edition), 25 August 2004.
16. News report, 'Manmohan Calls Hasina, Expresses Concern', *The Daily Star* (Internet edition), 22 August 2004.
17. News report, 'Turkish PM, Sonia, Advani, Rocca Express Concern', *The Daily Star* (Internet edition), 23 August 2004.
18. News report, 'Annan Condemns Attack on Rally', *The Daily Star* (Internet edition), 25 August 2004.
19. News report, 'Turkish PM, Sonia, Advani, Rocca Express Concern'.
20. News report, 'President, PM, Speaker Shocked', *The Daily Star* (Internet edition), 22 August 2004.
21. New report, 'Khaleda Visits Ivy at CMH', *The Daily Star* (Internet edition), 23 August 2004.
22. News report, 'One Man Probe Body Formed', *The Daily Star* (Internet edition), 23 August 2004.
23. News report, 'BNP Plans Campaign to Counter Backlash', *The Daily Star* (Internet edition), 25 August 2004.
24. News report, 'Shock Wave Runs through the Nation's Spine.'
25. News report, 'Hasina Critical of Security Steps', *The Daily Star* (Internet edition), 25 August 2004.
26. Ibid.
27. Shahedul Anam Khan, 'Saga of Bomb Blasts and Black Saturday'.
28. Editorial, 'Probe Body Must be Credible and Trustworthy', *The Daily Star* (Internet edition), 26 August 2004.
29. News report, 'Attack on AL Rally Part of a Plot to Mar BNP's Image', *The Daily Star* (Internet edition), 3 September 2004.
30. Ibid.
31. Editorial, 'Verdict before the Unearthing of Facts', *The Daily Star* (Internet edition), 4 September 2004.
32. News report, 'Probe Panel Submits Report on Grenade Attack at AL Rally', *The Independent* (Internet edition), 3 October 2004. The *Independent* is an important English-language daily of Bangladesh.
33. Ibid.
34. Julfikar Ali Manik, 'August 21 Grenade Attack: Judicial Probe Hints at Foreign Enemy Link', *The Daily Star* (Internet edition), 3 October 2004.
35. Editorial, 'Grenade hamlar tadanta report: Abilambe janashamkshe prakash kara hoke' (Grenade Attack Inquiry Report: Let it Be Revealed before the Public Without Delay), *Prothom Alo* (Internet edition), 4 October 2004.
36. Editorial, 'Make the Judicial Report Public: People Have a Right to Know', *The Daily Star* (Internet edition), 4 October 2004.
37. News report, 'Judicial Report: Foreign Country not Named for Diplomatic Reasons', *The Daily Star* (Internet edition), 4 October 2004.
38. News report, 'Probe Panel Submits Report on Grenade Attack on AL Rally'.
39. Khaled Mohiuddin, 'Prothom Alor Shange Shakshatkare Bicharpati Joynul Abedin: Bhougalik Rajnaitik Bibechanay Bideshi Char Chinhito Hoyechhe' (Justice Joynul Abedin in an Interview with *Prothom Alo*: Foreign Agents Identified on the Basis of Geographical and Political Considerations), *Prothom Alo* (Internet edition), 4 October 2004.

40. Ibid.
41. Jaideep Saikia, *Terror sans Frontiers: Islamist Militancy in North East India* (New Delhi: Vision Books, 2004), p. 81.
42. Abbas Ali Khan, 'Jamaat-e-Islami's Views on the Defence of Bangladesh', website of the Jamaat-e-Islami Bangladesh, www.jamaat-e-islami.org, as updated on 24 September 2002 and accessed on 21 December 2004.
43. Ibid.
44. News report, 'Morshed Khan Blasts India for "Unfair Trade"', *The Daily Star* (Internet edition), 8 September 2004.
45. Editorial, 'The Foreign Minister's Fury: Amateurish Outburst or a Policy Shift', *The Daily Star* (Internet edition), 10 September 2004.
46. News report, 'Morshed Khan Blasts India for "Unfair Trade"'.
47. Ibid.
48. Editorial, 'The Foreign Minister's Fury'.
49. News report, 'AL Pours Cold Water on Judicial Panel Report', *The Independent* (Internet edition), 5 October 2004.
50. Ibid.

Four
Beyond Red Herrings

We begin by trying to answer the first question raised in the last paragraph of Chapter Three: Did the Abedin Commission's report refer to an unnamed foreign country to tarnish India's image and rouse strong passions against it in Bangladesh besides diverting attention from the real perpetrators of the grenade attack on 21 August 2004? Then we move to the second question: If this was the case, who could the actual perpetrators be?

It is clear from the last chapter that Bangladesh's BNP-led coalition government is bitterly inimical to India and, if Awami League General Secretary Abdul Jalil's allegation is correct, Justice Abedin was earlier a functionary of the BNP. This lends plausibility to the charge that, taking its cue from the government, the Abedin Commission was out to stoke intense anti-India feelings. As to the question of whether it was trying to divert attention from those actually guilty, the search for an answer must begin with an examination of whether there is any justification at all for harbouring such a suspicion. For this, it would be necessary to look at the government's past conduct for instances reflecting such a tendency, which would make its reflection in the commission's report conceivable. One may, therefore, look at three major terrorist outrages that occurred in Bangladesh since October 2001, when the four-party coalition government assumed power and Begum Khaleda Zia became prime minister for the second time—the serial bomb blasts in four cinema halls in the district town of Mymensingh on 7 December 2002; the attempt to kill the outspoken scholar, writer and champion of the values of the liberation war, Prof. Humayun Azad, on 27 February 2004; and the grenade attack at the shrine of Hazrat Shahjalal in Sylhet on 21 May 2004 in which the British High Commissioner to Bangladesh, Anwar Choudhury, was wounded.

Late on the evening of 7 December 2002, serial bomb blasts in four cinema halls in the district town of Mymensingh left 17 persons dead and over 200 wounded. Reporting from Mymensingh, two correspondents of the *Daily Star*, Abul Kalam Azad and Aminul Islam, wrote, 'Neither police nor people have any idea about the men behind the blast and their motives. Police sources said that these bombs were powerful, remote-controlled devices. "These bombs were not locally made", said a high police official.'[1]

The Superintendent of Police, Mymensingh District, Motiar Rahman, told the *Daily Star* on 7 December that the police did not as yet have a clue as to the motive behind the blasts, adding, 'All the intelligence agencies are investigating it separately and we hope that the motive behind the attack will be revealed soon'. He would not say more than that the attacks were designed to create a reign of terror in the town and the whole country.[2] Arriving in Mymensingh on Sunday, 8 December, Begum Khaleda Zia, however, said that those who had launched an anti-Bangladesh smear campaign at home and abroad, and were engaged in a conspiracy to tarnish the country's image, seemed to have links with such terrorist incidents. She also said that the authorities had arrested some people for their alleged involvement with the blasts.[3] Her remarks, very similar to those she made about the forces behind the 21 August grenade attack at a discussion meeting in Dhaka mentioned in the first chapter, clearly referred to the arrests in Dhaka, in raids that began before dawn, of four important Awami League leaders, a columnist and writer, and a historian and columnist, on the same day. The arrested Awami League leaders were Sheikh Hasina's political secretary, Saber Hossain Chowdhury, Awami League leader Shafi Ahmed, Awami League Relief and Social Welfare Secretary, Mukul Bose, and the Dhaka City Awami League Organising Secretary Sheikh Fazlur Rahman. The columnist-cum-writer was Shahriar Kabir and the historian and columnist was a Professor of History at Dhaka University, Muntassir Mamun. Sunday, 8 December, saw the arrest of another 10 Awami League leaders and, in the late evening, of Tofail Ahmed, at Zia International Airport, Dhaka, upon his return from Singapore.[4] All except Tofail Ahmed were arrested under Section 54 of the Criminal Procedure Code (CrPC) for suspected involvement in 'anti-state activities'. Tofail, a member of the Awami League's Presidium and a former Minister, was arrested on the charge of killing a BNP activist, Anwar Hossain, in Bhola on 8 June 1996, featuring as one of the 13 accused in a case registered at Bhola police station.[5] The case, which had been closed with the submission of a final report by the police on 30 November 2002 stating that Anwar had been killed in police firing, was revived by his mother, who filed a petition in the High Court on 19 November 2002.

The courts, after rejecting the bail applications of the accused, filed by their defence lawyers, remanded them to police custody for three days.[6] On 9 December, the first day of their remand, the Detective Branch of the Dhaka Metropolitan Police interrogated Saber Hossain Chowdhury, Shafi Ahmed and Muntassir Mamun separately in three sessions. The charges? According to Deputy Commissioner of Police A.K.M. Mahifizul Haque, they had been arrested for aiding and abetting people to turn the country's law and order situation volatile, disrupting communal harmony, tarnishing the country's image abroad, and involvement in sabotage. He also told journalists that the police did not find any significant evidence to support the charges.[7]

On the same day, the Criminal Investigation Department (CID) interrogated Shahriar Kabir for his alleged association with two foreign journalists who had earlier been arrested for anti-State activities. Indeed, among those arrested, only Mukul Bose was accused of being involved in the Mymensingh bomb explosions. He was produced in the court of the Chief Metropolitan Magistrate, Dhaka, who remanded him in police custody for three days against a prayer for seven days.[8]

Diversionary arrests?

How does the fact that Bose alone had been charged with involvement in the bomb blast square with Begum Zia's statement that the authorities had arrested some people (note the plural) for their alleged involvement in the blast? Also, why were the rest arrested within hours of the bomb explosions in Mymensingh—Kabir and Mamun's homes were raided at 2 A.M. and 2.30 A.M. respectively[9]—particularly since the district police had made it clear that they had no idea who was involved? Given the background of vicious rivalry between the BNP and the Awami League, could the other arrests have been to harass Awami League leaders and intellectuals sympathetic to it besides diverting attention from the real culprits? It is important to ask these questions because at least Mamun, Kabir and Shafi Ahmed were arrested without specific charges against them. This is clear from the issue of a show-cause notice by a Division Bench of the Dhaka High

Court on Tuesday, 10 December, asking the Government to explain within three days as to why the arrest of the three, made without any specific charges against them, should not be declared illegal along with their subsequent remand.[10]

On the same day, another Division Bench of the High Court gave Tofail Ahmed ad-interim bail, and issued a show-cause notice on the government to explain within four weeks why he should not be given permanent bail. It also ordered the government not to harass him unlawfully.[11] As for Mukul Bose, his lawyers told the Chief Metropolitan Magistrate before whom he was produced that he had been away from the country for a heart bypass surgery and was not involved in the blast.[12] A Division Bench of the High Court gave Saber Hossain Chowdhury and Mukul Bose bail on 11 December but the police immediately detained the latter for a month under the Special Powers Act (SPA) of 1974.

Indeed, the entire approach of the police raises serious questions because, after the Mymensingh District police had said that they had no clue as to the identity of the people behind the blast and the motives, the Army picked up, early on the morning of Sunday, 8 December, 34 persons, including the President of the Mymensingh District unit of the Awami League, Alhaj Mohammad Motiur Rahman and his son, Mohit-ur-Rahman Shanta. They were taken to the army camp for interrogation. Anil Bandhu Das, President of the Jatiya Party (Monju) district unit, and Bazlur Rahman Tuhin, students' affairs secretary of the district unit of the BNP, who were also arrested, were later released.[13] On Sunday, 8 December, again, at least 10 ward-level leaders of the Awami League in Dhaka were also arrested.

The arrest of top Awami League leaders and of two of Bangladesh's most respected and outspoken intellectuals on grounds that were patently flimsy understandably created a stir all over the country. The fact that the authorities did not detain a single member, to say nothing of a leader, of the Jamaat and the IOJ or HUJIB, the country's most lethal terrorist organization, hardly attracted the kind of attention it would otherwise have. Given their well-known opposition to cinema shows, plays, music and theatre and their proneness to resorting to violence against their opponents, the government should have suspected them first rather than anyone else. Since the government did not even hint at the possibility of their involvement and straightaway arrested Awami League leaders and critical intellectuals, one can hardly be blamed for concluding that it wanted not merely to harass and intimidate the leadership and the rank-and-file of the Awami League and members of the intelligentsia but also to divert attention from the search for the real culprits.

The conclusion appears all the more plausible if one considers how very different has been the attitude of the police and other uniformed authorities towards fundamentalist Islamist terrorist groups even in cases like the grenade attack on an Awami League meeting near Habiganj in Sylhet District on 27 January 2005. The attack killed one of the country's most respected public figures, diplomat-turned-politician and Finance Minister in Sheikh Hasina's government S.A.M.S. Kibria, along with three others, and injured over 70. The outrage sent a wave of shock and anger throughout Bangladesh and created consternation abroad in a manner reminiscent of what followed the grenade attack on 21 August. Asked in the aftermath of the attack whether there was any militant organization in Habiganj, the Superintendent of Police, Sylhet, Abu Musa Mohammad Fakhrul Islam, said that the police suspected a group but were investigating because they did not want to harass anyone without evidence![14]

The second instance concerns the attempt to murder one of Bangladesh's most respected literary figures—Humayun Azad, poet, novelist, researcher, critic and linguist, and professor in Dhaka University's Bengali Department, on Friday, 27 February 2004. Known for his modern and secular outlook and outspoken opposition to fundamentalist Islamists, he had just come out of the Amar Ekushe Boimela[15] when he was brutally attacked with choppers by a group of young men who were lying in wait for him, and who then escaped by exploding a bomb as he lay seriously wounded and bleeding on the ground.

Azad was removed to the Dhaka Medical College Hospital by a group of students. He needed blood transfusion and, as his blood group, B-negative, was not found there, was shifted to the Combined Military Hospital at 10.45 P.M. By then, however, hundreds of students had gathered at the hospital and Dhaka University campus and academic circles were seething with anger. At 11 P.M. that very night, they went on a procession in the campus area raising slogans demanding the immediate arrest and trial of the criminals.[16] Anger spread the next day with the campus being a scene of continuous protest meetings, demonstrations, and processions. Civil society and opposition parties held fundamentalist Islamists responsible for the attempt on Humayun Azad's life, and accused the government of shielding the culprits.

Fundamentalist threats

Several staff members of publishing houses said on the night of the 27th itself that Azad was being threatened by fundamentalist Islamists after his latest book, *Pak Sar Zamin Saad Baad*, which dwelt on Pakistan's atrocities in Bangladesh during the liberation war of 1971 and the collaborationist role of the fundamentalists, had been published in the Eid issue of the widely-circulated Bengali-language daily *Ittefak* on 20 November 2003.[17] That night itself, Azad's incensed wife, Latifa Kohinoor, said at the Combined Military Hospital, 'fundamentalists have done this. Who else could do this? . . . You know an MP even spat venom against him in Parliament'. She asked Dhaka's mayor Sadeque Hossain Khoka and Bangladesh's Minister of State for Home Affairs, Lutfozzaman Babar, who had arrived at the hospital on hearing the news, 'Why didn't you take security measures to protect him after such an outrage in Parliament?'[18]

Latifa Kohinoor's reference was to a speech by the Jamaat MP Delawar Hossain Saydee in Bangladesh's National Parliament on 25 January 2004, demanding the enactment of a blasphemy law. Mentioning Azad's novel *Pak Sar Zamin Saad Baad*, whose title was taken from the first line of Pakistan's national anthem, he had said that it was not possible for a normal person to even think of such a novel. Through it, the author had committed the unpardonable offence of hurting Islam, the Quran, the Sunnah and their followers by ridiculing them in a vile manner. Had there been a blasphemy law in the country, no enemy of religion and morality would have dared to talk or write like this.[19]

Earlier, on 12 December 2003, a demonstration at Bangladesh's national mosque, Baitul Mukarram, in Dhaka, organized by the anti-Ahmadiyya front, the Hifazate Khatme Nobuwat Andolan Coordination Committee, had demanded that the government declare Ahmadiyyas non-Muslims. Threatening newspapers with dire consequences if these did not acknowledge the justness of their cause, speakers demanded Azad's arrest and trial as his novel was derogatory to Islam. Understandably, therefore, Bangladesh's academics and intellectuals believed that the fanatical, intolerant Islamists were behind the attack. Thus Prof. Sirajul Islam Chowdhury said on 28 February: 'I don't believe that this attack was due to personal enmity. Rather it is about his writing that criticizes fundamentalists. The fundamentalists have spoken against him publicly, giving us an idea about the identity of his enemies.'[20]

Writer Shahriar Kabir, himself a victim of brutal torture and harassment said, referring to the attack, 'Those who write against the fundamentalists are being attacked.' He added that there was an attack on himself and Shamsur Rahman in August 2000 and Muntassir Mamun's car was ransacked (in 2000). In the past, Ahmed Sharif, Sufia Kamal and Jahanara Imam had been declared apostates by fundamentalists. Since declaring a person an apostate meant that he or she could be killed, such a proclamation was tantamount to encouraging people to kill that person.[21] It was not just individual writers who suspected that fundamentalist Islamists were responsible for the attack. The *Daily Star* said in an editorial,

> The assailants who have committed a dastardly crime have yet to be identified. But it is not difficult to guess who they could be. Obviously ordinary criminals could not have any stake in liquidating an intellectual known for his very original views. The attack, one is forced to conclude, can be traced to some ideological origin. And there is no doubt that political intolerance, which we witness these days with much trepidation, was the driving force behind it. The victim must have exposed himself to the fury of obscurantism or fanaticism through his write-ups.
>
> It has been an attack on not only an individual but also the whole enterprise of intellectual freedom. The attack should be a wake up call to the truth that obscurantism has cast its ominous shadow on society and that intellectual freedom is its target.[22]

Remarkably, instead of arresting or interrogating any of the fundamentalist elements who had been threatening Azad and demanding his arrest, the police arrested the Joint Secretary of the Sir A.F. Rahman Hall unit of the Chhatra League (the students' organisation of the Awami League), Abu Abbas Bhuiyyan, from the Dhaka University campus at 11 A.M. on 28 February. According to a report in *Prothom Alo*, the police stated that Abbas was known as a 'terrorist'[23] in the university. They said they suspected his involvement in the attempt to kill Azad and were interrogating him in this connection.[24] The *Prothom Alo* report added,

> Questions have been raised about the police's role in investigating the murder. Many among the police have themselves alleged that an attempt

is on under the direction of a certain quarter to obscure what had actually happened. There was no case against Abbas though he is known as a 'terrorist'. The police had arrested 10 to 12 of his political associates before arresting him. As a result it was not unnatural for him to try to run and escape on seeing policemen.

Prime Minister Khaleda Zia saw a wider conspiracy behind the attack, albeit of a very different kind from the one writers and academics were talking about. Addressing a public meeting on 29 February at Savar, in the outskirts of Dhaka, she accused the Awami League of having perpetrated the attack ahead of its hartal programme and alleged that it was a ploy to disrupt the peace. Expressing shock over the incident, she said that Azad would be provided modern treatment facilities and the assailants arrested for punishment under the Speedy Trial Act.[25]

Azad, who was sent to Bangkok for treatment, recovered and travelled to Munich, Germany on 9 August 2004 on a PEN[26] fellowship to do some research on Heinrich Heine. His death there, following a heart attack on 12 August, did not end the controversy over the identity of his assailants.[27] Amidst the continuing flurry of allegations and counter-allegations what stood out was the fact that instead of arresting and interrogating people who had openly demanded his arrest and trial and carried out a vituperative campaign against him, the police had arrested a Chhatra League student leader, and that Begum Zia had accused the Awami League of conspiring to have him murdered. From this, it was for many a short step to the conclusion that the Government was trying to protect the culprits by diverting attention from them.

The same impression

One gets the same impression from the way Bangladesh's government has handled the investigation into a grenade attack at the shrine of Hazrat Shahjalal in Sylhet on 21 May 2004 which led to the death of three persons and injuries to over 70. Among the latter was the British High Commissioner to Bangladesh, Anwar Choudhury, himself of Bangladeshi origin, whose original home is in Sylhet. There was a general feeling that the target of the attack was Choudhury himself. An editorial in the *Prothom Alo* of 23 May declared, 'We are perturbed and mortified by the bomb attack on the British High Commissioner in Sylhet. . . . There is no doubt at all that the bomb attack had occurred with the Bangladesh-born British High Commissioner Anwar Choudhury as target. . . . One can say that he has escaped with his life because the bomb thrown by the attackers did not explode at the right time at the right place.'[28] In its editorial published on the same day, the *Daily Star* said that the attack 'which most probably had the British High Commissioner in Bangladesh as its target, was another grim reminder' of the 'ever-lengthening shadow' of terrorism over the country's image. It further stated, 'it is not known why Mr Anwar Choudhury, the first British High Commissioner of Bangladeshi origin, was targeted by terrorists who have had blood-letting as their broader agenda.'[29]

One reason could, of course, have been Britain's participation in the United States-led invasion of Iraq, which had angered a large section of people in the world, including many Muslims. Fundamentalist Islamists were particularly incensed and held, in Bangladesh and elsewhere, angry demonstrations against Britain and the US. A report in the *Prothom Alo* of 23 May quoted a 'reliable source' as stating that there was every possibility of an international terrorist group being involved in the incident. A senior police officer, it added, said on condition of anonymity that the police also held the same view. According to him, an international terrorist group may have been acting behind the scenes in the incident in the context of the developments in Iraq.[30]

The attack could also partly have been the result of the hostility of the fundamentalist Islamists, who are strongly entrenched in Sylhet, towards the shrine (mazar) because of their opposition to the observance of religious functions and the holding of Urs[31] around such places. According to a report in the *Daily Star* of 23 May 2004, a grenade attack on the Hazrat Shahjalal shrine on 12 January 2004 which killed five persons and injured 30[32] was suspected to have been their work. A brother of the shrine's caretaker, who filed the First Information Report at Sylhet's Kotwali Police Station on 13 January 2004, had said that for several days leading up to the attack, the shrine authorities had been receiving anonymous phone calls threatening disruption of the Urs.[33] The caretaker's family sources had also alleged that under pressure from the Jamaat, which had been trying to subvert the holding of the Urs, the authorities of the adjacent madrasa did not allow visitors to the shrine car parking facilities on their premises.[34]

Local leaders of the four-party coalition ruling Bangladesh, which includes two fundamentalist Islamist parties, the Jamaat and the IOJ, and whose main prop is Begum Khaleda Zia's BNP, however, pointed their fingers in a very different direction in respect of the 21 May attack. In an obvious reference to the Awami League, the leaders claimed that a 'force' defeated in the last elections had become so desperate to achieve their political ends that it was not even thinking of the national interest. Reading from a written statement at a press conference on the following day, the General Secretary of the district BNP, Ariful Huq Choudhury, said that, like people all over the country, those in Sylhet too were saddened by the inhuman and cruel act. A 'political force', however, was giving a political colour to this human matter and trying to shield the real culprits. It was stated at the press conference that those who had failed to embarrass the country and its present Government by travelling abroad at different times and making statements that damaged the country's interest may have chosen the path of this attack to attract the attention of foreigners.[35]

It is perhaps not without significance that, of the first nine persons arrested in connection with the attack, four were leaders of the Awami League's students' organization, the Chhatra League. They were: the convener of the organization's Sylhet city unit, Habibur Rahman Selim; a member of its national council, Alam Khan Mukti; and the Joint Secretary and Social Service Secretary of its district unit, Selim Ahmed Selim and Harun-ar Rashid respectively. Also arrested were the City Commissioner and General Secretary of the district unit of the Jubo League, Azadur Rahman and his elder brother Safiur Rahman Soleman, a businessman. The other three arrested were Khon Ali Muktadir, Sirajul Islam Mannan and Abdul Qaiyum.[36] It is perhaps also not without significance that, despite these and subsequent arrests, the case remained unsolved and the culprits unidentified. This, of course, is hardly surprising. The *Daily Star* report dated 23 May, cited in the paragraph before last, stated that major blasts that had killed 140 persons and injured about 1,000 throughout Bangladesh in the five preceding years stood unresolved, and not one of those involved had been punished because of the politicization of the investigations. According to the *Daily Star*, though no one claimed responsibility, 'Islamic militants' were supposed to have been behind most of these.[37]

The supposition, which rested on circumstantial and other evidence available, has subsequently had some sort of retrospective corroboration in the form of indications that it was the work of an organized group spreading terror in Bangladesh. These came to light during investigations into the grenade attacks on the Awami League's rallies in Dhaka on 21 August 2004 and Sylhet on 27 January 2005 in which S.A.M.S. Kibria and four others died, and 100 were injured. In its report submitted on 17 October 2004 to the Criminal Investigation Department of Bangladesh Police, Scotland Yard, which had been assisting in the investigations into the 21 May grenade attack, said that the grenade thrown at the British High Commissioner to Bangladesh, Anwar Choudhury, was of the same make, ARGES (from Armaturen Gessellschaft MBH), as the ones thrown at Sheikh Hasina's rally in Dhaka on 21 August, and the one found at Amin Bazar, Dhaka, the following day. Manufactured in Austria, these are used by the American, Chinese, Pakistani and Indian armies, among others. Later, bomb experts of Bangladesh's Rapid Action Battalion (RAB)[38] investigating the incident in Sylhet that led to the deaths of S.A.M.S. Kibria and four others, concluded that an ARGES grenade was used there too. Captain Mamtazur Rahman of the RAB said that operatives from the same chain seemed to have been involved in all the three attacks but declined to state who they could be.[39]

All this raises two questions. First, why should the organized group or chain be considered fundamentalist Islamist? Second, was the attempt to insinuate that the Awami League was responsible for the attack, and the arrest of four Chhatra League leaders, a Juba League leader and his brother, part of an attempt to divert attention from the real culprits responsible for the grenade attack? While the first question will require some discussion, the circumstances of the cases discussed, the conduct of the police, and statements made by people in authority including Khaleda Zia in the case of the attack on Prof. Humayun Azad, suggest that both the Bangladesh government and the BNP were trying to divert attention from those actually responsible for the cinema hall explosions in Mymensingh, the 21 May 2004 grenade attack in Sylhet and the attempt to murder Humayun Azad.

We had set out to examine the three cases of terrorist violence discussed above to see whether any of these reflected an attempt by the Bangladesh government and the BNP to shield the guilty by trying to blame the Awami League and its activists. The purpose was to see whether there was any ground at all for suspecting that they, as well as the Joynul Abedin Commission, were trying to do the same thing—and tarnish India's image into the bargain—in respect of the grenade attack in Dhaka on 21 August, by attributing it to foreign forces and their local agents. The answer, in the light of circumstances, is simple: yes, there was. This takes care of the first question asked at the beginning of this chapter, but leaves us with the second: Who could the actual perpetrators be? This prompts two other questions: What was their objective and how could the attack have helped to achieve it?

Taking up the second question, it will be interesting to recall an allegation made by Sheikh Hasina, who had demanded an international probe into the 21 August grenade attack, during a conversation with the media at her residence in Dhaka on 24 August 2004. Dismissing the appointment of the Joynul Abedin Commission as an eyewash, she had said that the government was afraid of any international probe as it would then be found to have masterminded the attack.[40] It would also be interesting to note that in his article in the *Daily Star*, referred to in Chapter Three, Brig. Gen. (Retd) Shahedul Anam Khan had observed, 'There can be no doubt that the aim of this particular attack was to destabilise the country.' Wondering who the beneficiaries of the ensuing instability would be, he had asked, 'Who stands to gain by eliminating the Awami League leadership? Do those who have engaged in the recent spate of bomb attacks, have external sponsors of are they home grown?'[41]

It is not difficult to identify the chief beneficiaries of the elimination of the Awami League's leadership, an act which could have been expected to leave the party rudderless and demoralized and, therefore, incapable of coping with a savage political offensive accompanied by a campaign of systematic terror and carefully targeted assassinations. They are the BNP and the fundamentalist Islamist parties like the Jamaat and the IOJ which are its allies in Bangladesh's four-party ruling coalition. Also to benefit would have been the Jamaat's militant student wing, Shibir, and terrorist organizations like HUJIB and the JMJB.

Though defeated in the elections held on 1 October 2001, having secured 62 seats against the Bangladesh Nationalist Party's 191, the Awami League emerged as the largest single party in Bangladesh in terms of votes and received over 40 per cent of the votes polled. The party has a nationwide organization with strong grassroots support, particularly in the villages. With its leadership, organization and support base intact, the party may well win the general elections to be held in 2006 and form the government, when the 'anti-incumbency factor' can be expected to work against the ruling coalition. It is hardly surprising that the BNP, given its bitter relations with the Awami League, and particularly the personal animosity between Sheikh Hasina and Begum Khaleda Zia, should abhor this prospect. Nor should it be surprising that Jamaat, the IOJ, HUJIB and the JMJB loathe it even more, given their intense hatred for the Awami League for having led the struggle for Bangladesh's liberation and its liberal, democratic, secular and modern ethos.

But would the BNP, which practices parliamentary politics and has the image of being a moderate party, go to the extent of getting the leadership of the Awami League physically liquidated? Why would it, as the BSS reported Justice Joynul Abedin asking in his report, attract public wrath and dig its own grave by committing such an act? Would a party that has a two-thirds majority in the National Parliament, start a process that would destabilize its own government? There is logic behind these questions and, without concrete and credible evidence, it would be wrong to hold the BNP responsible for the 21 August grenade attack. The same, however, cannot be said of the Jamaat, IOJ, or Shibir. Nor can one rule out the involvement of HUJIB or the JMJB.

The Jamaat's agenda

The Jamaat and the IOJ have agendas that go beyond the normal goals of parliamentary democracy. Of the two, the former, which has 18 members in the National Parliament against the latter's two and is represented in the coalition government's council of ministers while the latter is not, is clearly the more important. Though it talks of its belief in democracy and elections, the destruction of Bangladesh's current multi-party parliamentary form of government and the legal and constitutional system on which it rests is imperative for the realization of its goal, which is the establishment of a theocratic Islamic state, which follows the Sharia system of law. It is, therefore, necessary to pay more than passing attention to its creed.

The Jamaat's website[42], as updated on 24 September 2002 and as accessed on 21 December 2004 declares, in subsection '(a) Comprehensiveness' under the section heading 'Strategy for change', that the

Jamaat is an ideological and not merely a religious or political party. It has tried to influence almost all dimensions of life, intellectual, cultural, moral, educational, literary, economic and political. It stands, not for partial reform, but for total change. Its uniqueness comes from its comprehensiveness, which constitutes its distinctive merit and which is also responsible for some of the difficulties and complexities it has to face. Every vested group of the society has somehow been affected by its tasks. Its followers have come from all walks of life and its challenge has also been felt in all corners.

It continues in subsection '(b) Awakening among Muslims',

Secondly, Jamaat has a unique influence in bringing about an awakening among Muslims that Islam is not a religion in the limited sense of the word: It is a din, a complete way of life. The demands of faith are not fulfilled merely by offering ibadat, the link between Salah and total obedience to Allah in all walks of life must be restored. If Munkar and Fawahish are not eradicated with the offering of Salah, prayers are not fulfilling their role in society. The sovereignty of Allah must be established in all fields of human existence. Mosque and Parliament, taqwa and adl, dikr and shariah are inalienable dimensions of the same reality. Islamic fulfillment is possible only though complete submission.[43]

Under the subsection heading '(c) Social Reform', it had said that the Jamaat's comprehensive programme

seeks to make the mosque the hub of all Islamic activity. Heavy emphasis is placed on establishment of educational institutions, arrangements for adult education, communication of the basic teachings of Islam to the common people and trend setting reading rooms to create enlightenment.

The objectives of the Jamaat are made clearer in the section titled 'Characteristic of the Jamaat-e-Islami':

- The ultimate objective of the Jamaat-e-Islami is the establishment of the Islamic system in all spheres of life
- The Jamaat-e-Islami is of the opinion that Islam can be established only by those who know and practice Islam
- The membership of Jamaat-e-Islami can be obtained only by committed Muslims.

The motto of the Jamaat is stated as:

- Allah is our Lord
- Muhammad is our leader

- The Quran and the Sunnah is our ideal
- Jihad is our means
- Salvation is our end

The website states, in 'Basis of Society', under the sectional heading 'Vision and Commitment', that:

- Sovereignty belongs to Allah alone and Authority is a Trust to be exercised in accordance with Islamic injunctions as embodied in the Quran and the Sunnah.
- Jihad (legitimate struggle) is a paramount and inalienable duty. Its aim is to uphold the word of Allah and defend the Islamic order with all means at our command.

Again, the website states, in 'State policies', under the subsectional heading 'Framework for policies', in the section titled 'Vision and Commitment', that

[t]he Quranic code is the supreme law of the Muslim community and must be enforced in its entirety in all aspects of life. Islamic law is to be made the criterion by which to judge the public and private conducts of all, rulers and the ruled alike, and the chief source of all legislation.

All this makes it absolutely clear that the Jamaat seeks to replace Bangladesh's parliamentary democracy with a theocratic Islamic State, which will have no place for nationalism, secularism and socialism. The Jamaat's website says, in 'An introduction to the Jamaat-e-Islami Bangladesh',

Overwhelming majority of the population of Bangladesh are Muslims. They are intensely religious. But sometimes they are misled by nationalist, secularist and socialist leaders. . . . Politically, Bangladesh is a playground for all. There are pro-India, pro-Russia, pro-America and pro-China political parties in Bangladesh. There are some nationalist and some Islamic parties. The Jamaat-e-Islami is the vanguard of the Islamic movement in Bangladesh.

Needless to say, Shibir shares the Islamist worldview of the parent organization. On its website, 'Bangladesh Islami Chhatra Shibir: Brief Introduction' states,

We should study Quran and Hadith to know about Islam and should fight for the salvation of mankind in the cause of Allah by enjoining good deeds and forbidding evils [sic] deeds. This work cannot be accomplished single-handedly. An organized group is necessary for that, regarding which Hazrat Umar says, 'No Islam without party'.[44]

Describing Bangladesh as a poor country 'where about 80 per cent of the people live below poverty line', it describes life there as being 'totally devoid of peace, happiness, and an ideal picture. Children are growing up through unethical ways.' It then adds,

If this situation is allowed to continue, the future of the nation will be groping in the dark. To get rid of the grip of this ominous darkness a group of conscious and conscientious people must come forward. So Bangladesh Chhatrashibir, an organisation of young students has been established here to call the students to the way of Allah to mould the future generation of our country into men of ideal character.

Under the heading 'Aims and Objectives' on the same website, Bangladesh Islami Chhatra Shibir's aim is given as 'Earning the satisfaction of Allah through a recasting of the total life of man along the way given by Allah and shown by the Prophet (Rasul)'. Its 'Karmashuchi' or Programme has five points which, translated, read as follows:

One: To arouse in the young student community a feeling of responsibility to acquire knowledge of Islam and practice Islam fully in actual life by reaching the message of Islam to them.
Two: To organise under the organisation all students who want to participate in the struggle to establish the Islamic order of life.
Three: To take effective measures to impart Islamic knowledge to students organized under this organisation as people with ideal characters and capable of meeting all challenges from Jahiliyah[45] to prove the supremacy of Islam.
Four: To struggle to press the demand for changing the system of education on the basis of Islamic values to create ideal citizens and to provide leadership to the struggle for solving the real problems of the student community.
Five: To mount a comprehensive effort to bring about an Islamic revolution to liberate humanity from economic exploitation, political repression and cultural slavery.

The resemblance between the agendas of the Jamaat and Shibir and the Taliban is striking. In 1999, when the student militia still ruled

Afghanistan, Lt Gen. (Retd) Kamal Matinuddin of the Pakistani army, wrote,

> The aim of the Taliban is to establish an Islamic Government in Afghanistan where the *shariah* law, as interpreted by them, will be the law of the land. The country is to be called the Islamic State of Afghanistan and will be governed according to Sunni Hanafi *fiqah*. A nominated *shoorah* is to run the affairs of the state in keeping with the edicts of the *Amirul Momineen*.[46]

The Taliban too have a theocratic worldview. This is hardly surprising. As Olivier Roy points out, 'The ideology of the Afghan Islamists has been entirely borrowed from two biggest Islamist mainstream organisations, the Muslim Brotherhood and the Pakistani Jamaat-e-Islami.'[47] And the Jamaat-e-Islami Bangladesh and Jamaat-e-Islami Pakistan are both offshoots of Jamaat-e-Islami Hind, established in undivided India on 26 August 1941 by Syed Abul Ala Maudidi.

The views of the Jamaat, Shibir and Taliban converge not only on the issue of theocracy and the need to establish a dispensation based on the precepts of Islam but also in matters like the place of women in society, social practices and entertainment. What the Taliban did in Afghanistan is well known. Matinuddin wrote,

> Girls are being denied education; women have been prevented from working; if they leave their houses, they have to be covered from head to foot, with a veil (*burqa*); besides being veiled, women have to be accompanied by a male relative when they venture out on the streets. Shopkeepers have been directed not to sell goods to unveiled women. Rickshaw drivers are not to pick up women passengers unless they are fully covered. Women caught violating these rules are imprisoned, as are the shopkeeper and the rickshaw driver.[48]

Ahmed Rashid, the well-known authority on the Taliban, wrote that they banned 'every conceivable form of entertainment, which in a poor, deprived country such as Afghanistan was always in short supply anyway. Afghans were ardent movie-goers but movies, TV, videos, music and dancing were all banned.'[49] Photography and the display of portraits, pictures and posters were banned. The flying of kites and keeping of pigeons and other pets were forbidden and the birds were killed.[50]

The Jamaat has not yet been able to attain power in Bangladesh and, therefore, the question of its implementing similar measures does not arise. There are, however, strong indications that it fully supports what the Taliban did and, given a chance, would like to do the same in Bangladesh which, under their dispensation, would become a joyless land ruled by tyrannical Islamist fanatics. In the subsection 'The Approach', in the section entitled 'Objectives, goals and approach', on the organization's website, one is told, 'Everybody is welcome to join it [the Jamaat]. There are no restrictions on becoming an associate. However to become a member one is naturally expected to fulfil a set of conditions.' Condition (5) lays down that a member's 'living should not be sinful. For instance, it should not be dependent on usury, liquor, fornication, song, dance, perjury, graft, corruption and misappropriation.' Clearly, the Jamaat views singing and dancing not only as sinful but sufficiently so to be bracketed with fornication, graft, perjury and corruption! From this, it is not difficult to imagine that their treatment of those indulging in both would not be very different from that of the Taliban.

Cousins of the Taliban

A similarly puritanical, harsh and taboo-ridden attitude, which frowns on anything that makes life entertaining and pleasurable, marks the worldview of Shibir. In a Bengali write-up ('Bishwa Paristhiti Paribartane Jubo Samajer Bhumika' or 'The Role of the Community of Youth in Changing the World Situation') on its website[51], accessed on 6 February 2005, its President, Muhammad Selim Uddin writes,

> We live in a decadent world civilization. Decadence and decadence [sic] is the ultimate outcome of a secular society that knows only enjoyment and is averse to religion which controls values and morality. . . . A fearfully poisonous environment is prevalent everywhere. Where are our youths running to? What is their destination? . . . We have only to turn the pages of the papers every day to be frightened by the pictures of our young men and women. The community of our youth and young is falling into the clutches of a huge conspiracy and getting destroyed. . . . A flood of modelling and beauty contests has started. The beautiful girl is rushing to photo sessions of modelling companies in the hope of becoming famous overnight as a star. They are getting involved in an ugly and primaeval trade.

Like the Jamaat, the Shibir blames 'a secular society' for Bangladesh's wild decadence. The latter, according to Selim Uddin, is also the result of a long-term conspiracy that has led to an education system that is without morality and is based on Lord Macaulay's recommendation in 1835. According to Macaulay, the aim of Western education was to 'form a class who may be interpreters between us and the millions whom we govern; a class of persons Indian in blood and colour but English in taste, in opinions, in morals and in intellect.'[52] Selim Uddin continues,

> Youngsters educated under our system of education are becoming good Englishmen, Americans or Indians, not good Bangladeshis or Muslims. It is because religion is neglected, patriotism absent, morality abandoned and a sense of values banished under this system of education. Only worldly matters are increasingly getting importance here. It is only natural that a youth educated under a system of education that teaches the calculation of profit through the computation of interest, determination of the rate of profit or loss on the basis of adulteration, does not discourage bribery, would become self-centred, and a profiteer, usurer and bribe-taker. There is nothing surprising that human beings educated in an education [system] that places men as descendants of monkeys, keeps them unaware of the noble objective of the human world, should become inhuman and anti-human.

The disapproving reference to a system of education that 'places men as descendants of monkeys' signifies an obscurantist rejection of modern science as represented by Darwin's theory of evolution. Selim Uddin's piece reflects a medieval mindset, manifesting itself in a preference for gender segregation. He writes,

> Not just in the matter of syllabus and curriculum, socially our system of education [and] environment of education have been so arranged as to make people go astray. It is only most natural that a youngster educated in a coeducational system would at one stage couple up, maintain illicit relationships, get into rehearsals of love affairs and plunge into despair.

The media is also at the receiving end of Selim Uddin's flak. According to him,

> The owners of print and electronic media are finishing off our youth. The electronic media has a remarkable capacity for establishing unreality as

reality and falsehood as truth. Far more dangerous than the country's TV channels are cable networks dish antennae packed entirely with entertainment programmes. These channels have no programme which one can see for an hour at a stretch along with one's mother– father, brothers–sisters. They show pictures either of violence and rioting or of some half and fully naked persons or some song and dance performance. Thanks to the dish, all this is now spreading into every home.

Stating that now the Internet has come as a greater danger, and that the situation becomes far more frightening when youngsters watch obscene items on television alone, Selim Uddin adds, 'Having watched all this till late at night, an irrepressible, demonic desire rises in the minds of young men and women to practice the same. The result is a destructive decadence.' NGOs are as much his targets as they are the Jamaat's. He writes that when young men and women 'are fighting against hunger, poverty and unemployment, NGOs appear before them with two fistfuls of food, tempting salaries–allowances and their slogan, "What is the home, who is husband, [my] body is mine, desire is mine." NGOs are pushing them towards an unscriptural life free of the ties of home. They are destroying families and gradually snatching their nursed religious feeling and articles of faith.'

The message is clear. The Shibir regards modelling and beauty contests as part of a conspiracy to destroy the youth, and as 'an ugly and primaeval trade', which is an obvious reference to prostitution. It is against co-education which 'leads to illicit relations'. It is against showing 'obscene films' on television. It is against the secular system of education which is modelled on the system prescribed by Thomas Babington Macaulay, a member of Governor-General William Bentinck's Executive Council, and teaches Western science and the Western system of knowledge. Its hostility towards modern science is clearly reflected in Selim Uddin's observation, quoted above, that it is not surprising that a system of education that regards man as a descendant of monkeys would keep students 'unaware of the noble objectives of the human world' and make them 'inhuman and sub-human.' The kind of a system of education the Shibir wants becomes clear on reading one of the objectives listed under the sub-heading 'Education Policy' in the sub-section entitled 'Framework for Policies' in the section on 'Vision and Commitment' on the Shibir's website. It reads,

Specifically the two parallel streams of secular and religious prevailing today would be fused together so as to provide an Islamic vision for those engaged in education, and to enable them to reconstruct human thought, in all its forms, on the foundation of Islam.

The Jamaat has a compact and highly organized, but relatively small, following in Bangladesh, which is a moderate Islamic country where the large bulk of the population is tolerant and disinclined towards fundamentalist bigotry. The country's intelligentsia, active civil society and press are secular and modern in their outlook and quick to oppose fundamentalist excesses and violence. The Jamaat has, therefore, to couch its political message in a language that does not go drastically against the country's cultural grain, and that helps it to expand its base by winning over moderate elements who might be put off by strident fundamentalist Islamist rhetoric. Even so, an analysis of its literature and that of the Shibir makes it abundantly clear that they have essentially the same worldview as the Taliban and that, therefore, it is reasonable to suppose that they will try to turn Bangladesh into another Afghanistan if they ever achieve the political power to do so.

As we have seen, the Islamist theocratic order that the Jamaat and the Shibir seek to establish will have to be built on the debris of Bangladesh's present plural parliamentary system. For that, they will have to destabilize and destroy Bangladesh's democratic order as it exists today. Returning to the outrage of 21 August 2004, we find that a responsible cross section of people in Bangladesh felt that it was targeted not only at Sheikh Hasina and the Awami League leadership, but also at Bangladesh's democracy. Rehman Sobhan, Chairman of the Centre for Policy Dialogue, wrote in the *Prothom Alo* of 27 August 2004:

> The massacre in front of the Awami League's office on 21 August was not targeted at Sheikh Hasina's head alone, the gun was pointed at the future of Bangladesh's democracy as well. This massacre was not a scattered terrorist enterprise of a fistful of persons. It was a planned attack, which was pre-planned and which clearly had the aim of obliterating an important section of the Awami League's leadership along with Sheikh Hasina. . . . This planned attack by the assailants on the Awami League, the country's oldest political party and main opposition force, clearly indicates that they wanted to destroy the party as a political force. Or their aim was to weaken it so much that it cannot any more be a serious contender for power.
>
> One does not need to be a supporter of the Awami League to realise that an attempt to obliterate one of Bangladesh's two principal political parties means an attempt to strike at the foundation of the country's

democratic process. If this weapon is used to destroy one political party, then the same lethal weapon can be used in future against the other principal party or other democratic forces. In fact, we can fall into such a world of anarchy in which the rule of the terrorists will prevail, and guns and bombs will be the only weapons of political advancement.[53]

Earlier, *Prothom Alo* had declared in an editorial, 'An attack of this sort represents a conspiracy to nullify the democratic process itself.'[54] On the same day, the *Daily Star* had written in an editorial, 'The way the attack was carried out points to a very well-organised, well-planned and professionally executed operation. . . . By now it is certain to all of us that the neatly planned and executed, almost to a perfection, bomb attacks on the peaceful [Awami League] rally had the sole objective of destabilizing the country.'[55] On 21 August 2004 itself, the Dhaka University Teachers' Association had, in a statement, described the blasts as an attack on Sheikh Hasina which was also aimed at eliminating the Awami League's 'progressive and non-communal political practice'.[56]

We have seen that the Jamaat and the Shibir can establish their theocratic Islamist State only by destabilizing and destroying Bangladesh's democratic order as it stands today. We have also seen that scholars and editors, who ought to know what they are talking about, have described the grenade attack on 21 August 2004 as an attempt to destabilize Bangladesh, destroy its democracy and secular, non-communal politics. We, therefore, have a situation in which there is greater reason for suspecting the Jamaat and the Shibir's involvement in the grenade attack on 21 August than that of an unnamed foreign country and its unnamed agents. It is remarkable that this did not strike Justice Joynul Abedin.

An important question arises at this stage: Would the Jamaat and the Shibir use violence to achieve their objective of establishing a theocratic Islamist State in Bangladesh? We will examine the question in the next chapter.

Notes

1. Abul Kalam Azad and Aminul Islam, 'Cinema Hall Blasts Kill 17 in Mymensingh: 200 Also Injured in Series of Bombings', *The Daily Star* (Internet edition), 9 December 2002.
2. Ibid.

3. News report, 'Planned Terrorist Attack: Khaleda', *The Daily Star* (Internet edition), 9 December 2002.

4. News report, 'Swoop on City Residences of AL Leaders, Columnist: Tofail, Saber Chy, Shahriar, Muntassir Held', *The Daily Star* (Internet edition), 9 December 2002.

5. Ibid.

6. Ibid.

7. News report, 'DB Gets No Clue to Back Charges: Saber, Shafi, Muntassir Quizzed', *The Daily Star* (Internet edition), 10 December 2002.

8. Ibid.

9. News report, 'Swoop on City Residences of AL Leaders, Columnist: Tofail, Saber Chy, Shahriar and Muntassir Held'.

10. News report, 'Why Arrest of Shahriar, Muntasir [sic], Shafi Won't Be Declared Illegal: High Court Grants Tofail Bail', *The Daily Star* (Internet edition), 11 December 2002.

11. Ibid.

12. News report, 'DB Gets No Clue to Back Charges: Saber, Shafi, Muntasir [sic] Quizzed'.

13. Abul Kalam Azad and Aminul Islam from Mymensingh, 'Mymensingh Cinema Blasts: Army Picks Up Top AL, JP Leaders, 32 Others', *The Daily Star* (Internet edition), 10 December 2002.

14. Rajib Nur from Habiganj, 'Habiganje Sarbatmak Hartal Palan: Sabgulo Grenade Hamlar Madhye Mil Royechhe' (Total Hartal Observed in Habiganj: There is a Similarity about All Grenade Attacks', *Prothom Alo* (Internet edition), 29 January 2005.

15. Beginning in 1953 people of East Pakistan and subsequently Bangladesh have observed 21 February every year as Bengali Language Martyrs' Day or Language Martyr's Day. The occasion commemorates the death, on 21 February 1952, of four students—Rafiq, Barkat, Jabbar and Salam—in police firing on a peaceful demonstration against the Pakistan government's decision to have Urdu alone as the country state language. The brutal act sparked a massive upsurge throughout the province that not only compelled the federal government to recognize Bengali as a state language but also gave a decisive turn to East Pakistan's alienation from the federal government and established a tradition of mass movements that eventually contributed significantly to Bangladesh's emergence as an independent country. The observance of 21 February, often referred to as 'Immortal 21st February' or 'Amar Ekushe February' in Bengali, is a highly emotional occasion for Bangladeshis as it stands for the immense sacrifices they made to preserve their rich language and culture. Hence, the annual book fair in Dhaka, a major event in the country's cultural life, which is held in February is called 'Amar Ekushe Boimela'. In 1999, UNESCO gave global recognition to Bangladesh's heroic struggle in defence of its language and culture by designating 21 February is the International Mother Language Day.

16. News report, 'Humayun Azad Stabbed, Fighting for Life', *The Daily Star* (Internet edition), 28 February 2004.

17. Ibid.

18. Ibid.

19. News report, 'Blasphemy Ain Karar Prostab Dilen Delawar Hossain Saydee' (Delawar Hossain Saydee Proposes the Enactment of a Blasphemy Law), *Prothom Alo* (Internet edition), 26 January 2004.
20. Manik, Julfikar Ali, 'Writers Feel Insecure', *The Daily Star* (Internet edition), 29 February 2004.
21. Ibid.
22. Editorial, 'Attack on Humayun Azad: Intellectual Freedom at Stake', *The Daily Star* (Internet edition), 29 February 2004.
23. In Bangladesh, the term 'terrorist' is often used in respect of violent criminals as well.
24. News item, 'Humayun Azader Abostha Akhono Shankatjanak, Campus Uttal, Dhaka Bishwavidyalaye Shikshakder Class Barjan Aaj Theke, Hatyacheshta Abhijoge Maïmla' (Humayun Azad's Condition Still Critical, Campus in Tumult, Dhaka University Teachers to Boycott Classes from Today, Case Registered for Attempt to Murder), *Prothom Alo* (Internet edition), 29 February 2004.
25. News report, 'Shun Violent Agitation: PM Urges AL, Warns on Hard Line on Vandalism', *The Daily Star* (Internet edition), 1 March 2004.
26. International Association of Poets, Playwrights, Essayists, Editors and Novelists.
27. News report, 'Thousands Pay Tearful Homage to Writer Azad', *The Daily Star* (Internet edition), 20 August 2004.
28. Editorial, 'High Commissionerer Opor Hamla: Amra Kshubdha Stombhito' (Attack on the High Commissioner: We are Perturbed, Stunned), *Prothom Alo* (Internet edition), 23 May 2004.
29. Editorial, 'The Friday Massacre at the Shrine: Impunity Syndrome Playing Out', *The Daily Star* (Internet edition), 23 May 2004.
30. News report, 'British High Commissionerer Opor Grenade Chhonda Hoyechhilo: Arekjoner Mrityu' (A Grenade was Thrown at the British High Commissioner: Another Person Dies), *Prothom Alo* (Internet edition), 23 May 2004.
31. An Urs is a religious gathering.
32. News report, 'Blasts Rage, Probes Stall: 140 Killed Around the Country in the Last Five Years', *The Daily Star* (Internet edition), 23 May 2004.
33. News report, 'Sylhet Shrine Bombing: Another Dies, Bigot Link Suspected', *The Daily Star* (Internet edition), 14 January 2004.
34. Ibid.
35. News report, 'British High Commissionerer Opor Grenade Chhonda Hoyechhilo' (A Grenade was Thrown at the British High Commissioner).
36. Ibid.
37. News report, 'Blasts Rage, Probes Stall'.
38. Rapid Action Battalions are elite para-military formations with superior capabilities and weapons, established to cope with Bangladesh's critical law-and-order situation.
39. Julfikar Ali Manik, 'The Same Group Used the Same Arges Grenade', *The Daily Star* (Internet edition), 29 January 2005.
40. News report, 'Hasina Critical of Security Steps', *The Daily Star* (Internet edition), 25 August 2004.
41. Shahedul Anam Khan, NDC PSC, Brig. Gen. (Retd), 'The Saga of Bomb Blasts and Black Saturday', *The Daily Star* (Internet edition), 25 August 2004.
42. www.jamaat-e-islami.org.

43. Ibadat—worship; Salah—*namaaz*; Munkar—atheist; Fawahish—lust; taqwa— fear of God, and staying away from sin; adl—justice; dikr—remembrance of God; shariah—Islamic law.

44. shibirbd.tripod.com.

45. Jahiliyah actually means 'ignorance'. It is also used to connote the pre-Islamic era.

46. Kamal Matinuddin, Lt Gen. (Retd), *The Taliban Phenomenon: Afghanistan 1994–97* (Karachi: Oxford University Press, 1999), p. 42.

47. Olivier Roy, 'Has Islam a Future in Afghanistan?' in William Maley (ed.), *Fundamentalism Reborn: Afghanistan and the Taliban* (New York: New York University Press, 1998), p. 201.

48. Matinuddin, *The Taliban Phenomenon. Shoorah*—representative assembly; *fiqah*— jurisprudence; *Amirul Momineen*—Commander of the Faithful.

49. Ahmed Rashid, *Taliban: Islam, Oil and the New Great Game in Central Asia* (New York/London: I.B. Taurus, 2001[2002]), p. 115.

50. Matinuddin, *The Taliban Phenomenon*, p. 35.

51. Mohammad Selim Uddin, 'Bishwa Paristhiti Paribartane Jubo Samajer Bhumika' (The Role of the Youth Community in Changing the World Situation), www.shibir.com.

52. Quoted in Sugata Bose and Ayesha Jalal, *Modern South-Asia: History, Custom, Political Economy* (New Delhi: Oxford University Press, 1998), p. 84.

53. Rehman Sobhan, 'Sangbad Bisleshan: Ganatantra Akhon Atal Gahbarer Kinaraye' (News Analysis, Democracy is Now at the Edge of a Bottomless Abyss), *Prothom Alo* (Internet edition), 27 August 2004.

54. Editorial, 'Sheikh Hasinake Hatyar Cheshta: Aatogulo Mrityur Daye Sarkarkei Nite Hobe' (Attempt to Kill Sheikh Hasina: It is the Government that Has to Bear the Burden of So Many Deaths', *Prothom Alo* (Internet edition), 23 August 2004.

55. Editorial, 'Bleeding Politics: Leaders Must Rise to the Occasion', *The Daily Star* (Internet edition), 23 August 2004.

56. News report, 'Shock Wave Runs Through the Nation's Spine', *The Daily Star* (Internet edition), 24 August 2004.

Five

Scripted for Violence

On the Jamaat's website, in the section 'Objectives, Goals and Approach', under the sub-section heading 'The Approach', it is written that 'Jamaat-e-Islami is devoted to peaceful and upright means of struggle and a strict adherence to this principle marks its whole history.'[1] Recorded history, particularly that of Bangladesh's liberation war in 1971, however, tells a very different story. Jamaat not only opposed the liberation war but also participated in the savage, genocidal repression unleashed by Pakistani troops. In his book, *Ekattorer Ghatak o Dalalra Ke Kothaye*, which created a stir when it was first published in February 1987, Shahriar Kabir writes,

> Reading descriptions of the massacres, one can also be sure of another matter—members of the Peace Committee, Jamaat-e-Islami, Muslim League and militia like the Al Badr, Al Shams, Mujaheed, Razakar, EPCAF (East Pakistan Civil Armed Forces) had shown the same cruelty as the killer Pakistani Army in this act of barbarism.[2]

Leaders of the Jamaat played an important role in the formation of the Peace Committee mentioned above. According to a report in the *Dainik Purbadesh* of 5 April 1971, 12 fundamentalist leaders met Lt Gen. Tikka Khan (who had come to take over as Governor of East Pakistan) on 4 April 1971, and assured him total cooperation in restoring completely normal conditions in the entire province. They proposed the formation of a citizens' committee in Dhaka to remove 'baseless fears' from peoples' minds.[3] Besides its leader, Nurul Amin, the delegation included Prof. Golam Azam, Moulvi Farid Ahmed, Khwaja Khairuddin, A.Q.M. Shafiqul Islam, and Maulana Nuruzzaman. A 140-member Dhaka Citizens' Peace Committee (the Dhaka Nagarik Shanti Committee) emerged almost immediately after

Chief Justice B.A. Siddiqui of Dhaka High Court swore Lt Gen. Khan in as the Provincial Governor on 9 April. It was announced on 11 April that all peace committees in the city would function under this one whose convener was Khwaja Khairuddin.[4]

Violence under the auspices of the Committee began almost immediately thereafter. On 13 April, a huge procession organized by it started from Baitul Mukarram and, moving through the main streets of Old Dhaka, ended at New Market. Among those at its head were Khwaja Khairuddin, Golam Azam, Pir Mohsin Uddin (Dudu Mian), Syed Azizul Huq (Nanna Mian) and Mahmud Ali. After holding a meeting at New Market, the processionists set fire to the homes of Bengalis at places like Azimpur Colony, Shanti Nagar and Shankhari Bazaar and, chasing and killing a quite a few of them, left their bodies on the roadside.[5]

At a meeting in Dhaka on the following day, 14 April, the name of the Citizens' Peace Committee was changed into East Pakistan Central Peace Committee (Purba Pakistan Kendriya Shanti Committee) so that, it was stated, it could conduct its efforts to restore peace throughout East Pakistan.[6] A 21-member working committee was appointed to ensure that its decisions were quickly taken and implemented. Shahriar Kabir writes,

> Extending itself to union and village levels throughout the liberation war in besieged Bangladesh, this committee led, in cold blood and in a carefully planned manner, the most fearful genocide in history. In fact, this so-called peace committee had made a far greater contribution to the genocide than the Pakistani junta. Pakistani troops recklessly destroyed whatever human habitation they visited, but (members of) the peace committee killed with great skill and through the preparation of specific lists. Apart from themselves indulging in murder, rape, plunder and destructive activities, [members of] the peace committee had created armies like the Razakars, Al Badr, Al Shams and so on for these purposes. While the Pakistani troops could carry out their destructive activities in the areas around which they were stationed, the mass slaughter perpetrated by the peace committee was far more damaging because it had spread out all over Bangladesh which was trapped, as it were, in a net. Besides, the Pakistani troops killed according to directions [by the authorities], or to create terror and satisfy their desire for vengeance and lust; in the case of the peace committee, to these was added the desire to usurp the properties of those killed, wreak vengeance, earn praise from the military junta, and religious madness.[7]

According to Kabir, Golam Azam, whose name features above and who was the Ameer of the Jamaat from 1978 to 2000, played a critical role not only in the mass killings perpetrated by the Pakistanis but also in the infamous slaughter of intellectuals in December 1971. Kabir writes,

> Professor Golam Azam is also a principal actor in the killing of intellectuals. Professor Azam had presented a blueprint for the killing of intellectuals at a meeting with Rao Farman Ali[8] at the beginning of September, 1971. It was according to this blueprint that intellectuals were killed mercilessly later, that is, in December. Jamaat leaders like Abdul Khaleque, Barrister Korban Ali, Prof. Yusuf Ali, Abbas Ali Khan[9] were involved in the preparation of the blueprint. The various documents pertaining to the killing of the intellectuals that were discovered after the liberation, carried the clear directive: It will perhaps not be possible to retain East Pakistan. But one thing has to be done, intellectuals, engineers, scientists, doctors of this place have to be 'finished' for ever, so that they will not be able to run the country even if Pakistan loses it. Prof Golam Azam instructed his party cadres, that is, Al Badr and Al Shams, to implement the blueprint.[10]

Indeed, the Jamaat played a key role both in the mass killings perpetrated by the Pakistani Army and in the massacre of intellectuals and educated persons. On 27 December 1971, the Bengali-language daily *Dainik Azad* carried a long report under the heading 'They Would have Killed All Bengali Intellectuals had One More Week Passed—Badr Army's Master Plan'. The report said,

> Of those parties that helped the raiding Pakistani Army, the most despicable was the role of the Jamaat-e-Islami. . . . They had not stopped with helping the Pakistani Army's indiscriminate mass slaughter, they had set up a secret, armed terrorist organisation which was known to the general public as Badr Army. Everybody has now come to know that in the last moments before the surrender by the raiding Pakistani Army, this Badr Army had taken away a large number of intellectuals and killed them mercilessly. Sufficient information has been found indicating that had they a few days more, they would have succeeded in implementing history's worst spree of killing intellectuals by completely destroying Bangladesh's community of intellectuals.[11]

Maulana A.K.M. Yusuf was the founder of the Razakars, and organized the first batch of the militia, comprising 96 Jamaat activists, at an Ansar camp at Khulna's Khan Jahan Ali Road in May 1971. He also gave the organization its name.[12] He said at a meeting in Sylhet on 26 October, 'Some youths, ignorant about the history of Pakistan's creation and misled by India's false propaganda, have gone across the border and are carrying out despicable subversive activities on our soil with the help of Indian agents. Spread yourselves out into villages, markets and every corner to finish these subversive activities completely and to totally uproot Bengali nationalism from our soil.'[13]

Abbas Ali Khan, one of the principal organizers of the Peace Committee, mainly directed the activities of the Razakars during the liberation war.[14] A report in the *Purbadesh* of 25 June 1971 stated that a 15-member Peace Committee had been set up in Bogra District's Joypurhat subdivision[15] under the leadership of Janab Abbas Ali Khan. He said in his presidential address to a joint parade by Razakars and policemen in Joypurhat on Azadi (Independence) Day, 14 August, that the Razakars were determined to sacrifice their lives to uproot and destroy the separatists.[16] After lavishly praising the role of the members of the Peace Committee and the Razakars, he said at a meeting of the Peace Committee at Chandpur on 16 November 1971, 'Pakistan will survive undamaged for ever. Your responsibility is to destroy the enemies, root and branch, and for ever.'[17] In a broadcast on Dhaka Radio on 6 December 1971, he said,

> Those who spread rumours, create disorder, or carry on propaganda in favour of Hindustan or the so-called Bangladesh of fantasyland, are our enemies. Keep an alert eye on them. Destroy their poison fangs at the first opportunity. Get down to the task of defending our country shoulder to shoulder with our militia like Razakars, Badr, Shams and so on.[18]

The Razakars, Al Badr, Al Shams and their leaders

The Jamaat's student front organization was the Islami Chhatra Shangha. Its leaders were made the heads of Razakars in their respective districts. Chhatra Shangha leader Mohammad Yunus was made the Supreme Commander of Razakars, whose leaders used to be present at the meetings of the Peace Committee, present their views and implement the decisions taken. For example, a report in the *Dainik Sangram* of 21 August 1971 said that among those present at a meeting of the Chittagong District Peace Committee on 14 August was the

President of the local Chhatra Shangha and the head of the district Razakars, Mir Kasem Ali.[19]

Giving an account of the programme of the Chhatra Shangha on Al Badr day, on 7 November, the *Dainik Sangram* of 8 November 1971 said that on the occasion, a massive procession was taken out in Dhaka at the initiative of the Islami Chhatra Shangha. It also said that, earlier, a huge mass gathering was held in the compound of Baitul Mukarram. It was chaired by the President of the Dhaka City Islami Chhatra Shangha, Janab Shamsul Haq, and addressed by the organization's East Pakistan President, Ali Ahsan Muhammad Mujahid, and General Secretary, Mir Kasem Ali. According to the *Dainik Sangram*, issuing a stern warning against the infiltration of 'Hindustan's culture', Mujahid said, 'From tomorrow no library will be able to buy or sell books by Hindus or agents of Hindustan. From tomorrow, any book by Hindus or Hindustan's agents seen to bought or sold, will be burnt to ashes.' The Chief of the East Pakistan Islami Chhatra Shangha, the report added, also harshly warned Indian agents and said that they were continuously carrying out propaganda against Pakistani volunteers. Stating that 'we know their faces', he asked people to be on their guard against them.[20]

According to the report, 'the newly appointed general secretary of Chhatra Shangha, Mir Kasem Ali, said in his speech, "Pakistanis will not under any circumstance be ready to become slaves of Hindus. We will keep the unity and integrity of the country unimpaired even with the last drop of our blood."'[21] The 14 November 1971 issue of *Dainik Sangram* carried an article by the Supreme Commander of Al Badr, Matiur Rahman Nizami, entitled 'Badr Dibas, Pakistan O Al Badr'. He wrote,

> For the past two years a students' organization by young pilgrims of Pakistan for an Islamic renaissance has started observing the historic Badr Day. . . . These young pilgrims have made the biggest contribution to the observance of this day with great enthusiasm throughout Pakistan. . . . It is our conviction that the day is not far off when, standing side by side with our armed forces, our youth will raise the victorious flag of Islam the world over by defeating the Hindu Army and finishing off Hindustan.[22]

Earlier, Nizami had said at a gathering of students and scholars organized by the Chittagong unit of the Islami Chhatra Shangha at the local Muslim Institute on 2 August 1971,

Such a terrible situation would not have been created in the country if the patriotic masses had come forward in confronting the criminals from 1 March. Allah had entrusted faithful Muslims with the responsibility of protecting his beloved land Pakistan. Allah is defending the country through the Armed Forces after Muslims failed to do so.[23]

Another member of the high command and the President of the Chittagong University Islami Chhatra Sangha, Abdul Zaher Muhammad Abu Naser said, 'We will continue our efforts to foil every conspiracy by India and keep Pakistan alive.' Mir Kasem Ali said, 'We must search every area in villages and markets, find out enemies and destroy their last traces.'[24]

It is important to remember the names of those mentioned above as leaders of the Islami Chhatra Shangha and militia like Razakars, Al Badr and so on. Some of their names also feature in the list of 15 criminals opposing the 1971 liberation war identified by an 11-member National People's Inquiry Commission (Jatiya Ganatadanta Commission). Named in two lists, of eight and seven respectively, prepared by the Commission in two reports based on investigations conducted at the field level and depositions by eyewitnesses and victims, they were Abbas Ali Khan, Matiur Rahman Nizami, Muhammad Kamaruzzaman, Abdul Alim, Maulana Delwar Hussain Saydee, Maulana Abdul Mannan, Anwar Zahid, Abdul Kader Molla, Salahuddin Qader Chowdury, A.S.M. Solaiman, Maulana Abdus Sobhan, Maulana A.K.M Yusuf, Ali Ahsan Muhammad Mujahid, Mohammad Ayn Uddin and A.B.M. Khalek Majumdar.[25]

On the National People's Inquiry Commission were highly respected individuals from Bangladesh's literary, cultural and academic worlds, and civil society. They were: Begum Sufia Kamal (Chairperson), the most celebrated woman poet of Bangladesh, who died in 2003; Bangladesh's national poet Shamsur Rahman; litterateur Shaukat Osman; Professor Anupam Sen; Professor Khan Sarwar Murshid; Professor M.A. Khaleque; Justice Debesh Chandra Bhattacharyya (Retd); Justice A.M. Sobhan (Retd); Salauddin Yusuf, Member of Parliament; Air Vice Marshal Sadruddin (Retd); and barrister Shafique Ahmed (Coordinator).[26]

Matiur Rahman Nizami is now Ameer-e-Jamaat (head of the Jamaat-e-Islami Bangladesh), and President of its Central Executive Committee and Central Working Committee. He is also, at the time of writing, Bangladesh's Minister for Industries, with Cabinet rank in the four-party coalition government led by Prime Minister Khaleda Zia. Ali Ahsan Muhammad Mujahid is the Jamaat's Secretary General and Minister of State for Social Welfare, besides being a member of the Central Executive Committee and Central Working Committee respectively. Maulana A.K.M. Yusuf is Senior Nayeb-e-Ameer (Senior Assistant Ameer), a member both of the Central Executive Committee and the Central Working Committee. Maulana Abdus Sobhan, Maulana Delwar Hussain Saydee (the one who demanded a blasphemy law which would have sent Prof. Humayun Azad to jail for his writings), Muhammad Kamaruzzaman and Mir Kasem Ali are members of the Jamaat's Central Executive Committee as well as its Central Working Committee.[27] Abbas Ali Khan became the Acting President of the Jamaat when it was re-launched at a convention in Dhaka on 25–27 May 1979. He is also the author of 'Jamaat-e-Islami's Views on the Defence of Bangladesh', which we have noted above in Chapter Four and which, featuring on the Jamaat's website as updated on 15 October 2004, was accessed on 21 December 2004. Salahuddin Qader Chowdury is Parliamentary Affairs adviser to Prime Minister Khaleda Zia and is supposed to have a major say in the shaping of the government's policies.

One has so far referred to the savage role Al Badr, the Razakars, Al Shams and allied organizations, with which the current leaders of the Jamaat were closely associated in leadership positions, played in the genocide and in the slaughter of intellectuals during Bangladesh's liberation war. An eyewitness account such as Professor Hamida Rahman's graphic, heart-rending one of the discovery of the bodies of intellectuals and professionals killed and dumped in Rayer Bazar Beel (a marsh) alone can convey—that, too, not fully—the immensity of what members and leaders of these organizations did. She writes,

The dead bodies of two large men [were found lying] as we went a little further, nose severed, ears severed, somebody seemed to have scratched out the flesh from near their mouths, hands and feet tied. The two dead bodies had been lying there for two days. The terrible, distorted bodies of the two large men come floating before [my] eyes even now.

A little further ahead a girl's dead body [lay] at the feet of the mound of earth to the left. Her eyes were tied. The two napkins were still lying there. She had been wearing a black Dhakai sari and socks on one foot. There was no shape to her nose and mouth. It seemed that someone had scooped them out with a weapon so that she could not be recognized. She was fair and well-built. A part of her breasts was severed.

The dead body was lying on [its] back. The horrible sight can't be seen for long. I could not recognise her. Of course she was identified later; she was Salina Parvin, editor of *Shilalipi*.[28] Her relatives took her body away in the afternoon after being informed.

I saw a skeleton after I went a little further, with a little flesh left on the two legs and the ribs. Perhaps kites and vultures had eaten [the rest]. Yet there were long strands of hair on the skull, mingling with the dust and mud and bearing witness that the body was a woman's.

Going a little further ahead, I found quite a few people standing on high ground and leaning forward to look at something. A gentleman stretched his hand out and pulled me up as I started climbing. Looking ahead, I saw a terrible scene on the low-lying wetland. There were not one, not two but 12 or 13 [dead bodies of] strong and healthy persons. Lying one after the other. There were two dead bodies by the side, one whose heart seemed to have been torn away by someone. The man with the scooped out heart was Dr Rabbi. In the pile next were the chairman of the Ramna Union Yakub Ali and Serajuddin Hussain of *Ittefak*.[29] Someone standing by my side said that Munir Chowdhury's[30] body was also here. Kabir Chowdhury[31] had come and seen it in the morning. . . . None of them had his shirt on. They had all been made to take off their shirts and wear vests. Thereafter they were interrogated to the accompaniment of merciless torture. Then they had been thrown away after being shot in the chest. [32]

Prof. Hamida Rahman gave some idea of the number of people killed when she wrote, in the same account, 'Field stretched after field. Skeletons of the dead in the thousands and thousands mounds of earth besides every wetland bore witness to the number of people killed in this field.'

People who ordered and supervised these killings and who are now at the helm of the Jamaat in Bangladesh can hardly be expected to be squeamish about resorting to violence. In this context, it is important to consider the account of the Jamaat's blueprint for capturing power, contained in a short report said to have been prepared by it following an expanded meeting on the theme of 'Evaluation and Training' held on 11 and 12 April 2003, at the auditorium of the International Islamic University in Chittagong. The report features as the last appendix in the Bengali language book *Aghoshito Juddher Blueprint* or 'Blueprint of an Undeclared War' by Prof. Abu Sayeed, former State Minister of Information in Sheikh Hasina's Government, which was released at his residence in Dhanmondi, Dhaka, on 18 February 2005, the day on which the Ekushe Boimela or Ekushe (21st) Book Fair opened in Dhaka.

The report, as carried in Sayeed's book, clearly states that the Jamaat's plan of replacing the present constitution of Bangladesh by one based on the Quran and the Sunnah can only be implemented if it comes to power. Hence, if power cannot be attained through normal means, a plan and a programme will have to be implemented for capturing power throughout the world, with Bangladesh getting the top priority, through armed struggle. The Islamic system of administration will then be made a part of the constitution.[33] Elaborating on its plan for militancy, the Jamaat's report states, in the section entitled 'Fund Supply' that, apart from Islami Bank, Rabita Al-Alam Al-Islami (an important Saudi Arabian NGO) and Al-Arafa Bank, money will be distributed through Maulana A.K.M. Yusuf. A *quomi* (private) madrasa, a *dakhil* (primary) madrasa and a senior madrasa will receive Tk 50,000, 200,000 and 1 million respectively in the financial year 2003–2004.[34] The report says, in the section under the heading 'Training' that apart from the old training centres, new ones will be opened on Bandarban's[35] highest peak Tazim Dong, and also on Keora Dong, Chimbuk, and in the deltaic forest on the banks of the southernmost Handia Bhanga River under Satkhira–Shyamnagar Police Station in the Sunderbans.[36] The report states, in the section titled 'Arms Supply Areas', that earlier, arms used to be brought though Myanmar, St Martin Island and Teknaf and Chhatak in Sylhet. From now (the date of the report's adoption in April 2003), arms supply will remain uninterrupted from Myanmar and also from India through the Satkhira–Shyamnagar border area in the Sunderbans, the border areas of Bagerhat and Borguna and Dublachar. The arms will be given to designated persons through central and regional Ameers.[37]

The section under the heading 'Communication and Signal' (*Jogajog o Sanket*), prescribes the following colours for turbans worn by leaders and cadre: white for members of the Central Shoora[38] (Kendriya Shoora), sky-blue within white for responsible commanders and central leaders, red for team commanders of its operational cadre. Black is a symbol of mourning and green is a symbol of victory. Bearded messengers wearing half-shirts and caps maintain active communication through bicycles in *mofussil* areas, motorcycles in districts and sub-divisions, and by motorcycles, cars and jeeps in the capital city, Dhaka.

Maulana A.K.M. Yusuf presided over the inaugural session on 11 April 2003. The speakers included Golam Azam, Delwar Hussain Saydee, Al Haj Al Hussaini Al Madani, Dr Mustafizur Rahman, Maulana Keramat Ali (Ibne Sina), Prof. Mohammad Ali (International University) and Maulana Dr Shamsul Haq. Four hundred and eighteen delegates, including important imams, were present. Maulana Shamsul Haq presided over the day's second session in the afternoon. The President of the Kusthia unit of the Jamaat, Dr Anisur Rahman, presided over the first session on 12 April, and Dr Mustafizur Rahman over the second.

The report states that the Jamaat would quit the government as the opposition's movement against the latter became irresistible in the country, and, in its own way, build a dynamic and powerful organization and capture the political field on its own strength and programme. Apart from sharply castigating the government for its failures, people at the meeting criticized the Prime Minister for her 'un-Islamic activities', unbridled talk and the divergence between her words and deeds. They also criticized some 'influential' ministers and state ministers.

According to the Jamaat report, the meeting decided, as a part of the strategy to implement the blueprint, not to make any statement against Bangladesh's liberation. Anybody doing so would be summoned by the organization and punished. It, however, left no one in any doubt as to what the Jamaat would do after capturing power—the People's Democratic Republic of Bangladesh would be renamed the Islamic Republic of Bangladesh. In place of *Amar Sonar Bangla* the national anthem would be Sura Fatiha (the opening chapter of the Quran).[39]

Addressing a press conference at his residence at the Dhanmondi area of Dhaka after the release of *Aghoshito Juddher Blueprint* and *Brutal Crime Documents* in English, Professor Sayeed said that over 50,000 Islamist zealots belonging to more than 40 militant groups were receiving military training in 50 camps functioning across Bangladesh. They controlled vast stretches of the country with help from the Jamaat and a section of the BNP. Islamist militants, he said, had their people in all [government] departments and sections of society, including mosques, madrasas, educational institutions, the Secretariat, the judiciary, civil society, mass media and even the armed forces. Islamists had also developed a strong countrywide network to capture power through an Islamist revolution.[40]

Professor Sayeed said that the Islamist groups mushrooming in the country were now on a strong footing in terms of funds, arms and manpower. They had a net annual income of Tk 5 billion. Claiming that the Jamaat was involved with, and assisting, these groups, he called for it to be immediately banned for the sake of Bangladesh.[41]

The Jamaat, of course, has strongly repudiated the entire report. Denying that any meeting was held in Chittagong on 1! and 12 April 2003, a counter-statement sent by its publicity department on 19 February 2005 stated that the Jamaat did not believe in the politics of drawing up documents. The allegations of criticism of the Prime Minister or ministers were false. The former Information Minister had written the book on an assignment from someone as a part of the implementation of a blueprint to confuse people about the Jamaat, an idealistic Islamic organization, and turn Bangladesh into a so-called failed state and fundamentalist country. The International Islamic University of Chittagong had also, in a news release on the same day, denied that any such meeting had been held.

If by the politics of drawing up documents is meant the preparation of manifestos and programmes laying down a party's worldview, creed, package of policies and measures to implement it, the Jamaat can hardly claim not to be involved in it. A look at its website[42] would provide one with a most elaborate and carefully-expounded presentation of its ideology which, in turn, is an extension of its religious worldview in which every aspect of human life is defined and regulated. The sections under the heading 'An Introduction to Jamaat-e-Islami Bangladesh' and the subsections under the headings 'Vision and Commitment', 'Articles of Faith', 'The Goal', 'Basis of Society' and 'Framework for Politics' contain long and carefully-constructed tracts. The same goes for the section under the heading 'Objectives, Goals and Approach' and the sub-sections that follow under the headings 'The Challenge', 'The Response', 'The Ideology', 'Faith' and 'The Approach'. Under 'Strategy for Change', one finds the same painstaking exposition of its views as under sub-headings 'Procedures', 'Significance of the Strategy' and 'Jamaat's Problems'.

If one has to treat the Jamaat's claim that it is not involved in the politics of drawing up documents with a measure of skepticism, one has to repeat the treatment in respect of its claim that it held no meeting in Chittagong on 11 and 12 April 2003. The reason is the poor credibility of its leaders. Its Ameer, Bangladesh's Industries Minister, Matiur Rahman Nizami, said at a press conference at the party's central office in Dhaka on 22 July 2004 that Bangla Bhai, the leader of the JMJB, 'was created by some newspapers as the Government has found no existence of him'.[43] Yet an interview with Bangla Bhai had been tele-cast by the NTV channel run by Prime Minister Khaleda Zia's former Political Secretary, Mosaddek Ali Falu![44]

The Jamaat's Secretary General, Bangladesh's State Minister for Social Welfare, Ali Ahsan Mohammad Mujahid, also addressed the press conference where Nizami made his statement about Bangla Bhai. Referring to Sheikh Hasina's comments linking the Jamaat with militant organizations, he said, 'Jamaat-e-Islami never dreams for a Taliban-style revolution, rather it wants to establish an Islamic State in a systematic manner.'[45] The Jamaat's associate organization Khilgaon Islamic Library and Social Welfare Council[46] ended a three-day gathering at Paltan Maidan, Dhaka, on Friday, 18 February 2005, with a *ghazal* about flying the Taliban flag on Bengal's sky, which was sung with great gusto.[47] Speaking on the occasion, Jamaat leader Delwar Hussain Saydee had said, 'Secularism is the Satan's dispensation'. Sternly criticizing America, he had also said that it was trying to teach atheism to Bangladesh. Such secularism–atheism, however, would not be accepted in Bangladesh.[48] Besides, as we had seen in Chapter Four, there is very little difference between the kind of society the Jamaat wants in Bangladesh and that the Taliban established in Afghanistan.

Besides, there are indications that the Jamaat might already have started implementing the plan mentioned in *Aghoshito Juddher Blueprint* which, in the section under the heading 'Training' had mentioned the deltaic forest on the banks of the southernmost Handia Bhanga River under Satkhira–Shyamnagar Police Station in the Sunderbans as one of the areas where new training centres would be opened. A report in the *Daily Star* of 31 August 2005 stated, 'Law enforcers have started a combing operation in the Sundarbans to find out the hideouts of Islamist militants after intelligence reports revealed that they were being trained in deep forests.'[49] The paper quoted its staff reporter in Khulna as stating that top JMB leaders used to visit the training camps in the Sundarbans and that one Maj. (Retd) Jainul Abedin was imparting training, in the garb of a fisherman.

The storm troopers

Given the Jamaat's fundamentalist ideology and the fact that its attempt to trash the report of its meeting on 11 and 12 April 2003 in Chittagong lacks conviction, one can hardly rule out the possibility that the party, which has a background of involvement, through its front organizations, in the savage killings of 1971, was also behind the grenade attack on the Awami League rally in Dhaka on 21 August 2004, and the wave of violence currently sweeping Bangladesh. The possibility appears stronger when one considers that the Jamaat certainly has the organizational strength and striking power to unleash both widespread and clinically-targeted attacks. In 1971, the leaders of the Chhatra Shangha assumed the leadership of militias like Al-Badr, the Razakars, Al-Shams and so on. The Shangha disappeared after Bangladesh's liberation, with the surrender of the Pakistan Army in Bangladesh to the Indian Army and the Mukti Bahini in Dhaka on 16 December 1971. It was reincarnated, albeit without any announcement, as the Islami Chhatra Shibir by the Al-Badr high command on 6 February 1977.[50]

Since then, it has been growing steadily in strength inside Bangladesh, and is currently firmly entrenched in the universities of Chittagong, Rajshahi, Jahangirnagar, Khulna and Sylhet.[51] It has also been establishing links abroad. It became a member of the International Islamic Federation of Students' Organisations (IIFSO) in 1979. Its former President, S.A.M. Taher, was also the latter's Secretary General. It is also a member of the World Assembly of Muslim Youth (WAMY). It reportedly has close links with the ISI, which provides it with substantial funds, as do some Islamic countries, particularly Saudi Arabia. As we have seen, the Shibir is reportedly helping, in association with elements in Saudi Arabia, subversive Islamist activities in India, particularly in the regions bordering Bangladesh.[52]

The Shibir, according to Indian intelligence reports, actively helped the United Liberation Front of Asom (ULFA), which, implementing a blueprint provided by the ISI, targeted Hindi-speaking Assamese in the closing days of 2002 with a series of terrorist strikes.[53] On 27 January 2001, Bangladesh Police raided Darul Irfan Academy, a madrasa in Chandgaon, Chittagong, and seized documents revealing its links with the Arakan Rohingya National Organisation (ARNO), an extremist Islamist group active among Rohingya Muslims who have fled to the Chittagong Hill Tracts to escape persecution in Myanmar, and the ISI. The head of the madrasa, Khairul Bashar, was four times the chief of the Shibir's Chittagong District unit.[54] Inside Bangladesh, Shibir acts as one of the principal striking arms of the Jamaat. It was thus active in the brutal anti-Hindu riots that occurred in that country after the general elections of October 2001 that brought Begum Khaleda Zia's Government to power.

The violent and extremist ethos of the Shibir is clearly underlined by the importance it attaches to martyrdom. Its website[55] has a separate section under the heading 'Shahadat Option' or 'Martyrdom Option'. It has sub-sections under the headings 'Profiles of Shaheeds (martyrs)', 'Profiles of Injured Brothers', 'Information for Shaheed Museum' and 'Information for Shaheed Fund'. Besides, it has a page under the heading 'A Mashe Shaheed Hoyechhen Jara' or 'Those Who Have Become Martyrs this Month', with photographs of those of its activists killed in the same month in different years along with the dates of their deaths.

It is not surprising, therefore, that the Shibir maintains close links with terrorist outfits operating in South Asia and Afghanistan, acting on their behalf in Bangladesh, mainly by helping them to recruit and indoctrinate fanatical youth. Many of these youths were reportedly sent through Pakistan to Afghanistan during Taliban rule there, and a number of them fought directly under Osama bin Laden.[56] Inside Bangladesh, the Shibir is the kingpin of the Jamaat's terror network, which includes a number of terrorist outfits like HUJIB, the JMB and the JMJB. Its network has provided terrorists with an infrastructure for training and of camps and shelters for storing weapons and supplies. On 23 April 2004, Bangladesh's 11-party Left alliance alleged that the Jamaat and the Shibir were developing an 'Islamic militant network' across the country by taking advantage of the Jamaat's presence as a partner in the ruling coalition. Earlier, on 16 November 2000, the Convener of the Bangladesh Madrassa Teachers' Association, Maulana Mirza Nurul Huq, alleged that the Shibir was involved in terrorist activities in educational institutions in the name of Islam.[57]

Understandably, the Shibir, whose ranks include a number of criminals, has come to be known for its violent activities. Akhtar Hamid, 38, was arrested by the Rapid Action Battalion (an elite force created for tackling crime and lawlessness) in Dhaka on 17 January 2005. Brought to Chittagong for interrogation, Hamid, known as a 'godfather' and an accused in as many as 29 criminal cases, including some involving murder, abduction and extortion, made a confessional statement which led to the recovery of five guns, 10 rifle bullets, six cartridges and two daggers from his village home. He was handed over to the local police station, Maheshkhali, where a case was registered against him under the Arms Act.[58] There have been a number of such cases, as also clashes between activists of the Shibir and the Jatiyatabadi Chhatra Dal (the BNP's front organization among students) and the Awami League.

A typical clash occurred between activists of the Shibir and Chhatra Dal on the campus of Rajshahi University on 13 January 2004. The President, General Secretary, Organizing Secretary and the Assistant Organizing Secretary of the Chhatra Dal's university unit were critically injured and had to be hospitalized. Several activists of the organization also required hospitalization. Both sides used firearms during the clash, which began with a dispute over the sale of admission forms in the black market. Beginning at 5 P.M., the clash ended at 6 P.M., when the Shibir supporters drove the Chhatra Dal supporters out of the campus and occupied the residential halls. The *Daily Star*'s report on the incident quoted a senior police officer, who wished to remain unnamed, as saying that both sides used firearms but the Shibir used sophisticated ones.[59]

Besides such clashes, the Shibir has also been accused of being involved in some major acts of terrorism. On 16 June 2001, 22 persons were killed and many others, including Awami League MP Shamim Osman, were seriously injured, in a bomb blast at the Awami League's office in Narayanganj, south of Dhaka. While the ruling Awami League and its supporters alleged that the BNP and its ally, the Jamaat, were using 'foreign trained extremists' to create a law-and-order problem before the elections'[60], the police, on 29 June, arrested a Shibir activist for involvement in the blast. Earlier, on 9 April, the police had arrested nine Shibir activists at Satkania, Chittagong, for the murder, on 7 April, of two leaders of the Jubo and Chhatra League respectively. In another even more serious act of violence on 12 July in the same year, Shibir activists killed nine persons, including seven activists of the Chhatra League at Chittagong.[61]

One of the worst crimes committed by the Shibir, however, was the murder of Principal Gopal Krishna Muhuri of Nazirhat College at his Jamal Khan Road residence in Chittagong city on the morning of 16 November 2001. Of the 12 accused charge-sheeted, judge M. Hasan Imam of the Speedy Trial Tribunal sentenced four, all activists of the

Shibir, to death, two of them in absentia, on 6 February 2003. Of the four sentenced to death, Alamgir Kabir or Baittya ('Shorty') and Taslimuddin Montu were present in the court. Gittu Nasir and Azam were absconding. Also absconding were Habib Khan and Mohiuddin who, along with another Shibir activist, Chhota Saiful, and the accountant of the college, Mohammad Shahjahan, were sentenced to life imprisonment. All who had been sentenced to life imprisonment had to pay a fine of Tk 50,000 each, which the judge asked the Deputy Commissioner of Chittagong District to recover by attaching their properties.[62] The verdict is now under appeal and a large section of the public alleges that the government is doing everything possible to sabotage the prosecution. Among those sentenced to death, Gittu Nasir (full name Mohammad Nasiruddin) was killed in 'crossfire'[63] with a unit of the RAB in Chittagong District on 2 March 2005.[64]

According to the *Daily Star* report of 7 February 2003, Gopal Krishna Muhuri was killed at the behest of vested interests wanting to remove him from the principal's post. It is, however, difficult to accept this as a full and satisfactory explanation. Principal Muhuri was not only a highly respected scholar and humanist but had also played an important role during the liberation struggle and resolutely stood for its secular values. He was also a Hindu. If his politics and background made him an object of hate for the Jamaat and the Shibir, his killing could be expected to demoralize and terrorize Hindus, who are traditionally supporters of the Awami League, and whom communal elements represented by organizations like the Jamaat, the Shibir and HUJIB have regularly persecuted and killed.

Warriors of jihad

If the Shibir is the kingpin of the Jamaat's terror network, HUJIB has close links with it and is perhaps the most important component of Bangladesh's *jihadi* infrastructure. It has strong ties with both the Jamaat and Shibir, as well as the Islami Oikya Jote and Al Qaeda. In this context, one would do well to look at the five reports which Bangladesh's widely-circulated and highly-respected Bengali-language daily *Prothom Alo* carried in August 2004 under the series heading 'Brihattara Chattagrame Jongi Tatparata' or 'Militant Activity in Greater Chittagong'. Published under the joint byline of Saiful Alam Chowdhury and Abdul Quddus Rana, each report had a distinct focus, reflected in its sub-heading. The second article in the series[65], published under the sub-heading 'Desher Bibhinna Quomi Madrasar Chhatrader Prashikshan Dichhe Shasastra Rohingyara' or 'Armed Rohingyas[66] are Training Students in the Various Quomi Madrasas', states that a former Assistant Superintendent of Police of the Ukhia Circle had arrested a former commanding officer of the ARNO, Salim Ullah, and interrogated him from 22 January 2001, on ten days' remand. On the basis of the latter's statement, he had submitted a report to the then Superintendent of Police, Cox's Bazar. It said that the RSO (Rohingya Solidarity Organisation) and the ARNO were operating with the help of the Jamaat, with which they had established ties through certain foreign organizations. The report said that the Jamaat–Shibir had close links with a Myanmarese student organization, Iktadultullah Al Muslimeen, and with another organization of the RSO. The Saudi-based organizations WAMY and Rabita-Al-Alam-Al-Islami were present in Bangladesh, particularly Chittagong. Also, the Jamaat–Shibir implemented the Kuwait-based IIFSO's programme in Bangladesh. All the above organizations were interlinked. No organization in Bangladesh received any assistance from any of these without recommendation from Jamaat–Shibir.

The third article in the *Prothom Alo* investigative series, published on 16 August under the sub-heading 'Harkat-ul Jihad Akhono Shakriya' or 'Harkat-ul Jihad is still active'[67], said that the report based on the statement by Salim Ullah, arrested in 2001, made clear that the Jamaat had a role in the HUJIB's rise. It added, 'Investigation by *Prothom Alo* has revealed that Harkatul Jihad had first started training with Arakan's militant groups. Later, it established ties with the local Jamaat-e-Islami through these.' The report further stated that relations between these groups and Jamaat also developed on the basis of family ties. The district Jamaat unit Secretary Shahjalal Chowdhury's sister married a former leader of the RSO and HUJIB, Mohammad Alam. In addition, a militant Burmese leader and former General Secretary of the RSO, Nurul Islam Driver a.k.a. Zakaria, married the sister of a former Shibir President.

The report quoted Shahjalal Chowdhury as saying that the HUJIB had started working in the area with the help of Rohingya rebel groups and some teachers of *quomi* madrasas, but the Jamaat or Shibir had no role in their spread. He dismissed the allegations against the Jamaat as part of a conspiracy. What he said, however, does not withstand scrutiny. That the Jamaat and HUJIB have close links becomes clear on considering that Maulana Delwar Hussain Saydee, the Jamaat's[68] MP and a member of both its Central Executive Committee and Central Working Committee, is also a member of HUJIB's Advisory Council. His name features on the list of members of the latter given by Bertil Lintner in 'Bangladesh: Extremist Islamist Consolidation' in the *Faultlines* of July 2003.[69] HUJIB has also forged connections with the IOJ and the Islamic Shashantantra Andolan (Islamic Consti-tution Movement). The former's Chairman, Fazlul Huq Amini, and the latter's chief, Maulana Fazlul Karim, Peer of Charmonai, are members of HUJIB's Advisory Council.[70]

HUJIB is one of the most sinister organizations active in South Asia. It has close links with Al Qaeda, which is believed to have been behind its creation. The third article in the *Prothom Alo* series states,

> Harkat-ul Jihad, which is included in the US State Department's list of terrorist organisations, is still active in Bangladesh. It is known from more than one source that members of this militant organisation formed by those who have returned to Bangladesh after the Afghan War are now undergoing arms training in camps in Cox's Bazar, in the inac-cessible hills in Naikkhangchhari in Bandarban, in the no-man's land along the Bangladesh-Myanmar border, and certain hilly areas of Chittagong. They are supported by some *quomi* madrasas in the Chittagong and Cox's Bazar districts, certain Islamist political parties and quite a few rebel Rohingya militant groups.[71]

The report quotes the Bangladesh Police's special branch as saying that nearly 300 *mujahideen* from Bangladesh participated in the war in Afghanistan towards the end of the 1980s. Twenty-nine of them died there. In 1992, 17 *mujahideen* returned to Bangladesh and formed HUJIB under the leadership of Maulana Sheikh Farid of Khalishpur in Khulna (a south-western district of Bangladesh). They had, at that time, cultivated good relations with Rohingya rebel groups, particularly the RSO. Rohan Gunaratna, in his book *Inside Al Qaeda: Global Network of Terror*, also identifies the year of HUJIB's formation as 1992 and says that its purpose was to recruit volunteers to fight in Afghanistan and Kashmir. Significantly, he also stated, 'the Bangladeshi authorities now believe that Al Qaeda had funded it'. He goes on to say, 'The group also operates in north-eastern India in tandem with several small Islamist groupings. Osama was said to have sent his private secretary to attend a meeting of the Harkat-ul-Jihad-al-Islami in Bangladesh to draft a strategy to intensify their violent campaign in that region.'[72]

Besides, we have already seen that one of the six signatories to a *fatwa* (decree) issued on 23 February 1998 by the World Islamic Front for Jihad Against Jews and Crusaders, which has come to be commonly known as the World Islamic Front, was, according to Yossef Bodansky[73], Sheikh Abdul Salam Muhammad, 'Amir of the Jihad movement in Bangladesh'. Gunaratna, who states that Muhammad was from HUJIB and that his alias was Fazlur Rahman supplements Bodansky's information. Sheikh Farid, who is also known as Shaukat Osman, continues to head HUJIB with Imtiaz Quddus as General Secretary.[74]

In the 15 October 2002 issue of *Time* magazine, Alex Perry provided a graphic account of the arrival of Taliban and Al Qaeda fighters from Afghanistan in Chittagong on the night of 21 December 2001, by sea. He also quoted a military source as saying that most of the men stayed on in Bangladesh and did not just transit through. Though, according to Perry, the source could not say whether they just sought refuge or planned to set up a new base of operations, things started becoming clearer on 24 September 2001, when Bangladesh's domestic intelligence agency arrested four Yemenis, an Algerian, a Libyan and a Sudanese from three houses in Dhaka's upmarket Uttara area. They were allegedly involved in imparting arms training in a madrasa in Dhaka run by the Saudi Arabian charity organization Al Haramian.[75]

Fazle Karim, a HUJIB operative who was arrested by Kolkata Police on 7 October 2002, had revealed during his interrogation that Ayman Al Zawahiri, reportedly next to Osama bin Laden in the Al Qaeda's hierarchy, and some other Al Qaeda terrorists had entered Bangladesh in September 2002 with HUJIB's help.[76] Perry writes, about the same man:

> A veteran of Al Qaeda camps in eastern Afghanistan who told his interrogators he had twice met Osama bin Laden, Karim said he recognized two people he had trained with in Afghanistan while visiting HUJI hideouts in August. The pair told him they were a part of more than 100 Arabs and Afghans belonging to the Al Qaeda and the Taliban who had arrived by sea at Chittagong in winter.[77]

Jaideep Saikia provides a list of mosques and madrasas in Bangladesh housing Al Qaeda *jihadi*s, which he unearthed in the course of his research at University of Illinois at Urbana-Champaign in the United

States. According to him, 30–35 Al Qaeda cadres were staying at Mona Tola Quomi Madrasas, under police station Madhabpur in Habiganj District, and another 30 to 35 at Panchori and Manikchora Madrasa complex in Khagachari District in the Chittagong Hill Tracts. Five of them, commanded by Muhammad Zainuddin Khan, were staying at Chunarughat Quomi Madrasa, under Chunarughat Police Station in Habiganj District. Ten to 12 Al Qaeda *jihadis* were staying at Islampur Mosque, Companyganj, under Biyani Bazar police station, and 20–25 at the Lakertala Tea Estate Masjid complex, both in Sylhet District. Robir Bazar Tilagram Madrasa Complex in Police Station Kolaura, Maulvi Bazar District, housed about 15–16 of them.[78]

The US State Department declared HUJIB a terrorist organization on 21 May 2002. Its report *Patterns of Global Terrorism 2003*[79] includes the organization's name in the list of other terrorist groups—as distinct from the 37 designated as terrorist organizations. The HUJIB's mission is to establish Islamic rule in Bangladesh. The implications of this become clear on recalling that its supporters frequently raise the slogan 'Amra sabai hobo Taliban/Bangla hobe Afghanistan.' It means, in English, 'All of us will become Taliban/Bangladesh will become Afghanistan.' HUJIB's strength has been variously estimated. According to the report of the US State Department cited above, 'it has a cadre strength of more than several thousand members'. According to the survey *Bangladesh Assessment 2003* in the South Asia Terrorism Portal maintained by the Institute of Conflict Management, HUJIB reportedly has 15,000 members of whom 2,000 are 'hardcore'. The survey further stated, 'Bangladeshi Hindus and moderate Muslims hold them responsible for many attacks against religious minorities, secular intellectuals and journalists.'[80]

In January 1999, three activists of the HUJIB, armed with axes, burst into the apartment of Bangladesh's legendary poet and outspoken secular icon, Shamsur Rahman. The poet escaped unhurt though his wife was injured.[81] The attack led to the arrest of 42 members of HUJIB. Two men, a Pakistani and a South African, claimed that they had been sent to Bangladesh by Osama bin Laden with more than $300,000, which they distributed between 421 madrasas.[82] Interrogation of the three attackers, who were apprehended by Rahman's neighbours, and subsequent investigations, revealed that the attempt on his life was a part of campaign to eliminate 28 Bangladeshi intellectuals known for their secular outlook and opposition to fundamentalist Islam.[83] HUJIB has also been held responsible for the murder on 16 July 2000 of a journalist, also named Shamsur Rahman, and an abortive attempt to assassinate Sheikh Hasina, then Prime Minister of Bangladesh, on 22 July 2000. It has also been considered responsible for an explosion at Ramna, Dhaka, on 14 April 2001, when the Bengali New Year's Day was being celebrated by the well-known cultural organization Chhayanot through a musical soirée.[84] Ten persons were killed and around 100 wounded in that attack. According to the third report in the *Prothom Alo* series, one of HUJIB's leaders and the Vice-President of Shiddhirganj Madarinagar Quomi Madrasa, Maulana Akbar, was arrested for involvement in the crime. In the confessional statement he submitted before the trial court, he said that he and 10 other leaders of the organization, including Sheikh Farid, had planned the blast. He also stated that HUJIB had two training camps at Narsinghdi and Brahmanberia and that its leaders had more than one passport each.[85]

HUJIB activists have joined hands with the Jamaat and the Shibir not only in persecuting and killing Hindus but also in terrorizing Christians. Ten persons were killed and over 24 injured in an explosion in a Roman Catholic Church in Beniarchar in Gopalganj District during morning mass on 3 June 2001.[86] A top-ranking leader of the organization and the Vice-President of the Shiddhirganj Madarinagar Quomi Madrasa, and three of his accomplices, were arrested from Kakrail, Dhaka, on 8 June in connection with the blast.

As has been noted, HUJIB has also been active in promoting terrorism outside Bangladesh. On 22 January 2002, the Asif Reza commando force owned responsibility for the attack that very morning on police personnel in front of the American Centre in Kolkata which killed four policemen on the spot (another died later in hospital) and injured 17. It was a criminal group allied with HUJIB.[87] Interrogation of the principal accused, Aftab Ansari[88] alias Farhan Malik, is said to have established HUJIB's involvement in the outrage. It also yielded further information about the international linkages among the Pakistan-based Jaish-e-Mohammad and Lashkar-e-Toiba, and the HUJIs of Pakistan and Bangladesh. Ansari also played a key role in the abduction, on 25 July 2001, of the Kolkata-based businessman Partha Pratim Roy Burman, who was released five days later on 30 July after his family reportedly paid a ransom of Rs 37.5 million in Dubai, through the *hawala* route. Omar Sheikh, convicted by a Pakistani court for the murder of the American journalist Daniel Pearl, was one of the terrorists released from Indian jails to secure the return of the passengers and the aircraft of Indian Airlines flight IC-814 from Kathmandu to Delhi, which was hijacked to Kandahar on 24 December 1999. He sent $100,000 from the ransom amount to Mohammad Atta, who played a leading role in the terrorist strikes on 9/11.[89] HUJIB maintains close links with the United Liberation Front of Asom (ULFA) and makes it possible for the latter to run its training camps in the Chittagong Hill Tracts.[90]

Clearly, HUJIB's financiers abroad and friends in Bangladesh want it to coordinate the activities of all fundamentalist Islamist groups active in Bangladesh and the neighbouring countries. A Bangladesh Islami Manch (Bangladesh Islamic Platform) was set up under its leadership at a meeting in Ukhia in the Chittagong Hill Tracts on 10–11 May 2002, attended by 63 representatives of nine Islamic groups, the Islami Oikya Jote and the Muslim United Liberation Tigers of Assam (MULTA).[91] Also formed was a 'Jihad Council' to coordinate the activities of the nine.[92] By June, Bangladeshi veterans of the war against the erstwhile Soviet Union in Afghanistan were training members of the new alliance in at least two camps in southern Bangladesh.[93]

Interestingly, Maj. Gen. (Retd) Afsir Karim writes, in the January 2005 issue of *Aakrosh*:

> It is a well-known fact that the HUJI-B has been training Rohingya Muslims for the past few years; reports now suggest that it has started training small groups of Muslims in Thailand, Cambodia, Indonesia and Brunei in the madrasas controlled by it. The aim seems to be to train militants for assisting the IIF[94] and step up their movement of establishing the 'Sharia' law in Muslim majority pockets in these countries. At least 150–250 cells of al-Qaeda and IIF are reported to be active in Bangladesh. The JeI (Jamaat), IoJ and the HUJI-B have lately been joined by Hizbul Tehrir for training militant groups and working on the junior officers of the armed forces.[95]

Lintner lists 19 training establishments run by HUJIB.[96] South Asia Terrorism Portal's write-up on the organization states, 'The Harkat reportedly maintained six camps in the hilly areas of Chittagong where its cadres were trained in the use of arms. Unconfirmed reports also hold that it maintains six training camps near Cox's Bazar. According to the third report in *Prothom Alo*'s series of five articles on militant activity in the Chittagong Hill Tracts, a number of local sources revealed that four military training centres were functioning in the Charia Hill area, Meghar Mahlooma Bazaar, Phatika and Mirer Khal under the direction of HUJIB. It also stated that the Sardar of Kutupalang refugee camp at Ukhia-Teknaf border, Nurul Islam Majhi, said on 17 June 2004 that Harkat-ul-Jihad had started regular training from 2000 at Ukhia border under the former RSO leader Abu Yunus. There used to be regular training at Madhurchhara at Rajpalang. But following police expeditions against them, the militants had fled and were being trained along with Rohingya Muslim groups at Harinmara, Dharmachhara and Garjania.[97] There are other camps also. Lintner writes,

> According to an eyewitness in Ukhia, a small town south of Cox's Bazaar, hundreds of armed men are staying in one of these camps near the Myanmar border. While some of them speak Bengali, the vast majority appears to be Arabs and others of Central and West Asian origin. The militants have warned villagers in the area that they will be killed if they informed the media or raised the issue with the authorities.[98]

The bulk of HUJIB's funds comes from abroad. It has very close links with the ISI, and receives and has received financial assistance from Pakistan, Saudi Arabia and Afghanistan—from the last during Taliban rule—through Muslim NGOs in Bangladesh, including Adarsha Kutir, Al Faruk Islamic Foundation and Hataddin.[99] Addressing a press conference at his residence at Dhanmondi in Dhaka on 5 March 2005, Prof. Abu Sayeed, an Awami League leader and State Minister for Information in Sheikh Hasina's government, cited a 1999 report by Bangladesh Police's Criminal Investigation Department stating that Al Qaeda had given HUJIB Tk 20 million for conducting militant training in 421 madrasas across Bangladesh.[100] According to Haroon Habib's dispatch in *The Hindu* of 2 March 2001[101], an investigation by the *Daily Star* had revealed that tens of millions of taka were being channelled to Bangladesh every year to fund fanatics and politically-motivated clerics whose dream was to turn Bangladesh into a theocratic Islamist State. The *Daily Star* found that the funds, which were brought into the country legally in the absence of an effective monitoring system, were ostensibly meant for imparting religious education, but were in reality used to finance extremist activities whose perpetrators drew their strength from Begum Khaleda Zia's main-stream Bangladesh Nationalist Party. Investigations revealed that foreign fundamentalist groups were channelling funds through some of the 21 local NGOs in the country, which also benefited from illegal cross-border transactions and 'over-invoicing' of exports. The report quotes sources in the NGO Affairs Bureau in the Prime Minister's Office, which supervises the activities of NGOs, as stating that in the preceding one year, 'Islamic NGOs had spent Tk 150 crore [1.5 billion] in the name of Islamic education'. They also said that in some cases 'show-cause' notices had been served on several NGOs for spending tens of millions of taka without the bureau's authorization. Some foreign banks had also been served with similar notices for violating rules and releasing funds without authorization. There was, however, no follow-up action; nor were the rules streamlined. Besides, a section of accountancy firms specialized in 'adjusting' financial irregularities and hoodwinking the thinly-manned bureau.

Apart from the money fundamentalist Islamists receive from Saudi Arabia and the Gulf countries, their investments and enterprises yield huge revenue and profit. In the Dr Abdul Gafur Memorial Lecture entitled 'Bangladeshe Moulabader Arthaniti' (The Economics of Fundamentalism in Bangladesh), organized by *Samaj, Arthaniti O Rashtra* (Society, Economy and State), a biannual subject-based research journal, delivered in Dhaka on 21 April 2005, Prof. Abul Barkat, who teaches economics at Dhaka University, stated that the organizations run by fundamentalist Islamists make a yearly net profit of Tk 12 billion.[102] The figure, he had explained, was arrived at by applying the 'heuristic method'. 'Though this method', he explains, 'involved dependence on conjectures to a considerable degree of supposition, the basis of the suppositions is sufficiently scientific. In this case, the opinions of specialists in various accounts and fields had been taken. In cases, accounts may have reflected more or less of what is true (nobody knows the real truth; it has not been revealed). Though formal information (which is not correct) is available in respect of several accounts–institutions, such information is either unavailable or unpublished in the majority of cases. The audit reports and/or annual reports available in some cases are not fully true/correct.'[103]

Divided into numerous groups and sub-groups, and engaged in implementing diverse programmes, the driving force behind militant communalism received huge amounts of foreign funds in the 1970s and 1980s, which 'they invested in building up their associated economic–political model. In most cases, the institutions they have invested in are making huge profits, a part of which they are spending on organisational activities, a part in expanding the associated institutions and, from time to time, a part in creating new accounts–institutions.'[104]

According to Professor Barkat, the fundamentalists used at least 10 per cent of the profit of Tk 12 billion on organizational purposees like conducting regular party activities, providing pay and allowances to party workers, and running military training centres. Professor Barkat states that this money enabled them to—and they actually did—maintain about 500,000 party cadres.

Professor Barkat, who is General Secretary of the Bangladesh Economic Association adds that out of the annual net profit of Tk 12 billion, financial institutions (banking, insurance, leasing companies and so on) account for 27 per cent or Tk 3.25 billion, commercial establishments (retail and wholesale selling and departmental stores, etc.) 1.3 billion or 10.4 per cent, the pharmaceutical industry and health undertakings including diagnostic centres 1.25 billion or 10.4 per cent. Further, educational institutions (schools, colleges and universities) account, according to him, for Tk 1.1 billion or 9.2 per cent, the communications sector (trucks, buses, steamers, ships, cars, CNG-run three-wheelers) Tk 900 million or 7.5 per cent, land and real estate for Tk 1 billion or 8.3 per cent, news media and information technology Tk 700 million or 5.8 per cent and, lastly, NGOs Tk 2.5 billion or 20.8 per cent.[105]

Professor Barkat holds that the growth rate of the fundamentalist sector of the economy averaged 7.5–9 per cent every year while that of the mainstream national sector averaged 4.5–5 per cent. Fundamentalists accounted for about 1.53 per cent of Bangladesh's total national investment, 3.3 per cent of the total revenue income and 3.7 per cent of the total export earnings a year, 6 per cent of the government's annual development budget and 12 per cent of its internal resources.[106] 'Hence', he argues, 'there could be no scope for a second view on the fact that, other things remaining unchanged, the communalization of the economy would increase henceforth.'[107]

Fundamentalists ran approximately 450 NGOs, a platform, Professor Barkat said, they used to reach the masses and, subsequently, to blend their political goals with the economic interests of the people.[108] Also significant is the growth pattern of primary education. 'While the number of primary educational institutions have doubled over the last 33 years, that of *dakhil* madrasas has increased eight times', and the number of students in the two categories of institutions doubled and become 13 times higher respectively. Not only that, while the government spent Tk 3,000 per year per secondary student, madrasas spent Tk 5,000.[109] According to Professor Barkat, one must remember in the context of the impact of communalization of education and necessary educational reform that the students of most madrasas came from poor low-income families.[110]

Both the proliferation of madrasas and the amount spent on each student is significant. At this rate, in the next decade or so the overwhelming majority of Bangladeshi youth will have their primary education in madrasas and will emerge as dyed-in-the-wool fundamentalists steeped in the *jihadi* mindset. The significance of this can hardly be overemphasized. Like most other extremist Islamist organizations, HUJIB draws its rank-and-file and leaders from the *quomi* (private) madrasas that are mushrooming in Bangladesh. There were about 64,000 of these in that country—of which 7,122 were, in 1999, *aliya* madrasas run with government assistance[111]—which offer subjects like English, science, mathematics and history along with Islamic religious instruction. The rest were *quomi* madrasas, the overwhelming majority of which only provided religious instruction according to the Deobandi school of Islam, besides teaching languages like Urdu, Persian and Arabic. Their students were not being prepared for jobs and professions in modern societies.

Deobandi madrasas, which feed militant and fundamentalist Islamist organizations with recruits, have been mushrooming. Saiful Alam Chowdhury and Abdul Quddus Rana describe, in the first of their five reports in *Prothom Alo,* a madrasa in the Chittagong Hill Tracts, located in the midst of hills and shrubbery, and with no human habitation within half a kilometre.

Located on a hillock, it is housed in a tin shed with four rooms, only one of which has three–four benches. Except a signboard at the foot of the hillock, there is nothing to indicate the existence of a madrasa here. Innumerable madrasas like this one in Ghonarpara, which has to be approached by travelling several kilometres on foot from Narkel Bagan (Coconut Grove) in Rajarkul Union under Ramu Police Station, have been established in the almost deserted foothill areas of Cox's Bazaar District. At some places, madrasas have mushroomed within 50–100 yards of one another. None of these has received Government recognition.

Conversation with residents of the adjoining areas and students and teachers of the madrasas revealed that *jihadi* training was being conducted with foreign money in these madrasas at the foothills. . . . Investigations have revealed that Arabic is taught during the day and militant training conducted at night in the madrasas and mosques on both sides of roads in Ramu and Ukhia Upazilas.[112]

The report quoted Maulana Haroon, who directed instruction at Chakmarkul Jamia Islamia Darul Ulum Madrasa, as saying that there were over 2,000 *quomi* madrasas in Cox's Bazar District. They all functioned under the Hathhazari and Patia madrasas.[113]

Tactical retreat

HUJIB began receding into the background following the uproar over the killing of five and wounding of over 20 policemen in front of the American Centre in Kolkata on 22 January 2002. The process became even more marked after the US declared it a terrorist organization on 21 May 2002. This was, however, a purely tactical move. As has been seen, it has remained active behind the scenes. Besides, fundamentalist Islamist terrorist outfits keep mushrooming and their number, put at over 40 by Professor Sayeed, is 53 according to the latest estimate.

Of these organizations, Jamaatul Islamia is active in Faridpur, Magura and Madaripur Districts. Hijbut Tawhid has established its presence in Barisal, Madaripur, Kushtia, Chuadanga, Jheniadah and Gopalganj Districts. It shot into the limelight on 27 September 2003 when its activists went berserk in Paglabazar in Narayanganj District and attacked local people who prevented them from distributing leaflets titled 'Call for Real Islam', with hammers. One of the victims, Abdul Malek, died in Dhaka Medical College Hospital. Nine others were injured. The leader of Hijbut Tawhid, Bayjid Khan Panni was arrested in a house in Sector Seven of Dhaka's posh Uttara area.[114]

More important than any of these, however, is the Shahadat al-Hiqma (SAH), which, according to its chief Sayed Kawsar Hussain Siddiki Raja, often called merely Kawsar, was a 'political party' with 10,000 'commandos' and 25,000 fighters.[115] Kawsar, who has a long history of brushes with the police, was arrested for cheating on 24 September 2002.[116] Released on bail on 21 December 2002, he began organizing the SAH. The latter, however, was banned on 9 February 2003, after he had announced, at a press conference in Rajshahi on the preceding day, its plan to launch an armed struggle to turn

Bangladesh into an Islamic state.[117] Police filed the first sedition case against him on 20 March 2003, and pressed charges against him and 11 of his associates five days later. He had by then gone underground, but was arrested under Section 54 of the Criminal Procedure Code, which applies to sedition and anti-State activities, on 6 November 2004 for storming the Boalia police station.[118]

On 18 January 2005, Rajshahi police, which had arrested Kawsar, sought clearance from Bangladesh's Home Ministry in Dhaka to file a second sedition case against him. Since people arrested under Section 54 of the Criminal Procedures Code cannot be kept behind bars for more than three months, and since the clearance had not come by then, it sought a 15 days' extension of his custody from a Metropolitan Magistrate's court in Rajshahi on 9 February. Granted the extension, it sought and received another 15 days remand as the Home Ministry's clearance had still not come. The delay is perhaps not without significance given the perceived softness of Bangladesh's Home Ministry towards violent fundamentalist Islamist militias (more about this in Chapter Six), and some of the revelations Kawsar has made. He had once laid claim to support from Dawood Ibrahim but had later said that this was not the case and that he had mentioned the mafia don's name to attract attention. Rajshahi police, however, had quoted him as saying that SAH had the support of several lawyers and businessmen of Rajshahi and Chapainawabganj as well as a Shibir leader of Khulna.[119]

Notes

1. From www.jamaat-e-islami.org, as updated on 24 September 2002 at 11 P.M. and as accessed on 21 December 2004.
2. Shahriar Kabir, *Ekattorer Ghatak o Dalalra Ke Kothaye* (The Agents and Killers of Seventy-one: Who is Where?), 2nd ed. (Dhaka: Muktijuddher Chetana Vikash Kendra [Centre for Spreading the Consciousness of the Liberation War], 1987), p. 10.
3. Quoted in ibid., pp. 30–31.
4. Ibid., pp. 31–32.
5. Ibid., pp. 32–33.
6. Ibid., p. 33.
7. Ibid., pp. 34–35.
8. Maj. Gen. Rao Farman Ali was Civilian Affairs Advisor to the Governor of East Pakistan during the liberation war in 1971.

9. We have seen his name in the preceding chapter as the author of the Jamaat's defence policy.

10. Ibid., p. 57. Kabir quotes here from the cover story, 'Ekattore Bhool Karini: Golam Azam o Jamater Rajniti' (We Did Not Make a Mistake in Seventy-one: Golam Azam and Jamaat's Politics), of the 17 April 1981 issue of the weekly magazine *Bichitra*, which had created a sensation.

11. Quoted in Kabir, *Ekattorer Ghatak o Dalalra Ke Kothaye*, pp. 114–15.

12. Ibid., p. 61.

13. Ibid., p. 62.

14. Ibid., p. 58.

15. Joypurhat is now a district.

16. Ibid., p. 59.

17. Ibid., p. 60.

18. Ibid.

19. Ibid., p. 102.

20. Ibid., p. 138.

21. Ibid., p. 139.

22. Ibid., pp. 139–40.

23. Ibid., p. 130.

24. Ibid.

25. Shahriar Kabir, 'Bangladeshe Aamra ebong Ora' (We and They in Bangladesh), *Ananya* (Dhaka), 2005, p. 15.

26. Ibid.

27. Their respective names and positions in the Jamaat have been taken from the latter's website, www.jamaat-e-islami.org, as updated on 12 December 2004 and accessed on 21 December 2004.

28. *Shilalipi*, literally 'Writing on Stone', was a highly acclaimed literary magazine.

29. One of Bangladesh's important Bengali-language dailies.

30. Munir Chowdhury was one of Bangladesh's most outstanding playwrights.

31. Munir Chowdhury's brother and a well-known intellectual steeped in the secular tradition of the liberation struggle. He is Bangladesh's National Professor.

32. Hamida Rahman, 'Katasurer Badhyabhumi' (The Killing Ground of Katasur), *Dainik Azad* (Dhaka), 2 January 1972.

33. Abu Sayeed, *Aghashito Juddher Blueprint* (Blueprint of an Undeclared War), 2nd ed. (Dhaka: Agami Prakashani, 2005), p. 253.

34. Ibid.

35. A district in the Chittagong Hill Tract division.

36. Ibid.

37. Ibid.

38. The highest decision-making body.

39. Sura Fatiha is recited at every performance of *namaaz*. The Quran has 114 Suras.

40. News report, 'Cops seize books from Abu Sayeed's house', *The Daily Star* (Internet edition), 19 February 2005.

41. Ibid.
42. www.jamaat-e-islami.org.
43. News report, 'Bangla Bhai media creation, Nizami reiterates'.
44. News report, '"Bheetikar Shakti" Talibani Pataka Odate Chaye: Markin Rashtra-doot Harry Thomaser Prati Paltane Challenge' ('Frightening Force' Wants to Raise Taliban Flag: Challenge Thrown at American Ambassador Harry Thomas from Paltan), *Dainik Janakantha* (Internet edition), 20 February 2005.
45. News report, 'Bangla Bhai Media Creation'.
46. In Bengali, it is Khilgaon Islami Pathagar o Samajkalyan Parishad.
47. News report, '"Bheetikar Shakti" Talibani Pataka Odate Chaye'.
48. Ibid.
49. News report, 'Agency Reports Militant Camps in Sundarbans: Combing Operation Begins: 16 More Held', *The Daily Star* (Internet edition), 31 August 2005.
50. Kabir, *Ekattorer Ghatak o Dalalra Ke Kothaye*, p. 79.
51. South Asia Terrorism Portal, 'Islami Chhatra Shibir' (www.satp.org/satporgtp/countries/Bangladesh), as accessed on 18 December 2004.
52. Ibid.
53. Jaideep Saikia, *Terror sans Frontiers: Islamic Militancy in North-East India* (New Delhi: Vision Books, 2004), p. 80.
54. South Asia Terrorism Portal, 'Islami Chhatra Shibir', as accessed on 18 December 2004.
55. www.shibir.com.
56. South Asia Terrorism Portal, 'Islami Chhatra Shibir', as accessed on 18 December 2004.
57. Ibid.
58. News report, 'Rab Seizes Arms from Shibit Cadre's House: Hands Him over to Police', *The Daily Star* (Internet edition), 20 January 2005.
59. News report, 'JCD, Shibir Men Trade Gunfire on RU Campus: 50 Hurt in Daylong Fight, Rooms Ransacked, Classes Suspended Today and Tomorrow', *The Daily Star* (Internet edition), 14 January 2004.
60. Haroon Habib, 'Islamic Militancy on the Rise in Bangladesh', *The Hindu* (New Delhi), 20 June 2001.
61. Ibid.
62. Shahidul Islam, 'Four on Death Row for Killing Muhuri: Life Imprisonment for Four', *The Daily Star* (Internet edition), 7 February 2003.
63. The term 'crossfire' is used in Bangladesh to mean 'exchange of fire', usually between law-enforcers and alleged criminals. It is widely alleged that the expression 'killed in crossfire' is an euphemism for cold-blooded killing by police or paramilitary personnel.
64. News report, '"Gittu Nasir", 2 Others Killed in Crossfire', *The Daily Star* (Internet edition), 3 March 2005.
65. Saiful Alam Chowdhury and Abdul Quddus Rana, 'Brihattara Chattagrame Jongi Tatparata—2: Desher Bibhinno Quomi Madrasar Chhatrader Prashikshan

Dichhe Shasastra Rohingyara' (Militant Activity in Greater Chittagong: Armed Rohingyas are Training Students of Various *Quomi* Madrasas in the Country), *Prothom Alo* (Internet edition), 15 August 2004.

66. Rohingyas are Muslims from Myanmar who fled to Bangladesh following persecution by their country's military regime.

67. Saiful Alam Chowdhury and Abdul Quddus Rana, 'Brihattara Chattagrame Jongi Tatparata—3: Harkatul Jihad Akhono Shakriya' (Militant Activity in Greater Chittagong: Harkatul Jihad is Still Active), *Prothom Alo* (Internet edition), 15 August 2005.

68. Jamaat's website, as updated on 12 December 2004 and as accessed on 21 December 2004.

69. Bertil Lintner, 'Bangladesh: Extremist Islamist Consolidation', in *Faultlines: Writings on Conflict and Resolution*, 14 July 2003. Also at www.satp.org/satporgtp/ publication/faultlines/volume14/Article1.htm.

70. Ibid., p. 24.

71. Chowdhury and Rana, 'Brihattara Chattagrame Jongi Tatparata—3'.

72. Rohan Gunaratna, *Inside Al Qaeda: Global Network of Terror* (New Delhi: Roli Books), p. 219.

73. Yossef Bodansky, *Bin Laden: The Man Who Declared War on America* (Rocklin, CA: Prima Publishing, 1999), p. 226.

74. Gunaratna, *Inside Al Qaeda*, p. 219.

75. Alex Perry, 'Deadly cargo', *Time*, 15 October 2002.

76. P.G. Rajamohan, 'Harkat-ul-Jihad-al-Islami Bangladesh (HuJI-BD)', Institute of Peace and Conflict Studies website, www.ipcs.org/ipcs/databaseIndex2. jsp?database=1004&country2=Harkat-ul-Jihad-al-Islami%20Bangladesh% 20(HuJI-BD).

77. Perry, 'Deadly cargo'.

78. Jaideep Saikia, *Terror sans Frontiers*, p. 116.

79. See US Department of State website, www.state.gov/it/rts/pgtrpt/2993, Appendix C, posted on 29 April 2004.

80. South Asia Terrorism Portal, 'Bangladesh Assessment 2003', www.satp.org/ satporgtp/countries/bangladesh/index.htm.

81. Eliza Griswold, 'The Next Islamist Revolution?', *The New York Times Magazine* (Internet edition), 23 January 2005.

82. Ibid.

83. South Asia Terrorism Portal, 'Bangladesh Assessment 2000', www.satp.org/ satporgtp/countries/bangladesh/assessment2000.html.

84. Air Cdr (Retd) Ishfaq Ilahi Chowdhury NDC PSC, 'The Rise of Extremism in Bangladesh', *The Daily Star* (Internet edition), 15 September 2004. Chowdhury and Rana, 'Brihattara Chattagrame Jongi Tatparata—3'.

85. Chowdhury and Rana, 'Brihattara Chattagrame Jongi Tatparata—3'.

86. South Asia Terrorism Portal, 'Bangladesh Assessment 2002', www.satp.org/ satporgtp/countries/bangladesh/assessment2002.htm.

87. Jaideep Mazumdar, 'Harkat Cadres Part of Asif Reza Force', *The Hindustan Times* (New Delhi), 24 January 2002.

88. On Tuesday, 26 April 2005. Kolkata City Sessions Judge Basudeb Majumdar pronounced Aftab Ansari and six of his associates guilty of waging war against the state, overawing the Government of West Bengal, conspiracy and murder. See news report 'Ansari, 6 others convicted in USIS attack case', *The Pioneer* (New Delhi), 27 April 2005.

89. K.P.S. Gill, 'Bangladesh: A Lengthening Shadow of Terror', in *Islamist Extremism & Terrorism in South Asia*, January 2004, South Asia Terrorism Portal, www.satp.org/satporgtp/kpsgill/2003/chapter10.htm.

90. Rajamohan, 'Harkat-ul-Jihad-al-Islami Bangladesh'.

91. Ibid.

92. Lintner, 'Bangladesh', p. 20.

93. Ibid., p. 20.

94. The World Islamic Front for Jihad against Jews and Crusaders that Osama bin Laden set up in February 1998, is referred to both as 'World Islamic Front' and 'International Islamic Front'.

95. Afsir Karim, Maj. Gen. (Retd), 'Editorial Perspective: Changing Contours of Terrorism', *Aakrosh: Asian Journal on Terrorism and Internal Conflicts* 8(26), January 2005, p. 9.

96. Lintner, 'Bangladesh', p. 27.

97. Chowdhury and Rana, 'Brihattara Chattagrame Jongi Tatparata—3'.

98. Lintner, 'Bangladesh', p. 20.

99. Gill, 'Bangladesh'.

100. News report, 'Time to Think about Banning Jamaat Politics', *The Daily Star* (Internet edition), 6 March 2005.

101. Haroon Habib, 'Foreign Funds Fuel Growth of Bangladesh Zealots', *The Hindu* (New Delhi), 2 March 2001.

102. Abul Barkat, 'Bangladeshe Moulabader Arthaniti' (The Economics of Fundamentalism in Bangladesh) (Dhaka: Jatiya Sahitya Prakashani, 2005), p. 19.

103. Ibid.

104. Ibid., p. 17.

105. Ibid., p. 18. See table.

106. Ibid., p. 19.

107. Ibid.

108. Ibid. See n. 5 on p. 7.

109. Ibid., p. 13.

110. Ibid.

111. Ibid.

112. Chowdhury and Rana, 'Brihattara Chattagrame Jongi Tatparata—4: Cox's Bazaar o Bandarbane Cholchhe Islami Jongider Prashikshan, Ashankhya Masjid Madrasa Ghire Gode Uthechhe Prashikshan Kendra' (Militant Activity in Greater Chittagong: Training of Islamist Militants Continues in Cox's Bazar

and Bandarban, Training Centres have Developed Around in Innumerable Mosques and Madrasas in Deserted Hills). Upazila can be translated as 'sub-district'. Several *upazilas* make a district, or Zila, pronounced in Bengali as 'jela'.

113. Ibid.
114. Haroon Habib, 'The Menace of Militancy', *Frontline* (Chennai), 24 October 2003.
115. South Asia Terrorism Portal, 'Bangladesh Assessment 2003'.
116. News report, 'Sedition Charge Against Al-Hiqma Chief: Home's Nod Didn't Come in 15 Days', *The Daily Star* (Internet edition), 27 February 2005.
117. Ibid.
118. Ibid.
119. Ibid.

Six

Awakened Terror

Of all the fundamentalist Islamist terrorist organizations that have come to the fore in Bangladesh after HUJIB lowered its profile, the most prominent and dreaded is the JMJB. Its Operations Commander, who goes by various names—Siddiqul Islam, Azizur Rahman, Azizul Islam, Siddiqur Rahman[1]—but is commonly known as 'Bangla Bhai' or 'Bengal Brother', had, until the banning of both the JMJB and JMB on 23 February 2005, cast a pall of terror over the whole of north-western Bangladesh. According to the well-known NGO, Ain o Salish Kendro, there were 22 murders and a number of cases of people being tortured between 1 April and 31 July 2004. A woman, Rabeya, killed herself on 14 May 2004 after being raped by a JMJB militant the previous day.[2]

According to the JMJB's Shaekh (spiritual leader) Maulana Abdur Rahman, his organization had been active secretly since 1998. It was formed as the JMB, but began publicly calling itself the JMJB after a gunfight between its cadres and the police at a village in Joypurhat district on 15 August 2003. This clash, in which six police personnel were injured and three shotguns and 60 rounds of ammunition taken away from the police, led to the arrest of the Maulana's brother Ataur Rahman Ibne Abdullah, and 18 others.[3] The JMB, however, continued to function under its own name as well and the two organizations overlap almost totally both in structure and personnel. A JMB activist is often one of the JMJB as well and vice versa.

If the JMJB's doctrine and activities reflect the character of Islamist fundamentalism in Bangladesh, the entire train of events connected with its rise reflects the kind of circumstances that led to the growth of religious extremism in the country. The first was the establishment of a complex body comprising distinct but linked organizations functioning, disappearing and reappearing (sometimes with different names) according to directions from a Jamaat-dominated centre.

The second was the availability of support and huge amounts of funds, initially mostly from abroad, for conducting organizational work, propaganda and the training of militant cadres in subversion and commando operations. The third was support from Bangladesh's authorities at various levels and, fourth, their close links with Islamist terrorists in India facilitated by the highly porous nature of the India–Bangladesh border.

Beards and veils

To begin with, it is important to examine the kind of Islam the JMJB stands for. The organization compelled men to grow beards and wear the Muslim cap, and women to wear *burqa*s or *hijab*s in areas where it called the shots. Those who defied were subjected to physical abuse and/or had their properties damaged.[4] Like the Taliban, the JMJB is against almost all kinds of entertainment. It was behind bomb attacks on several musical, theatrical and dance performances and village fairs in north-western Bangladesh between 22 November 2004 and 15 January 2005.[5] A bomb attack on a horse-racing event on 22 November 2004 in Bogra District injured 20 persons. A string of similar attack on stages erected for dramatic and musical performances and gambling on 15 December injured at least 15 persons in the same district. Bomb blasts at two separate cultural events at Jamalpur and Sherpur Districts left, respectively, 25 and 10 persons—two of the latter critically—injured on 12 January 2005. Blasts at *jatra* performances in Bogra and Natore—in the former, when a woman was dancing on the stage—killed two and injured 70 on 15 January.[6] The widespread suspicion that the JMJB was responsible for these was confirmed by a militant belonging to the outfit, Shafiqullah, who was arrested on 16 January with a huge quantity of explosives. He stated that the JMJB was behind the attack in Bogra district at midnight on 14–15 January which killed one and injured 40. He also said that the organization's operatives would continue with bomb attacks on 'anti-Islamic' social and cultural organizations as well as NGOs including Brac[7] and Karitas.[8] The leader of 12 militants arrested in Natore, Forman Ali, told the police that his organization, the JMB, hated NGOs, 'as they are spoiling our women and plotting to control our country'.[9]

Shortly after Shafiqullah and Forman Ali's statements, Brac and Grameen Bank, two of the largest and most respected NGOs in

Bangladesh, known for their significant contribution to rural development, came under a series of bomb attacks. One on Brac's office at Kalai Upazila in Joypurhat District on 13 February 2005 left two employees critically injured. Another bomb attack on a Brac office in Porsha Upazila, Naogaon District, on 15 February, injured four. On the same day, two employees of the Grameen Bank were wounded in a similar attack on its office in a village in Ullapara Upazila of Sirajganj District. On the morning of 16 February, three powerful hand grenades were recovered from Brac's office in Rangpur town in Rangpur District.[10]

If there was any scope for doubting the JMJB's involvement in these attacks, it was removed by the Bangladesh Home Ministry's press note of 23 February 2005, on the government's action in banning it and the JMB. The note referred, by way of explaining the background to the government's tough decision, to the several incidents of bomb- and other attacks on social, cultural and religious events, and on several branches of Brac and the Grameen Bank, that had occurred in different parts of the country.[11]

As can be seen from the above, the JMJB, like the Taliban in Afghanistan, imposed its will in social and cultural matters through violence. People were compelled to cooperate. JMJB activists prepared lists of those who did not. Announcements were made that they would be proclaimed accomplices of the *Sarbaharas*.[12] According to several local leaders of the JMJB in Rajshahi, their list of those so identified contained the names of over a hundred persons belonging to different professions.

One gathers that besides collecting *ushr*[13], JMJB activists were extorting donations of between Tk 500 and 2,000 from local people for waging a jihad to establish 'Allah's law in Allah's land'.[14] Those who did not make a donation were threatened with identification as extremists, and with despatch to camps and torture.[15] The identification of a person as an extremist was a totally arbitrary process. On 30 June 2004, JMJB supporters abducted Yasin Ali Mridha, 22, Publicity Secretary of the Maria unit of the Awami League—whom they had earlier declared an extremist outlaw, along with three others—from his cousin's house in Bagmara Upazila. It was 8 P.M. at night. They took him to the Kudepara Ahadia Dakhil Madrasa and brutally beat him to death.[16] On 19 January 2005, JMJB activists attacked Mokbul Hussain Mridha, Chairman of the Sreepur Union Council and a local Awami League leader. The latter escaped with a bullet injury. The

JMJB men attacked an angry village mob that chased them after the shooting, with bombs, killing one person and injuring 30. Three of the JMJB men were then lynched.[17]

Those identified as supporters of the *Sarbaharas* were tortured brutally, sometimes to death, and their screams blared over loud-speakers to terrorize those in the entire neighbourhood. This happened with Golam Rabbani Mukul, a cultural activist, who was killed on 11 April 2004.[18] In another case, JMJB militants announced over loud-speakers on 19 May 2005 night that they would publicly slaughter in Naogaon the next morning two villagers who, they alleged, had links with Purba Banglar Communist Party (PBCP). The killing of two others, they said, was suspended as they could not gather 'evidence' against them. The JMJB asked its activists in different camps to be present at Vertigram camp in Atrai Upazila of Naogaon District at 10 A.M. on 20 May to witness the punishment. Reporters were called on their cellphones to be present at the scene and provide coverage.[19]

In the event, they killed three: Abdul Qaiyum, better known as Badshah Mia, Khejur Ali and Bashar. Badshah's body, which bore marks of savage torture, was strung up by the feet from a tree. The fate of the fourth person was not known. It was a gruesome event. According to eyewitnesses, scores of JMJB activists beat the victims with hockey sticks and bamboo poles for hours as loudspeakers re-layed their screams and groans.[20]

If the savagery of the JMJB's cadres recalls that of Al Badr, the Razakars and Al Shams during Bangladesh's liberation war in 1971, its worldview is almost identical with that of the Jamaat, Shibir, HUJIB, and the largest Islamist organization in western Bangladesh, AHAB. The latter's Ameer, Dr Muhammad Asadullah al-Galib (hence-forth, Galib), a teacher of Arabic at Rajshahi University, was arrested on 23 February 2005, the day the JMB and JMJB were banned. AHAB has stated in the Internet edition of its monthly magazine *Al-Tahreek*, which Galib had been running for eight years prior to his arrest, that it followed the 'Salafi Path'.[21] The Salafiyya movement stands for Islam's return to its purest roots and adherence to the way of life of the Prophet's immediate followers. It represents a reductionist view of the religion and holds that the ideal Islamic state can only be a replica of the first Islamic state. Hasan-al-Banna, who established the Ikhwan-al-Muslimeen in Egypt in 1928, described his movement as a 'Salafiyya message, a Sunni way, a sufi truth, a political organisation, an athletic group, cultural–educational union, an economic company, and a social idea'.[22] We have seen in the preceding chapter that Islamist fundamentalist make an estimated profit of Tk 12 billion from their huge complex of investments and enterprises, including NGOs.

Not only do the JMJB, JMB and AHAB have similar views on Islam, they belong to a network of organizations that cooperate with one another and are closely linked to the Jamaat and Shibir. Bangla Bhai was an activist of the Shibir when he was a student.[23] The organization's Shaekh, Maulana Abdur Rahman, was a Shibir activist when he was a student, and later, an activist of the Jamaat.[24] Galib has close links with the JMJB. A report in the *Daily Star* of 26 February 2005 quoted Bangladeshi intelligence agencies as saying that AHAB mosques, built with funds from the Saudi Arabian organization Hayatul Igachha (HI) and the Kuwait-based Revival of Islamic Heritage Society (RIHS), were used as JMJB strongholds.[25] Earlier, another report in the same paper had quoted police and intelligence sources as saying that AHAB was just a mass platform for JMB and most AHAB members had been involved in JMB's activities. Statements by militants arrested after the banning of the JMJB and JMB that Galib was their leader, and that he used to meet them at AHAB mosques clearly corroborated this.[26]

Galib's empire

According to a report in the *Janakantha* of 1 March 2005, thanks to the RIHS' patronage, Galib had built nearly 650 mosques, madrasas, orphanages and other such institutions since 1992.[27] According to another report, AHAB ran nearly 700 madrasas across Bangladesh.[28] Apart from showing how Islamist militant groups in Bangladesh cooperated with one another and used one another's resources, such reports reveal how money from the Middle East has been used to further Islamist militancy in that country. Both RIHS and HI have large offices in the upmarket Uttara neighbourhood in Dhaka. According to Anisuzzaman, a 'reliable source' had said that both organizations, particularly the RIHS, were instigating militant activity.[29] Significantly, under Executive Order 13224, the US Treasury Department had, on 9 January 2002, designated and blocked the assets of the Afghan Support Committee (ASC) and the Afghanistan and Pakistan offices of the RIHS and identified two individuals associated with these groups as financiers of terrorism. The individuals were Abu Bakr Al-Jaziri,

ASC's finance chief, and Abd al-Muhsin Al-Libi, office director of the RIHS and the ASC manager in Peshawar. The Executive Order, however, stated that there was 'no evidence at this point' that the diversion, through fraudulent means, of the money meant for widows and orphans to Al Qaeda was done with the knowledge of the RIHS in Kuwait.

Both RIHS and HI began functioning under a militant leader from India, Abdul Matin Salafi, who came to Bangladesh in the early 1980s as a Muballig (religious preacher). Galib, Maulana Samad Salafi of Rajshahi, Nurul Islam of Sirajganj and Shaekh Abdur Rahman of Jamalpur became his favourites because of their militant and extremist views. His activities, however, soon began to alarm the Bangladeshi authorities and, in 1988, he was forced to leave the country on three hours' notice following a high-level decision by the Ershad Government. He was also blacklisted.[30] It has been alleged that before departing, Abdul Matin Salafi had left vast amounts of Saudi rials and Kuwaiti dinars with Galib, lest these be confiscated by the Bangladeshi government.[31]

According to Anisuzzaman, Abdul Matin Salafi has maintained close links with Galib without being in Bangladesh and has been providing the latter with funds raised in the Middle East.[32] They have been working together on a secret mission to promote Islamist militancy and establish an Islamist state in Bangladesh. The method is violence. In his book *Daoat o Jihad* (literally 'Invitation and Jihad', it is generally translated as 'Call to Jihad'), a transcription of a speech he delivered at an AHAB conference in 1991, Galib advocated armed struggle for an Islamic revolution in the country.[33] He said toward the end, 'At every village, there will be a team of mujahids committed to reconstituting the society and reforming their personal, family and social lives according to the dictums of the Holy Qu'ran and Hadith. We want pure Islamic politics, not political Islam'.[34] In his speech, he mentioned the names of many past and present *mujahids* and recounted their deeds of heroism to inspire his audience to join in an armed uprising.[35]

A report in the *Daily Star* quotes a teacher at a Salafi madrasa as saying that AHAB had its own way of recruiting imams and *muezzins* for its mosques. Not just anybody could be an imam, because incumbents of these positions in their mosques were trained to bring about a social revolution through teaching and had to know how to recruit new members.[36] Anisuzzaman, however, wrote that a department of the RIHS appointed imams and *muezzins* in mosques built by the organization, to ensure that militant activity in those mosques remained secret. According to him, militant and physical training was given in these mosques after midnight on special days in the month.[37]

The JMJB's participation in violent activities is well known. That this was an offshoot of its doctrinal orientation becomes clear on recalling a news report in the *Daily Star* of 31 January 2005 stating that the JMJB had been, for the two preceding days, circulating, in the Bagmara Upazila of Rahshahi District, leaflets calling upon Muslims to prepare for jihad. The leaflets, entitled 'Sacrifice and Jihad for Allah', stated that organizations committed to jihad to foil the 'conspiracies of Kafirs' and preserve 'the glory of Islam' flourished in Bangladesh as in many other countries. They urged people to extend to such organizations any help they could.[38]

Earlier, on 30 June 2004, the police had arrested 32 JMJB militants in a raid on a mosque in an outlying village in southern Barguna District. It had also seized a number of books, leaflets and other printed material inspiring people to participate in jihad. A handwritten guide entitled 'Surprise Action' inspired militants to attack the Prime Minister's Office, police stations, and paramilitary and other forces in case of resistance. Also among the items seized was a booklet on how to use AK-47 rifles and attack police stations, and maps of important areas. The books seized included *Jongi Prashikshaner Kalakoushal* (Tactics of Militant Training), *Eso Kafelay Jai* (Come, Let's Go on Pilgrimage) and *Jihad Santras Noy Rahamat* (Jihad is not Terrorism but a Blessing) edited by Mawlana Abdullah Al Azhar, and *Musalmander Guerrilla Juddher Poddhoti* (Methods of Guerrilla Warfare by Muslims) edited by Mawlana Mashruf Al Azhar.[39]

A look at Galib's emergence, which attracted considerable attention, along with that of Abdur Rahman and Bangla Bhai, as Islamic militant activity in north-western and western Bangladesh became a public and media concern, is instructive. It tends to corroborate the accounts in Chapter Two of attempts being made, albeit abroad, to revive the Jamaat in Bangladesh and seek the latter's reunion with Pakistan. The effort, which also involved Bangladesh's Islamization, came to be made openly almost immediately after the assassination of Sheikh Mujibur Rahman on 15 August 1975. We have already seen that on 3 May 1976, Abu Sadat Muhammad Sayem, who had become Chief Martial Law Administrator on 7 November 1975, issued a proclamation repealing the provision in Article 38 of Bangladesh's Constitution which forbade the formation of parties on a religious basis. This made it possible for political parties like the Jamaat and the Muslim League, which had been declared illegal, to participate in politics again.

Then a student in Dhaka University, Galib left an organization called Jomiyat-e-Ahle Hadith in 1978 and set up one called Ahle-Hadith Juba Sangha (AHJS). While doing so, he said that there was a need to wage jihad against Islamic fallacies, including the *mazar* culture, to establish Islamic rule in the country. In 1980, he left Dhaka University, where he had a teaching job, and joined Rajshahi University as a lecturer. Rajshahi now became the base of the AHJS, which launched its public activities in 1990. In 1994, Galib formed AHAB, its women's wing, a welfare organization called Tawhid Trust, and a publication wing called Hadith Foundation Bangladesh.[40]

With huge amounts of funds available, the AHAB, JMB and JMJB —in the case of the last since it was founded—steadily expanded both their organizational infrastructure and following. According to Maulana Abdur Rahman, Shaekh of JMJB, the latter's highest decision-making body was the Majlis-e-Shura. He was the Ameer while Bangla Bhai was one of the seven members. Its members and supporters formed three tiers. The first comprised of Ehsars recruited as full-time activists whom it had trained all over Bangladesh and on whom it spent Tk 700,000 per month and who acted according to the directives of the higher echelons.[41] The second tier comprised Gayeri Ehsars, part-time activists who numbered over 100,000. The third tier was made up of those who cooperated indirectly with the JMJB.

AHAB sought to cast the lives of people in its Islamist mould from their childhood. All students of its madrasas had to work with one of its front organizations. Those upto Class Seven had to be affiliated to its children's wing, Sonamoni (*sona* is gold; *moni* a jewel or a precious stone; both in Bangladesh and in West Bengal children are affectionately addressed as Sonamoni). Students of higher classes had to join AHJS and remain there until they were old and fit enough to join AHAB itself.

While the availability of huge amounts of funds greatly helped the AHAB, JMB and JMJB to expand their organizations and support bases, the JMJB's fight against the violence and lawlessness unleashed by extremist Left parties, particularly the PBCP, inclined a large section of the people and politicians in western and north-western Bangladesh to welcome its emergence and support its activities. The JMJB, of course, furthered its own agenda while combating Left extremists. Haroon

Habib quotes (without naming) a leading secular writer and education-ist at Rajshahi University as saying that JMJB activists were taking advantage of the villagers' aversion to Left extremists, and that their ultimate goal was spreading their 'ultra-Wahhabi doctrine among the rural folk'.[42] Not only the people but also leaders of the BNP and Jamaat strongly supported Bangla Bhai. Several of them participated in the rally and meetings held by armed JMJB militants in Rajshahi city on 23 May 2004 as a show-of-force exercise.[43]

Support for the JMJB and Bangla Bhai extended up to the higher echelons of the BNP to say nothing of the Jamaat, with which it has had close links. A cabinet minister, a deputy minister and several legislators from the Greater Rajshahi area strongly backed Bangla Bhai. They told Prime Minister Khaleda Zia, after she had ordered his arrest in May 2004, that the failure of the police to provide pro-tection from Left extremists prompted the people of the Greater Rajshahi area to launch the JMJB and hunt the extremists down in cooperation with law-enforcement agencies. Halting the JMJB in its tracks would only fuel Left extremist activity. The same newspaper report that stated this also quoted an official in Bangladesh's Home Ministry as saying that two religion-based parties, including the Jamaat, not only backed Bangla Bhai and the JMJB but also helped both with manpower and light weapons.[44]

Graphic coverage in Bangladesh's lively media of the violence unleashed by Bangla Bhai and his men, and accounts in the inter-national media of growing Islamist violence in Bangladesh targeting secular politicians and intellectuals, however, led to strong pressure being brought on Begum Zia's government for taking firm action against the JMJB. At the international level, pressure came from donor countries and their diplomatic representatives in Bangladesh, who were increasingly alarmed by the spread of fundamentalist Islamist activity in a country known for its practice of moderate and tolerant Islam. At the national level, pressure came not only from the opp-osition parties and the intelligentsia but also from within the BNP. A section of the latter's senior ministers and leaders felt that there could be no room for a private army like the JMJB conducting an anti-PBCP drive parallel to that by the law-enforcement agencies of the state.

Their demand for firm action against Bangla Bhai was, however, neutralized by the section of the BNP and Jamaat that came out strongly in his favour. As a result, no effective action was taken against him and both the organization of which he was the 'Operations

Commander' and he himself remained at large even after Prime Minister Khaleda Zia had ordered his arrest and the Cabinet Committee on Law and Order had asked the Home Ministry to take immediate action against him.[45] The fact that the police in the affected areas were hand-in-glove with Bangla Bhai and the JMJB was doubtless also an important factor. Even senior officers reportedly did little to prevent savage public executions despite prior information. Told by a correspondent of the *Daily Star* over the telephone on 19 May 2004 that JMJB militants had abducted four men and were asking people, over the loudspeaker, to come and witness their public execution on 20 May, the Superintendent of Police (SP), Naogaon District, said that he had no information about the matter. When the correspondent insisted that such announcements were being made, he was told in exasperation, 'Police are on the alert. I don't know how you got this information!'[46]

It did little credit to the SP or to the intelligence wing of the district police establishment he headed that he did not have prior information of the planned murders. He should at least have taken steps to stop the murders or warn the SPs of the neighbouring districts of the possibility of such a development in their districts as well, after his conversation with the *Daily Star*'s correspondent. His failure to do so was clearly tantamount to grave dereliction of duty.

On the following day, the police did nothing to stop the murders though the screams of the victims being tortured to death were blared over loudspeakers. Nor was any action taken subsequently against any of the JMJB camps where the gruesome executions took place. Golam Mostapha, brother of cultural activist Golam Rabbani Mukul who was tortured to death on 11 April 2004, has alleged that the police did not record his complaint against 12 JMJB men, including Bangla Bhai, accusing them of murder. He further added that though the police did not even visit the spot of the murder for investigation, it recorded a case in which no one featured as an accused![47] A torture victim said that Bangla Bhai and his men hung people by their feet and tortured them in front of the police, and that the SP, Rajshahi District, Masud Mia, did not listen to any complaint against the JMJB.[48]

The extent to which police in the Greater Rajshahi area were complicit with the crimes committed by JMJB militants and the warm ties even its senior officers had with the latter became clear from the JMJB's demonstration on 23 May 2004. On that day, travelling by hundreds of motorbikes, three micro buses, 60 buses and half a dozen trucks, and armed with large choppers, curved knives, hockey sticks, bamboo poles and weapons inside bags, about 5,000 of its activists went around Rajshahi town in a procession and held meetings where speakers reiterated their determination to 'eliminate the outlaws' and threatened to kill journalists for what they claimed was fabricated reporting. One of the speakers, Prof. Lutfur Rahman, said, 'We are pledge-bound to eliminate the outlaws. We will stay as long as the outlaws are here. But reporters are falsely accusing us of killing, torturing and oppressing people. They do not know that their pen might stop some day.'[49]

Several hundred policemen, who were deployed at several points of the city, watched silently. They not only took no action against the armed processionists but seemed at places even to be escorting them around and acting as their security guards. Asked why no action was taken against the processionists even though they were armed, an Assistant Commissioner of Rajshahi Metropolitan Police said, 'Why should we act against somebody if he wants to hold a peaceful gathering?' Asked about the hockey sticks, large choppers and poles, he shot back, 'Are these weapons? People can, of course, carry these to protect themselves.'[50]

The Deputy Commissioner (DC) of Rajshahi District, Aziz Hasan, the Deputy Inspector General (DIG) of Police, Rajshahi Range, Noor Mohammad, and the SP, Rajshahi District, Masud Mia, received the leaders of the procession, who submitted a memorandum addressed to the State Minister for Home, Lutfozzaman Babar. It said that the JMJB brought peace back to outlaw-infested areas but a section of the press and political parties were misleading the nation. Stating that curbing terrorism was 'not the work of the Government alone', it said that the 'brave people of Bagmara' had united against the terrorists and were 'helping the law-enforcers eliminate the outlaws as none of the ruling or opposition parties was able to resist them'. It claimed that all political leaders, 'including ministers and law-makers irrespective of parties', were supporting the JMJB.

While the DC and DIG said they would send the memorandum to higher authorities, SP Masud Mia reportedly told the leaders that the police welcomed the help they were providing in eliminating *Sarbaharas* from Rajshahi. He added, 'We must cooperate with you in the coming days so that people can rest without fear.'[51] Explaining the police's soft attitude towards the JMJB, he is further reported to have said, 'Those who have come forward to resist the *Sarbaharas* who used to terrorize people through killings in broad daylight are, of course, common people. Why would the *Sarbaharas* fear such people unless they carried poles?[52] Indeed, Masud Mia is even said to have denied the existence of Bangla Bhai. He has been quoted as saying, 'There is nobody called Bangla Bhai, nor any party called the JMJB. It is the local people who have forged resistance. I have come to know of Bangla Bhai through newspapers.' To be fair to him, however, he is not the only person to have denied Bangla Bhai's existence. Rajshahi range DIG Noor Mohammad did so as well, on 23 June 2004.[53]

The police being hand-in-glove with the JMJB, it is hardly surprising that investigation into such cases as were registered against it made little headway. Even by the time both the JMJB and JMB were banned, on 23 February 2005, the police had made virtually no progress in investigating the 22 cases of murder and the more numerous instances of torture that had occurred between 1 April 2004 and 31 July 2004. It had merely submitted one final report in one case and a chargesheet in respect of another.[54] The DIG, Rajshahi Range, Noor Mohammad, attributed the poor progress to lack of complainants, evidence and witnesses.[55] It should, however, be clear from what has been said above that this was not the case. Complaints were not registered at police stations. Also, policemen who are unwilling to look for evidence are unlikely to find it.

An important reason why police officers and men backed the JMJB so much was, of course, that they had a common enemy in the PBCP. Lacking in both firepower and manpower, they were unwilling to arrest Bangla Bhai and take tough measures against the JMJB, because they felt that they would be vulnerable without his and his organization's support. A senior police officer said in May 2004, 'We have information that the outlaws, now much more active, have gathered sophisticated firearms, including AK-47 rifles.'[56] The same report quoted the SP of Naogaon District, Fazlur Rahman, as saying that he had information that PBCP cadres were marking police stations for attack.

The divergence of views at the highest levels of the government over Bangla Bhai's arrest, which has been noted earlier in this chapter, and the support the JMJB's Operations Commander received from the local leaders of the BNP and Jamaat, must also have inhibited the police. If nothing else, they must have taken the hint when all JMB militants who were arrested following the clash with the police at a village in Joypurhat district on 15 August 2003, in which six policemen were injured and three shotguns and 60 cartridges were snatched from the police,[57] were released after a few days. Not only that, 'higher authorities' reportedly transferred several police officers responsible for the arrests.[58]

The question of intervention from above has a crucial bearing on the fight against Bangla Bhai, the JMJB and the JMB. The measures taken till the time of writing have certainly not been enough to put them out of action for ever. Bangla Bhai and Maulana Abdur Rahman remain at large, as do thousands of their followers. They can revive the organization—under another name if the present ban is not lifted—should the present drive against them peter out after a few months. The chances of this happening can hardly be brushed aside. Pressure to relax the drive can come from both local and national levels. We have already noted the conduct of the police at the local level. While some just looked the other way when Bangla Bhai and his men extorted money, murdered and tortured, others extended active help.

One of the latter was, allegedly, the SP of Rajshahi District, Masud Mia. He was seen to be particularly close to Bangla Bhai, who had reportedly visited him at his office on 24 April 2004 and was photographed as he came out. The Rajshahi SP had allegedly helped the JMJB chief to escape on several occasions even after Prime Minister Khaleda Zia had ordered his arrest.[59] Following repeated intelligence branch reports about his links with the JMJB leader, the police was asked to investigate the matter. A special report, drawn up on the basis of the investigations, is said to have stated that the unwillingness of the SP to arrest Bangla Bhai had enabled the latter to escape on several occasions.

Masud Mia, of course, has strongly denied the allegation. He told the *Daily Star* in the course of an hour-long conversation, 'Why should I help Bangla Bhai? He is a criminal. You made him the most powerful criminal. So where is he hiding now?' Asked about the special report, he questioned the manner in which it was obtained and said, 'You [journalists] must have supplied the allegations against me.' Not just that, he denied having met Bangla Bhai and asserted that the photographs showing the latter coming out of his office had been artificially produced—a charge the photojournalists concerned strongly refuted, saying that they had bromide copies of the photographs.[60]

It is, of course, not the police alone who have been helping Bangla Bhai and his men. Court documents have been disappearing mysteriously.

One set of these related to a bomb attack in a Bogra village. These documents, which should have been kept at the court of the first class magistrate trying the case, were, according to a report, kept illegally at the DC's office under lock and key. The report stated that the DC could not be reached despite repeated efforts.[61] Earlier, documents of a case filed under the Explosive Substances Act, in which three JMJB activists had been arrested following a statement by Shafiqullah recorded by a first class magistrate, had also been lost. It was the same Shafiqullah who had said that the JMJB was behind the blast at a *jatra* performance in Bogra on 14–15 January midnight and who had added that the organization's activists would continue with bomb attacks on 'anti-Islamic' social and cultural organizations and NGOs.[62]

Clearly, Bangla Bhai's supporters were—and perhaps still are—strongly entrenched in all sections of the administration in the Greater Rajshahi area and could hamper—if not frustrate—action against him and the JMJB and JMB. The same, it seems, applied to the government at the national level. A person who had came under scrutiny in this context was none other than the country's Home Secretary, Muhammad Omar Farooq. On 24 February, the day after the JMB and JMJB were banned, a number of BNP legislators from northern Bangladesh said that the crackdown on Islamist militants had come too late and doubted whether it would succeed. They also questioned the wisdom of retaining Home Secretary Omar Farooq in office. They blamed him for not helping the government to initiate measures against the emerging fundamentalist groups in time and alleged that he patronized fundamentalists and had links with the Jamaat.[63] Stating that it was the invisible hand of the Home Secretary that was behind the confiscation of Prof. Abu Sayeed's *Aghoshito Juddher Blueprint* (Blueprint of an Undeclared War) and *Brutal Crime Document* on 18 February 2005, Shahriar Kabir had, in an article in the *Dainik Janakantha* of 24 February 2005, cited a report about the Home Secretary in the 28 January 2005 issue of the weekly, *Saptahik 2000*. According to it, conversations with people on the spot in Dhamrai, the Home Secretary's 'own area', had revealed that the fact that he was a Jamaatist was an 'open secret'. He had close ties with the Jamaat's policy-making circles. Even many senior leaders of the BNP did not want to trouble him because his reach went very far. Kabir further stated that the opposition parties had complained many times that the fact that the Home Secretary was a Jamaatist made the arrest and prolonged detention of militant leaders impossible. Not only that, even the 'self-proclaimed militant fundamentalist Bangla Bhai remained at large as late as nine months after the Prime Minister herself had ordered his arrest'.[64]

One can clearly see in these developments signs of the rise of a fundamentalist Islamist state within Bangladesh's present parliamentary democratic state. It was powerful enough to frustrate the execution of even the Prime Minister's orders for the arrest of a fundamentalist Islamist leader like Bangla Bhai. One could, of course, argue that accounts of the Bangladeshi government's collusive links with Bangla Bhai were exaggerated, and that the government finally banned the JMJB and JMB and arrested Galib. That, however, was hardly enough. Bangla Bhai and Maulana Abdur Rahman remained at large, as did thousands of their followers. As we have seen both the JMB and JMJB are part of a complex of interconnected fundamentalist Islamist organizations, which the Jamaat has done much to set up and which it dominates. With the drive against the JMJB and JMB gathering momentum, all their activists had to do was to melt into the ranks of HUJIB or the Shibir or Jamaat itself and wait for the drive to slacken and an opportunity to revive both organizations under different names or to combine the two in a new one to present itself.

The fear that the drive would soon peter out was expressed almost immediately after it was launched on 23 February 2005 with the banning of the JMB and JMJB and Galib's arrest. As we have seen, it was known from the time that the JMJB started its killings and Bangla Bhai shot into public attention, that the government was not keen to act against him and his outfit. In fact, important ministers did not even accept that he or his organization existed. The denial of Bangla Bhai's existence by Bangladesh's Industries Minister Matiur Rahman Nizami, Ameer of the Jamaat, on 22 July 2004 has already been noted. Lutfozzaman Babar, State Minister for Home, had told the BBC as late as 26 January 2005, 'We don't know officially about the existence of the JMJB. Only some so-called newspapers are publishing reports on it. We don't have their Constitution in our record.'[65] And this, after having said at a press conference on the same day, 'We do not know any Bangla or English Bhai . . . No Bhai is important to us. We have made a clear and clean order to arrest him.'[66] Even Prime Minister Begum Zia had herself denied his existence during a conversation with editors in August that year.[67]

It was widely believed that pressure from donor countries, particularly the United States and the European Union, which became particularly acute after the attacks on the offices of Brac and Grameen

Bank, had compelled Bangladesh's government to take tough measures. State Home Minister Babar told the BBC on the night of 23 February itself, 'We did not receive any international pressure to ban them. The Government has done it out of its own sense of responsibility.' But the fact that the ban was imposed on 23 February, the day when a meeting of donor countries organized by the European Union, the World Bank and the United States' State Department, began at Watergate Hotel in Washington, DC, was no secret. Nor was it a secret that the purpose was to discuss a strategy for aid to Bangladesh against the background of rising Islamist militancy, violation of human rights, the declining law and order situation, and poor governance in that country.[68]

While the government of Bangladesh was under strong external compulsion to act, fundamentalist Islamist parties allied with the BNP along with Bangla Bhai's supporters within the BNP, opposed the drive immediately after it was launched. Senior leaders of the Jamaat, IOJ and Bangladesh Jatiya Party[69] questioned the role of the police in arresting 'religious-minded people' and framing them as militants. Some of them even said that some influential BNP leaders had ordered the crackdown to cover up the government's failure to arrest the real culprits behind the grenade attack on the Awami League rally on 21 August 2004. In a joint statement, IOJ leader Allama Azizul Huq and IOJ Chairman Fazlul Huq Amini protested against the drive and declared that coalition partners should have been contacted before it was launched.[70] Later, the party asked the government to stop raiding the *quomi* madrasas and harassing their activists throughout the country, threatening to take a tough stand if it did not.[71] This was hardly surprising. The IOJ supports each of the 15,000 *quomi* madrasas in Bangladesh and the importance it attaches to them became clear when Amini said at a rally on 1 March 2005 that an Islamist revolution would be brought about in Bangladesh through these.[72]

The pressure soon began to have an effect. A report in the *Daily Star* on 5 March 2005, which dwelt on the opposition to the drive, stated that 'internal tension' had somewhat slowed it down. The result was soon in evidence. Forty-two JMJB cadres who had earlier received bail were released from Rajshahi Central Jail on 7 April 2005.[73] According to lawyers, delay by the police in conducting investigations had paved the way for their enlargement on bail. Needless to say, their release made their conviction most difficult. Many villagers who had fled home after being tortured by JMJB cadres had returned after the latter's arrest. They had started fleeing again, fearing reprisals for having talked to the press about their torture. One therefore hardly need be surprised if they did not dare to provide evidence and the cases against JMJB cadres fell flat because of lack of evidence.

There are other instances. According to a report, investigation into the murder of Prof. Mohammad Yunus, who was killed while he was on a morning walk on 24 December 2004, had virtually stopped after the police had found out, following preliminary probes, that one of his killers was an activist of the Shibir.[74] The activist, an accused in several cases of murder and extortion, and one of the four who had attacked the victim, was the only one whom an eyewitness to the murder could identify. According to the police, who refused to name him, two other sources had corroborated the eyewitness's version. If this could happen in the case of Professor Yunus, a highly respected academic who was President of the Bangabandhu Parishad at Rajshahi University and a Vice-President of the Bangladesh Economic Association, whose murder had sent shockwaves throughout Bangladesh, one can imagine how powerful was the pressure that the Islamist fundamentalists exercised—and do at the time of writing—on Bangladesh's BNP-led coalition government.

The pressure that had led to slow investigations was effective largely because of the BNP's electoral calculations. To some extent at least, its massive tally of 191 out of the 300 elected seats in the National Parliament in the elections on 1 October 2001 was due to the solid votes it received from the Jamaat and the IOJ. These votes would be lost to it in the next elections, scheduled to be held in 2006, if these two parties walked out of the alliance. While the BNP had never been a fundamentalist Islamist party, and while many of the senior leaders were seriously worried about the increase in the strength of the Jamaat and the IOJ through skilful use of governmental machinery, they abhorred the prospect of the Awami League returning to power.

The BNP's dealing with Bangla Bhai, the JMJB and JMB, therefore, mirrored the broader dilemma it faced in coping with Islamist forces in Bangladesh. In sharp contrast, the latter were—and are—very clear about their goal of turning the country into a fundamentalist theocratic Islamist state and have been—and are—relentlessly moving in that direction. Their effort is a part of the global Islamist movement spearheaded by Al Qaeda and the Taliban. Maj. Gen. (Retd) Afsir Karim writes, 'Bangladesh Muslims are generally followers of moderate Islamic norms and the fundamentalist trends noticeable lately are not a part of natural process, but [represent] a deliberate attempt by the Al-Qaeda-led Islamic jihadi groups to change cultural values. Al Qaeda is in the process of creating bases and opening a new area of operations here with the aim of extending [its] influence over certain parts of South and South-East Asia.'[75]

The assistance that the Jamaat and allied organizations provide to secessionist groups active in north-eastern India with the help of Bangladesh's DGFI, which in turn works in close coordination with Pakistan's ISI, has, since 1998, become a part of Al Qaeda's greater South Asian and South-East Asian designs. The India connection of Bangladeshi *jihadis*, however, goes deeper than that. Islamist militants in Bangladesh have established bases in India and are provided sanctuary by their counterparts as well as Indian rebels they help. As we have seen, Galib's mentor is an Indian, Abdul Matin Salafi, who left him with huge funds when he was peremptorily expelled from Bangladesh in 1988. Also, we have seen that he allegedly remained regularly in touch with Galib from outside Bangladesh, sending him money raised in the Middle East. According to Anisuzzaman, money came to Galib across Bangladesh's border with India along the Chapainawabganj and Rajshahi Districts. Anisuzzaman also wrote that the name of India's Lalgola border was heard in this connection and it was also said that Galib had a shelter there.[76]

Galib is alleged to have visited India, Pakistan and Afghanistan with fake travel documents. He reportedly had close relations with Afghan and Kashmiri mujahideen and entertained a number of them at his Naodapara madrasa in the early 1990s. As early as March 1993, intelligence agencies informed the higher echelons of the government of Bangladesh of his activities and sought permission to arrest him for interrogation. Nothing came of it. In 1998, he visited India on a business passport and spent 11 days with his spiritual leader, Maulana Abdul Matin Salafi. He, however, had gone without a 'no objection certificate' from the university authorities. For this, he was served a show-cause notice by the then Registrar of the University, Prof. Muhammad Yunus who, as has been seen, was murdered while he was on his morning walk on 24 December 2004.[77]

Investigations by the intelligence branch of the police in West Bengal in India, revealed that Galib had visited several madrasas in the border districts of North 24 Parganas, Malda and Murshidabad. But neither he nor his associates had valid travel documents. He, however, always had valid visas when he visited Aligarh Muslim University in Uttar

Pradesh on research work. West Bengal's intelligence branch suspected that he had links with the banned Students' Islamic Movement of India (SIMI) and also perhaps the Jamaatul Mujahideen in India.[78] Significantly, with the police hot on his trail, Bangla Bhai had reportedly slipped into West Bengal in the early hours of 3 March 2005, crossing the border somewhere in Naogaon District. The sources who said this to a reporter of the *Daily Star* added that Galib would return to Bangladesh once he received the 'green signal' from two Cabinet ministers from the northern part of the country who had been protecting him.[79] Indeed, seeking refuge in India's border districts seems to be a common practice with Bangladeshi Islamist fundamentalists on the run. According to a report, the Shibir activist who had been identified as one of the four murderers of Professor Yunus of Rajshahi University, had at least on occasion jumped bail and fled to India. He had returned to Rajshahi three days before the murder.[80]

Clearly, the border areas of West Bengal and Assam are in danger of becoming, in the parlance of guerrilla warfare, safe rear areas for Bangladesh's fundamentalist Islamist militants. This is yet another indication of the planned and highly methodical way in which the latter, led by the Jamaat, are going about to capture power in Bangladesh with the aim of turning it into an Islamist state like Afghanistan under the Taliban, and making it the staging ground for the Islamization of the whole of South and South-east Asia. It is this that gives to the continued influx of illegal Bangladeshi migrants, who constitute support bases for fundamentalist Islamist terrorists, into the border districts of India a dangerous dimension and precludes regarding it as an economic migration in search of jobs and livelihood.

Notes

1. Haroon Habib, 'A Threat from Militant Islam', *Frontline*, 2 June 2004 and 'Govt divided on Bangla Bhai arrest', *The Daily Star* (Internet edition), 23 May 2004.
2. News report, 'Dozens of Bangla Bhai Cases Stalled', *The Daily Star* (Internet edition), 27 January 2005.
3. News report, 'Cops, Militants Trade Fire at Joypurhat', *The Daily Star* (Internet edition), 16 August 2004, and Julfikar Ali Manik, 'JMJB Mentor Rahman Evades Probing Eyes', *The Daily Star* (Internet edition), 25 February 2005.
4. Eliza Griswold, 'The Next Islamist Revolution?', *The New York Times Magazine* (Internet edition), 23 January 2005; and Haroon Habib, 'A Threat from Militant Islam'.

5. Shariful Islam, 'Jatra Attacks Instill New Fears in Rural Life', *The Daily Star* (Internet edition), 21 January 2005. *Jatra* is an open-air opera or dramatic performance.

6. Ibid.

7. 'Brac' stands for Bangladesh Rural Advancement Committee.

8. News report, 'Cultural Outfits, NGOs, JMJB's Next Target', *The Daily Star* (Internet edition), 31 January 2005.

9. News report, 'Two More JMJB Men Held', *The Daily Star* (Internet edition), 7 February 2005.

10. News report, 'Grameen Bank under Bomb Attacks: Home Ministry', *The Daily Star* (Internet edition), 17 February 2005.

11. News report, 'JMJB, Jamaatul behind the Bomb Attacks', *The Daily Star* (Internet edition) 24 February 2005.

12. *Sarbahara* is the accepted Bengali term for 'proletariat'. It is commonly used in Bangladesh to describe members of the Purba Banglar Communist Party or Communist Party of East Bengal, a Maoist political party.

13. *Ushr* is a tax on agricultural income, and *zakat* a tax on wealth. The payment of both is mandatory under Islam.

14. News report, 'Rajshahite Aaj Jagrata Muslim Janatar Samabesh' or 'Jagrata Muslim Janata's Meeting in Rajshahi Today', *The Daily Star* (Internet edition), 23 May 2005.

15. Ibid.

16. Anwar Ali, 'Bangla Bhai Men Kill Awami League Leader at Madrasa', *The Daily Star* (Internet edition), 1 July 2004.

17. News report, '50 Injured as Bangla Bhai Men Clash with Police', *The Daily Star* (Internet edition), 25 January 2005.

18. News report, 'No Progress in Cases against JMJB', *The Daily Star* (Internet edition), 7 February 2005.

19. News report, 'Bangla Bhai Men Slaughter Two Today', *The Daily Star* (Internet edition), 20 May 2005.

20. News report, 'In Cold Blood They Beat Them Dead', *The Daily Star* (Internet edition), 21 May 2005.

21. News report, 'AHAB Men on the Run, JMJB Flouts Ban', *The Daily Star* (Internet edition), 26 February 2005.

22. Quoted in Khalid Bin Sayeed, *Western Dominance and Political Islam: Challenge and Response* (Karachi: Oxford University Press, 1995), p. 38.

23. Ibid.

24. Julfikar Ali Manik, 'JMJB Mentor Rahman Evades Probing Eyes'.

25. Ibid.

26. News report, 'Govt Finally Cracks Down on the Militants, Galib Arrested' *The Daily Star* (Internet edition), 24 February 2005.

27. Anisuzzaman, 'Madhyaprachyabhittik Duti Sangsthar Karjakram Niye Goendara Udbigna' (Detectives Worried over the Programmes of Two Middle East-Based Organizations), *Prothom Alo* (Internet edition), 1 March 2005.

28. News item, 'AHAB Men on the Run, JMJB Flouts Ban'.

29. Anisuzzaman, 'Madhyaprachyabhittik Duti Sangsthar Karjakram Niye Goendara Udbigna'.

30. Ibid. See also news report, 'Govt Finally Cracks Down on the Militants, Galib Arrested'.
31. Anisuzzaman, 'Madhyaprachyabhittik Duti Sangsthar Karjakram Niye Goendara Udbigna'.
32. Ibid.
33. News item, 'AHAB Men on the Run, JMJB Flouts Ban'.
34. Ibid., as quoted.
35. Ibid.
36. News report, 'AHAB Men on the Run, JMJB Flouts Ban'. A *muezzin* sounds the call to prayer from a mosque.
37. Anisuzzaman, 'Madhyaprachyabhittik Duti Sangsthar Karjakram Niye Goendara Udbigna'.
38. News report, 'Bangla Bhai Men Circulate Leaflets Calling for Jihad', *The Daily Star* (Internet edition), 31 January 2005.
39. News report, 'Islamic Militants Nabbed in Raid on Barguna Mosque', *The Daily Star* (Internet edition), 1 July 2004.
40. News report, 'Govt Finally Cracks Down on Militants, Galib Arrested'.
41. Ibid.
42. Habib, 'A Threat from Militant Islam'.
43. Arifur Rahman, Anu Mustapha and Mamunur Rashid, 'Bangla Bhaiyer Shasastra Cadre-ra Police Paharay Rajshahi Dapiye Bedalo' (Bangla Bhai's Armed Cadres Stomped Around in Rajshahi under Police Protection), *Prothom Alo* (Internet edition), 24 May 2004.
44. News report, 'Govt Divided over Bangla Bhai's Arrest', *The Daily Star* (Internet edition), 23 May 2004.
45. Ibid.
46. News report, 'Bangla Bhai Men Slaughter Two Today'.
47. News report, 'No Progress in Cases Against JMJB'.
48. News report, 'Dozens of Bangla Bhai Cases Stalled'.
49. Rahman, Mustapha and Rashid, 'Bangla Bhaiyer Shasastra Cadre-ra Police Paharay Rajshahi Dapiye Bedalo'; and news report, 'Police Escort JMJB in Rajshahi Showdown', *The Daily Star* (Internet edition), 24 May 2004.
50. Rahman, Mustapha and Rashid, 'Bangla Bhaiyer Shasastra Cadre-ra Police Paharay Rajshahi Dapiye Bedalo'.
51. News report, 'Police Escort JMJB in Rajshahi Showdown'.
52. Rahman, Mustapha and Rashid, 'Bangla Bhaiyer Shasastra Cadre-ra Police Paharay Rajshahi Dapiye Bedalo'.
53. News report, 'Eating Own Words', *The Daily Star* (Internet edition), 24 February 2005.
54. News report, 'Dozens of Bangla Bhai Cases Stalled'.
55. Ibid.
56. News report, 'Cops Reluctant to Capture Bangla Bhai', *The Daily Star* (Internet edition), 25 May 2004.
57. News report, 'Cops, Militants Trade Fire in Joypurhat, 19 Held', *The Daily Star* (Internet edition), 16 August 2004.
58. Julfikar Ali Manik, 'JMJB Mentor Rahman Evades Probing Eyes'.

59. News report, 'Rajshahi SP Helped Bangla Bhai to Flee', *The Daily Star* (Internet edition), 1 March 2005.
60. Ibid.
61. News report, 'Documents of Another Case against JMJB Men Missing', *The Daily Star* (Internet edition), 18 February 2005.
62. Ibid.
63. News report, 'BNP MPs Hail the News, Doubt Home Secy's Role', *The Daily Star* (Internet edition), 25 February 2005. The Home Secretary, Omar Farooq, has since retired, but has been given another important assignment by the Bangladesh Government.
64. Shahriar Kabir, 'Abu Sayeed-er Boi Jabdo Korle Ki Jamaater Shadojantra Bandho Hobe' (Will the Confiscation of Abu Sayeed's Book End Jamaat's Conspiracy?), *Dainik Janakantha* (Internet edition), 25 February 2005. Bangla Bhai remains at large at the time of correcting the proofs of this book in October 2005.
65. News report, 'Mystery Shrouds Bangla Bhai's Power', *The Daily Star* (Internet edition), 27 January 2005.
66. News report, 'Eating Own Words'.
67. Ibid.
68. News report, 'Washington Meet Begins', *The Daily Star* (Internet edition), 24 February 2005.
69. The Bangladesh Jatiya Party (Bangladesh National Party) was formed by H.M. Ershad, who ruled Bangladesh from 1983 to 1990.
70. News report, 'Drive against Militants: Strain Within the Coalition over Govt Crackdown', *The Daily Star* (Internet edition), 5 March 2005.
71. Ibid.
72. Ibid.
73. News report, '42 Bangla Bhai Men Released from Jail', *The Daily Star* (Internet edition), 8 April 2005.
74. News report, 'Prof Yunus' Murder Probe Stalled after "Shibir Link" Found', *The Daily Star* (Internet edition), 20 March 2005.
75. Afsir Karim, Maj. Gen. (Retd), 'Editorial Perspective: Changing Contours of Terrorism', *AAKROSH*, January 2005.
76. Anisuzzaman, 'Madhyaprachyabhittik Duti Sangsthar Karjakram Niye Goendara Udbigna'.
77. News report, 'An RU Teacher with a Long Militant Track', *The Daily Star* (Internet edition), 18 February 2005; and news report, 'Govt Finally Cracks Down on Militants, Galib Arrested'.
78. News report, 'India Starts Probing Galib's Links in West Bengal', *The Daily Star* (Internet edition), 6 March 2005.
79. News report, 'Bangla Bhai Slips into India', *The Daily Star* (Internet edition), 5 March 2005.
80. News report, 'Prof Yunus' Murder Probe Stalled after "Shibir Link" Found'.

Seven
The Sledgehammer

Is the Islamist thrust in Bangladesh irreversible? For an answer one needs to look at the dynamics of the thrust, which derives its strength from two parallel processes. The first is the BNP's attempt to stay on in power by defeating the Awami League and its allies in the general elections due before October 2006. The second is the efforts by the Jamaat, which spearheads the fundamentalist Islamist offensive in Bangladesh, and the IOJ, another constituent of the country's BNP-led four-party ruling coalition, to use their participation in the government to push their Islamist agenda and capture power.

As we shall see, the BNP as well as the fundamentalist Islamist parties have relied heavily on violence and state repression to achieve their respective goals. Their common target is the Awami League, which stands for a secular Bangladesh with a modern ethos. The Jamaat and IOJ's objectives are both political and religious. Therefore, they attack not only the Awami League and its front organizations but all sections and people whose views and activities they consider un-Islamic—the minorities, cultural groups, liberal intellectuals, writers, film-makers, playwrights, poets, NGOs, women's organizations and judges who have pronounced against obscurantist practices.

Violence as an instrument of political domination is of critical importance to the complex of Islamist parties and terrorist organizations clustered around the Jamaat because their respective mass bases are very small. The Jamaat, which won 17 seats, received only 4.28 per cent of the total votes polled in the 2001 elections.[1] The other fundamentalist Islamist parties fared even worse. The Islami Oikya Jote, which won 2 seats, received only 0.68 per cent of the votes polled. The Jamaat-e-Ulema Islam Bangladesh, the Bangladesh Khelafat Andolan and the Islami Shashantantra Andolan (Islamic Constitution Movement), none of which won a single seat, received 0.03 per cent, 0.02 per cent and 0.01 per cent of the popular vote respectively.

The Jamaat, Shibir, IOJ, HUJIB and other Islamist organizations have, therefore, to rely on force and terror to impose their version of a reductionist, Talibanized Islam on Bangladesh's moderate and culturally plural Islamic society and polity. As it is, their *jihadi* doctrine, intolerance and fanaticism, links with Al Qaeda and the Taliban, glorification of martyrdom and their minatory posture and rhetoric tend to incline their militant cadres, trained in the use of arms, towards violence. If the confluence of necessity, doctrine and ethos is significant, so is the fact that most of the victims of the violence that has occurred during the last decade have been opponents of Islamist fundamentalism or proponents of secular and modern values.

The BNP is not a fundamentalist Islamist party, though it has a section that is close to the Jamaat. Its support base is almost as—if not as—large as the Awami League's. It has come to power twice through elections. Since the size of its following did not prevent it from losing the 1996 general elections, its resort to large-scale violence is clearly the result of two things. The first is its determination to win the next general elections at any cost, which also accounts for its attempt to pack all key institutions of governance, including the judiciary, with its own supporters. The second is its desire to settle scores with the Awami League and the latter's front organizations, with which it has a relationship of visceral mutual hatred.

Sheikh Hasina gave a chilling account of the violence unleashed on the Awami League when she said, while addressing two rallies at Bakerganj and Patuakhali town in Barisal and Patuakhali Districts on 2 April 2004, that 26,000 leaders and workers of her party had been killed across the country since the BNP-led coalition government had assumed office. She said that the government had unleashed repression on the Awami League's supporters 'soon after it had come to power' and added, 'To hang on to power it has been trying to strangle the opposition by killing our leaders and workers.'[2] The figure Sheikh Hasina mentioned is doubtless very high and one cannot rule out the possibility of its being exaggerated. Nevertheless, the number of Awami League leaders and supporters killed by armed cadres of the BNP, Jamaat, Shibir, IOJ, JMJB, JMB, HUJIB and the police and RAB is certainly very substantial. This is clear from the massive and virulent offensive launched against the leaders and activists of the Awami League and its front organizations, like the Chhatra League, Jubo League and Sramik League, almost immediately after the elections. One form of offensive comprised attacks on individuals and their homes. Another was arrest and imprisonment on a mass scale on the basis of trumped-up charges. Yet another was victimization of government personnel who were perceived to be pro-Awami League when Sheikh Hasina was Prime Minister.

The attacks began almost immediately after the BNP-led coalition government came to power and became more frequent and widespread with the passage of time. Visiting Kushtia Awami League Joint Secretary, Syed Nizam Uddin, who had been seriously injured in an attack by BNP supporters, Sheikh Hasina said at BIRDEM hospital, Dhaka, as early as 17 January 2002, that the government was attacking her party leaders and arresting them by filing 'false' cases against them.[3]

On 26 January 2002, Sheikh Hasina circulated among foreign television channels, websites and local Bangladeshi media recorded copies of a speech by her on the BNP-led government's performance during its first 100 days in office, which the government and private television channels had declined to telecast as an 'address to the nation'. The long list of allegations it contained included one that leaders and workers of the Bangladesh Chhatra League were being brutally killed. She also referred to an NGO, Democracy Watch, as having stated that 610 persons were killed for political reasons and some 530 women murdered in the first 100 days of the new government.[4]

Forced to flee

Leaders and workers of the Chhatra League were certainly at the receiving end of large-scale violence on university and college campuses all over the country and even in their own neighbourhoods. On most campuses, they were attacked by supporters of the Jatiyatabadi Chhatra Dal (Chhatra Dal) BNP's student front organization, and the Shibir, and forced not only to suspend their activities but also to leave the halls of residence in which they stayed. They were not even allowed to sit for examinations, to say nothing of being permitted to return to the halls or organize political activity, for months on end. In Dhaka University, the administration designated 3 December 2001 for their return to their halls of residence under the supervision of the authorities. No one, however, turned up during the period announced for reporting. The Chhatra League General Secretary, A.K.M. Azim, told reporters that there was no 'atmosphere for co-existence' in the halls, and that non-students and outsiders, sheltered by the Chhatra Dal, continued to occupy these.[5]

Things were worse outside the capital city of Dhaka. Chhatra League leaders and activists could not return to their halls of residence (or conduct their organizational activity) at Islamic University, Kushtia, from which Chhatra Dal and Shibir cadres had evicted them soon after the installation of the BNP-led coalition government seven months earlier. Attacks by Chhatra Dal and Shibir cadres kept them away. A report in the *Daily Star* of 26 May 2002 quoted campus sources as saying that 100 Chhatra Dal activists had been beaten and 15 stabbed on the campus during those seven months, with the victim of the latest knife attack being Chhatra League leader Ashique Iqbal, who was stabbed by Shibir activists when he turned up at an examination hall on 14 May 2002.[6]

Nor were Chhatra League leaders safe near their homes. To cite just one example, Ripon Kumar Mollik, General Secretary of the Islamia Degree College in Chittagong city, was shot dead in front of his home on the night of 29 January 2002.[7] Ironically, on that very day, 75 Awami League and Chhatra League leaders and workers of Chandanaish Upazila in Chittagong District were granted bail, and 11 sent to jail, by the judge at Sadr Court No. 3, Chittagong. Another 109 had been given bail on 28 January.[8] Two hundred other leaders and activists of the two organizations had been given bail on 27 January and four sent to prison.[9] They were part of 600 Awami League and Chhatra League leaders and activists who had surrendered *en masse* in the court of a first class magistrate, Abdul Hye, on 27 January 2002[10] as part of a 'non-violent protest and movement' against the BNP-led government's 'repression and harassment of opposition leaders and activists'.[11]

The filing of cases against as many as 600 leaders and activists of a political party and its students' organization in only one *upazila* of one district, appears, *prima facie*, an act of political vendetta, particularly when seen in the context of the violence unleashed on the same elements throughout Bangladesh. The impression is reinforced by the fact that all except a handful of the accused were given bail when their cases came up for hearing, which suggests that the charges did not have much to sustain them. Any residual doubt is removed on considering the reaction of lawyers allied to the BNP and the Jamaat to the granting of bail. They boycotted the hearing from the second day (28 January), alleging bias on the part of the judge, and staged a procession in the court premises on the third.[12] Their action reflected anger over the court's order, an attempt to intimidate the judge and put him under pressure from the government controlled by their parties. Clearly, they had expected the judge to humour them by denying bail to the accused, as the police and the administration seemed to have done by framing most of them.

Given such incidents and the sustained onslaught on Chhatra League leaders and activists on campuses across Bangladesh, one cannot regard as a wild exaggeration the statement by the Chittagong Awami League leader Moslemuddin Ahmad on 26 January 2002, that over 10,000 Awami League and Chhatra League activists in Chandanaish had fled their homes after hooligans backed by the ruling BNP-led coalition, and a partisan section of Chittagong's administration, had unleashed violence and repression on them following the elections.[13] Ahmad, who was talking to reporters, also sounded credible when he said that it was the same story at Sandip, Sitakunda, Anowara, Raozan and Fatikchhari Upazilas of Chittagong District. By the same token, Afsaruddin Ahmad, the Awami League's candidate from the Chandanaish (Chittagong–3) constituency in the October 2001 elections, also sounded credible when he claimed that the victims had no alternative to seeking refuge in Chittagong city and elsewhere.[14]

The utterly partisan way in which the administration and, in particular, the police acted will become clear from the following two representative examples. On 26 January 2002, the court of Dhaka's Chief Presidency Magistrate granted bail to Haji Mohammad Selim, a former Awami League MP arrested under Section 54 of Bangladesh's CrPC, upon executing a bond for Tk 10,000 and providing two guarantors. Haji Selim, however, could not be released as his bail prayer in a murder case had been rejected on 23 January.[15] A few words about that case will be revealing. A BNP leader, Shamsul Haque Santi, was murdered in Dhaka's Lalbagh area on 9 June 1996. On the same day, his mother filed a complaint with the police accusing Nasiruddin Ahmed Pintu, a BNP MP at the time of writing who was then a Senior Vice-President of the Chhatra Dal, and five others, of the crime. Over four-and-a-half years later, and after the BNP-led government had come into power, the officer investigating the case filed a charge sheet dropping Pintu's name and mentioning Haji Mohammad Selim and 11 others as accused, raising the total number of accused to 17.[16]

That the entire development was politically motivated is strongly suggested by the government's subsequent conduct. On 2 April 2005, the Chief Metropolitan Magistrate, Dhaka, Jahangir Alam, dismissed a case registered on 15 April 1998 against Pintu and a dozen others for assaulting policemen and Awami League supporters earlier on the same day. His action came almost a year after Bangladesh's Home Ministry had instructed the District Magistrate, Dhaka, in writing, on 18 March 2004, to withdraw the charges against Pintu and 12 of his accomplices as these were 'politically motivated'.[17]

The argument that Pintu was victimized in the first instance because the case against him was registered when the Awami League was in power is fetching but based on an assumption unsubstantiated by evidence. Even such an argument was not available in another striking case. On 22 March 2005, the Chief Metropolitan Magistrate, Dhaka, Jalal Ahmed, granted a petition for the withdrawal of a case filed against Pintu on 26 December 2001 for attempting to snatch, at gun-point, the auction documents of a bankrupt company's property. The magistrate's action came over a year after Bangladesh's Home Ministry had instructed the District Magistrate, Dhaka, in writing, on 18 March 2004, that it wanted the case withdrawn as it was 'politically motivated'.[18]

Pintu, who was arrested on 26 December 2001, had been granted bail on 24 January 2002. A report in the *Daily Star* of 27 December 2001 had stated, quoting 'sources', that his arrest reflected the BNP government's decision to take a hard line against criminals engaged in terrorism and extortion, especially those in its own ranks, and that it would soon launch a massive drive to arrest all such elements irrespective of their party affiliations. According to the report, Bangladesh's Home Ministry had for long been seeking permission from the 'highest authority' for acting against Pintu and his accomplices. Several BNP leaders holding key ministries and positions at the PMO, however, continued to lobby in his favour. The report further quoted 'sources' saying that the Prime Minister had several times in the past warned him against persisting with his criminal activities, to no effect.[19]

The implication of the Home Ministry's instruction of 18 March 2004 to the District Magistrate, Dhaka, is clear: the 'highest authority' in Bangladesh—which obviously meant Begum Khaleda Zia[20]—had ordered Pintu's arrest out of political motives, and the Home Ministry was undoing that great wrong! Or was it that, having once sanctioned his arrest, it withdrew the charges against him, as the party needed his services? Incidentally, the BNP government did not withdraw criminal charges against Pintu alone. According to an editorial of the *Statesman* of Kolkata and Delhi, the lawlessness in Bangladesh was 'the result of Begum Zia's avowed policy of sheltering criminals in her coalition and dropping cases of murder, rape, and looting that have been filed against them. Even those who had been convicted of these charges and were serving jail terms have been released and their number exceeds 65,000. One of her senior party leaders, charge-sheeted for his involvement in the murder of a leading journalist, had, ironically, been rewarded with the information ministry.[21]

The *Daily Star* cited a higher number. Referring to the alarming rise in crime that led to drastic measures and a growing number of deaths of alleged criminals in exchanges of fire, euphemistically described as 'crossfire', with police or RAB personnel, it observed in an editorial on 13 May 2005,

> The rot goes deeper, indeed. There is the factor of blanket dropping of cases by the BNP government pertaining to 72,000 who were accused on 'political considerations' of assorted crimes during the preceding AL rule. The wholesale release of the accused was an unthinking re-action on the part of the BNP government to the AL's perhaps sweeping haul-ups, because among the let-offs might well have been real criminals who needed to be proceeded against under any government.[22]

Double standards

Very different standards were applied to the cases of political opponents like the Convenor of the Shechchasebak (Volunteer) League and former Awami League legislator, Alhaj Mockbul Hossain. Arrested from his residence in Mohammadpur, Dhaka, in the early hours of 2 December 2001, he was produced in the court of the Chief Metropolitan Magistrate, Dhaka, Biman Bihari Barua, at noon on the same day but not, as the law prescribed, during open hearing of cases. Instead, the police took the case file directly to Barua's chamber without the knowledge of his lawyers, which, according to the latter, prevented them from filing a petition for his release on bail. Besides, while he was initially shown as arrested under Section 54 of the CrPc without any warrant being produced and specific charges being framed against him, the police had forwarded to the court documents for his detention under the Special Powers Act, 1974, alleging that he had planned to attack government, semi-government and non-government offices during the Awami League-sponsored *hartal* on 1 December 2001, and that he had been involved in killings and, with his accomplices, in land-grabbing.[23]

Since Mockbul's case provides yet another telling example of the frequent misuse of both Section 54 of Bangladesh's Criminal Procedure Code and the Special Powers Act of 1974, it would be useful to take a brief look at both. The former permits arrests without an order from any magistrate or any warrant if the police feel that a person has been involved in the commission of a cognizable offence or there is credible information about, or reasonable grounds for suspecting, his involvement in such an offence. It has a wide range of applicability. It can be invoked against people possessing housebreaking implements without valid reason or suspected receivers of stolen property, as also against those in respect of whom there is credible information or reasonable grounds for suspecting that they have committed abroad an offence that is punishable in Bangladesh. There has been widespread criticism of the Section because of its misuse by governments by taking full advantage of the provision for arrest on the basis of mere suspicion, which has often been used to harass political opponents. Not surprisingly, there have been cases in which people detained under Section 54 of the CrPC have subsequently been charged with specific offences, or under the Bangladesh Special Powers Act, 1974, or released without being charged at all.

The Bangladesh Special Powers Act, 1974, covers a wide range of offences from the counterfeiting of currency notes and government stamps to any deed likely to prejudice the sovereignty and defence of Bangladesh, the maintenance of Bangladesh's friendly relations with other countries, or endanger public safety and the maintenance of public order. It also covers acts that create or excite feelings of enmity or hatred among different communities, interfere with, or encourage or excite interference with, the administration of law and maintenance of order and prejudice the maintenance of essential supplies and services, cause fear and alarm among the public or any section of it, and prejudice the economic and financial interests of the state.

The law empowers the government to control subversive associations and prohibit the formation of communal associations or unions, provides for preventive detention and the constitution of advisory boards to review grounds thereof in individual cases, and trial by special tribunals. It also provides for sentences of death and life imprisonment for offences like smuggling, counterfeiting and sabotage. Preventive detention under the Act can extend to six months, and beyond this period if the Advisory Board sanctions it.

Misuse of the Act has been rampant and, in many cases, as in Mockbul's, people arrested under Section 54 of the CrPC have subsequently been detained under the Bangladesh Special Powers Act, 1974. Equally misused is Section 167 of the Bangladesh CrPC, which allows custodial police remand for total period of 15 days where the magistrate concerned is satisfied that there are grounds for believing that the accusation or information about a person's involvement is well founded. Needless to say, remand in police custody frequently means torture to extract information or a confession, and in many cases magistrates do not adequately record their reasons for granting it.

It is, therefore, not surprising that in a landmark judgement on 7 April 2003, the High Court barred the government from detaining a person under the Special Powers Act after his arrest on the basis of suspicion.[24] The bench, comprising Justice Hamidul Huq and Justice Salma Masud Chowdhury, also held that a person arrested under Section 54 CrPC could not be placed under police remand for interrogation without permission from a Metropolitan Sessions Judge or a District and Sessions Judge. It provided that the accused should be interrogated by the Investigating Officer in prison instead of the interrogation cell, in the presence of his relatives and lawyers, and behind a glass partition so that they could see whether he or she was being tortured.

In a series of guidelines mandatory for the authorities, the bench further laid down that an accused had to be medically examined before and after police remand under Section 167 of the CrPC. Further, the court would take action against an Investigating Officer if medical examination of an accused bore out his or her charge of torture during police remand. The High Court bench further prescribed that police officers arresting a person at his house or place of work had to show their identity cards and immediately inform his or her relatives. If anyone was arrested on the street or anywhere else, his or her relatives had to be informed within three hours—through a special messenger, if necessary.

The court directed the government to amend Sections 54 and 167 CrPC within six months and said that the guidelines would apply until then. It also recommended that the necessary legal amendments be made to increase the punishment for malicious prosecution from three to seven years. The government, however, appealed against the judgement to the Supreme Court and the matter is pending before the latter. Meanwhile, misuse of both Sections 54 and 167 of the CrPC as well as the Special Powers Act of 1974 continues, and perhaps the best-known case is that of the writer, columnist, human rights activist, freedom fighter and advocate of a secular Bangladesh, Shahriar Kabir.

The case of Shahriar Kabir

Kabir was arrested at Zia International Airport upon his arrival from Kolkata on 22 November 2001 under Section 54 of the CrPC without any specific allegation being levelled against him. His detention for one month under the Special Powers Act, 1974, ordered on 25 November, was later increased to four months. During his period of detention, he was denied even the basic right of a family visit every 15 days. He was initially not allowed access to legal protection or to his lawyers, with the jail authorities flouting even the High Court's ruling on lawyer's visits. Two lawyers were eventually allowed to see him, and that too in the presence of the police, which prevented him from confidentially discussing the case with them. Even this visit was granted after a group of lawyers had demonstrated at the jail gate and threatened to take further legal action.

In prison, he was denied the separate accommodation normally granted to respected citizens like lawyers, journalists, politicians and socially prominent people. He was kept with common criminals and brought to court in handcuffs. Mahfuz Anam, editor of the *Daily Star*, who cited these facts in a moving and powerfully argued signed article calling for Kabir's release, asked:

> What is Shahriar's crime? He went to Kolkata. He interviewed some people who claimed to have crossed the border following attacks on some minorities after the October 1, 2001 election. He gave [an] interview to BBC in which he spoke out against the oppression on the minorities. According to the FIR filed by the police, when arrested at ZIA[25] he was in possession of some video films. These video films are supposed to contain interviews with members of Hindu community who said they were forced to leave home because of attacks on them.

There is also reportedly some footage of demonstrations in India in which slogans were raised against repression on Hindus in Bangladesh and some placards were seen which read, 'We do not accept the border'. The police nowhere accuses Shahrir of organizing any of these demonstrations, inciting people to violence, writing anti-Bangladesh placards, nor in any way being involved with any of the activities which was recorded in the video.[26]

Anam continued, 'So where is his treason? Is it treason to find out what has happened to members of Hindu community who could be CITIZENS OF BANGLADESH [Anam's capitals]?' Anam referred to a response Altaf Hossain Choudhury, Bangladesh's Home Minister, had given on the issue of Kabir being kept with common criminals: 'What is so special about him?' He then observed,

It is a sad commentary on the sophistication of our Governments that they forget what is proper and what is not once they assume power. Shahriar is an author of more than 70 books. He has done nothing else in his life except write—either books or columns, articles for journals. For the most part of his life he has been a journalist with *Bichitra* [Miscellany] in its earlier incarnation as a magazine under the Dainik Bangla trust. That is what is special about him. If the minister cannot distinguish between a petty criminal (and that is the way he is being treated) and Shahriar Kabir then it is indeed a sad day.

Anam further wrote,

It is now 57 days that a writer, columnist and a civic rights activist has been denied all his fundamental rights. He has been kept in prison with criminals, terrorists and murderers for the simple reason that he spoke his mind about an issue that embarrassed the government. So is embarrassing the government the new definition of treason? The government has not been able to provide any credible evidence against Shahriar for the crimes he has been accused of. In fact there is a lot of speculation regarding what triggered the government to act the way it did. Some believe the pressure was from one of the coalition partners.

Those familiar with Bangladesh's history and politics would instantly recognize that the coalition partner concerned was the Jamaat. Kabir and the Muktijuddher Chetana Bastabayan o Ekattorer Ghatak Dalal Nirmul Jatiya Samanway Samity (National Coordination Committee for the Realization of the Consciousness of the Liberation War and the Annihilation of the Killers and Agents of Seventy-one) have been relentlessly exposing acts of mass savagery the Jamaat's leaders and activists, who sided with Pakistan, perpetrated in Bangladesh during the liberation struggle of 1971, which the Jamaat had vehemently opposed.

On 20 January 2002, Kabir was released from jail on six months' interim bail granted by a bench of Dhaka High Court.[27] His case is emblematic of the BNP-led government's vindictiveness, total disregard for the rule of law and vulnerability to pressure from parties like the Jamaat. An editorial in the *Daily Star* that followed Mahfuz Anam's Commentary piece said,

> We are not trying to pronounce any judgement in the case: all we are seeking to do is underline the fact that the whole state machinery seemed arrayed against him [Kabir] with abuse of power (not permitting family visit and access to legal protection) being in evidence against a single individual. The sheer enormity of the state power as vested in the Constitution obligates a government to be highly responsible in the exercise of such power. Protection of the fundamental rights of citizens by the state is the supreme test of rule of law. The state as the custodian of the rule of law cannot allow itself to be impinging on the civil liberties and human rights of individual citizens without denigrating itself to ordinary levels.[28]

That the hounding of Shahriar Kabir was the result of sheer vindictiveness on the part of the BNP-led government becomes absolutely clear when one considers that relentless persecution of dissidents and political opponents has been the hallmark of its functioning. Apart from murder, assault, burning of homes and trumped-up criminal cases, the levelling of corruption charges against Awami League leaders and activists on a mass scale has been yet another instrument of the BNP and Jamaat's no-holds-barred effort to destroy the party. The two White Papers on alleged corruption by the Awami League's former leaders and activists released on 23 January 2002, and a third released on 4 May 2002, poignantly illustrate the process.

The first and second parts, together running into 793 pages, were drawn up by a special cell under a former secretary to the government of Bangladesh, M. Muniruzzaman, and listed 40 cases of graft, irregularities and abuse of power committed when the Awami League was in power from 1996 to 2001. According to the document, former

Prime Minister Sheikh Hasina and almost all senior members of her cabinet were involved in 'irregularities and financial mismanagement'. Former ministers like Mohammed Nasim, Amir Hossain Amu, Shah A.M.S. Kibria, A.S.H.K. Sadique, Anwar Hossain Manju, Abdur Razzak, Prof. Rafiqul Islam, A.K.M. Mosharraf Hossain, Dr Mohiuddin Khan Alamgir, and Maulana Nurul Islam were among those named as being involved. Also accused of being involved were many government officials as well as different 'local and international private organisations'.

Haris Chowdhury, Prime Minister Khaleda Zia's political secretary with the rank of a state Minister, said at a press conference while releasing the White Papers on 23 January 2002, 'On the basis of the information discussed in the White Paper, it appears that huge irregularities, graft and other illegal activities took place at the highest level of the government.' He added that 'in some cases, the head of the Government [former Prime Minister Sheikh Hasina] was involved in illegal activities'. Since 'corrupt persons take proceeds from large financial transactions to foreign banks', it was, he added, 'specially required to engage an international investigation organisation to look at those allegations'. Replying to a question, Chowdhury said, 'If necessary, we will go for an international investigation into the incident.'[29]

The third part of the White Paper, released on 3 May 2002, again by Haris Chowdhury, listed 20 cases of alleged graft, irregularities and abuse of power costing the public exchequer a total of Tk 27.01 billion. The former Ministers allegedly involved were Shah A.M.S. Kibria, Mosharraf Hossain, M.A. Mannan, Abdul Matin Kashru, Syeda Sajeda Chowdhury, Zillur Rahman and Amir Hossain Amu, besides a number of serving and retired civil and military officials.[30] The most striking part of the third part, however, was the allegation that five generals of Bangladesh's army illegally received a total of Tk 8 million as special allocation from the Upazila Parishad Development Assistance Fund during the Awami League's rule. Of them, serving and retired Chief of Army Staff, Lieutenant Generals Harun-or-Rashid and Lieutenant-General (Retd) Mustafizur Rahman, received Tk 2.5 million and 2 million respectively. Major Generals Jibon Kanai Das, Nazrul Islam and Masedur Rahman received Tk 1.5 million, 1 million and 1 million respectively.[31]

Releasing the third part of the White Paper, Haris Chowdhury described it as 'only a sample of the large-scale graft committed by them

[Awami League leaders and government officials]. It is not possible to project all those in such a limited purview.' He also asserted that the disclosures of corrupt practices were not aimed at earning cheap popularity. They were meant to ensure accountability and transparency in the administration and as a 'warning' for the future. Interestingly, he also said while releasing the first part that 'This white paper is not an outcome of a political vendetta', rather, it was a 'warning for the future'.

Watchful response

There was never any doubt that corruption was rampant during the Awami League's rule. Besides, the Awami League's filing of 69 corruption cases against former BNP ministers and senior leaders after coming to power in 1996 had caused raised eyebrows because these had not led to a single conviction even five years later when the party was dislodged from power after the elections of 1 October 2001. Nevertheless, responsible opinion in Bangladesh reacted to the BNP's exercise with caution, making it quite clear that judgement would depend on how things unfolded. An editorial in the *Daily Star* stated, after the publication of the first two parts of the White Paper, that their release could be viewed as an attempt to wreak political vendetta, to gain political mileage by putting the opposition on the defensive, or to set up 'a good example of clean leadership, both by means of establishing accountability for past misconduct as well as warning the present incumbents of the consequences of corruption'.[32] Stating that 'our heart' was in 'the third way of viewing' the White Paper, the editorial declared,

> Now, the nation will keenly watch out for the direction the handling of the White Paper takes in order to judge for itself as to which of the motives will have triumphed in the end. Except for a few, most of the AL ex-ministers (some officials not excluded) had figured in speculative stories linked to [acts of] omissions and commissions when they were in government. So, it is not surprising that their names have surfaced but the credibility and effectiveness of BNP's 'clean-up' initiative will critically hinge on the moral high ground from which it handles the cases. The transparency of the procedures will be central to the travesty or otherwise of the justice which the BNP is professedly trying to bring the AL leaders to.

The editorial continued,

> It has been a commonplace charade in South Asia for a government of
> the day to file corruption cases against members of a predecessor
> government, largely because the latter had done so while being in power
> itself. Then somewhere down the line the pursuit of such cases slackens
> with most of the initial roar whimpering into the ethereal wilderness.
> What is worse, it degenerates into political wheeling-dealing leading
> up to the exoneration of corruption in lieu of joining the ruling party
> bandwagon.

The manner in which the BNP began implementing the White Paper
soon began to raise serious questions. A report published in the *Daily
Star* the day the third part was released said that the government had
not filed any case in respect of the 40 corruption charges it had levelled
against senior Awami League Ministers and Sheikh Hasina in the
first and second parts. Nor had it changed or modified the defective
procedures which had, as identified in the White Paper, facilitated
corruption.[33] It had not engaged an international investigation organization, which Haris Chowdhury had said it might do, to probe some
of the charges. What tended to further undermine the credibility of
the first and second parts of the White Paper was that while the Bureau
of Anti-Corruption (BAC)—incidentally, an appendage of the Prime
Minister's Office—had filed 30 cases until the day the third part was
released, not one of these related to charges mentioned in the earlier
White Papers.[34]

Significantly, the only allegation on which the BNP-led government had acted was that the Awami League government had printed
textbooks with politically-biased contents to 'brainwash' students!
After coming to power, it had lost no time in changing the contents of
18 textbooks to insert that it was President Ziaur Rahman (then a
major in the East Bengal Regiment) who had announced Bangladesh's
independence from Kalurghat Betar Kendra (radio station), Chittagong,
on 26 March 1971.[35] Understandably, its record in implementing the
first two parts of the White Paper raised serious questions, as did its
decision to review—with a view to phasing them out rapidly—the 69
corruption cases filed by the Awami League government in 1996
against former BNP ministers and key functionaries, many of whom
were now in Begum Zia's cabinet.

The *Daily Star* observed in a thought-provoking editorial on 26 April
2002,

It is not our responsibility as a newspaper to pass any judgement on the veracity, validity or overall merit of the cases nor do we venture any pretence to even a quasi-judicial opinion on the subject. All we would like to say is this: the process through which the cases are being withdrawn smacks of political intervention . . .

One reads several implications into such a blanket withdrawal or deactivation of corruption cases by an executive decision instead of judicial opinion sought a priori and received by the government to act on it with unquestionable legal propriety. In the first place, this does not show any respect for the rule of law, in fact, it is repugnant to the cornerstone of constitutional rule in our country. Secondly, it has all the portents of encouraging corruption within the ruling party. Ministers, State Ministers, Deputy Ministers and MPs might revel in the knowledge that since power alternates between BNP and the AL, they are always in with a chance for impunity or reprieve at the end of the day even though corruption charges would be formally levelled against them with the reversal of fortunes.[36]

Credibility undermined

Released in the midst of growing cynicism about the BNP-led government's seriousness about fighting corruption, the third part of the White Paper only served to further undermine its credibility. What contributed the most to this was its allegation of corruption in the grant of Tk 8 million to five generals of Bangladesh's army. Apparently, there had been nothing wrong in the allocation and utilization of the amounts given to the generals as well as the maintenance of accounts. According to reports, Begum Zia herself expressed 'deep anguish' over the matter and rebuked the PMO officials concerned for the 'mistake'. She also reportedly summoned Haris Chowdhury, and reprimanded him for not having briefed her about the contents of the third part of White Paper before releasing it.[37]

Haris Chowdhury's plea that he had no prior idea of the contents of the third part of the White Paper, which had come to him in a 'sealed form' had few takers. The *Daily Star* said in an editorial that it was strange that as political secretary to the Prime Minister with the rank of a state Minister and as 'someone specially assigned to make the White Paper public he would be totally unaware of any sensitive part of it'.[38]

Stating that there was 'an impression in the press circles', drawn from a question a reporter asked Haris Chowdhury, that there had been 'some name-doctoring' in the white paper', the editorial observed that he could not plead innocence about the contents of the white paper if that was true. Both disbelief and reprimand was implicit in its observation, 'Furthermore, the report had been circulated among a number of officials ten days before its release. Yet it appears that the Prime Minister was not properly briefed on the subject. A cell wrote the paper and that was the end of it.'

The editorial further commented,

Setting aside the question of lack of coordination even in matters of [a] sensitive nature, there is a serious concern over violation of some other principles. To drag the names of the army top brass into any controversy amounts to breaking institutional norms. Discipline being the cornerstone of the national defence organisation such an approach was patently undesirable.[39]

What was perhaps most damaging to the White Paper, however, was the observation that the Prime Minister's political secretary had 'played politics' with it, allowing army generals to be drawn into a controversy and that 'the whole process of preparing the white paper' had been 'thrown open to question'. A White Paper was supposed to be 'the epitome of transparency' because it sought 'to clean up society. Unfortunately this does not seem to be the case'.[40]

Not surprisingly, the White Papers have come to be regarded as both an exercise in vindictiveness and a part of the BNP–Jamaat government's attempt to destroy the Awami League as a political force. The second impression was reinforced by the savage manner in which the police—obviously under instructions from above—dealt with even completely peaceful demonstrations staged by the Awami League. As early as 3 December 2001, police fired teargas shells and frequently interrupted a completely peaceful rally by the Awami League, addressed by leaders like former ministers Motia Chowdhury and Tofail Ahmed, in front of the party's central office on Bangabandhu Avenue, Dhaka.[41] The partisan role of the police was sharply underlined not only by its disruption of a completely peaceful rally, but by its having done so in the name of an order prohibiting processions and rallies in Dhaka—at a time when no such order existed.[42]

Police action became increasingly vicious with the passage of time. Thus, former Awami League ministers Mohammad Nasim, Motia Chowdhury and the Chief Whip of the Opposition in Parliament, Abdus Shahid, were injured on 9 January 2002 when the police fired teargas shells at, and attacked with batons, a peaceful sit-in by the party close to its central office in Dhaka. The indiscriminate and savage attack with batons followed after a threat by the police to run two double-decker buses of the Bangladesh Road Transport Corporation over the demonstrators had failed to disperse the latter.[43] The police then besieged the Awami League office as wounded and bleeding leaders retreated into it.

Even the widespread national and international criticism of the policies and actions of the BNP-Jamaat government that followed the grenade attack on the Awami League's rally on 21 August 2004 led to no change in police methods. As noted in Chapter Three, some of the demonstrations organized by the Awami League, the JSD and the 11-party Left alliance to protest against the outrage were savagely attacked by both the police and supporters of the government. Widespread criticism of even these had no effect. In one event, both policemen and BNP supporters viciously attacked a procession of the Jubo Mahila League (Young Women's League—a front organization of the Awami League) on 15 February 2005, the last day of a *hartal* called by 14 parties, including the Awami League, to protest the killing of former Finance Minister Shah A.M.S. Kibria and to press their demand for the government's resignation. It began when a procession by the Jubo Mahila League attempted to damage a vehicle which was plying on the road in Dhaka's Shyamoli area despite the *hartal*. Shouting slogans in support of the Chhatra Dal and the Jubo Dal, about 10 to 15 young men tried to drag the President of the organization's Dhanmondi branch, Srijani Akhtar Shiuli, into a lane by her hair. A clash followed as other supporters of the Jubo Mahila League rushed to protect her and began throwing stones at Chhatra Dal and Jubo Dal supporters. Thereupon the latter pounced on them with sticks, molested them, and beat some of them mercilessly after throwing them on the ground. Jubo Mahila League leaders like Shamim Akhtar, Lovely Yasmin and Sathi Akhtar suffered bleeding head injuries.[44]

The *Prothom Alo* report which mentions all this quotes eye-witnesses as saying that the police attacked the women with *lathis* as they tried to save themselves from the assailants. Faced with a two-pronged attack, they sought refuge in the houses by the road. The police and

Chhatra Dal workers surrounded the home of the Officer-in-Charge of the Mirpur police station, Intezar Rahman, where some of the women had sought shelter. Locking the doors of the other houses from the outside, they asked for women police to come. The young men, who had all this time been abusing the women inside the houses in the most vulgar language, dragged them out by their hair when the women police arrived and further molested them before handing them over to the police. Some of the women had their clothes torn in the process. Both police and the attackers stopped photojournalists who tried to snap the incident. The women who had taken refuge at the residence of the OC of Mirpur police station were taken to the Mohammadpur police station where they were reportedly beaten once again.[45]

The leaders and activists of the Awami League and its front organizations were not the only targets of savage attacks by the police and supporters of the ruling coalition acting in tandem. Even government officials and employees perceived to be supporters of the Awami League—particularly those who had joined the Janatar Mancha (People's Dais) were hounded. The Janatar Mancha was erected in March 1996 in front of the National Press Club in Dhaka. It was from here that the Awami League had urged government servants to 'revolt' against the BNP government whose first term in office ended with the elections later that year. More than 1,000 officials and employees of different administrative cadres, government offices and autonomous bodies, led by Dr Mohiuddin Khan Alamgir (henceforth Alamgir), a secretary to the government who became State Minister for Planning in Sheikh Hasina's government, responded and participated in the Janatar Mancha.[46] The BNP-led coalition government which came to power following the elections on 1 October 2001 asked 46 middle-level officials and 50 employees, who had served the government for 25 years or more, but who had joined the agitation led from the Janatar Mancha, to retire voluntarily. Refusal to do so, the government had told the employees, who had earlier been served with show-cause notices for joining the agitation, would lead to termination of their service.[47]

While the government was trying to make up its mind as to what it should do with officials and employees who had put in less than 25 years of service, and was even toying with the idea of offering them 'golden handshakes', it seems to have been very clear about what it intended to do with Alamgir. He was arrested on 15 March 2002 under

Section 54 of the CrPC at Zia International Airport upon his return from Singapore. Twenty-four days after the arrest, on 8 April 2002, police filed a sedition case against Alamgir and six others including the former Home Secretary and incumbent Election Commissioner, Shafiur Rahman, at the court of the Chief Metropolitan Magistrate, Dhaka.[48] They were charged with instigating government officials and employees to join the agitation led from the Janatar Mancha—an agitation which was to continue until a caretaker government was formed to conduct the elections. As a result, the government relinquished power to a caretaker government on 30 March 1996. According to the complaint filed by the police, the Mayor of Dhaka, Mohammad Hanif, and Alamgir were the architects of the plan to set up the Mancha.[49]

Alamgir, who was, by several accounts, horribly tortured in jail, was finally released by the High Court on bail on 18 September 2002.[50] The cases against him, which had come to include corruption charges, continued. As late as 9 November 2004, the High Court stayed for six months the proceedings in the sedition charge against him and six others in the lower court. It issued a rule on the government to show cause, within three weeks, why the lower court's order rejecting the seven accused's petition to be discharged from the sedition case should not be set aside.[51]

Without going into the merits of the cases lodged against Alamgir and others, one can conclude from the abuse-prone nature of the Section 54 CrPC under which he was arrested, and the manner in which he was detained, that the government was out to persecute him to the utmost of its capacity. This could only be due to two reasons. First, the government wanted to settle scores with Alamgir for leading the revolt of its officials and employees in 1996. Second, it wanted to make an example of him to ensure that officials and employees did not respond to a call for revolt if the Awami League or any other opposition party issued one before the next elections, and that they did not dare to question any order they might be asked to carry out.

Sacking of a president

The manner in which the BNP-led government has unleashed a no-holds-barred offensive against the Bikalpa Dhara Bangladesh (BDB), a political party formed by former President A.Q.M. Badruddoza Chowdhury (henceforth Chowdhury), indicates that it wants the same message conveyed to its MPs, leaders and activists—that revolt and defection to the BDB as well as refusal to obey the party's orders unquestioningly would invite dire consequences. In the case of Chowdhury, one of the best known physicians of Bangladesh, once a close confidante of President Ziaur Rahman and the founding general secretary of the BNP, the process began with his resignation as President of Bangladesh on 21 June 2002. It is important to examine the circumstances of his resignation and the events that followed for what these reveal about the BNP as a political party. He resigned in the evening after the BNP's parliamentary party had, at a meeting that same morning, passed a unanimous resolution condemning his activities as anti-party and threatening to impeach him if he did not quit on his own.

The anger of some of the young MPs, who called the shots at the meeting, had two immediate causes. The first was Chowdhury's failure to visit the grave of former President Ziaur Rahman on 30 May 2002, the 21st anniversary of his assassination, and the second was his failure to mention, in his message on the occasion, that it was President Zia who had declared Bangladesh's independence. Earlier, several incidents had soured relations between Chowdhury and Begum Zia and the coterie around her. The first such incident was his visit to the Awami League leader, Abdus Samad Azad, apparently to see if the latter's party could be persuaded to end its boycott of Parliament. Seen by many as an attempt to neutralize the allegation of bias he had attracted earlier by calling upon Begum Zia at her residence, in violation of protocol, it attracted flak from BNP hardliners who deprecated what they considered to be an attempt to strike a 'neutral' posture. These elements had earlier criticized him for not preventing his son, Mahi B. Chowdhury, then a BNP MP, from extending a grand welcome to Sheikh Hasina when she visited Munshiganj, his constituency. They were also annoyed because his messages published in the various supplements to newspapers taken out by the government on different occasions, did not end with the slogan 'Bangladesh Zindabad' which was supposed to indicate allegiance to the BNP.[52]

Begum Zia was also not amused when he refused to endorse the appointment of Dr Aftab Ahmad, whom she had chosen as the Chairman of the Public Service Commission, as he had reservations about the person. The fact that he later approved her selection of Dr Zinnatun Nesa Tahmida Begum for the same position clearly did not mollify her. Finally, the coterie was angry because its members thought he sought and received unduly extensive television coverage.

That such small matters could cause resentment among those calling the shots in the BNP points to the culture of sycophancy and intolerance that had come to pervade the party; that these should be considered adequate grounds to warrant Chowdhury's removal as President indicated a total absence of a sense of proportion. Besides, annoyance over what they perceived to be Chowdhury's efforts to project himself as a 'neutral President' suggests that they expected Bangladesh's head of state to be an instrument of the party and not a symbol of the unity of the entire country. Understandably, there was sharp media criticism of his ouster. In an editorial, the *Daily Star* observed on 22 June that the BNP's action had reduced the status of the President of the Republic to that of 'a person who has to be endorsed by the party and not necessarily the people. One may understand the sentiments of the party workers, but it is the parliament and not the party that elects the President. It means that to the BNP the two mean the same.'[53] Stating that the action had 'diminished the status of the head of the State', it added,

> The repercussions will be heavy and long. The next President will certainly remember that he is not the neutral head of the State symbolically representing all people but a party member put in high office who can be removed if the party desires and without any concern as to what the Parliament, let alone the country, may have to say.

The distinguished editor of the *Daily Star*, Mahfuz Anam, wrote in a signed column that what should have brought praise to Chowdhury had 'now subjected him to the worst humiliation of his life. Not only was he castigated and his integrity questioned', his 20 years' contribution to the founding, building and strengthening of the BNP, was 'thrown to the wind by a well-orchestrated political attack at its most vicious'.[54] Anam added,

> Perhaps the most tragic was the fact that there was not a single person in the BNP parliamentary party (BNPPP) to utter one word of support for a man with whom many of the BNP leaders have worked shoulder to shoulder over the last 20 years. Many who denigrated him are not worth even remotely comparing with him in terms of talent, ability, devotion and service to the country and community.

Wondering what kind of morality and ethics the silence 'of our veteran leaders' reflected, Anam asked whether they knew that a 'similar fate may befall them, and [at] that moment nobody will say one word of support for them'? Strongly criticizing the fact that the founding general secretary's two decades of dedicated work and self-less contribution had been 'neutralised' because of his 'crime' of trying to be a 'neutral' President, he added, 'The BNP, during its first term in office, had successfully built an image of being a party, which was tolerant, willing to be accommodative and one that was respectful of institutions.' Stating that it was a yearning for the return of such a party 'at the helm of affairs' that led to the Awami League being shown the door, he added that to 'most voters, and many sincere sup-porters, what they are seeing of BNP today is shocking them, to say the least'.

If the circumstances of Chowdhury's removal from the office of the President indicated that the BNP had degenerated into a vicious and vindictive party run by petty-minded satraps without any regard for propriety, democratic norms and the sanctity of institutions, the manner in which he and his associates were hounded when they started forming their own party after leaving the BNP, recalled the methods of the Nazis and Fascists. On 10 March 2004, two BNP MPs, Mahi (representing Munshiganj-1 constituency) and a retired Army Major, M. Abdul Mannan (representing Dhaka-10), resigned from the BNP and Parliament to join the new political formation, Bikalpa Dhara Bangladesh (BDB)[55], to be started by Chowdhury. This prompted the government and the BNP to launch a no-holds-barred offensive to nip the new organization in the bud.

Policemen and hoodlums

About 10.30 P.M. on 10 March 2004, police personnel and 'other un-known people' attacked BDB activists and employees of the firm setting up loudspeakers near the dais at Muktangan in Purana Paltan, Dhaka, from which the former President of Bangladesh was to announce, the next day, the national committee of the new organ-ization at a large gathering of his supporters.[56] The police demolished the dais and took away the loudspeakers despite the fact that Dhaka City Corporation had permitted the sponsors to hold the gathering at Muktangan. The claim by Dhaka Metropolitan Police that the sponsors had not been permitted by it to use loudspeakers did not justifiy such action because it could easily have shut down the loudspeakers if these were used at the gathering without permission. Also, the sponsors, who had applied for permission, could legitimately argue that they were having the loudspeakers installed in anticipation of permission being granted, and would not have used them in case it was not.

That the purpose of the entire exercise was to abort the proposed gathering on 11 March becomes clear on considering two developments. The first was the explosion of a series of bombs by 'unknown attackers' in front of Chowdhury's house and clinic—KC Clinic—around midnight on 10 March.[57] The second was the manner which the police and armed supporters of the BNP prevented BDB's rally on 11 March by means of three distinct sets of operations. In one of these, the police blocked several roads and prevented Chowdhury, Mahi, and Mannan from proceeding to the venue of the gathering at Muktangan.[58] Thwarted in his bid, the 73-year-old former President of Bangladesh addressed a small rally of his supporters at a place called Kuril where he described the government's action against the Muktangan rally as 'undemocratic and outrageous' and tantamount to 'sheer hooliganism'. The rally over, he began walking along with his supporters only to be stopped again by the police at the Mohakhali[59] railway crossing. There he addressed his supporters again. As soon as he had finished, about 60 men armed with iron rods and sticks pounced on the gathering shouting, 'Soldiers of Zia unite!', 'Get them out' and 'There is no place for B. Chowdhury on the soil of Shaheed[60] Zia!'[61] While some of them chased and assaulted fleeing BDB supporters, one of them sought to run Chowdhury over with his motorbike while his associates hit him in the back with stones. Mahi and Mannan were hit in the leg and forehead respectively as the police watched.[62]

Meanwhile, the second set of operations were being conducted by a section of ruling party activists, who occupied Muktangan and assaulted and drove away anyone they suspected of being a BDB supporter. Those assaulted included Dr Zakir Hossain, a candidate in the Bangladesh Supreme Court Bar Association's presidential election. While the violence at Muktangan was thoroughly deplorable, it pales when viewed alongside the third set of operations that took place on and near the bridge over the Dhaleshwari river on the Dhaka–Mawa highway. A large crowd of armed BNP activists, who had been waiting near the bridge, attacked BDB supporters travelling from Munshiganj to attend the rally. Beating them up savagely and at will, they injured at least 300 persons, besides damaging 40 buses.[63]

Commenting on the incidents on 10 and 11 March 2004, the *Daily Star* wrote in an editorial published on 12 March,

> It suddenly appears that political dissent is an unpardonable sin that has to be punished in the crudest of ways. How else can one explain intolerance of this kind?
>
> Manifestation of such political vandalism is repugnant to all democratic norms and, therefore, unacceptable. The question that arises for obvious reasons is, what brand of democracy is the ruling alliance practising? The general masses get the impression that such attacks couldn't have been carried out without some kind of nod from the party in power. [64]

Stating that it was difficult to 'wish away' such popular belief when the powers that be 'failed to demonstrate a minimum adherence to the rules of the game', it added,

> But the BNP was not quite known for such treatment of its political adversaries and defectors in the past. Even a lay person should be able to surmise that such activities cannot portend anything auspicious for the party, or society as a whole. Why this journey backwards?

Targeting Mannan

The government and armed activists of the BNP acted in tandem not only to prevent BDB supporters from conducting political activity in public but also to disrupt the business and vocational activities of their leaders. Mannan, who had become the BDB's General Secretary, was a special target. The scuttling of the rally on 11 March was followed by Customs men raiding his company's depot at Dewanhat on 13 March and taking away 4,500 bottles of the Sun Crest soft drinks which it manufactured and sold, along with many documents. On the same day, Chhatra Dal and Jubo Dal activists forced the closure of eight of his garment manufacturing factories in Chittagong, while there was a bomb attack on his house in Gulshan, Dhaka.[65] On 15 March 2004, about 60 armed supporters of the BNP arrived in 13 micro-buses and four motorbikes at Mannan's soft drink factory at Hemayetpur in Savar. Forcing their way in by firing guns and exploding bombs, they went on the rampage, injuring six workers, ransacking the office of the Senior General Manager and the Senior Factory Manager, destroying a date-punching machine, a computer, over 100 mango juice bottles and hundreds of cans and lights in the production room. They also destroyed two micro-buses and one mini-truck. According to Major (Retd) Mannan, the attack cost the factory Tk 100 million in lost property.[66] The next day, 16 March, the government froze the accounts of five companies owned by Major (Retd) Mannan while Chhatra Dal activists forced workers out of the building of his company, Elite Chemicals, which was under construction, and locked it.[67]

Mannan, however, was not alone in being victimized. Several BDB followers alleged that threats from BNP activists and law-enforcement authorities had kept them away from their homes and offices. They alleged that National Board of Revenue (NBR) officials had started visiting their offices and examining whether they were doing their business legally and paying their taxes regularly.[68] The word was that the government had ordered the police, NBR and other agencies to go for a massive crackdown on the business and political activities of BDB supporters.

Fascist tendencies

The entire train of events from the BNPPP's resolution calling for Badruddoza Chowdhury's resignation from the Presidency to the scuttling of the BDB's attempts to hold a rally on 11 March, and the official persecution of Mannan and other supporters of the new organization underlined the strong Fascist tendencies emerging within the BNP. These tendencies were further reflected in the government's rejection of every application by the BDB to hold rallies at a specific venue. This forced Chowdhury, Mannan and Mahi to announce BDB's conversion into a political party from the office of the Dhaka Reporters' Unity (DRU) on 8 May 2004.[69] Indeed, Chowdhury, Mannan and others came to the DRU office straight from the High Court where they had filed a writ petition against the government for obstructing the BDB from holding meetings and denying it permission to use whichever venue it chose for a meeting.[70]

Chowdhury told reporters that failing to get permission to hold a meeting at Paltan Maidan, Engineers Institution, Muktangan and Mohanagar Natyamancha, he had decided to launch his party simultaneously with the filing of the writ petition. The party, which was launched with Chowdhury as its founding president and Mannan as secretary-general, had as its central plank faith in the independence and sovereignty of Bangladesh and democracy at all levels. His party, Chowdhury said, was committed to fighting terrorism, corruption and poverty, the major problems facing Bangladesh.[71]

The BDB had a tough line to hoe from the very beginning. The High Court doubtless admitted Mannan's writ petition and asked the government to explain within two weeks why its denial of permission to the BDB to hold a meeting at Paltan Maidan or Mohanagar Natyamancha, should not be declared illegal. It also directed the government to explain why it should not be asked to dispose of, preferably within a week, the organization's fresh application to hold a rally at Paltan Maidan on 25 May.

A new pattern, however, soon emerged. Activists of the Chhatra Dal and the Jubo Dal began violently disrupting any public meeting that the BDB held on its own or in collaboration with the Jatiya Oikya Mancha[72] (JOM) headed by Bangladesh's former Foreign Minister and eminent lawyer, Dr Kamal Hossain. This followed the launching by the two parties of a programme of 'mass dialogues' throughout Bangladesh to draw up, in consultation with the public, a set of guidelines for combating terrorism and corruption. To cite two examples, the dialogue at Rangpur on 19 October 2004 was disrupted by activists of the two front organizations of the BNP, who injured 30 persons in the process. Activists of the Jubo Dal and Jubo League scuttled yet another dialogue at Mymensingh on 25 October 2004.[73] Blaming the four-party ruling alliance for the attack, Chowdhury and Dr Kamal Hossain said at the end of the incident, that it was afraid of the people's power. Though desperate, it would, however, never be able to suppress the people's demand for the government's ouster.[74]

Commenting on the incident on 25 October, the *Daily Star* observed in an editorial on 27 October 2004,

We are once again shocked at the despicable behaviour of the ruling party activists at the mass dialogue meeting of Bikalpa Dhara Bangladesh (BDB) and Jatiya Oikya Mancha (JOM) on Monday. All that these two parties were doing was conducting a perfectly legitimate political dialogue in a transparently peaceful manner. But they were subjected to such gangsterism that it has sent shock waves throughout the country. To set the government party 'maastans' (goons) against a peaceful political meeting is an act of outright mayhem and terror in itself. [75]

The editorial further observed that the way the whole disruption was carried out, and the venom spewed by the 'ruling party minions', suggested that it was all 'pre-planned and well-tutored'. It added, 'We wonder what the approach of the government is to legitimate dissent. The idea appears to be to crush all dissent at the seminal stages before it can blossom.'[76]

What accounted for such a dictatorial approach was the fear of losing power at the next elections. This becomes reasonably clear on considering some of the other steps the BNP government took. One was to attempt to pack the judiciary with its own supporters, and another an amendment to the Constitution meant, to all appearances, to ensure that the next election to the National Parliament was held under a dispensation willing to stretch the rules to facilitate its victory. The step was the appointment of the Chief Election Commissioner in a manner that lent strong credence to the allegation by the Awami League and other political parties that the government was planning to rig the next elections to the National Parliament due before 1 October 2006.

Packing the judiciary

The judiciary, as has been seen above, has played a very important role in providing relief to those hounded by the government and preventing the latter from riding roughshod on all dissent—political, intellectual and cultural. It has also come out frequently against arbitrary, obscurantist practices. An outstanding example of the latter was a judgement by a division bench of the High Court comprising Justices Golam Rabbani and Najmun Ara Sultana, on 1 January 2001. The judges had issued a suo moto rule following the publication in newspapers, on 2 December 2000, of the story of an incident in Naogaon district in November concerning a woman, Shahida Islam, whose husband, Saiful Islam Atikha, had verbally divorced her during a quarrel 18 months earlier. The quarrel over, they had continued to live as husband and wife and even had a child. Eighteen months later, a neighbour and influential man in the village, Maulana Haji Azizul Islam, had decreed that she could not continue to live with Saiful as, under Islamic law, she could remarry her husband only after she had married another person and had a divorce with the latter. While Saiful was away, she was forced to marry another person who divorced her the next day. Saiful, however, then refused to take her back.[77]

While the district administration subsequently prosecuted the mullah concerned, and five others, the judges admonished it for failing to take immediate steps to help the woman, the victim of an unlawful dictat and warned the officials, including police personnel, that they should be vigilant against such incidents.

Further, the judges observed that a *fatwa* meant a legal opinion, which meant the 'legal opinion of a lawful person or authority'. Bangladesh's legal system empowered 'only the courts to decide all questions relating to legal opinion on the Muslim and other laws in force'. They therefore proclaimed that all *fatwa*s, 'including the instant one', were 'unauthorised and illegal'. The judges also recommended the introduction in all schools and madrasas of the teaching of Muslim family law which prohibited *hilla* or forced marriage and the issuing of directions to imams and preachers in all mosques to discuss the ordinance in their Friday sermons.[78]

Posterity will remember this judgement as one of the most enlightened and courageous ever pronounced in Bangladesh. It not only exposed the tyranny of the mullahs in the countryside—of which women were the main victims—and the callousness of the administration, but also the commendable role of the judiciary. Understandably, Bangladesh's clergy as well as lay fundamentalist Islamists were incensed. The Jamaat, several Islamist groups and hundreds of the *ulama* condemned the judgement as un-Islamic and pronounced the two judges 'murtads' or apostates.[79] The IOJ and ICM launched a violent agitation against the judgement, with the head of the former's faction which is in the ruling coalition, Mufti Fazlul Huq Amini, threatening to launch a Taliban-style movement against the 'enemies of Islam'.[80] These and other organizations attacking the judgement held a massive rally in Dhaka on 2 February 2001, an occasion which saw several clashes in the city between the supporters and opponents of the judgement and the killing of a police constable inside a mosque. Declaring NGOs as the 'number one enemy' of Islam and Bangladesh, clerics accused the Awami League government of appointing judges with a bias against Islam.[81] A few weeks later, Bangladesh's Supreme Court stayed the judgement, which remains suspended.

Since the subordinate judiciary in Bangladesh has proved vulnerable to government pressure, the Jamaat, IOJ and ICM need a higher judiciary packed with pliable judges whom they can influence to push their fundamentalist agenda. Equally, the BNP needs judges who would not stand in the way of its bid to subdue all opposition to its rule in order to return to power in the next elections. It is, therefore, not surprising that allegations that it was packing the higher judiciary began shortly after the BNP-led coalition came to power following the general elections on 1 October 2001. It was reported in May 2002 that the government had agreed to confirm as a permanent judge only one—Najmun Ara Sultana—of the four additional judges[82] of the High Court whom the Chief Justice had recommended for confirmation.[83]

The Supreme Court Bar Association (SCBA) reacted sharply. It said in a statement that the government had violated constitutional norms by not accepting the Chief Justice's recommendations in respect of three judges. Stating that disregarding the assessment of the Chief Justice, who was responsible for evaluating the performance of the judges, was tantamount to interference with the independence of the judiciary, the SCBA demanded the immediate confirmation of the services of the three judges left out. The Law Minister, Moudud Ahmed, however, countered its arguments by stating on 27 May 2002 that the provision of appointing judges with the advice of the Chief Justice, which featured in Bangladesh's 1972 constitution, had been removed by the Fourth Amendment when the Awami League was in power in 1975. He added that the Awami League government had also appointed judges by 'ignoring' the Chief Justice's advice.[84]

Controversy raged, with Abdul Matin Khasru, Law Minister during the Awami League regime, denying the next day that his party's government had appointed judges by disregarding the Chief Justice's advice and stating that the government's action amounted to a clear case of interference with the independence of the judiciary.[85] A committee of senior lawyers of the SCBA finally managed to meet President Badruddoza Chowdhury on 29 May 2002, and requested him to confirm the three additional judges.[86] Nothing came of it and, as we have seen, the President himself was forced to resign from his office on 21 June. Eventually the controversy over the non-confirmation of judges subsided. The belief remained however, that the confirmations were denied on political considerations. This in turn was due to the fact that the file on the confirmation of the four additional judges had been sent to the Prime Minister's Office and Begum Zia had personally seen it and decided to confirm only one of them.

This, no doubt, makes matters a trifle intriguing. The Jamaat and the IOJ, now members of the BNP-led ruling coalition, had viciously condemned Justice Najmun Ara Sultana for being active on the bench that had pronounced the courageous and path-breaking judgement on *fatwa*. What then could explain the fact that she was the only judge to be confirmed? When asked, a senior Bangladeshi leader[87] told this writer that this was because she was the first woman to be appointed an additional judge of the High Court and denying her confirmation would have been widely condemned at home and abroad, particularly in the context of the *fatwa* judgement. On the other hand, confirming her as a permanent judge and denying confirmation to the other three would make it easier for the government to deny the charge that the decision was politically motivated.

The major consequence of the confirmation controversy was a marked souring of relations between the government and the SCBA, which began to view former's intentions with increasing suspicion. Not surprisingly, therefore, another storm burst upon Bangladesh's legal world when the government announced the appointment of 19 additional judges to the High Court on 23 August 2004[88], two days after the grenade attack on the Awami League's rally in Dhaka. The appointments, which took the number of judges appointed to the High Court since 2002 to 45, came to be regarded as the worst ever made in Bangladesh on political grounds. The appointees included a daughter and nephews of a former minister and BNP MPs. Another was a Shibir leader. Another had contested an election for the presidency of the SCBA as a BNP candidate but had been defeated.[89] Understandably, there was widespread resentment among the lawyers. At an emergency requisitioned meeting on 23 August itself, the SCBA resolved not to address the new judges as 'My Lord'. The new form of addressing them, it stated, would be decided in consultation with the association.

Lawyers revolt

The SCBA President, Rokanuddin Mahmud, said at the meeting that 'respect comes from inside and it cannot be demanded'. Stating that rumours were rife that people with false educational qualifications and records of having served jail terms were appointed, he said, 'in the past, the judges were intellectuals but things have changed'.[90] His organization was not the only one to protest. The Sammilita Ainjibi Samanyay Parishad (United Lawyers' Coordination Committee), boycotted the courts on 25 August. At another meeting on 29 August, the SCBA decided to serve notices on Law Minister Moudud Ahmed and the Chief Justice of the Supreme Court, Justice J.R. Mudassir Husain, asking both to explain what considerations applied to the judges' appointment. It decided that Supreme Court lawyers would boycott the Chief Justice's court indefinitely from 30 August since he had ignored their plea to cancel the swearing-in of the new judges, and that any member, including the Attorney General, who defied the decision would be expelled from the SCBA. Further, it asked the Chief Justice to convene a full court reference, with representatives from the bar, to consider the appointments.[91]

On the other hand, Jatiyatabadi Ainjibi Forum (Nationalist Lawyers Forum), identified with the ruling party, decided on 30 August to extend 'all out cooperation' to ensure the Supreme Court's functioning despite the SCBA's boycott call which, it said, was issued out of 'political considerations'. At an emergency meeting on that day, its Supreme Court unit decided not to 'tolerate any interference with the delivery of justice to the common people'. It also added that the SCBA's decision represented an attempt by 'some Awami League lawyers with vested interests' who wanted 'to direct [the country's] politics in a wrong direction by using the Supreme Court's premises as an office to carry out their political activities'.[92]

The Islamic Lawyers Association, identified with the Jamaat and associated organizations, also opposed the boycott decision.[93]

The boycott was by all accounts an impressive success, which reflected the widespread misgivings caused in all sections by the appointments. The *Daily Star* wrote in an editorial on 1 September,

> The recent appointments can be called into question both on grounds of qualification and procedure. The appointees lack the credentials and experience that High Court judges typically possess, and there can be little argument that they do not have the reputation and background that one would expect for such an august appointment.
>
> Similarly, the way in which the appointments were made was extremely unconventional, calling into question the integrity of the entire

procedure. There was no consultation, as is customary, with senior members of the bar, and no transparency as to who had made the recommendations and on what basis the appointments were made. The Chief Justice swore in all the nineteen judges in one day, raising the question of how he could have considered the applications in such a short time, and questions have been asked as to the necessity of rushing through such an appointment just before the court is about to break for recess.

Finally, that the Government would attempt to push through such controversial measures not three days after August 21, at the same time it is preaching the need for national unity, beggars the imagination. [94]

The editorial, however, made clear that it did not consider the boycotting of the court of the Chief Justice the correct response and wondered whether the SCBA 'could not have found a more appropriate means of expressing its opposition to the appointments' that 'did not bring the office of the Chief Justice into controversy'. Simultaneously, it urged the Chief Justice to heed the bar's request to convene a full court reference with representatives of the bar to reconsider the appointments.

The Chief Justice, of course, did nothing of the sort. The agitation was automatically suspended as the court went into recess two days after the boycott of the Chief Justice's court began. The controversy, however, continued to simmer, and exploded into a crisis within a week of the reopening of the courts on 24 October 2004. On 30 October, two highly-respected Bengali-language newspapers of Bangladesh, *Prothom Alo* and *Bhorer Kagaj*, reported that Faisal Mahmud Faizee, one of the 19 judges appointed on 23 August, had tampered with the mark sheet of the LLB examination for which he sat from the Chittagong University in 1989.[95] On that very day, the SCBA asked Faizee not to sit on his bench and the Chief Justice of the Supreme Court to withdraw his name from the roster of judges hearing cases.[96] The Chief Justice did that the next day, while senior judge Asghar Khan, who sat on the same bench as Faizee, refused to do so any more.[97]

Faizee's was not the only case that tended to vindicate the questions about the appointment of the 19 judges. The records of some others also raised eyebrows. An editorial in the *Bangladesh Observer* of 1 November 2004 commented that 'the Government's political appointment [of judges] is backfiring in more ways than it could imagine'. It continued,

First, a judge of the High Court implicated in a bribery case had to go. Now another judge of the HC is alleged to have got the job on production of a fake certificate of [having passed the] LLB examination. It is difficult to imagine that such a thing can happen in reality, rather they seem to be characters and incidents out of a fiction.[98]

Stating that such things were bound to happen if politicization was taken to the extreme, the *Bangladesh Observer* added that the SCBA, which had launched several campaigns protesting against the appointment of the judges, stood vindicated, as various charges had been levelled against some of the judges. At least one of them was punished by a military tribunal and another was an accused in a murder case. The editorial went on to say that 'Appointment of party loyalists to government service could not be totally ruled out' but should be made only in cases where comparable candidates were available. The making of appointments based on purely political considerations was 'certain to compromise the quality of service'.[99]

Meanwhile, Faizee's case took a new turn when the Division Bench of Justices M.A. Matin and A.F.M. Abdur Rahman, on 8 November 2004, following a petition filed on the same day by his father, Mohammad Faiz, served notices on *Prothom Alo* and *Bhorer Kagaj*, asking why contempt charges should not be drawn up against them for running reports about the Additional Judge's alleged tampering with his LLB mark sheet. It also asked the two papers as to why they should not be punished for maligning the High Court by publishing the reports.

Stunning judgement

On 21 March 2005, the Division Bench gave a stunning verdict which ran totally contrary to modern concepts of the freedom of the press and judicial accountability. Holding that the papers had failed to prove that Faisal Mahmud Faizee had tampered with his LLB mark sheet, it fined the editor and publisher of *Prothom Alo*, Matiur Rahman and Mahfuz Anam respectively, and two of its reporters Enamul Haq Bulbul and Masud Milad Tk 1,000 each. Failure to pay would mean serving a month in prison. The same punishment was awarded to the former editor of *Bhorer Kagaj*, Abed Khan and its publisher Saber Hossain Chowdhury. The paper's reporter, Samaresh Baidya, was, however, awarded two months of rigorous imprisonment and a fine of Tk 2,000 because of his role not only in writing the story but also in carrying a photograph of Justice Faizee.[100]

The court observed that *Prothom Alo* and *Bhorer Kagaj* reports were 'false' since it was not proven that Justice Faizee's LLB certificate was fake.[101]

Referring to the heading of the *Prothom Alo* report—'A judge's LLB certificate is fake'—the court observed that it found no basis for the paper to reach such a conclusion or give such a headline. The content of the report had nothing to do with the forgery of the certificate. The report neither substantiated the headline nor disclosed who had committed the forgery.[102]

While the papers had not been able to prove conclusively that Justice Faizee's mark sheet had been tampered with and his certificate was forged, the evidence at hand did not establish that his mark sheet had not been tampered with. The fact, as affirmed in the judgement itself, was that he was one of the 2,400 examinees in 1989 whose results were re-investigated by the University authorities following allegations of tampering. Justice Faizee had applied for the Bangladesh Bar Council's[103] certificate of enrolment as an advocate on the basis of a provisional LLB certificate. Even his father Mohammad Faiz reportedly could not produce his LLB certificate while filing his contempt case against *Prothom Alo* and *Bhorer Kagaj.*[104] The High Court ignored not only these facts but also the legitimate question whether such a person should be made a High Court judge, particularly when, according to reports, the investigation had not yet been completed. A High Court judge should not only be a person of unimpeachable integrity but his background must contain nothing that may raise misgivings. The judgement not only overlooked this fact but also sought to severely restrict contact between media persons and judges. The former could not communicate with a judge directly in person or over the telephone but had to take permission from the Registrar of the Supreme Court to do so. Also, it wanted the press to draw up, in association with the SCBA, guidelines governing court reporting.[105]

The High Court's judgement, against which an appeal by the newspapers and journalists who were held guilty lies with the appellate division of Bangladesh's Supreme Court at the time of writing, enabled Justice Faizee to return to the bench from 10 April 2005. It, however, created serious disquiet in the press and did not make for Justice Faizee's acceptance by the majority of the bar. The press was upset because the verdict ignored the wider question of the judiciary's credibility and integrity and resorted to an argument that amounted to giving the judge the benefit of the doubt. The *Daily Star* observed in an editorial on 23 March 2005,

> We, as members of the free and independent press, are unable to accept the judgement as it will greatly curb people's right to know about one of the three pillars of modern state, namely the judiciary. It is our view that the judgement effectively forecloses all possibilities of public scrutiny of a very important component of democracy. By preventing any public knowledge of how the judiciary is functioning, the judgement in question has greatly diminished the possibility of judiciary's own capacity of strengthening itself through transparency regarding its composition and functioning. . . .
>
> The judgement cites Lord Morris' judgement of 1899 (just 105 years ago, as if nothing has changed since then) about the need for contempt laws. He is quoted as saying that contempt laws regarding scandalizing of court may be 'necessary in small countries, consisting principally of coloured population'. It is regrettable that such racist language should find any place in our court's consideration even as a passing reference. . . .
>
> Our respect for the judiciary remains firm and unconditional. We have relentlessly fought for the independence of the judiciary and have all through supported the idea of its complete separation from the executive. We pledge to continue to do so in spite of a judgement that clearly goes against the freedom of the press. We do so because we have no doubt in our mind that an independent judiciary is the best guarantee for a free and independent press. The opposite is equally true. We in the independent and free press know it. Does the judiciary? The judgement, sadly, does not indicate it.[106]

The judgement further widened the gulf between the judiciary and the overwhelming majority of the bar that had emerged with the SCBA's agitation against the appointment of the 19 new judges on 23 August 2004. Its seriousness first became manifest on 1 March 2005 when the Chief Justice Syed J.R. Mudassir Husain and many of the judges did not attend the SCBA's annual break-up party. Stating that the Chief Justice had said that he did not attend because some of the judges had not been 'invited properly', the SCBA's President said that all the judges, including the controversial 19, had been invited, as in the previous years, in an appropriate manner. Adding that he did not understand the rationale behind the decision, he observed that the movement against the appointment of the 19 judges may have had something to do with the absence.[107]

Things deteriorated further following Justice Faizee's return to work at the High Court on 10 April 2005, when he was allotted a single bench. While the lawyers continued with their agitation, the Bangladesh Bar Council cancelled his enrolment certificate on 24 April for providing false information during his enrolment and his failure to disprove the allegations made regarding his LLB examination certificate.[108] It also decided to file a criminal case against him for giving a wrong date of birth in the affidavit he had submitted when he had applied for the Council's certificate that enabled him to practice law as an advocate. Since Justice Faizee had not replied to the show-cause notice the Council had served on him in November 2004, and since Chittagong University authorities had not come to his defence, the Council took it for granted that the allegation against him was true.[109] It also alleged that Justice Faizee had mentioned 15 September 1965 as his date of birth in his application form and supporting affidavit for the Council's certificate, while his Secondary School Certificate (SSC) attached to the application had the date as 15 September 1963.

On 5 May 2005, Justice Faizee filed a writ petition at the High Court challenging the Bar Council's show-cause notice and cancellation order.[110] Faizee argued that he had not replied to the show-cause notice as it was clearly issued without jurisdiction and because a contempt petition about the genuineness of his LLB certificate was pending with the High Court at that time. There was no basis to the cancellation, he said, as the Vice Chancellor of Chittagong University had stated that his LLB certificate was still valid. Faizee further argued that the Bar Council had earlier accepted his claim that the SSC had wrongly recorded his date of birth and had issued him a certificate of enrolment.[111]

On 7 May the High Court issued a rule asking the Bar Council to explain within eight weeks why its cancellation of Justice Faizee's certificate of enrolment, as well as its show-cause notice to him, should not be declared illegal. It also stayed the cancellation of the order until the rule was finally disposed of. This by no means put a lid on the SCBA's agitation, and matters headed towards another crisis when, on 16 May, Bangladesh's Minister for Law, Justice and Parliamentary Affairs, Moudud Ahmed, asked this rhetorical question in the National Parliament, 'Doesn't it fall into a [category of] contempt of court when a section of lawyers are blocking the CJ's entrance?'

He added, 'We hope that the Supreme Court will take steps to keep its dignity intact'.[112] The Speaker, Jamiruddin Sircar, said in the National Parliament on the same day, 'Blocking the entryway of the Chief Justice and asking him to withdraw a certain judge was unconstitutional', and that the Chief Justice should draw up contempt proceedings against those involved.

Reacting sharply to these statements, the SCBA decided at an emergency general meeting on 17 May to cancel Moudud and Sircar's membership.[113] While this gave a new turn to the agitation, the High Court, on 23 May, exactly a week after Moudud and Sircar's remarks in the National Parliament, banned agitations on the premises of the Supreme Court or any other court.[114] Taking suo moto cognizance of the agitation, the court, in an unprecedented ruling, prohibited gatherings, congregations, picketing, or laying of a siege at the entrance of any court, besides slapping a ban on boycotting and abstaining from attending any court on the basis of any decision taken by the SCBA.[115]

Moudud and Sircar's statements about SCBA's allegations, made in the National Parliament, clearly indicated that the government was determined not to remove even one of the 19 additional judges it had appointed. The conduct of the Chief Justice, Syed J.R. Mudassir Husain, and a section of both the High Court and appellate divisions of the Supreme Court showed that, far from standing firm against the government's moves, they would either fall in line or support these actively. The result was bound to be a subservient judiciary, which seems to have already come about—at least to a certain extent.

Constitutional carrot

In the government's bid to ensure a tame and pliable judiciary, the ruthless bulldozing of all opposition (the stick) is accompanied by a generous offering of the carrot. Thus, among other things, the Constitution (Fourteenth Amendment) Bill passed by the National Parliament on 16 May 2004 raised the retirement age of Supreme Court judges from 65 to 67.[116] The Awami League and the 11-party Left alliance immediately alleged that the BNP-led alliance had amended the Constitution 'to ensure that its own man became the chief of the next caretaker government, to manipulate the coming elections'. Elaborating, the Deputy Leader of the Opposition in Parliament, Abdul Hamid, who was the Speaker of the last National Parliament, said, 'The age

limit of the Supreme Court judges has been increased because they
want to see a particular judge as head of the caretaker government'.[117]
The judge referred to was the Chief Justice who, under the 13th amendment to Bangladesh's Constitution, will head the caretaker government
that will hold the next general elections.[118]

The explanation by the Minister for Law, Justice and Company
Affairs Moudud Ahmed that the upper age limit was raised to prevent
a vacuum in the top tier of the judiciary that would be caused by the
retirement of 25 Supreme Court judges over the next four years had
few takers in the Opposition ranks.[119] And its hollowness became
evident within months. Underlying his explanation was the argument
that judicial vacancies had to be filled only after being sure of the juri-
dical competence and integrity of the appointees, and the government
wanted to do precisely that by prolonging the tenure of the existing
judges and taking its time over the selection of new ones. The wholesale appointment of 19 additional judges—some of them with records
that raised eyebrows—to the High Court on 23 August 2004 made
nonsense of such an argument. The appointments and the BNP-led
coalition government's ill-concealed hostility to the media criticism
and agitation by lawyers that followed were completely irreconcilable
with any concern for a competent, independent and credible judiciary
known for its honesty. Rather, in the context of the government's earlier
moves, the appointments seemed to represent a blatant attempt to
pack the judiciary with supporters of the ruling coalition to destroy
its independence.

Seen retrospectively against this background, the increase in the
retirement age of Supreme Court judges effected by the 14th amendment to Bangladesh's Constitution is entirely compatible with the
claim that it was done with an ulterior motive. That this impression is
not unwarranted is clear from an observation in an editorial in the
Daily Star of 18 May that 'raising the retirement age for judges at a
time like this, marked by a climate of suspicion and distrust, could
raise a question whether it has been done with an eye to the make-up
of the caretaker government that will hold the next elections, or to
maintaining a status quo on the Bangabandhu murder case.'[120]

The impression that the motive was to secure a friendly caretaker
government is reinforced by the fact that, apart from the provision
raising the retirement age of Supreme Court judges, there was nothing
in the Constitution (Fourteenth Amendment) Bill that made a real

difference. There was nothing earthshaking about the increase in the number of women MPs, to be elected by the 300 elected MPs, from 30 to 45. As previously, the Bill made sure that the party with the greater number of seats had a larger share of indirectly elected women MPs. It ignored the demand by women's organizations that women should be directly elected from reserved constituencies.[121] Referring to the issue, the *Daily Star* commented in its editorial on 18 May 2004, 'It is worth noting that this amendment has been rejected by virtually every major women's group in the country. What is the sense of passing legislation ostensibly for women if it is opposed by the very constituency it claims to help?'[122]

Referring to the provision for mandatory display of the portraits of the President and Prime Minister in government offices, the editorial wondered whether an amendment 'was at all necessary'. It observed, 'The amendment detracts from the importance of the Constitution by including something that could better be addressed through an executive order. It is more a matter of custom and precedent than that of a constitutional provision.' Nor did this amendment benefit the common people. This is also true of provisions like the one enabling the Chief Election Commissioner to swear in MPs if the constitutionally designated person was unwilling or unable to do so within three days after a general election, and the one raising the retirement age of the Comptroller and Auditor General from 62 to 65 years. Nor did any of these changes make the Constitution a more comprehensive and durable document. As the *Daily Star* editorial rightly observed, 'The ultimate test of a good constitutional amendment lies in adding value to the Constitution and in ensuring that it lasted through the vagaries of politics and the changing of guards. On both counts, the amendment falls short of the criteria.'[123]

Then why the amendment?

Friendly caretaker

In the absence of any other credible explanation, the one that tends to stick is that the BNP-led government wants a 'friendly' caretaker regime. This explanation is further reinforced by manner in which it has appointed the new Chief Election Commissioner (CEC), which has also sparked a massive controversy. It has been a long-standing demand of the opposition parties, including the Awami League, that the CEC should be appointed in consultation with the Opposition and should command the confidence of all parties. The BNP-led government, however, contemptuously dismissed the demand and, on 23 May 2005, appointed Justice M.A. Aziz, a senior judge in the appellate division of the Supreme Court, in place of M.A. Syed who retired as CEC on 22 May.[124] On the following day itself, Sheikh Hasina alleged that the government had unilaterally appointed the new CEC to clear the way to rigging the general elections the next year.[125] She added, 'Sensing defeat in the next general elections, the BNP-led alliance has politicized the appointment of the CEC.'

Neither she nor any other Opposition leader seemed to have been impressed by Aziz's assertion before journalists, on assuming office, that his first priority was holding free and fair elections, that he was 'nobody's man', that he was rather 'a friend of everybody' who would try his 'best to serve the nation'.[126] The reason clearly was the manner of his appointment, which suggested that he was a BNP or Jamaat loyalist. That such a person was unilaterally appointed despite the Opposition's demand for consultation suggested that the appointments to the Election Commissions that would follow would also be along party lines. Since of the three Election Commissioners, Safiur Rahman retired on 24 June 2005 and Munsef Ali and A.K. Mohammad Ali will both retire on 18 April 2006[127], the BNP-led government will have been able to appoint its own men in all the posts to ensure a completely pliant EC by the time the next parliamentary elections are held by October 2006.

Importance of the EC

What this means in practical terms will become clear on considering the outcomes of two prestigious contests—the parliamentary by-election in Dhaka-10 constituency on 1 July 2004 and the Chittagong City Corporation elections on 9 May 2005. The first, a contest between retired Army Major and former MP M.A. Mannan, who had resigned from the National Parliament and BNP and joined the BDB, and Mosaddek Ali Falu, regarded as close to Begum Khaleda Zia, was a farce. Dwelling on the day's polling, a report in the *Daily Star* of the following day stated that the ruling alliance's intimidation of voters and polling agents, false voting and the absence of the Army at every polling centre marred the much talked-about by-election. The report went on to add,

> Gangs of marauding youths, most of them aged between 18 and 25, forced their way into the polling centres and stuffed ballots [papers] into boxes . . . drawing flak from the Awami League and the other opposition parties that threw their might behind the Bikalpa Dhara.
>
> Thousands of activists mobilized by [ruling] alliance leaders arrived in Ramna-Tejgaon constituency [Dhaka-10] from outside by buses and trucks early yesterday and rushed to most of the 103 polling centres.[128]

The absence of the Army was particularly shocking as the High Court on 29 June had directed the government to deploy the required number of Army personnel at each polling centre. It made a critical difference, as the police was totally inactive. The BDB's polling agents were forced out of most centres, and Mannan himself received the same treatment when he went near one. Mannan filed a complaint with the EC at 1.40 P.M. calling for the cancellation of the election. The EC rejected his demand, though Safiur Rahman, acting as CEC, admitted that the High Court's order was flouted and BDB had no polling agent at most centres. He also said that polling was 'unrealistic' in many centres.[129] What was most striking in this context was the unseemly haste with which the EC secretariat published the gazette notification of the result and Speaker Jamiruddin Sircar administered the oath of office to Falu—the entire process took less than three hours.[130]

Elections to the Chittagong City Corporation (CCC) presented a very different picture. Awami League-supported Nagarik (Citizens) Committee candidate A.B.M. Mohiuddin Chowdhury (henceforth Mohiuddin) seeking his straight third term as Mayor, roundly defeated his principal rival, the BNP-led alliance's candidate Mir Mohammad Nasiruddin (Mir Nasir) by a margin of 91,481 votes. With 55.82 per cent of the electorate voting, Mohiuddin secured 350,891 votes against Mir Nasir's 259,410.[131] While the results no doubt reflected Mohiuddin's very considerable popularity and the voters' resentment against the aggressive campaign launched by the BNP-led alliance, these factors had the impact they did because the EC had firmly foiled the massive government-backed attempts to rig the polls in Mir Nasir's favour.

On 2 May 2005, the government removed the Commissioner of the Chittagong Metropolitan Police (CMP), Amjad Hossain, after the EC, had on the same day, ordered it to do so on finding him guilty of not discharging his duties properly and harassing Nagarik Committee poll workers.[132] The EC warned the Chittagong Divisional Commissioner who tried to interfere with the polling by taking, at a high level meeting, decisions which the Returning Officer (RO) alone was authorized to take.[133] The day before the polling, it blasted the RO who had appointed as polling officials unqualified persons, including supporters of a BNP-backed professional body. On seeing newspaper reports to this effect, the CEC, M.A. Syed, rang up the RO and ordered the replacement of such officials with qualified polling officials.[134] Syed even told the RO, Golam Quddus, that he would have changed him had there been time for that. Besides, the EC forced the RO, who was also the Additional Divisional Commissioner of Chittagong, to shift to the original location a polling centre he had moved elsewhere without the EC's approval.[135]

While lauding the EC for what it did to ensure a free and fair election in Chittagong, one must also recognize that it succeeded because the government did not flout its directives the way it defied the High Court's order for troop deployment during the Dhaka-10 by-election. And it is difficult to believe that the change in the government's attitude had nothing to do with the world waking up to the dangerous drift of events in Bangladesh after the grenade attack in Dhaka on 21 August 2004, and the growing international pressure on the BNP-led coalition government to curb violence and observe democratic norms. The question is: will it show, during the run-up to the general elections next year, the same respect it accorded to the EC during the run-up to the CCC polls? The question is important because even in respect of the CCC elections the government did whatever it could to hamstring the EC. Though the latter's secretariat is responsible for supervising election-related functions and bringing any attempt to rig the election to its notice, it did almost nothing of the sort. The EC came to know of the irregularities through the media and took corrective action.[136] The role of its Secretary, its administrative head, who did not attend any of its meetings during the run-up to the CCC polls,

also raised many questions, as did the excruciatingly slow pace of announcing the results and the mysterious interval of one-and-a-half
hours that separated the completion of the counting and the final
declaration of Mohiuddin as the winner.

This, of course, was not the first occasion when the conduct of the
EC secretariat had raised eyebrows. The haste with which it had issued
a gazette notification declaring Mosaddek Ali Falu the winner in the
by-election in the Dhaka-10 parliamentary constituency on 1 July
2004, which had been reduced to a farce through BNP's blatant rigging,
had also attracted adverse attention. Technically, the question should
not arise as it will be a neutral caretaker government and not the BNP-
led coalition that will be conducting the elections. But what happens
if the caretaker government defies the EC and rigs the elections in the
ruling coalition's favour? It is in this context that one has to consider
seriously the Opposition's allegation that the increase in the retirement
age of Supreme Court judges under the 14th Constitution Amendment
Act, passed on 16 May 2004, has been aimed at ensuring a caretaker
government friendly towards the BNP. Things will be even easier for
the latter if a friendly EC looks the other way while the elections are
hijacked by the BNP-led coalition. It is precisely this apprehension
that explains the strong reaction of the opposition parties to the BNP-
led coalition government's appointment of a CEC in contemptuous
disregard for their demand for the selection of a person acceptable to
all political parties. Indeed, the ruling coalition can have a completely
subservient EC since, as we have seen, all of the latter's members are
set to retire months before the next general elections and the
government can well appoint in their place party loyalists who will
act as the government's rubber stamps.

The kind of appointments the government makes will be closely
watched. Meanwhile, all that one has witnessed so far strongly suggests that the BNP-led coalition is making a no-holds-barred effort to
destroy the Awami League as a political force and make sure that it is
going to win the next general elections. Of course, intention is always
difficult to establish beyond reasonable doubt. But the question
remains: Why otherwise would the coalition and its supporters have
done the shocking and grossly improper things they have done? The
other question that remains is: Will they succeed?

Notes

1. See the Bangladesh Election Commission's website, www.bd-ec.org/stat/parliament.
2. News report, '26,000 Awami League Men Killed During Coalition Rule, Rallies Told', *The Daily Star* (Internet edition), 3 April 2004.
3. News report, 'Hasina Asks Govt to Stop Attacks on Awami League Men, Arrest BNP Terrorists', *The Daily Star* (Internet edition), 18 January 2002.
4. News report, 'Hasina Terms 100-Day Rule an Episode of Disaster', *The Daily Star* (Internet edition), 27 January 2002.
5. News item, 'Rehabilitation Move: BCL Activists Didn't Go to DU Halls', *The Daily Star* (Internet edition), 4 December 2001.
6. Ahmed Rahat, 'JCD, Shibir Resistance: BCL Out of IU Campus for Seven Months', *The Daily Star* (Internet edition), 26 May 2002.
7. News report, 'BCL Leader Gunned Down in Chittagong', *The Daily Star* (Internet edition), 30 January 2002.
8. News report, '75 More AL and CL Members Granted Bail in Ctg', *The Daily Star*, (Internet edition), 30 January 2002.
9. News report, '200 AL, BCL Men Granted Bail', *The Daily Star* (Internet edition), 28 January 2002.
10. Ibid.
11. Shahidul Islam, '1100 False Cases after Oct. 1 Polls: 600 AL, BCL Men to Surrender to Court in Chittagong', *The Daily Star* (Internet edition), 27 January 2002.
12. News report, '75 More AL, BCL Men Granted Bail in Ctg'.
13. News report, '1100 False Cases after Oct. 1 Polls'.
14. Ibid.
15. News report, 'Haji Selim Granted Bail', *The Daily Star* (Internet edition), 27 January 2002.
16. News report, 'Haji Selim's Bail Petition Rejected', *The Daily Star* (Internet edition), 24 January 2002.
17. News report, 'Govt Absolves Pintu in Another Criminal Case', *The Daily Star* (Internet edition), 3 April 2005.
18. News report, 'Petition for the Withdrawal of Extortion Charge against Pintu Granted', *The Daily Star* (Internet edition), 23 March 2005.
19. News report, 'A Fall from Grace', *The Daily Star* (Internet edition), 27 December 2001.
20. Those familiar with Bangladesh would have no trouble realizing that the reference was to Begum Zia.
21. Editorial, 'Lawless Bangladesh: Khaleda's Recipe for Disaster', *The Statesman* (Kolkata and Delhi), 24 February 2004.
22. Editorial, 'We Better Avoid Ruse: Judicial Investigation by a High Court Judge Imperative', *The Daily Star* (Internet edition), 13 May 2002.
23. News report, 'Mockbul Arrested, Gets One Month's Detention', *The Daily Star* (Internet edition), 3 December 2001.
24. News report, 'Detention Under SPA Not Allowed After Arrest on Suspicion: HC', *The Daily Star* (Internet edition), 8 April 2003.

25. ZIA is the acronym for Zia International Airport, which is Bangladesh's airport near Dhaka, named after the assassinated President of Bangladesh and distinguished freedom fighter, Ziaur Rahman. Begum Zia is his widow.

26. Mahfuz Anam, 'Commentary: An Appeal for Shahriar's Release', *The Daily Star* (Internet edition), 18 January 2002.

27. News report, 'Shahriar Released on Bail: "A Freedom Fighter Cannot Be a Traitor"', *The Daily Star* (Internet edition), 21 January 2002.

28. Editorial, 'Rule of Law Vindicated for Now: Government Behaviour Was High-Handed All the Way', *The Daily Star* (Internet edition), 22 January 2002.

29. News report, 'White Paper Released: Hasina, Most Ministers Linked to 40 Cases of Graft', *The Daily Star* (Internet edition), 24 January 2002.

30. News report, 'Third Part of the White Paper on 20 More Cases', *The Daily Star* (Internet edition), 4 May 2002.

31. Ibid., and also news report, 'Special Funds for Five Top Army Officers', *The Daily Star* (Internet edition), 4 May 2002.

32. Editorial, 'BNP's White Paper and Awami League's List: Form an Independence Commission and Put it in Charge of Investigation and Prosecution', *The Daily Star* (Internet edition), 25 January 2002.

33. News report, 'All Charges, No Cases', *The Daily Star* (Internet edition), 3 May 2002.

34. Ibid.

35. Ibid.

36. Editorial, 'Blanket Shelving of Corruption Cases Diminishes Rule of Law: Independent Anti-Corruption Commission is the Answer', *The Daily Star* (Internet edition), 26 April 2002.

37. News report, 'Generals in White Paper Fuel Furore in BNP', *The Daily Star* (Internet edition), 9 May 2002.

38. Editorial, 'The White Paper Fall-out: Government Must Establish Culpability', *The Daily Star* (Internet edition), 10 May 2002.

39. Ibid.

40. Ibid.

41. News report, 'Police Bar Awami League from Protest Rally, Snatch Mike,' *The Daily Star* (Internet edition), 4 December 2001.

42. Ibid.

43. News report, 'Police Besiege Awami League Office, Baton Motia, Nasim', *The Daily Star* (Internet edition), 10 January 2002.

44. News report, 'Hartale Policer Pituni, Nari Michhile Chhatra Daler Hamla, Dhakashaho Bibhinno Sthane Bikshipta Shangharsha, Hai Selim Haspatale' (Police Beatings During Hartal, Chhatra Dal Attack on Women's Procession, Haji Selim in Hospital), *Prothom Alo* (Internet edition), 16 February 2005.

45. Ibid.

46. News report, '106 Asked to Retire for Joining AL-Backed Janatar Mancha', *The Daily Star* (Internet edition), 30 January 2002.

47. Ibid.

48. News report, Sedition Case against Alamgir, Shafiur', *The Daily Star* (Internet edition), 9 April 2002.

49. Ibid.

50. Haroon Habib, 'A Year of Troubles', *Frontline*, 25 October 2002. Also see report on the 'Working Group on Arbitrary Detention', discussed at the 60th session of the United Nations Human Rights Commission with Leila Zerrougui as chairperson/rapporteur, on 15 December 2003 (EC/CN.4/20004-3), paragraph 26, p. 11.

51. News report, 'Sedition Case against Janatar Mancha Leader Stayed for Six Months', *The Daily Star* (Internet edition), 10 November 2004.

52. News report, 'How He Irked the BNP', *The Daily Star* (Internet edition), 22 June 2002.

53. Editorial, 'The President's Resignation: It Raises Questions that Have Serious Implications', *The Daily Star* (Internet edition), 22 June 2002.

54. Mahfuz, Anam, 'Commentary: The President is Neutral, Show Him the Door: The BNP Gives a Bizarre Twist to the Highest Constitutional Office', *The Daily Star* (Internet edition), 25 June 2002.

55. 'Bangladesh Alternative Stream', in English.

56. News report, 'Midnight Bomb Attack on B. Chy's Office: Police Raze Rally Stage to Ground', *The Daily Star* (Internet edition), 11 March 2004.

57. Ibid.

58. News report, 'BNP Men Attack B. Chy, Cops Join to Foil Rally', *The Daily Star* (Internet edition), 12 March 2004.

59. A Dhaka neighbourhood.

60. The English for 'Shaheed' is 'martyr'.

61. News report, 'BNP Men Attack B. Chy, Cops Join to Foil Rally'.

62. Ibid.

63. Ibid.

64. Editorial, 'What Brand of Democracy is this? Retaliatory Strike Abomindable', *The Daily Star* (Internet edition), 12 March 2004.

65. News report, 'Govt Takes a Hard Line on B. Chy's Forum', *The Daily Star* (Internet edition), 16 March 2004.

66. News report, 'Major Mannan's Beverage Factory Bombed, Rampaged', *The Daily Star* (Internet edition), 16 March 2004.

67. News report, 'Mannan's Five Bank Accounts Frozen', *The Daily Star* (Internet edition), 17 March 2004.

68. Ibid.

69. News report, 'Chy Launches Political Party: Bikalpa Dhara Bangladesh to "Unite Nation"', *The Daily Star* (Internet edition), 9 May 2004.

70. Ibid.

71. Ibid.

72. National Unity Platform in English.

73. Shameem Mahmud and Aminul Islam, 'BNP Activists Disrupt BDB, Oikya Manch Meet in Mymensingh', *The Daily Star* (Internet edition), 26 October 2004.

74. Ibid.

75. Editorial, 'Dissent Under Threat: The Govt Mustn't Allow this to Happen Any More', *The Daily Star* (Internet edition), 27 October 2004.

76. Ibid.

77. News report, 'Verbal Divorce of Wife: HC Declares "Fatwas" Illegal', *The Bangladesh Observer* (Internet edition), 2 January 2001.

78. Ibid.
79. Taj Hashmi, 'Failure of the Welfare State, Islamic Resurgence and Political Legitimacy in Bangladesh—IV, Jamaat Emerging as an Alternative to Secular Organisations, *Holiday* (Internet edition), 16 February 2002.
80. Ibid.
81. Ibid.
82. The number of additional judges coming up for confirmation as permanent was five. The Chief Justice did not recommend one of them as he had been accused of corruption.
83. News report, 'Confirmation of Judges: CJ's Recommendation Ignored', *The Daily Star* (Internet edition), 22 May 2002.
84. News item, 'Non-confirmation of Judges: Senior Lawyers Fail to get President's Date', *The Daily Star* (Internet edition), 28 May 2002.
85. News report, 'Sr Lawyers Meet President Today on Judge Issue', *The Daily Star* (Internet edition), 29 May 2002.
86. News report, 'President Urged to Confirm Appointment of Three Judges', *The Daily Star* (Internet edition), 30 May 2002.
87. I was asked not to reveal his identity as he feared reprisals.
88. News report, 'Appointment of 19 Judges: Lawyers to Boycott Chief Justice's Court from Today', *The Daily Star* (Internet edition), 30 August 2004.
89. Ibid.
90. Ibid.
91. Ibid.
92. News report, 'Pro-Government Lawyers to Ignore Bar Decision', *The Daily Star* (Internet edition), 31 August 2004. Also, see news report, 'Lawyers Boycott CJ's Court', *The Daily Star* (Internet edition), 1 September 2004.
93. News report, 'Pro-Government Lawyers to Ignore Bar Decision'.
94. Editorial, 'High Court Appointments: Transparency and Consultation Must Always Be Key', *The Daily Star* (Internet edition), 1 September 2004.
95. Editorial, 'Judges Certificate Case: HC Convicts Editors, Publishers, Reporters of Contempt, *The Daily Star* (Internet edition), 22 March 2005.
96. News item, 'Certificate "tampering": SC Bar Asks HC Judge to Stand Down: Tells Chief Justice to Remove Justice Faizee', *The Daily Star* (Internet edition), 31 October 2004.
97. News report, 'HC Judge Withdrawn: His Bench Colleague Refuses to Sit with Him', *The Daily Star,* (Internet edition), 1 November 2004.
98. Editorial, 'Disgraceful Appointment', *The Bangladesh Observer* (Internet edition), 1 November 2004.
99. Ibid.
100. News report, 'Judge's Certificate Case: HC Convicts Editors, Publishers, Reporters of Contempt', *The Daily Star* (Internet edition), 22 March 2005.
101. Ibid.
102. Ibid.
103. Bangladesh Bar Council is a corporate body constituted under the Provisions of the Bangladesh Legal Practitioners and Bar Council Order of 1972. Its functions include admitting people on its rolls as advocates, holding

examinations to this end, and removing from its rolls those guilty of professional misconduct or failure to pay their dues.

104. News report, 'Judge Faizee's Bar Certificate Cancelled: Bar Council Decides to File Criminal Case against Him for Furnishing False Info', *The Daily Star* (Internet edition), 26 April 2005.

105. News report, 'Judges Certificate Case: HC Convicts Editors, Publishers and Reporters of Contempt'.

106. Editorial, 'Judgement Likely to Curb Freedom of Press', *The Daily Star* (Internet edition), 23 March 2005.

107. News report, 'CJ, Judges Keep Off Bar Break-Up Party', *The Daily Star* (Internet edition), 2 March 2005.

108. News report, 'Judge Faizee's Bar Certificate Cancelled'.

109. Ibid.

110. News report, 'HC Stays Cancellation of Faizee's Enrolment', *The Daily Star* (Internet edition), 8 May 2005.

111. Ibid.

112. News report, 'Judges, Bar Agitation Brew Storm at JS', *The Daily Star* (Internet edition), 17 May 2005.

113. News report, 'SC Bar to Cancel Sircar, Moudud Membership', *The Daily Star* (Internet edition), 18 May 2005.

114. News report, 'HC Bars Agitation at Court, Boycott', *The Daily Star* (Internet edition), 24 May 2005.

115. Ibid.

116. Haroon Habib, 'A Controversial Amendment', *Frontline*, 18 June 2004.

117. Ibid.

118. Ibid. The Chief Justice at the time of enacting the amendment was K.M. Hasan. It was, however, known then that he was due for retirement on 27 January 2004. The Chief Justice at the time of writing, J.R. Mudassir Husain, has done nothing to annoy the BNP–Jamaat alliance.

119. Ibid.

120. Editorial, '14th Amendment: Does it Add Value to the Constitution?', *The Daily Star* (Internet edition), 18 May 2005.

121. Haroon Habib, 'A Controversial Amendment'.

122. Editorial, '14th Amendment: Does it Add Value to the Constitution?'

123. Ibid.

124. News report, 'Justice Aziz Becomes CEC: Pledges to Uphold Free, Fair Elections', *The Daily Star* (Internet edition), 24 May 2005.

125. News report, 'Hasina Says Aziz Picked to Rig National Polls: Rules Out Cooperation with the New CEC', *The Daily Star* (Internet edition), 25 May 2005.

126. Ibid.

127. News report, 'Justice Aziz Becomes CEC'.

128. News report, 'Prestige By-poll Well Managed: Absence of Army at Centres, False Balloting, Alliance's Intimidation Mar Election', *The Daily Star* (Internet edition), 2 July 2004.

129. Ibid.

130. News report, 'Dhaka-10 By-polls: Observers Demand Result Cancellation', *The Daily Star* (Internet edition), 7 July 2004.
131. News report, 'Emphatic Win for Mohiuddin', *The Daily Star* (Internet edition), 11 May 2005.
132. News report, 'CCC polls: CMP Chief Removed as EC Finds Him Guilty', *The Daily Star* (Internet edition), 3 May 2005.
133. Shakhawat Liton, 'EC Wins Kudos for Tough Stand', *The Daily Star* (Internet edition), 11 May 2005.
134. Ibid.
135. Ibid.
136. Ibid.

Eight
The Fundamentalist Challenge

This chapter dwells on the efforts of the Jamaat, IOJ and other funda-mentalist Islamist organizations to use their participation in the BNP-led government to push their Islamist agenda and capture power. They have, by every indication, launched a two-pronged process. The first element of their strategy is the creation of a wave of Islamist fanaticism on whose crest they can ride to power, swamping all their opponents. In the process they are further strengthening their organization and increasing their resources to prepare themselves for the final takeover. The second element is installing their own men in strategic positions in the government—thereby creating a state within a state—and taking over institutions like universities, colleges and schools to propagate their brand of reductionist Islam.

The creation of a climate of fanaticism is very important from their standpoint because that alone can fetch them the mass support they now so woefully lack. Central to the creation of such a climate is the designation of a person or a group—religious, ethnic or political—as the enemy and giving a strident call for its suppression, if not annihi-lation. In most such cases a group already exists as a demon in the minds of those whipping up fanaticism. Even otherwise, generation of hatred for opponents is inherent in the glorification of one's own religion or nationality. As Stanley J. Tambiah points out,

> When any group or community constructs its own myths of origin, stories of victories and conquests, and the lives of exemplary culture heroes, it also directly or indirectly denigrates and blackens the traditions of the opponent neighbours and contestants against whom its accom-plishments are measured.[1]

Islamist fundamentalists, who are now organized under the banner of the Jamaat, IOJ and associated organizations, have been targeting minorities—Hindus, Buddhists and Christians—and identifying them, in deed if not in words, as enemies. Even the Ahmadiyya sect of Muslims has not been spared. The result has been predictable. According to Rosaline Costa, Director, Hotline Bangladesh, a human rights organization, non-Muslims, who constituted 33 per cent of Bangladesh's population at the time of its liberation from Pakistani rule in 1971, now constitute 9.9 per cent.[2] In this the fundamentalists are hand-in-glove with a section of the BNP which is pathologically anti-Hindu and anti-India, and with criminal elements. The primary target of the Islamists have been the Hindus, their *bete noir* since even before the creation of East Pakistan and its post-liberation emergence as Bangladesh. There have been several riots following the one in Khulna in 1950. There were widespread attacks on Hindus in 1964 following the theft of the Prophet's hair from the Hazratbal Mosque in Kashmir, and in 1992 (when the BNP was in power) following the demolition of the Babri Mosque in India. Needless to say, the rise of Hindu fundamentalism in India and the hate campaign conducted against Muslims by organizations like the Vishwa Hindu Parishad and the Bajrang Dal have greatly helped Bangladesh's Islamist fundamentalists and their allies.

Turn for the worse

Things have taken a turn for the worse since the ascent of the present BNP-led four-party coalition to power. Rioting against Hindus, who are generally regarded as supporters of the Awami League, broke out even before the results of the elections on 1 October 2001, which the BNP-led alliance swept, were announced. According to a statement by the then Home Minister of Bangladesh in the country's National Parliament, 266 persons were killed and 213 women raped over a period of 25 days. While the figures are bad enough, the actual numbers killed and raped are clearly much higher. For one, governments always play down the number of victims on occasions like riots. For another, without rioting on a much larger scale, 15,000 Hindus would not have left their homes and crossed over to the border areas of West Bengal for safety, while about 100,000 would not have been prevented from doing so by police and paramilitary personnel. Referring to the atrocities—beatings, killings, torching of homes, shaving of heads and sexual violence—a report by the India Abroad News Service (IANS) quotes an official of the Hindu–Boudhya–Christian Oikya Parishad (Hindu–Buddhist–Christian Unity Council) as saying, that these had 'surpassed all previous records. Cruelty in some cases has overshadowed atrocities in 1971.'[3] It further cites a report in The *Daily Star* which quoted a school teacher in southern Bhola as saying that hundreds of Hindu women aged between 8 and 70 were raped on the night of 2 October 2001 in Annada Prashad village. He said that all houses in the village were systematically looted, forcing the Hindus to flee. Some were forced to pay protection money.[4]

That the schoolteacher's statement was not an exaggeration becomes clear on considering Rosaline Costa's statement that 98 per cent of the Hindu women interviewed at Bhola had been raped.[5] It was the same in most other places where rioting had occurred. The police did little to help those attacked and joined the attackers in some cases. The *Daily Star* report cited by the IANS dispatch in question quoted a local woman in Bhola as saying, 'You know the policemen camping at nearby Vaskar Bari are the attackers' friends, they were invited by the rapists.'[6] That her accusation is credible is indicated by Costa's statement that local police did little or nothing to investigate the attacks on the minorities.[7] The IANS report quotes *Janakantha* as saying that nearly 4 million members of the minority community (read Hindus) were tortured in post–2001 election period in Bangladesh. Referring to communal violence in Jessore, the report quotes *Prothom Alo* as stating that Hindus were still living in fear and endured the tortures silently as they felt it would not be safe to report the matter to the police or the administration. What was most striking, it added, was the inaction of the law-enforcers. The authorities seemed to have closed their eyes.[8]

Though large-scale rioting has not occurred since the one that began on 1 October 2001, Hindus continue to be persecuted and have to leave their homes and flee to India. According to a news report in the *Daily Star* of Saturday 11 May 2002[9], a gang of about 40 criminals, riding motorbikes and allegedly supporters of the BNP, drove into Basantapur village in Natore on Wednesday 8 May night, firing guns and exploding crackers,[10] and attacked 13 Hindu families. They beat up the men, harassed and threatened to rape the women if the villagers disclosed their identities to newsmen. The attackers, who ransacked the houses, looted a huge amount of cash and moveable property like gold ornaments, returned the next day and warned the villagers of dire consequences unless they were paid more money. The report said that the gang had on 4 May asked the families to pay them sums ranging from

Tk 20,000 to 50,000, and that this was the fourth attack on the Hindus of Basantapur village. It further stated that the police had arrested four BNP cadres and had set up a temporary camp near the village to avoid a repetition of such incidents.

Police action, however, has always been tardy and half-hearted, with the result that many of those arrested after various incidents have subsequently been acquitted or enlarged on bail. Not surprisingly Hindus have had no respite in Bangladesh. A report in the *Prothom Alo* of 27 March 2005[11] showed how local criminals were trying to force six Hindu families in Belghoriahat in Bagmari Upazila of Rajshahi District to leave their homes and go away. They were threatening to lock the families inside their houses and set them on fire, stoning the houses every night, throwing human excreta inside the rooms and making obscene remarks at their women whenever they ventured out of their homes. According to the families, a local criminal, Akbar, and his associates were doing all this to capture their property. They also said that the District Magistrate of Rajshahi, to whom they had appealed for protection on 20 March, had asked the police personnel at Bagmara police station to inquire into the matter and take stern measures. The report observed that the police had not visited the village until 26 March.

The worst act of savagery, however, occurred on 19 November 2003 in a remote village in Banshkhali Upazila, 30 km from Chittagong city. A gang of 20 persons set a two-storey earthen house on fire, burning to death 11 members of the family of Tejendra Sushil, including a 4-day-old baby. The only survivor was Bimalendra Sushil, a son of Tejendra and also a village physician, who had escaped by jumping out of the window. While many felt that the ghastly crime was no more than the work of robbers angry because they could not break into the first floor, others held that this was a part of a minority cleansing strategy. Sheikh Hasina was clearly one of them. According to her, the killings marked an attempt to implement a blueprint, drawn up by the BNP-led government immediately after assuming office, to persecute the minority communities.[12]

Not the only ones

Hindus are not the only victims. Buddhists, mainly indigenous hill people inhabiting the Chittagong Hill Tracts (CHT), have perhaps been a bigger target. Saradindu Mukherji quotes Brian Eads who wrote in the *Observer*, London, of 20 July 1978 that:

Bangladesh security forces are waging a terror campaign against the non-Bengali tribes of CHT which threatens the very existence of the Buddhist minority of half a million people. Official silence makes it impossible to give exact figures, but sources in the hill tracts last week gave me precise details of killings, rapes, summary arrests and detentions without trial since the end of last year. The killings and rapes are said to run into hundreds, the arrests and detentions into thousands.[13]

Religious persecution of the Buddhists is an integral part of a wider scheme to change the CHT's demographic and religious character by colonizing the homeland of the indigenous people, collectively called Jumma[14] people, by Bengali Muslims. The process began when Bangladesh was East Pakistan. The CHT was deprived of its 'Excluded Area' status in 1963[15] and thrown wide open to colonization by Bengali Muslims from Noakhali, Chittagong, Sylhet and Comilla. Saradindu Mukherjee writes that it was 'the massive Bengali settlement on the Jumma land which caused the first forced displacement of about 100,000 tribesmen in the CHT'[16], and that rioting by Bengali Muslims evicted a single group of 60,000 tribals in 1961, pushing them into Burma and India, where they remained. The attack on the Buddhist Jummas stopped only when the Sri Lankan and other governments protested to Pakistan.[17]

If anything, the situation became worse after the liberation of East Pakistan and the emergence of Bangladesh. Sheikh Mujib and other Awami League leaders had become hostile to the indigenous people because the Chakma king Tridib Roy and a section of the Jummas had supported Pakistan during the liberation war. Sheikh Mujib's assassination on 15 August 1975, however, brought further misery to the CHT. The creation of the CHT Development Board by Ziaur Rahman in 1976 led to accelerated influx by Bengali Muslims and suffering for the Jumma people. Driven to desperation, Jummas, organized under the Parbatya Chattargam Jana Sanhati Samiti (PCJSS), formed an armed wing, the Shanti Bahini in 1973, and re-sorted to armed action in 1976.[18] The military action that followed drove a large number of Jummas to seek refuge in India where they were housed in camps. As President, Ziaur Rahman however tried to arrive at a political settlement and open a channel of communication with the Shanti Bahini. His assassination on 30 May 1981 put an end to the process. H.M. Ershad, who became President through a military coup, declared two amnesties in 1983 and 1985 respectively and established a Parbatya Jila Sthaniya Sarkar Parishad or Hill District Local Government Council.[19] It did not work because it did not have enough power. It was only after Sheikh Hasina became Prime Minister in 1996 that a real attempt to find a solution led to the peace agreement of 2 December 1997 between the PCJSS and the Bangladesh government. Despite bitter attacks and threats of a nationwide agitation by the BNP, Sheikh Hasina's government had the Chittagong Hill Autonomous Regional Council Act passed by Bangladesh's National Parliament in May 1998, which formed an autonomous council. A vicious campaign launched by the BNP and the Jamaat and its affiliates, however, hindered a full-fledged implementation of the accord particularly in respect of the return of the refugees and their rehabilitation. Tension continued.

The situation has deteriorated further since the formation of the BNP-led coalition government, which has combined ethnic cleansing of the Jummas with a massive drive to Islamize the CHT. Even Buddhist monks are not spared. Islamist fundamentalists beheaded the highly respected monk Bhikkhu Gyanojyoti Mahasthobir in Raozan in Chittagong District on 21 April 2002. Later in the same year, the Venerable Bhikkhu Khela Chong was beaten up and hanged by the Bangladeshi Army at Kaokhali in Rangamati District. Kumar Sivasish Roy of the Jumma People's Network UK stated in a paper presented at a conference in June 2005 that 'Al-Rabita [Rabita Al-Alam Al-Islami], a Saudi government funded NGO, is the main Islamic missionary organisation in the region. Supported by the military, it is entrusted with the task of the Islamisation of the CHT.' According to him the Jamaat worked actively with the military in the region.[20]

Meanwhile, 82,000 Jumma families which have been listed as internally displaced still await government assistance, and refugees, who have returned from India, have not been properly rehabilitated.[21]

Even Christians, who had faced no problems until recently, and who as 'people of the book' are entitled to religious freedom under Islam, are now under attack. The most heinous case occurred on 3 June 2001 when a bomb attack on a church in Beniarchar in Gopalganj District left 10 persons dead and 24 wounded. A top-ranking leader of HUJIB, also Vice-President of the Shiddhirganj Madarinagar Quomi Madrasa, and three of his accomplices were arrested from Kakrail, Dhaka, on 8 June in connection with the blast.[22] There have been several attacks on Christians since the BNP-led government came to power, and Islamist fundamentalists have killed at least five Christian functionaries since 2003.

Open season on the Ahmadiyyas

Much more severe has been the persecution of the Ahmadiyyas, who have been living in Bangladesh since 1912. They faced no serious attacks until 1987, when an organization called the International Khatme Nabuwat Movement Bangladesh (IKNM)[23] attacked and captured several Ahmadiyya mosques in and around Brahmanbaria town in Brahmanbaria District. The community again faced violence in 1992, when there were three attacks on its mosques and religious establishments in different parts of Bangladesh. After a lull of sorts, the attacks resumed in 1997. There were two serious incidents in 1999. Seven Ahmadiyyas were injured in an attack on a mosque of the community in Kushtia District on 7 January. Seven Ahmadiyyas were killed and number of them were permanently crippled on 8 October 1999 when a bomb exploded in an Ahmadiyya mosque in Khulna during Friday prayers. No one was arrested. While a number of incidents occurred during 2000, a well-organized and well-coordinated campaign of persecution backed by violence began to take shape in 2003. The worst incident occurred after Friday prayers on 31 October 2003. A mob led by a local Jamaat leader arrived at the residence of Shah Alam, the imam of a local Ahmadiyya mosque in Jessore District, and asked him to renounce his faith. Upon his refusal, the leader and a few of his associates assaulted Alam mercilessly in front of his wife and daughter. He succumbed to his injuries four hours later. No one had been arrested for the crime until 17 June 2005.[24]

The incident was especially important for two reasons. It demonstrated the Jamaat's leadership role in the anti-Ahmadiyya movement and the BNP-led four-party coalition government's tacit support. This support became evident when the Home Ministry banned 20 Ahmadiyya publications on 8 January 2004. The Ahmadiyyas submitted two written appeals to Prime Minister Khaleda Zia to rescind the ban but without result. Finally, the Ahmadiyya community and seven human rights organizations filed a writ petition before the High Court on 20 December and obtained a stay order on the government's decision the following day.

If there could still be any doubt about the government's role, it was removed by the totally partisan conduct of the police and the civil administration during a number of attacks launched by the IKNMB and a more recent creation, Amra Dhakabashi (We, the Inhabitants of Dhaka). On 11 March 2004, an armed mob of 10–12,000 IKNMB supporters, which had earlier been a part of the anti-Ahmadiyya rally at Bogra town following Friday prayers, marched toward an Ahmadiyya mosque at Seuzgari in Bogra District.[25] Intercepted by the police, its leaders demanded that the police search the mosque and hand over Ahmadiyya publications to them. They also demanded that the police replace the existing signboard on the mosque— 'Ahmadiyya Mosque'—by the one brought by them which declared: 'A place of worship of the Kadiyanis in Bogra; no Muslim should be deceived into considering it a mosque'. The police not only took five leaders of the IKNMB mob inside the mosque, ignoring the protests of the Ahmadiyyas who had gathered to protect their mosque, but, ordered by the Additional Superintendent of Police leading them, also had the existing signboard replaced by the one the mob had brought.[26]

Far more shocking was what happened in Khulna between 17 and 19 April 2005. On 17 April, a mob of nearly 15,000 IKNMB supporters, led by the organization's Nayeb-e-Ameer, Mufti Nur Hussain Nurani, and central leader, Mohammad Muntassir Ahmed, approached the Ahmadiyya mosque at Sundarban Bazar in Shyamnagar Upazila of Satkhira District to put up on it a signboard stating, 'It is a place of worship for Kadiyanis, Sundarban Bazar', and advising Muslims not to mistake it for a mosque. As the Ahmadiyyas present at the site tried to prevent the mob from doing so, its members began throwing stones, injuring 50 persons, including women and children, some seriously. Significantly, it is police personnel who requested the mob to hand over the signboard to them and placed it on the mosque in the presence of Deputy Inspector General of Police Sohrab Hossain, Khulna Superintendent of Police Abdul Rahim and a magistrate Mian Masuduzzaman. Immediately after this, the mob looted 10 Ahmadiyya homes located around the mosque, taking away cash, jewellery and other valuables.[27]

Apparently encouraged by the role of the police on 17 April, a mob arrived on 18 April and, besides besieging the mosque, ransacked the home of local Ahmadiyya missionaries Abdul Wadood and Ahmed Ali Molla, and beat up Wadood's son.[28] The next day, the IKNMB supporters looted six more Ahmadiyya houses and assaulted three members of the community.[29] Meanwhile, encouraged by police inaction, Khulna's religious bigots threatened to attack members of the Ahmadiyya community at Koira Upazila on 24 April.[30]

There are several aspects of the attacks from 17 to 19 April that merit special attention. First, one attack at least, on the 17th, occurred in the presence of as high an official as a Deputy Inspector General of Police, who did nothing to stop it. Second, the fact that senior officers were present on both occasions clearly suggests that the incidents cannot be blamed on complicity on the part of low-level officers present on the spot. Third, the argument that their action was guided by their desire to avoid a violent confrontation with the IKNMB crowd would not wash. On every earlier occasion when they had been stopped by the police, armed IKNMB supporters did no more than shout slogans standing in front of police cordons. Fourth, any claim that the police contingent was neither large enough nor adequately equipped to deal with the crowd and, therefore, wanted to defuse the situation by doing what the mob wanted it to do, would also not wash. The police had ample prior notice to organize an adequate presence. At a press conference at Sundarban Bazar local Ahmadiyya leaders had said on 10 April that over 4,000 members of their community were in a state of panic following the distribution of leaflets by the IKNMB asking them to leave the area and urging the government to declare them non-Muslims.[31] Not only that, the Shyamnagar Upazila Nirbahi Officer (sub-district executive officer), Solaiman Mondol, had visited the area and assured them that all possible measures would be taken to protect them.[32]

At a press conference in Dhaka on 12 April, central leaders of the Ahmadiyya Muslim Jamaat had urged Bangladesh's government to take proper measures to protect the community's mosque at Sundarban Bazaar. The community's central missionary, Abdul Awal Khan Chowdhury, had observed, 'We are justifiably apprehensive from our past experience that the local administration will prove inadequate to protect the Ahmadiyya community and its establishments from disgrace.'[33] The Nayeb-e-Ameer of the Ahmadiyya Muslim Jamaat, Professor Meer Mobashsher Ali, said, 'The law enforcement authorities in Bogra had tarnished the image of the country and the Government by putting up a signboard undermining the community by the Khatme Nabuwat Movement on March 11. So we are taking the matter to the notice of the Government five days ahead of the attack.'[34]

All this suggests that the police's role in Sundarban Bazar on 17, 18 and 19 April 2005 reflected orders received from the highest echelons of the government of Bangladesh. This in turn tends to convey a very important message when viewed against the widespread condemnation in Bangladesh and abroad of the attacks on the Ahmadiyyas. On 19 May 2004, the US Assistant Secretary of State for South Asia, Christina Rocca, had said at a press conference at the American Centre in Dhaka that 'Bangladesh has a long tradition as a moderate and tolerant society. The problems that the Ahmadis are facing are causing us concern because it looks as if that things might be getting off [the] tracks a little.'[35] Referring to the ban on Ahmadiyya publications she said, 'We have to see how it plays out, we hope it will be reversed. We are watching it very carefully and it is a [matter of] considerable concern on the part of the United States.'[36]

Nearly six months later, ambassadors of six European Union countries—the Netherlands, Germany, France, Italy, Sweden and Norway—visited the Ahmadiyya mosque at Nakhalpara in Dhaka on November 5 2004, the day on which the IKNMB had threatened to take it over along with the community's mosques at Missionpara in Narayanganj and Brahmanbaria town in Brahmanbaria district. Police on that day thwarted the designs of the IKNMB supporters though at Brahmanbaria the Ahmadiyyas had to conclude their prayers without *azaan*. The Netherlands' ambassador Kees Beemsterboer said on behalf of the entire delegation which he led, 'We are not here to take a stand against anyone. Our main intention is to stand by the Constitution of Bangladesh that guarantees the freedom of religion and expression to all its citizens.'[37]

The attacks at Sundarban Bazar took place despite Christina Rocca's expression of disquiet and the stand taken by the EU envoys. This assumes a special significance when viewed in the context of Bangladesh's dependence on foreign aid and the widespread belief that its banning of several fundamentalist Islamist organizations on 23 February 2005 was aimed at mollifying donor countries that were meeting in Washington, DC, on the same day to consider the future of aid to the country in the light of the rise of Islamist fundamentalism and the abuse of human rights there. The message that comes through once again is clear: Bangladesh's BNP-led government is in no position to act against Islamist fundamentalists beyond a point. Nothing underlines this more starkly than the fact that the Special Powers Act of 1974 and Section 54 of the Criminal Procedure Code (CrPC), which have been liberally used against its political opponents and members of the intelligentsia, have never been invoked against leaders of the IKNMB. This again is hardly surprising considering that both the Jamaat and the IOJ, whose links with the IKNMB are no secret, are part of the BNP-led coalition government that rules the country.

If there is any doubt about the Jamaat being behind the attack on the Ahmadiyyas a look at history will remove it. The Jamaat in Bangladesh is an offshoot of the Jamaat-e-Islami which was established in India in 1941 by Maulana Abul Ala Maududi who held that Islam, as revealed to the Prophet, did not distinguish between the spiritual and the temporal worlds. Going over to Pakistan and establishing the Jamaat's headquarters on the outskirts of Lahore, he demanded the creation of an Islamic state in that country. On 18 January 1953, he prevailed upon a conference of 31 members of the *ulama* in Karachi to demand that the Constitution should declare 'Kadiyanis' to be a non-Muslim minority, that Zafarullah Khan, an Ahmadiyya, be removed as Pakistan's Foreign Minister, and that Ahmadiyyas be removed from all important positions in the government.[38] In February 1953 began massive, brutal attacks on Ahmadiyyas, hundreds of whom were killed. Martial law was imposed on 6 March and Maududi was arrested on 28 March 1953. A military court sentenced him to death on 8 May for his role in inciting violence, a sentence that a civilian court later reduced to 14 years of rigorous imprisonment.[39]

Maududi, of course, did not have to serve the full term of his sentence. He was released on 29 April 1955[40] following the emergence of a new political situation in which the Pakistani establishment sought to enlist the support of Islamist fundamentalists to counter the massive movement in what was then East Pakistan for full regional autonomy and a democratic constitution. Meanwhile, a provincial unit of the Jamaat had been established in East Pakistan in 1951. It, however, became an active organization only after Golam Azam, a professor at Carmichael College, Rangpur, joined it in 1954 as a *muttafiq* or 'associate' and rose rapidly in its ranks.

Given this background and the fact that pressure from the Pakistani unit of the Jamaat had led the government of Zulfiqar Ali Bhutto to declare the Ahmadiyyas non-Muslims in 1974, it is clear that the ideology of the Jamaat would require it to demand that all Ahmadiyyas in Bangladesh be declared non-Muslims and, as a coalition partner whom the BNP does not want to or dare not antagonize, should be able to prevent strong, effective action against the IKNMB's violent and

lawless activities. Indeed, another coalition partner, the IOJ, is a constituent of the IKNMB.

That the attack on the Ahmadiyyas is a part of a wider design to
Talibanize Bangladesh becomes clear on considering that the IKNMB
and its allied and affiliated organizations have also been trying to
neutralize by intimidation two major obstacles in the way of realizing
the design—liberal intellectuals and writers, and the enlightened
media. Thus, at a rally outside the Baitul Mukarram mosque[41] on 24
December 2004, anti-Ahmadiyya elements proclaimed Dr Kamal
Hossain an enemy of Muslims because he was arguing a case in the
High Court in defence of Ahmadiyyas.[42] Earlier, another anti-
Ahmadiyya rally at the same venue on 12 December 2003 had
demanded the arrest and trial of the writer and scholar Humayun
Azad for having written the novel *Pak Sar Zamin Saad Baad* as well as
the President of Bangladesh's National Press Club at Dhaka on the
ground that the two had said things derogatory to Islam.[43] At the
same rally, M. Asadullah, Joint Secretary of the Jamia Talaba Arabia,
which was a part of the Hifazate Khatme Nabuwat Andolan Coordination Committee, an anti-Ahmadiyya alliance, thundered, 'No newspaper will be spared now if it publishes any write-up against us.'
Indeed, threats have been held out against the press at all levels. At an
anti-Ahmadiyya rally in Jyotindranagar in Satkhira District's
Shyamnagar Upazila on 20 April 2005, IKNMB leaders threatened
local journalists with dire consequences for running what they described as false and fabricated reports about their organization. They warned the journalists not to support the Ahmadiyyas, 'otherwise Touhidi
Janata (people believing in one God) will teach you a good lesson'.
Needless to say, the administration took no action against anyone.[44]

The Jamaat's veto power

As in the case of criminal activity by fundamentalist Islamists mentioned in the earlier chapters, the administration's inaction in cases
involving atrocities on minorities clearly indicates that the Jamaat
enjoys veto power in the BNP-led coalition government. This is made
clearer by the Talibanizing process under way in Bangladesh's social
and cultural life ever since Begum Zia assumed power in October
2001. Among the principal targets have been films and plays disapproved of by fundamentalist Islamists. The first to face the chopper

was the sensitive and technically outstanding film *Matir Moina*[45], directed by Tareque Masud and produced by Katherine Masud. The first Bangladeshi film to be shown at the Cannes Film Festival, it received a standing ovation at its premiere on 16 May 2002, as the opening film in the prestigious Directors Fortnight section.[46] On 17 May it was released by MK2, an internationally renowned distribution house which had brought Abbas Kiarostami's films before a global audience. *Variety*, the leading journal of the US film industry, described *Matir Moina* as an accomplished and emotionally involving film, 'an intimately observed story of divisions within a family that reflect the wider clash between moderate and extremist views'.[47]

The letter of May 9 2002 to Mr Tareque Masud, by which Bangladesh's Film Censor Board (FCB) conveyed to him its decision to ban his film, said that the film should not be projected in public as it contained religiously sensitive material.[48] This clearly ran counter to the perception in informed circles. The *Daily Star* observed in an editorial,

> Given the fact that the film depicts madrassah education in a very sensitive light and presents the socio-religious contradictions in any society trying to adjust to the modern world, one is left wondering what caused the ire of the censors. In fact, the film takes a very sympathetic view of madrassah education which contrasts radically with Western depiction of Muslim religious education in such institutions. . . . The Censor Board is confusing depiction of Madrassah education as criticism of our religion. . . . Given that the Board had earlier greenlighted it and chose to withdraw its consent afterwards displays that a malaise deeper than cinematic ethic is involved.[49]

The FCB's decision is intriguing, considering that on 28 April it had recommended that the film be released for showing without cuts. As many as six of the eight FCB members present during the screening had endorsed the decision; one had made no comment and only one had submitted a note of dissent calling for a verification of the rendition of the verses from the Holy Quran in the film.[50] Also, remarkably, there was no bar on the film being shown abroad; the government just did not want it to be shown in Bangladesh.

Ultimately, however, domestic and international pressure was too strong for the Bangladesh government to resist. Allowed screening with minor cuts, it was initially released in Modhumita cinema hall in Dhaka in October 2002, which was followed by a record four-week, packed-house run in Balaka cinema hall in Dhaka in July–August 2003. The Jamaat and the fundamentalist cluster around it, however, remained bitterly critical of it and opposed its screening wherever they could. Thus, activists of the Shibir prevented the showing of *Matir Moina* and another symbolic and sensitive film, *Lal Shaloo*, at a film festival organized at Chittagong University on 25 and 26 March 2005. Under their pressure, the organizers had to show commercial entertainment films in their places. Interestingly, the President of the Shibir's Chittagong University unit denied the allegation and said that the Shibir as an organization was not involved in preventing the screening of the two films. Significantly he said nothing about what Shibir supporters did in their personal capacity.[51]

It is not difficult to see why the Islamist fundamentalists, who had collaborated with the Pakistani army during the liberation of Bangladesh, were so opposed to the release of *Matir Moina* for domestic showing. Tareque Masud has made three outstanding documentaries, *Muktir Gaan* (Song of Liberation), *Muktir Katha* (Story of Liberation) and *Narir Katha* (Story of Women) about the liberation war, and is known for his modern and liberal views that are anathema to the fundamentalists. The attack on him and his film is a part of the wider attempt to wipe out both the memories and values of the liberation struggle along with those who seek to keep these alive and create a Bangladesh where the traditional and the modern interact creatively. The need to erase the genuine memories of the freedom struggle and intimidate, physically eliminate or isolate those who uphold these arises, in turn, from the efforts of the fundamentalists to now project themselves as freedom fighters and to Talibanize Bangladesh, which in turn requires the imposition on the whole country of their reductionist and obscurantist version of Islam.

An integral part of such an attempt is the elimination or suppression of any form of entertainment incompatible with the Talibanesque version of morality. Obviously in keeping with such an approach, the government, on 19 May 2002, ordered the closure of eight popular TV pay channels and five 'free-to-air' channels 'to resist the adverse impact of alien culture on religious and social values'. The channels banned were HBO, Star Movies, Star World, MTV, Channel V, MGM, Hallmark, AXN, RAI TV, PTV, TVE and SNTV. Besides, cable operators promised not to show films from VCDs, while ATN Bangla said it would not telecast objectionable foreign films in future.[52] Unfortunately, in its zeal to please the fundamentalists, the government had bargained without popular reaction, which was instant and angry. In less than 24 hours, it had to lift the ban on all channels except MTV and Channel V.

Jailing of a playwright and other outrages

The Islamist fundamentalists, however, refused to give up and continued acting as cultural censors and executioners, coming down hard on everyone or every piece of artistic creation they considered, rightly or wrongly, to have insulted their religion. This is clearly established from the fate of the Bengali play *Katha Krishnakali*, which tells the story of a young girl trafficked to India for prostitution, and its author Sambit Shaha, a Hindu. His arrest on 16 August 2002 followed the staging of the play in Faridpur town, about 100 km from Dhaka on 6 August, which led to angry demonstrations by hundreds of fundamentalists claiming that it insulted Prophet Muhammad because it had a sequence showing a man playing the latter's role. Shaha's assertion that the original script of the play had no reference to the Prophet[53] seemed to be corroborated by the fact that there had been no trouble when the play was first staged in Dhaka several months earlier; nor had there been any in several towns where it had been staged since then. Notwithstanding all this, the police arrested Shaha and five others involved in the play's production as frenzied protests by fundamentalists continued.[54]

That the fundamentalists targeted not just the play but everyone and every organization standing for a plural society that permitted dissent and freedom of thought, belief and expression, became clear when a fundamentalist organization, Touhidi Janata (also spelt Tawhidi Janata), held out death threats to journalists who had supported the theatre group that had staged *Katha Krishnakali*. Thugs with machetes and axes attacked one of them, Belal Chowdhury, a reporter with *Thikana*, a local Faridpur newspaper, who was seriously injured and had to be removed to Dhaka for treatment.

Shaha's arrest provides yet another example of Begum Zia's government surrendering to pressure from Islamist fundamentalists. Encouraged by such incidents, the latter have relentlessly sought to eliminate from Bangladesh's life everything that does not conform to their Talibanized version of Islam. Paila (spelt Pahela by some) Baishakh, the first day of the Bengali year, is a major occasion in

Bangladesh's social and cultural life. The *Daily Star* observed in an editorial on 14 April 2003, 'Pahela Baishakh has truly become a symbol of our cultural heritage.' It added that a very striking aspect of the day was that its appeal was not confined to members of any particular community. It was a day of celebration for all people.[55] The Jamaat and its associated bodies, however, have always severely disapproved of its observance. As has been seen in Chapter Five, HUJIB, which has close links with the Jamaat, was held responsible for the explosion that killed 10 persons and injured over 100 at Ramna Park on 14 April 2001, when the well-known cultural organization Chhayanot was observing Bengali New Year's Day through a musical *soirée*. In an obvious reference to the incident and the Jamaat's views, the editorial observed, 'Unfortunately, there are fanatics who have failed to realise the social, cultural and economic significance of Pahela Baishakh. They have made attempts to take the fun out of the lives of the citizens by resorting to barbaric means.'[56]

Given the popular enthusiasm for the celebrations, however, the Jamaat and other fundamentalist parties have never launched an open offensive against these. They have confined themselves to sniping from the wings. Recently, however, there have been indications that the administration, over which they now exercise considerable control, is acting on their behalf to take the zest out of the celebrations. Thus, in a release on 12 April 2005, the Chittagong Metropolitan Police urged all guardians to 'discourage their sons and daughters' from going into an overdrive during the celebrations of Pahela Baisakh. Referring to past instances when 'people of all ages, even some overenthusiastic elders, and castes' had become 'so much involved in Bangla Nabo Barsha (Bengali New Year) celebrations' that they forgot their 'civic responsibilities and the [*sic*] religious bindings', it warned that such behaviour was 'tantamount to violation of the law of the land and obstruction of normal civic life.' 'These', it said ominously, were 'punishable offences.'[57] It was only strong criticism in the media and by the public that forced the police to climb down.

Earlier, a bomb attack on a Valentine's Day celebration at the Dhaka University campus on 15 February 2005 had injured 16 persons, including 12 students.[58] On 17 February, while the police were still to make any arrest, six student organizations, all fronts for opposition parties, including the Chhatra League, told a protest rally at the university campus that the Shibir was responsible for the blast. They demanded the immediate arrest of—and punishment to—those behind the attack.[59] Needless to say, Islamist fundamentalists had been severely frowning upon celebrations during occasions like Valentine's Day. Fundamentalists are also trying to crack down on women's participation in sports. Referring to a women's football tournament under way, a central leader of the Islamic Shashantantra Andolan (Islamic Constitutional Movement), Nur Hossain Nurani, accused the four-party alliance government of failure in protecting Islamic values. The tournament, he said, could not be called sport. It was, he said, 'a vulgar display of women's physique'.[60]

The fundamentalists failed to stop the women's football tournament but succeeded in preventing women from participating in the Eighth National Long-Distance Swimming Championship. Four women swimmers, including the ace performer Sabura Khatun, had to pull out of the annual event of the Bangladesh Swimming Federation following threats of dire consequences held out by the Anti-Islamic Activities Prevention Committee (AIAPC).[61] Here too the Jamaat's hand can be seen from the fact that the general secretary of the party's Chandpur District Committee is a leader of the AIAPC![62] Since women swimmers had no trouble participating in the previous year's competition, the incident once again shows how pressure from Islamist fundamentalists is slowly and inexorably leading Bangladesh towards Talibanization.

Infiltrating education

What is worse, a planned effort is on to pack Bangladesh's university faculties with supporters and activists of the Jamaat and the Shibir. A report by Ekramul Huq Bulbul and Masud Milad in *Prothom Alo* of 12 August 2004, states,

> The allegation has been levelled of Jamaatification of the Chittagong University by violating all rules. Most applicants did not get appointed as teachers despite getting four first classes in their educational life. Yet there has been the unprecedented occurrence of appointment of supporters of the Jamaat-e-Islami, a partner in the present four-party coalition government, despite their being without a single first class.[63]

According to the report, aggrieved by such developments, a section of the teachers supporting the BNP decided to meet Prime Minister

Khaleda Zia and place before her the irregularities in the appointment of teachers and non-teaching staff in the university. Further, the report says that according to investigations by *Prothom Alo*, of the 122 teachers appointed during this period, 57 had been appointed by ignoring the recommendations of the Departmental Planning Committee and the number of posts advertised. The situation had become so desperate that even a leader of the BNP-supported Democratic Teachers' Forum, Dr Abdul Moktader, a teacher in the Finance Department, expressed his resentment, 'We are now a minority. The University has become devoid of intellectual excellence as a result of wholesale and irregular appointment of Jamaat-supported teachers.'[64]

Reacting to the charge of Jamaatification, the Vice-Chancellor reportedly stated that it was someone's personal political reaction. Told by *Prothom Alo* that the appointments made in excess of the number of posts had flouted the decision taken at the 239th meeting of the University's Syndicate ruling out appointments in excess of posts advertised, the Vice-Chancellor had said that he was not aware of the decision.[65]

There have also been allegations both of irregular appointments and the appointment of inadequately qualified Jamaat and Shibir supporters as well as those of the BNP at Rajshahi University. On 23 December 2004, for example, the Department of Computer Science and Technology's (CST) selection board appointed 10 teachers without the approval of the University's Recruitment Planning Committee. According to four protesting members of the latter, the university's rules precluded recruitment to posts in which people had been working on an ad hoc basis, and the CST Department already had 13 teachers appointed temporarily four years earlier.[66]

The report also stated that the Department of Social Work appointed five teachers against three advertised posts on 21 December 2004. Of them only one had been placed in the first class in four examinations. Of the other four, one was a Shibir leader and a relative of a pro-Jamaat teacher in the same department, one was a Shibir loyalist, the third was a relative of a pro-Jamaat teacher in Dhaka University's Social Welfare Institute, and the fourth was a Chhatra Dal leader of Dhaka University.[67]

Other examples can be cited. Clearly, the Jamaat is using its participation in the BNP-led coalition government to infiltrate into faculty positions which would further facilitate the spread of its ideology among students. Simultaneously, it is also using it to promote the growth of madrasas, many of which are nurseries for *jihadis*. Thus, according to *Bangladesh Economic Review* statistics, the number of general educational institutions receiving government funds has increased by 9.7 per cent, and the number of madrasas by 22.22 per cent, from 2001 to 2005.[68] On the other hand, the number of general institutions and madrasas had risen by 28 and 17 per cent respectively when the Awami League was in power from 1996 to 2001. Again, the number of teachers in general schools and colleges rose by 12.27 per cent, and those in madrasas by 16.52 per cent during 2001–2005.[69] The number of students in general institutions rose by 8.64 per cent, and in madrasas by 10.12 per cent, during this period. This followed a sharp increase of 1,084,950 in the number of madrasa students, taking the total to 2,959,867 during 1996–2001 when the number of students of general institutions had risen by 1,954,316 to 7,797,163.[70]

With huge resources at its disposal, the Jamaat is clearly proceeding according to a well-conceived plan. At one level it is using its participation in the government to prevent action against its militant cadre, and to take over the institutions of higher learning which had been the bastions of intellectual resistance to it. At another level it is producing masses of Islamist cadres through the proliferating madrasas. At the ground level, it as well as its allied and affiliated organizations are attracting new recruits and whipping up a religious frenzy among them by targeting the minorities. Every 'victory' against the latter, with the help of a conniving law-and-order machinery, is used to infuse amongst Jamaat supporters a feeling of the inevitability of their ultimate victory. Finally, with the intelligentsia, civil society and those political parties committed to secularism and religious tolerance terrorized into silence or rendered incapable of functioning through a planned campaign of assassination and assault, and an administration won over through bribes and infiltration and paralysed by orders from the top, it will launch a massive and violent mass movement that will make victory in an election a mere formality.

This once again raises the old question: Will it succeed? To begin with, one must consider what makes a violent mass movement wax.

The pull of mass movements

According to Erich Fromm in *Fear of Freedom*, the most powerful factor driving a person to a militant mass movement like the Jamaat's is the search for security. According to him, despite the biological separation caused by birth, the child 'remains functionally one with the mother for a considerable period'.[71] Slowly, however, it becomes aware of its separateness from its mother and others. With physical, emotional and mental development an 'organized structure guided by the individual's will and reason develops. If we call this organized and integrated whole of the personality the self, we can also say that the [sic] *one side of the growing process of individuation is the growth of self-strength* [Fromm's italics].'[72] The other side is an increasing feeling of aloneness which leads to a growing feeling of insecurity. 'The primary ties' which link a child to its mother 'offer security and basic unity with the world outside oneself. As long as one was an integral part of that world, unaware of the possibilities and responsibilities of individual action, one did not need to be afraid of it. When one has become an individual, one stands alone and faces the world in all its perilous and over-powering aspects'.

The way to overcoming a feeling of loneliness and insecurity 'is to relate spontaneously to the world in love and work, in the genuine expression of one's emotional, sensuous, and intellectual capacities', becoming 'one again with man, nature and himself, without giving up the integrity and independence of his individual self'.[73] Not all, however, can do so. Many seek security in sadistic domination or masochistic submission. According to Fromm,

> The annihilation of the individual self and the attempt to overcome thereby the unbearable feeling of powerlessness are only one side of the masochistic strivings. The other side is the attempt to become a part of a bigger and more powerful whole outside of oneself, to submerge and participate in it. This power can be a person, an institution, God, the nation, conscience or a psychic compulsion. One surrenders one's own self and renounces all strength and pride connected with it, one loses one's integrity as an individual and surrenders freedom; but one gets a new security and a new pride in the participation in the power in which one submerges. One also gains security against the torture of doubt.[74]

Fromm makes clear that the wish to inflict pain on others is not the essence of sadism. All the different forms of sadism 'go back to one simple impulse, namely, to have complete mastery over another person, to make him a helpless object of our will, to become the absolute

ruler over him, to become his God, to do with him as one pleases'.[75]
Fromm points out that, often, masochistic and sadistic tendencies are
present in the same person. Psychologically,

> both tendencies are the outcomes of the one basic need, springing from
> the inability to bear the isolation and weakness of one's own self. ...
> The sadistic person needs his object just as much as the masochistic
> needs his. Only instead of seeking security in being swallowed, he
> gains it by swallowing somebody else. . . . People are not sadistic or
> masochistic, but there is a constant oscillation between the active
> [sadistic] and passive [masochistic] side of the symbiotic complex, so
> that it is often difficult to determine which side of it is operating at a
> given moment.[76]

Both sadism and masochism facilitate the rise of totalitarian mass
movements—the former by inclining people to dominate others and
the latter by inducing submission. Sometimes the same person exer-
cises dictatorial power over one set of people and surrenders his or
her self to another, or to an organization. Hitler, for example, considered himself to be a tool of destiny. One thus has authoritarian hier-
archies in which each rung comprises people who combine sadistic
control over those below with masochistic surrender to those above.

Erich Hoffer identified an impulse similar to that of masochistic
submission when he said,

> A rising mass movement attracts and holds a following not by its
> doctrine and promises but from the refuge it offers from the anxieties,
> barrenness and meaninglessness of an individual existence. It cures
> the poignantly frustrated not by conferring on them an absolute truth
> or by remedying the difficulties and abuses which made their lives
> miserable, but by freeing them from their ineffectual selves—and it does
> so by enfolding and absorbing them into a closely knit and exultant
> corporate whole.[77]

He underlines a different and equally powerful cause when he says
that people join mass movements because they seek

> a new life—a kind of rebirth—or, failing this, a chance to acquire a
> new element of pride, confidence, hope, a sense of purpose and worth
> by an identification with a holy cause. An active mass movement offers
> them opportunities for both. If they join the movement as full converts,
> they are reborn to a new life in its close-knit collective body, or if

attracted as sympathizers they find elements of pride, confidence and purpose by identifying themselves with the efforts, achievements and prospects of the movement.[78]

Understandably, people who join such movements lack pride and confidence in themselves and a sense of achievement. They see themselves as irremediably spoiled, failures without any prospect for self-advancement. Their ranks include misfits, the unemployed, the new immigrants, internal or external, who are lost in an unfamiliar milieu, and criminals who seek to shed their sense of guilt by espousing what they consider to be a noble cause. Their ranks also include the new poor who 'throb with the ferment of frustration. The memory of better things is as fire in their veins.'[79] Coming from a ruined middle class, the new poor formed the chief support base of the Nazi and Fascist movements in Germany and Italy respectively.

Roots of insecurity

The feeling of insecurity that dogs the lives of people in Bangladesh has many origins. Apart from floods and cyclones, unemployment and lawlessness have assumed alarming proportions. A report in the *Daily Star* of 13 October 2004 states that an 'unbridled rise in joblessness' was stoking frustration among the youth besides making for snowballing crime. According to it, out of the country's population of about 138.1 million in 2003, 68.3 million constituted its workforce. About 27.2 million out of the latter were either unemployed or underemployed.[80] With a million new entrants to the job market every year, and the already low investment level bound to become lower because of the violence unleashed by fundamentalists, the country's formal employment sector could hardly be expected to expand rapidly enough to make a dent in the employment problem. If anything, the problem will become worse, considering that the education provided in a large section of madrasas does not qualify people to play a productive role in a modern economy.

The impact of severe and growing unemployment becomes clear on recalling (from Chapter Two) how rapidly-increasing unemployment contributed to Hitler's rise in Germany. In Bangladesh, growing economic insecurity is compounded by physical insecurity spawned by endemic lawlessness, enough evidence of which is available in the preceding chapters. Along with planned and systematic violence unleashed by Islamist fundamentalists, and the activities of criminal gangs involved in robberies, dacoities, abduction for ransom and con- tract killing, there are the operations of organized syndicates involved in gun-running and drug smuggling.

Nothing underlines the seriousness of the situation more tellingly than the number of murders, which is extremely high for a country of Bangladesh's size and population. According to press reports and human rights groups, about 4,500 people were murdered in 2003, up from 4,000 in the previous year. Home Ministry statistics, however, showed that 3,503 persons were murdered in 2002 and 3,550 in 2003.[81] On average, 350 persons were murdered every month between January and June 2004, pace police sources who also claim a little improvement in the situation between July and September when, on average, 300 people were murdered every month. Human rights groups, however, claim that 395 were murdered in September, 779 in August and 776 in July.[82]

Bangladesh has emerged as the biggest centre for gun-running in South and South-east Asia. In 2003, the Bangladesh Army and the paramilitary Bangladesh Rifles (BDR) seized a large number of fire- arms, along with huge quantities of ammunition and explosives, in three districts—Bandarban, Khagrachhai and Rangamati—in the Chittagong Hill Tracts (CHT). The arms included sophisticated anti- aircraft machine guns, rocket launchers, grenade launchers, Chinese and US made AK-47s, M-79 and M-16 rifles, and grenades.[83] On 27 June in the same year, the police recovered over 100,000 bullets and 200 kgs of explosives in an abandoned truck in a remote village in Bangladesh's north-western Bogra District.[84] The police arrested the truck owner, who was suspected to have close ties with a front organ- ization of the All-Tripura Tiger Force (ATTF), a secessionist outfit active in the north-eastern Indian state of Tripura. In June 2003, again, the BDR recovered a huge cache of arms, ammunition and high frequ- ency communication devices from the CHT, which has a 172-km border with India and Myanmar.[85] In September and October 2003, the BDR recovered five time-bombs, 130 kg of plastic explosives, 226 hand grenades, 310 grenade launchers, 50 time-bomb detonators, and 14 containers of chemicals in the dense forests of Bandarban District. On 30 November 2003, the police recovered four AK-47 rifles, two revolvers, 20 hand grenades, four time bombs, 1,000 AK-47 bullets,

2 kgs of plastic explosives and walkie-talkie sets, after a gunfight with a criminal gang in Dhaka.[86]

These recoveries, however, pale into insignificance when viewed alongside the massive arms haul in Chittagong on 2 April 2002. The inventory reportedly included 690 7.62-mm AK-56-1 and 600 7.62-mm AK-56-2–type assault rifles, 400 9-mm carbines, 100 tommy automatic rifles, 40 150-mm T-69 rocket launchers, 2,000 launching tubes (Ugo rifles), 2,752 magazines of AK 56-1 and 2,400 magazines of AK-56-2–type assault rifles, 800 magazines of 9-mm automatic carbines, 400 magazines for tommy rifles, 400,000 7.25×25 ball pistol bullets, 739,680 bullets of T-56 pistols, 840 40-mm rocket heads of T-69 launchers and 25,020 NV hand grenades.[87]

Understandably, there has been much speculation about the intended destination of the consignment. According to a report datelined 6 July 2004 by Anthony Davis in *Jane s Intelligence Review*, the world's leading defence magazine, the consignment, shipped from Hong Kong, was augmented with additional supplies at Singapore. It was meant for ULFA and the NSCN(I-M).[88] Shahriar Kabir, however, believes that newspapers had published two views regarding whom the arms and ammunition were meant for. One view holds that it was meant for the secessionists of north-eastern India; the other, to create a civil war in Bangladesh. Newspapers have also said that, besides the armed forces, the cadres of no other party except the Jamaat have the training to use such ultra-modern weapons. In the past, reports have appeared in newspapers on different occasions about the Jamaat using rockets and other such ultra-modern arms.[89] Davis' views seem to be supported, albeit by implication, by those of Adm. William J. Fallon, Commander of the US Pacific Command. Asked to explain the basis of his apprehension, expressed at a press conference in Dhaka on 17 April 2005, that some international terrorist groups might have shifted their activities to Bangladesh, taking advantage of the situation on the ground, he cited several recent arms recoveries in that country which, he thought, were destined for radical groups.[90]

Two important conclusions follow from Admiral Fallon's remark. First, 'some international terrorist groups' must certainly include Al Qaeda and its associates, and suggests that the US government is not convinced by the government of Bangladesh's loud protests against media and intelligence reports about their presence in its territory. Second, since these groups cannot but operate under the umbrella of the Jamaat and its satellite organizations, arms and ammunition meant for them must also have been meant for their hosts in Bangladesh. This in turn indicates two things. First, with its large and sophisticated arsenal, huge funds and the capacity for violence unleashed frequently by the Shibir and its other affiliates, the Jamaat has become a powerful and feared organization despite its limited mass base. Second, it is, therefore, an automatic destination for a large number of psychologically weak and insecure people, particularly since siding with it would also bring God's blessings as it seeks to establish an Islamic state. With the passage of time, its front organizations like the Shibir and IKNMB are likely to grow unless the Jamaat is defeated politically and its capacity for violence and spreading terror neutralized through stern administrative action.

Such action has to be really strong because it must prevent corruption in the administration and the police force from undoing its effects. Among other things, corruption enables both criminals and those who seek to bring down a system through violence and terror to bribe their way to their goals or escape the state's efforts to bring them to justice. Equally, it undermines the state's efforts to counter such elements because money for buying arms and ammunition, sophisticated communications and surveillance equipment and so on is diverted to private pockets. Not surprisingly, a major cause of the Kuomintang army's collapse before the People's Liberation Army's advance during the Chinese revolution was the gargantuan corruption that hollowed it out from within.

The point about corruption needs to be made, since it is rampant in Bangladesh. For the fourth year in succession Bangladesh was declared the most corrupt country in the world by Transparency International's corruption perception index released on 20 October 2004.[91] According to a World Bank survey, almost every company in Bangladesh is compelled to pay bribes which consume 3 per cent of their total sales revenue.[92] According to yet another survey—this one by the Transparency International Bangladesh, a chapter of the Berlin-based organization—every year people pay Tk 67.96 billion in bribes to 25 service-sector institutions.[93]

As has been seen in the preceding chapters, the BNP-led four-party coalition government cannot or will not act strongly against any fundamentalist Islamist organization. Such action as is taken under international pressure—for example, the banning of the AHAB, JMB and JMJB and the arrest of Dr Galib and others—has been regularly undone by 'delays' in investigation leading to the grant of bail to the accused and/or sloppy investigation and evidence-gathering leading to acquittal. Thus, on 7 April 2005, 42 cadres of the banned JMJB were released from Rajshahi Central Jail after being granted bail. According to lawyers, the police's delay in investigation paved the way for the grant of bail to the accused, who had been charged in two cases of murdering four persons, one case of attempted murder and another of assaulting police personnel. According to reports, many villagers who had been tortured at JMJB camps last year and returned home only after the arrest of the organization's cadres, had started fleeing after hearing of the release.[94] On 4 August 2005, 12 Islamist terrorists arrested on the charge of attacking a *jatra* show and injuring three performers at Boraigram Upazila, Natore District, on 15 January 2005, were released by the District Judge. This happened after the Investigating Officer submitted a petition saying that they should be discharged as the investigation showed that they were not guilty![95]

Clearly, the Jamaat and other violent Islamist fundamentalist organizations cannot find more congenial conditions for their growth than they have under the present BNP-led government in Bangladesh. As of now, they are not strong enough to have even an outside chance of capturing power on their own through elections. For the overwhelming majority of people in Bangladesh have no use for their distorted version of Islam. Proud of the eclectic Bengali culture, to which both Hindus and Muslims have contributed, the rich language which has been its matrix and which they have defended with their lives during the historic language movement; fond of music, dancing, cinema, the theatre, and the *jatra*; and used to a society where women are increasingly assertive of their rights and playing an important role in several walks of life, they are bound to resist the Talibanization of their country to the last. To come to power, Islamist fundamentalists will have to break their will to resist by terrorizing them thoroughly by a systematic campaign of murder, intimidation and the assassination of key political and social leaders and personalities in field of culture who stand for modernity, moderation and secularism.

As has been seen in the earlier chapters, the process has already begun. The fundamentalists are, however, meeting strong resistance from Bangladesh's active civil society, press and political parties. Organizations like the Nirmul Committee and the Supreme Court Bar Association, NGOs like Ain o Salish Kendra, and several organizations set up to protect human rights and the sanctity of the electoral process, have been fighting the Islamist offensive every inch of the way, undaunted by the heavy odds they face.

Whether fighting fundamentalists, Left extremists, crime syndicates or corruption, the press in Bangladesh has shown a courage and commitment which should be an example to its counterparts anywhere in the world. It has had to pay a heavy price in the process. Seven journalists, including outstanding figures like Manik Shaha, Dipankar Chakravarti and Humayun Kabir Balu have been killed since 2001. Six hundred and seventy-eight of them have had to suffer repression, and 1,236 received death threats during the same period.[96] A four-member delegation of the New York-based Committee to Protect Journalists (CPJ) poignantly highlighted the situation when, after a week-long fact-finding visit, it described Bangladesh at a press conference in Dhaka on 5 March 2004 as the most violent country for newspersons in Asia.[97] Ann Cooper, CPJ's Executive Director, who led the delegation, said that physical assaults and intimidation were almost commonplace, particularly in rural areas where journalists were threatened, beaten severely, or murdered just for reporting.[98]

Given determined resistance by civil society and the press, it will not be easy for the Jamaat and associated fundamentalist bodies to take over and Talibanize Bangladesh. Not only that, their plans will be disrupted if the Awami League-led alliance returns to power in the parliamentary elections due next year. We have seen in Chapter Seven that the appointment of a new Chief Election Commissioner following the retirement of his predecessor, and other changes in the commission's personnel have drawn widespread criticism. Two developments since then have made it amply clear that the allegation that the ground is being prepared for the wholesale rigging of next year's elections cannot be easily brushed aside. The first was the way in which the by-election in the Narsingdi constituency, which was boycotted by the Awami League, was rigged on 22 June 2005. This by-election, in which the BNP candidate Khairul Kabir Khokon defeated his nearest rival Shahadat Hossain Munna, an independent, by 86,005 votes to 60,198, was marked by low polling, fake voting and the capturing of polling centres.[99] Khokon's supporters captured polling centres and voted in place of genuine voters. They chased and assaulted Munna and his supporters at the Narsingdi Government Girls School. In many centres, polling officers either colluded with or were intimidated by them. The police watched passively, bursting into action only to attack a procession taken out by Munna in the afternoon.

Referring to the day's events, the *Daily Star* observed in an editorial on 24 June 2005:

> We are simply shocked at the lack of tolerance by the ruling party sup-porters towards the opponent in a by-election which was not even contested by the main opposition party. They could easily have shown restraint. And specially since the issue of holding free and fair elections is a national concern, the by poll should have passed off without any incident.[100]

Remarkably, the Election Commission did little to prevent rigging at Narsingdi. Nor has it done anything about the second development, which tends to suggest that a massive nationwide attempt to rig the elections by manipulating the voters list is afoot. In a report sent to former Chief Election Commissioner M.A. Syed on 23 September 2003, the European Union had observed that the figure of 74.7 million registered voters was too high in a population of 130 million. Extra-polating census data, the report concluded that the maximum number of potential voters in Bangladesh would be 61.51 million.[101] The impli-cation is clear: over 13 million nonexistent voters are on the list and their votes will be cast by those preparing to rig the elections.

Reforming the poll process

Given such straws in the wind, it is important to ensure that the 2006 parliamentary elections are both free and fair. It is in this context that the Awami League-led 14-party combine's agenda for electoral and caretaker-government reform, announced on 15 July 2005, merit the most serious consideration. The agenda contains a five-point proposal for amending the provisions relating to the formation and jurisdiction of the caretaker government that will take over the country's government three months before the elections, a 15-point proposal to make the Election Commission truly independent, and an 11-point proposal for re-forming electoral laws and regulations.[102]

Briefly summarised, the chief adviser and advisers to the caretaker government should be appointed on the basis of a consensus arrived at after consultations with political parties. They should be members neither of any political party nor of any of its affiliated bodies. The caretaker government, which will conduct only routine work, should have jurisdiction over the Defence Ministry. During the tenure of the caretaker government the President should act in all matters of state on the advice of the Chief Adviser.[103]

The Chief Election Commissioner (CEC) and other Election Commissioners (ECs) should be appointed, and the number of the latter decided on, in consultation with political parties. The EC should have an independent secretariat with full control over its finances and staff including the right to appoint and dismiss. It should have full authority over the appointment of returning and presiding officers and control over the law-enforcement agencies during the elections. The government must arrange for adequate staff for the EC during the elections. Those conducting the elections will be under EC's authority for a specified period before and after the elections. During this period the EC should have the authority to take immediate disciplinary action against them and the government will have to implement its decisions. The EC should have full independence in announcing election schedules, framing election rules and postponing or cancelling elections.[104]

The proposals provide for the preparation of voter lists with complete transparency, introduction of voter identity cards and electronic voting machines, and the drawing up of new voter lists for residents of the CHT and for expatriate Bangladeshis. Religion-based politics should be banned, and also the use of religion in seeking votes. The EC should constitute all-party observer teams at the local level during the elections. At the national level, members of the election observer team should be appointed six months before the elections and their names supplied to contestant political parties and candidates with the announcement of the election schedule.[105]

All candidates will have to provide the EC with personal information like their academic qualifications, sources of income, and a description of their assets and liabilities. Black money hoarders, loan defaulters and those who had opposed the liberation war as well as war criminals should be barred from contesting the elections. The proposals include the banning of religion-based politics, electioneering at religious places including mosques, temples and churches.[106] The proposals are comprehensive and, if made into statute, will go a long way towards ensuring free and fair elections and keeping fundamentalists and criminals away from the seat of governance. Their adoption, however, will only be the beginning of the beginning. Much will depend on what happens during the elections and who comes to power afterwards. Reversing the Talibanization of Bangladesh will not be easy, considering the manner in which the Jamaat and other fundamentalist bodies have infiltrated the institutions of governance and strengthened themselves since 2001. And the effort will certainly fail if the next government is not much tougher than the Awami League was in combating the Jamaat and other fundamentalist bodies when it was in power between 1996 and 2001.

Notes

1. Stanley J. Tambiah, *Levelling Crowds: Ethnonationalist Conflicts and Collective Violence in South Asia* (New Delhi: Vistaar Publications, 1997), p. 292.
2. James Morrison, 'Terror in Bangladesh', *The Washington Times*, 26 August 2003. Morrison quotes her as saying this to correspondent Julia Duin.
3. Ershadul Huq (IANS), 'Bangla Rapists Prey on Minors, 70-year-olds', *The Pioneer* (New Delhi), 27 November 2001.
4. Ibid.
5. Morrison, 'Terror in Bangladesh'. Also see her prepared testimony before the United States Commission on International Religious Freedom, New York, 30 April 2004, at www.uscirf.gov/events/hearings/2004/april/04302004_wTest_Costa.html.
6. Ibid.
7. Ibid.
8. Ibid.
9. News report, 'Fresh Attack on Hindu Families in Natore', *The Daily Star* (Internet edition), 11 May 2002.
10. Low-intensity bombs are called 'crackers' in India and Bangladesh.
11. News report, 'Chinhito Santrashi Chakrer Sampatti Dakhaler Paintara: Gram Na Chhedey Gele Baghmarar Shankhalaghuder Prannasher Hoomki' (Manoeuvring to Capture Property: Death Threat to Minorities of Baghmara), *Prothom Alo* (Internet edition), 27 March 2005.
12. Abdullah Al-Mahmud, '11 Burnt to Death as Robbers Torch House', *The Daily Star* (Internet edition), 20 November 2003.
13. Saradindu Mukherji, *Subjects, Citizens and Refugees: Tragedy in the Chittagong Hill Tracts (1947–1998)* (New Delhi: Indian Centre for the Study of Forced Migration, 2000), p. 60.
14. The term Jumma, derived from the pattern of rotational agriculture, called *jum*, that they follow, connotes Chakmas, Chaks, Khiyangs, Bawms, Khumis, Lushais, Mros, Marmos, Pankhas, Tanchanyas and Tripuras—all indigenous people. The word *jum* is also spelt as *jhum*.
15. Ibid., p. 33.
16. Ibid., p. 34.
17. Ibid.
18. Ibid., p. 44.
19. Ibid., p. 58.

20. Kumar Sivasish Roy, 'Message from the Jumma People's Network, UK, for the European Human Rights Conference on Bangladesh', London, 17 June 2005.
21. Ibid.
22. South Asia Terrorism Portal, 'Bangladesh Assessment 2002'.
23. 'Khatme Nabuwat' means 'last Prophet'. According to Islam, Muhammad is the last Prophet. Literally translated, International Khatme Nabuwat Movement means 'International Last Prophet Movement', which really means a movement to assert that Muhammad was the last Prophet—a fact which, the IKNMB asserts, is denied by the Ahmadiyyas. The Ahmadiyyas reject the allegation.
24. Meer Mobashsher Ali, 'The Ahmadiyya Case: Extreme Violation of Human Rights', paper presented at the European Human Rights Conference on Bangladesh, London, 17 June 2005. Professor Ali is the Nayeb-e-Ameer or the Deputy National Ameer of the Ahmadiyya Muslim Community of Bangladesh.
25. News report, 'Anti-Ahmadiyya Campaign: Cops Help Bogra Bigots Pull Down Mosque Signboard', *The Daily Star* (Internet edition), 12 March 2005.
26. Ibid.
27. News report, '50 Hurt as Bigots Attack Ahmadiyyas at Satkhira: 10 Houses Looted', *The Daily Star* (Internet edition), 18 April 2005.
28. News report, 'Satkhira Tense: Bigots again Besieged Satkhira Mosque', *The Daily Star* (Internet edition), 19 April 2005.
29. News report, 'Khulna Bigots Threaten to Attack Ahmadiyyas: Six More Houses Attacked, 3 Beaten Up in Satkhira', *The Daily Star* (Internet edition), 20 April 2005.
30. Ibid.
31. News report, 'Ahmadiyyas in Satkhira Seek Govt Protection', *The Daily Star* (Internet edition), 11 April 2005.
32. Ibid.
33. News report, 'Ahmadiyyas Renew Demand for Protection', *The Daily Star* (Internet edition), 13 April 2005.
34. Ibid.
35. News report, 'Ban on Ahmadiyya Books: Dhaka's Tradition as a Moderate Muslim State Going Off Track', *The Daily Star* (Internet edition), 20 May 2004.
36. Ibid.
37. News report, 'Strong Watch Keeps Bigots at Bay: Six EU Members Visit Ahmadiyya Mosque', *The Daily Star* (Internet edition), 6 November 2004.
38. Shah Ahmed Reza, 'Jamaat-e-Islamir Chhechallish Bachhar' (Forty-six Years of Jamaat-e-Islami), in Shahriar Kabir (ed.), *Ekattorer Ghatak Jamaat-e-Islamir Ateet or Bartaman* (Past and Present of the Jamaat-e-Islami, the Executioners of Seventy-one), 2nd ed. (Dhaka: Muktijuddha Chetana Bikash Kendra, 1992), pp. 48–49.
39. Ibid., p. 49.
40. Ibid., pp. 49–50.
41. Bangladesh's national mosque.
42. News report, 'Anti-Ahmadiyya zealots threaten tough action', *The Daily Star* (Internet edition), 25 December 2004.
43. News report, 'Anti-Ahmadiyya Outfit Threatens Newspapers with Dire Consequences', *The Daily Star* (Internet edition), 13 December 2003.

44. News report, 'Satkhira Ahmadiyyas under Renewed Threat: Zealots Ask SP to Rehang Removed Signboard within a Week', *The Daily Star* (Internet edition), 21 April 2005. 'Touhidi Janata' is the name of a fundamentalist Islamist organization in western Bangladesh.
45. The official English title of the movie in 'Clay Bird'. Literally, however, it should have been the 'Clay Mynah'—the mynah being a bird of the starling family.
46. Naeem Mohaiemen, 'Remove the Ban on Matir Moina', *The Daily Star* (Internet edition), 24 May 2002.
47. Quoted in ibid.
48. News report, 'Matir Moina Denied Certificate', *The Daily Star* (Internet edition), 15 May 2002.
49. Editorial, 'Govt Bans Matir Moina, Hopefully for the Moment: Are We Becoming What Some Quarters are Accusing Us of?', *The Daily Star* (Internet edition), 16 May 2002.
50. News report, 'Matir Moina denied certificate'.
51. News report, 'Chattogram Bishwabidyalaye Mulabadbirdodhi Chalachtrer Padarshani Hote Daye ni Shibir' (Shibir Did not Allow the Screening of an Anti-fundamentalist Film in Chittagong University', *Prothom Alo* (Internet edition), 27 March 2005.
52. News report, 'Chop on Channels: HBO, Star Movies, MTV, Channel V and AXN Among Satellite Channels Banned', *The Daily Star* (Internet edition), 20 May 2002.
53. News report (Associated Press), 'Bangla Arrests Playwright for "Offensive" Play', *The Asian Age* (New Delhi), 18 August 2002.
54. Haroon Habib, 'Extremists Protest Against Stage Play', *The Hindu* (New Delhi), 28 September 2002.
55. Editorial, 'A Truly Festive and Unifying Occasion: Let's Live Up to Its Message'. *The Daily Star* (Internet edition), 14 April 2003.
56. Ibid.
57. News report, 'CMP Restricts New Year's Celebrations', *The Daily Star* (Internet edition), 13 April 2005.
58. News report, 'Valentine Day Party at DU Foiled by Blast', *The Daily Star* (Internet edition), 15 February 2005.
59. News report, 'DU Students Continue Protest Against Bomb Attack', *The Daily Star* (Internet edition), 18 February 2005.
60. News report, 'Women's Soccer: Zealots Blast Govt for Failure to Protect Islamic Values', *The Daily Star* (Internet edition), 12 October 2004. Nur Hosain Nurani is also a leading light of the IKNMB, a fact which underlines the close links that exist among fundamentalist Islamist organizations in Bangladesh.
61. News report, 'Women fall victim to bigots', *The Daily Star* (Internet edition), 1 December 2004.
62. Ibid.
63. Ekramul Huq Bulbul and Masud Milad, 'Chattagram Bishwabidyalay Shikshak Niyoge Jamaatikaran' (Jamaatification in the Appointment of Teachers in Chittagong University), *The Daily Star* (Internet edition), 12 August 2004.
64. Ibid.
65. Ibid.

66. News report, 'RU Syndicate May Okay Controversial Recruitment Today', *The Daily Star* (Internet edition), 25 December 2005.
67. Ibid.
68. Rejaul Karim Byron and Shameem Mahmud, 'Madrasas Mushroom with State Favour', *The Daily Star* (Internet edition), 4 August 2005.
69. Ibid.
70. Ibid.
71. Erich Fromm, *Fear of Freedom* (London: Routledge & Kegan Paul, 1960), p. 19.
72. Ibid., p. 23.
73. Ibid., p. 120.
74. Ibid., p. 134.
75. Ibid., p. 135.
76. Ibid., p. 136.
77. Erich Hoffer, *The True Believer: Thoughts on the Nature of Mass Movements* (New York: HarperPerennial, 1989), p. 41.
78. Ibid., pp. 12–13.
79. Ibid., p. 26.
80. News report, 'Youth Lost to Joblessness', *The Daily Star* (Internet edition), 13 October 2004.
81. Shariful Islam, '3 Years of Coalition Rule: Crime Takes on Terror Proportion', *The Daily Star* (Internet edition), 8 October 2004.
82. Ibid.
83. News report, 'Chronicle of Gunrunning', *The Daily Star* (Internet edition), 3 April 2004.
84. Ibid.
85. Ibid.
86. Ibid.
87. News report, 'Cop in Question to Probe Gun Running', *The Daily Star* (Internet edition), 5 April 2005.
88. Cited in news report, 'Jane's Report on Ctg. Ams Haul: Weapons Loaded at HK, S'pore, Headed for Indian Insurgents', *The Daily Star* (Internet edition), 28 February 2005.
89. Shahriar Kabir, 'Bangladeshe Aamra ebong Ora' (We and They in Bangladesh), *Ananya* 2005, p. 35.
90. News report, 'US Army's Pacific Chief Fears Int'l Terrorist Activities in Bangladesh'. *The Daily Star* (Internet edition), 18 April 2005.
91. News report, 'Most Corrupt for the Fourth Time', *The Daily Star* (Internet edition), 21 October 2004.
92. News report, 'Bribes Eat Away 3 per cent Sales of Business, Says World Bank Survey', *The Daily Star* (Internet edition), 30 September 2004.
93. News report, 'People Pay Tk 6,796 cr in Bribes a Year: TIB Finds the Sum Goes to 25 Service Sector Entities', *The Daily Star* (Internet edition), 21 April 2005.
94. News report, '42 Bangla Bhai Men Released From Jail', *The Daily Star* (Internet edition), 8 April 2005.
95. News report, '12 Militants Accused of Natore Jatra Blast Case', *The Daily Star* (Internet edition), 5 August 2005.
96. Shariful Islam, '3 Years of Coalition Rule'.

97. News report, 'Bangladesh Most Violent for Newsmen in Asia: CPJ Urges Govt to Probe Threats, Try Killers', *The Daily Star* (Internet edition), 6 March 2004.
98. Ibid.
99. Shameem Mahmud and Akbar Hossain, 'Low Turnout, Fake Voting Mark Narsingdi By-polls', *The Daily Star* (Internet edition), 23 June 2005.
100. Editorial, 'Narsingdi By-election: It Could Have Been Peaceful', *The Daily Star* (Internet edition), 24 June 2005.
101. News report, 'Unusual Voter Rise: EC Pays no Heed to EU Allegation', *The Daily Star* (Internet edition), 4 August 2005.
102. News report, 'AL, Allies Announce Agenda for Caretaker, EC Reforms', *The Daily Star* (Internet edition), 16 July 2005.
103. Ibid.
104. Ibid.
105. Ibid.
106. Ibid.

Postscript

I had pointed out in Chapter Eight that the 'BNP-led four-party coalition government cannot or will not act strongly against any fundamentalist Islamist organization. Such action as has been taken under international pressure—for example, the banning of the AHAB, JMB and JMJB and the arrest of Dr Galib and others—has been regularly undone by 'delays' in investigation leading to the granting of bail to the accused and/or sloppy investigation and evidence-gathering leading to acquittal.' We saw in the same chapter that 12 Islamist terrorists, arrested on the charge of attacking a *jatra* show and injuring three performers at Boraigram Upazila in Natore District on 15 January 2005, were released by the District Judge on 4 August 2005. This happened after the Investigating Officer submitted a petition saying that they should be discharged as the investigation showed they were not guilty! Further, as seen in Chapter Six, 42 JMJB cadres were released on bail from Rajshahi Central Jail on 7 April 2005. According to lawyers, delay by the police in conducting investigations had paved the way for their enlargement on bail. Needless to say, their release made their conviction most difficult. Many villagers who had fled after being tortured by JMJB cadres, had returned home after the latter's arrest. They started fleeing again, fearing reprisals for having talked to the press about their torture. One, therefore need hardly be surprised if they do not dare to give evidence and the cases against JMJB cadres cannot be proven.

Understandably, such developments boosted the morale of the bulk of the JMB, JMJB and AHAB supporters who had remained active and at large despite the government's ban, and enabled its leaders, including Bangla Bhai and Abdur Rahman, to plan a dramatic terrorist strike. The latter occurred on 17 August 2005, when a series of bomb explosions, initially estimated as numbering 459[1] but later close to 500, shook 63 of Bangladesh's 64 districts. The entire exercise lasted 30 minutes with the blasts going off everywhere between 11 and 11.30 A.M. in a frightening display of capability for carrying out synchronized nationwide strikes. In Dhaka, bombs exploded at 28 points including the Bangladesh Secretariat, Supreme Court complex, Prime Minister's Office, Dhaka Judges Court, Dhaka University, Dhaka Sheraton Hotel, Zia International Airport, airport rail station, a location close to the US Embassy, police headquarters at Ramna, Hotel Sonargaon, National Press Club, New Market and the Bangladesh Bank.[2]

A report by Anwar Ali from Rajshahi, carried in the *Daily Star* of 19 August, reinforces the view that the conspicuous lack of effective action in respect of incidents of terrorist violence had enabled their perpetrators to grow in strength. He states,

> After Wednesday's series of blasts rocking the whole country, senior officials of the law enforcement agencies observe that the operatives would not have built their stronghold had the previous incidents been dealt with seriously.
>
> Most militants were arrested only to be released on bail later to go ahead with their activities. In some cases, the incidents were not even investigated further.
>
> Militant lynchpin Asadullah Al Galib was arrested following certain pressure, but his followers JMB chief Abdur Rahman and Siddiqul Islam alias Bangla Bhai are still at large.[3]

The report added that intelligence agencies had recommended the banning of the RIHS.

Here it would be interesting to recall that not only do the JMJB, JMB and AHAB have similar views on Islam, they belong to a network of organizations that cooperate with one another and are closely linked to the Jamaat and the Shibir. Bangla Bhai was an activist of the Shibir when he was a student.[4] The organization's Shaekh, Maulana Abdur Rahman, was an activist of the Shibir when he was a student, and later of the Jamaat.[5]

Significantly, the *Daily Star* report mentioned above stated that the

> Jama'atul Jihad, Jama'atul Mujahideen, Ahle Hadith Andolon Bangladesh (Ahab), Ahle Hadith Jubo Shangha, Jagrata Muslim Janata Bangladesh (JMJB), Harkatul Jihad, Hizbut Tawhid, Tawhidi Janata, Islami Jubo Shangha, Islami Shangha, Al Falah A'am Unnayan Shanstha and Shahadat al Hiqma are believed to be missions of the Al Mujahideen.

According to Anwar Ali's report, Al Mujahideen remains an obscure entity. That Abdur Rahman, JMB's Shaekh, could be behind the attack was clearly suggested by another report by Zayadul Ahsan in the *Daily Star*, which stated that the confessions of those recently arrested, intelligence reports and information gathered until the publication of Ahsan's report (18 September 2005) indicated that most of the recent attacks on NGOs and cultural programmes, and the bomb blasts in Bangladesh, including those on August 17, were carried out under the leadership of Abdur Rahman. The newspaper's investigation revealed that most militant organizations across Bangladesh are somehow woven with the same thread by Rahman.[6]

This is shocking because, as early as 2003, decoded diaries of militants had revealed that Al Mujaheedin had training centres in as many as 57 districts with bases in AHAB mosques and madrasas. Ahsan's report quoted Khalilur Rahman, then an Inspector with Joypurhat Criminal Investigation Department (CID), as saying that they had 'well equipped training centres in all the northern and some southern districts' in which they operated.[7]

Yet, the government took no action against the centres and the organizations running them. The reason was clearly signals from the top. Speaking in the National Parliament on 15 March 2005, Begum Zia denied the presence of the Taliban and Al Qaeda in Bangladesh and dismissed reports about their activities as nothing but opposition propaganda aimed at causing a rift in the four-party alliance. She also said that Islamic organizations had long been working to spread the message of Islam and its ideology. 'They've also made an important contribution to maintaining social integrity and harmony. There's no allegation against them,' she added.[8]

Her remarks were almost identical to those by Industries Minister Matiur Rahman Nizami in Parliament and at a public meeting in Dhaka the same day. He claimed that neither the Jamaat nor any other known Islamic organization had links with militancy.[9]

No clearer message could be sent to police personnel in Bangladesh.

It soon became clear, however, that Nizami's words had nothing to do with the truth. On 16 September 2005, police, according to a report, arrested Maulana Shahidullah Faruk, JMB's section commander in Chapainawabganj, and Mohammad Tufan, an explosives expert from Shibganj in Chapainawabganj, with large quantities of bomb-manufacturing material and four firearms, from a house belonging to Jamaat men in Tanore in Rajshahi. The report described Faruk as a son of Maulana Meserullah Nasir Uddin, a Jamaat activist and madrasa teacher, and his elder brother Obaidullah as the treasurer of the Tanore Upazila unit of the Jamaat.[10]

In a press release on 17 September, the Jamaat said that Maulana Nasir Uddin was neither a leader nor an activist of the party but his son Obaidullah was Vice-President of its Tanore Upazila unit. It also claimed it had no links with Shahidullah Faruk, JMB's section commander in Chapainawabganj. Obaidullah, it further stated, lived separately from his father and his brother Faruk. The press release, however, admitted that the house from which firearms and bomb-making materials were recovered, was Maulana Nasir Uddin's. It reiterated the claim, made on numerous occasions earlier, that the Jamaat was not involved in any militant or violent activity. In another press release, the Shibir also claimed it had no link to Shahidullah Faruk and Tufan.[11]

Unfortunately for the Jamaat, indications of its links with the JMB kept coming up. Investigations brought to light the fact that Abdullah Ibn Fazal, father of the JMB's Shaekh, Abdur Rahman, was among those who had become notorious for collaborating with the Pakistani army during the liberation war. As a student, Abdur Rahman had joined the Islami Chhatra Shangha (now Shibir) and was sent to Saudi Arabia at the party's expense for higher education at Madina University.[12] On completion of his studies, Abdur Rahman returned home and after trying his hand at various things, gravitated towards interpretation and translation as his main occupation. This brought him into close contact with many diplomatic representatives from Middle Eastern countries. It would appear that these links as well as his background led him to Afghanistan, where he was inducted into the *jihadi* movement. After completing his training, he returned to Bangladesh and formed the JMB.[13]

There have been other more interesting developments. Referring to the Jamaat's report on its meeting on the theme 'Evaluation and Training', I had written in Chapter Five that it stated, in the section under the heading 'Fund Supply' that, apart from Islami Bank, Rabeta Al-Islami (an important Saudi-based charity) and Al-Arafa Bank, money would be distributed through Maulana A.K.M. Yusuf.[14] A report in the *Daily Star* of 4 September 2005 quoted a person investigating the 17 August blasts as saying that a huge sum of money was spent on buying explosives for these and that it was drawn from a personal account with a Chittagong branch of Islami Bank. One Mohammad, the JMB's Chittagong region chief, collected the money after it was sent from the organization's Dhaka Chapter to the Agrabad branch of Islami Bank, he said. Mohammad (believed to be a pseudonym), a student of the Islamic studies department at Dhaka University, also functions as the treasurer of an Ahle Hadith mosque in the port city. He and some other JMB activists had procured a large quantity of powdered explosives from Chittagong and sent these to Dhaka in several lots in between May and August, the investigator said, requesting anonymity.[15]

On 23 August 2005, a former Islamic Foundation director, Maulana Fariduddin Masud, who was detained for suspected links with the 17 August blasts, accused the Jamaat's Ameer, Bangladesh's Industries Minister Motiur Rahman Nizami, of involvement in the explosions. 'Vital clues to the blasts will come out if Nizami is grilled,' Masud said, when police produced him before a Dhaka court on 23 August amid tight security and petitioned for him to be taken on a seven-day remand. The Court of the Chief Metropolitan Magistrate, Dhaka, placed him on a five-day remand.[16]

The Jamaat has denied Masud's statement. But even if Masud is wrong, the fact remains that a number of militants arrested over time have revealed that they either belonged to the Jamaat or its various wings, or were past members. The most startling suspected Jamaat–militant link was unearthed at Joypurhat in August 2003. After an overnight gunfight, police arrested 39 suspected militants, 29 of whom confessed they were activists of the Shibir and that the latter had assigned them to work for JMB. Jamaat activist Montejar, whose residence the militants were using as a training camp, escaped arrest. Police found a list of Jamaat–Shibir activists and different Jamaat publications in his house. Though the Jamaat said it had expelled Montejar two years prior to the incident, police found from Montejar's diary that he had recently applied to become a Rukon, a mid-level position in the Jamaat. Police also recovered a letter to Montejar from the district Ameer of Jamaat. They seized some leaflets, letters and receipts of subscriptions to the JMB's Jihad Fund. A significant number of persons who paid subscription to the fund were Jamaat members.[17]

Not only were all those arrested in August 2003 released shortly thereafter, no action was taken on a report by the Special Branch (SB) of the police, submitted in October 2003, that expressed serious apprehension over the progress being made by religious extremists. The report went so far as to say that they might even challenge the country's sovereignty at one stage, and that the HUJIB, Islami Biplobi Parishad,

Hijbut Tahrir, Jama'atul Mujahideen, Hijbut Tawhid and Shahadat al Hiqma were involved in militancy and were trying to turn Bangladesh into a theocratic state.[18] No action was taken on its recommendation that these outfits be banned. As has been seen, it was only on 23 February 2005, the day foreign donors met in Washington, DC, to discuss aid to Bangladesh in the context of its horrendous human rights record and the growing threat posed by fundamentalist Islamist organizations to its society and polity, that the JMJB, JMB and AHAB were banned.

One need not be surprised that the continued disregarding of their advice would discourage intelligence agencies from following the activities of the Islamist fundamentalists closely and that this would affect the collection of intelligence regarding the latter. Poor intelligence was a major factor in the failure to prevent the blasts of 17 August. The *Daily Star* observed in an editorial, 'Intelligence failure of epic proportions', on 19 August, that

> The less said about the counter intelligence capability of the relevant intelligence agencies the better. But we will be remiss if the entire responsibility of the failure was laid at the doors of the agencies. We feel that much of the blame must lie squarely on the government for lack of proper direction and also on the shoulders of those responsible for tasking and utilizing our intelligence assets. Whatever is the capability of these agencies, in most cases their efforts are misutilized, mostly on political purpose. Instead of performing the counter intelligence work, they are utilized either to snoop on the political opponents or cover someone who has fallen foul of the administration and needs to be sorted out. It is thus no wonder that the real anti-state elements and the evildoers are left free to go about their business of endangering the lives of the citizens.[19]

In a searing indictment, the editorial added, 'The intelligence and the security apparatus have totally failed to protect the people and the government of the day; the responsibility for this failure must fall squarely on those at the helm of affairs.' It is typical of the politicization of the intelligence agencies that had taken place that, although leaflets in Bangla and Arabic bearing the imprimatur of the JMB and declaring that it was 'time to implement Islamic law in Bangladesh' and that there was 'no future with man-made law'[20] had been found, they hesitated for a long time before holding the organization responsible. In fact, some intelligence officers had even tried to insinuate that it was the Awami League that had engineered the blasts to defame the ruling four-party coalition.[21] This, no doubt, reflected the BNP's habit of blaming every explosion on 'a certain quarter', which wanted to destroy Bangladesh's image abroad.

There is no indication that the BNP government will mend its ways. Rather, things point in the other direction. Prime Minister Khaleda Zia told Bangladesh's National Parliament on 8 September 2005 that the BNP had allied only with those religion-based parties that believed in democracy and the constitution.[22] Needless to say, the two allies are the Jamaat and the IOJ and Begum Zia's statement was tantamount to endorsing what both parties have been saying about themselves.

Her statement could not but have a powerful influence on the administration's attitude to the Jamaat and the IOJ. On 14 September, the police arrested two Shibir leaders from Sadallahpur, Gaibandha District, Mahmudul Islam and Ershadul Haque, aged around 25–26, from the premises of Bangladesh's National Parliament, with CDs and books on jihad. Jamaat leaders lobbied intensely for their release and pressured the police not to publicize the incident. The Jamaat MP, Abdul Aziz, whom the two said they had come to meet, spoke to the Speaker, Jamiruddin Sircar, who also heard from other Jamaat MPs. Aziz even went to the Tejgaon police station to get the two released. Under pressure, the police not only stopped interrogating them but produced them in court the next morning under Section 54 CrPc without pressing any charge against them. The court released them on bail.[23]

The cavalier manner in which the whole matter was treated makes one wonder whether it at all struck the top leaders of the BNP-led coalition government that the two might have come to reconnoitre the Parliament premises for a terrorist strike. And this after the events of 21 August 2004 and 17 August 2005, to say nothing of the other terrorist outrages in Bangladesh! In another, and perhaps more shocking case, the police, on 23 September 2005, released Abdul Hakim Gazi, a school teacher they had arrested the previous night from his house, as the alleged mastermind behind the August 17 blasts in Khulna, on condition that he would help them arrest six local bombers.[24] The latter, JMB activists all, had reportedly manufactured around 60 bombs, carried out blasts in Khulna and gone into hiding. Besides, the police seized some paper cartons, cotton yarn, electric wire, power explosives, jagged fragments of marble and JMB booklets from Gazi's house. Though a police officer claimed that Hakim had been asked not to leave his house without permission and was told that he would be under constant legal watch and could be taken into custody at any time, the fact remains that it should not have been necessary to release him for his help in capturing those who had actually set off the blasts. The bombers could have been arrested on the basis of the information provided by him.

The consequences are likely to be serious. The continuing ban and crackdown on them notwithstanding, JMB terrorists have started reorganizing themselves in northern districts of Bangladesh, holding secret meetings in remote *char* areas[25] and in the houses of their patrons, to plan future attacks. According to intelligence agencies, at least 100 trained JMB militants were holding regular meetings in several remote villages under Gangachhara Upazila of Rangpur. Not only that, terrorist leaders had chosen some 200 students from different madrasas, colleges and universities across the country to train them in 'warfare' and form suicide squads with them.[26]

Anwar Ali, the *Daily Star*'s Staff Correspondent in Rajshahi, quoted a JMB source as saying that in the previous three months (the report was published on 31 August 2005) several thousand students were divided into 130 groups and tested at three-to-ten–day training camps to select 200 'skilled militants' in the districts. The chosen students would be divided into 10 groups, which 20 skilled militants with war-fare experience abroad will train, in 'open and free frontier areas' of Satkhira, Chittagong and Cox's Bazar, the source said. Of the 200, 50 students were from the Rajshahi, Natore, Naogaon, Chapainawabganj and Bogra Districts. Five experts from Chapainawabganj, Gaibandha, Jamalpur, Satkhira and Cox's Bazar selected them at secret training camps, the JMB source said, seeking anonymity. Fifty 'smart students' being trained in guerrilla warfare were likely to be picked up, in five groups, for training abroad.[27]

The BNP will have a major problem on its hands if suicide bombings begin in Bangladesh. Even otherwise, it may have trouble as the 2006 parliamentary elections approach. According to a report, the Jamaat was trying to get the four-party coalition to give it as many as 100 seats to contest in the elections. Its scarcely concealed involvement in the 17 August bomb blasts was meant to demonstrate its capacity to unleash terrorist violence, and as a message to the BNP that the rejection of its request and/or termination of its alliance with the Jamaat would mean serious trouble. The serial blasts also represented an attempt to persuade other Islamist parties to join ranks with it if they did not want trouble.[28]

Meanwhile, the allegation that the BNP-led coalition is planning to rig the 2006 elections on a massive scale is being widely levelled at the time of writing. The *Daily Star* of 21 September 2005 reported Begum

Zia's Foreign Affairs Advisor, Reaz Rahman, telling diplomatic correspondents in Dhaka on 19 September that she had assured the Bush administration that the next general elections in Bangladesh would be free and fair and that foreign observers would be allowed to monitor the polls. The assurance was given when the US Secretary of State Condoleezza Rice met Begum Zia in New York on September 15. The outcome of the meeting, Rahman said, was most positive.[29]

On the very same day (21 September), the *Daily Star* carried another report, according to which, of the 328 persons recruited through the Public Service Commission to the posts of Upazila Election Officers ahead of the next parliamentary elections, at least 150 were from a list of Chhatra Dal leaders of different universities and colleges. The report quoted 'sources' as saying that there might be many more persons loyal to the government in the controversial appointments. Top Chhatra Dal leaders had sent the names to Hawa Bhavan, Bangladesh's 'alternative source of power', presided over by Begum Zia's son Tarique Rahman.[30] Given the important role these officers will play in the elections, Begum Zia can hardly blame the Awami League and other opposition parties for believing that these appointments are part of a comprehensive plot to rig the polls. The Awami League has already made it clear that it will not participate in the elections if the reforms in the electoral system the opposition parties have demanded are not implemented. It is now clear that if the elections are to be free and fair, changes are required not only in the system but also in the personnel already appointed. And the elections would be reduced to a farce if these changes are not effected and the Awami League and allied parties boycott them.

Notes

1. News report, '459 Blasts in 63 Districts in 30 Minutes: 2 Killed, 100 Hurt, All Explosives were Time Bombs, Jamaatul Mujaheedin Leaflets Found', *The Daily Star* (Internet edition), 18 August 2005.
2. Ibid.
3. Anwar Ali, 'Jamaatul Tentacles Spread in Five and a Half Years: Law Enforcers' Laid Back Attitude Made It Possible', *The Daily Star* (Internet edition), 19 August 2005.
4. Ibid.
5. Julfikar Ali Manik, 'JMJB Mentor Rahman Evades Probing Eyes'.
6. Zayadul Ahsan, 'Inside Militant Groups–7: Abdur Rahman Spawned All', *The Daily Star* (Internet edition), 28 August 2005.

7. Ibid.
8. News report, 'Donors Asked not to Interfere, Says PM in JS, Denies Islamist Militancy', *The Daily Star* (Internet edition), 16 March 2005.
9. News report, 'Blasts Prove Govt Denials Wrong', *The Daily Star* (Internet edition), 18 August 2005.
10. News report, 'Bomb-making Materials Seized from Jamaat Man's House: 2 JMJB Men Held in Rajshahi with Detonators, Gun, Chemicals', *The Daily Star* (Internet edition), 17 September 2005.
11. News report, 'Tanore Militant Den: Nasir's Son a Jamaat Man, Admits Party', *The Daily Star* (Internet edition), 18 September 2005.
12. Ahsan, 'Inside Militant Groups–7'.
13. Ibid.
14. Mentioned in the report as Jamaat's Naib-e-Ameer.
15. Shariful Islam, 'August 17 Serial Blasts: Huge Sums Drawn from Ctg bank for Buying Explosives', *The Daily Star* (Internet edition), 4 September 2005.
16. News report, 'Serial Bombing: Arrested Moulana Points Finger at Nizami: Fund Sources of Militants being Probed', *The Daily Star* (Internet edition), 24 August 2005.
17. Zayadul Ahsan, 'Inside the Militant Groups–5: Militants Claim Jamaat Background', *The Daily Star* (Internet edition), 25 August 2005. An earlier news report, 'Cops, Militants, Trade Fire in Joypurhat, 19 Held', in *The Daily Star* (Internet edition) of 16 August 2003, put the number of those arrested at 19.
18. Zayadul Ahsan, 'Inside the Militant Groups–6: Agency Advice on Ban on Them Ignored Since 2003', *The Daily Star* (Internet edition), 26 August 2005.
19. Editorial, 'Intelligence Failure of Epic Proportions: The Government Must Take the Entire Blame', *The Daily Star* (Internet edition), 19 August 2005.
20. News report, '459 Blasts in 63 Districts in 30 Minutes'.
21. News report, 'Agencies Admit Failure', *The Daily Star* (Internet edition), 18 August 2005.
22. News report, 'Nucleus of Anti-State Plot to be Unearthed: Bombings Acts of Those Who Want to Portray the Country as Extremist One, PM tells JS', *The Daily Star* (Internet edition), 9 September 2005.
23. News report, '2 Shibir Men Held at JS, Freed after "Lobbying": Cops Tightlipped about the Contents of the Books, CDs Seized from Them', *The Daily Star* (Internet edition), 16 September 2005.
24. News report, 'Khulna "Mastermind" Freed on Farcical Condition', *The Daily Star* (Internet edition), 25 September 2005.
25. A *char* is a stretch of land formed by sand deposits arising from a river bed.
26. News report, 'JMB Regrouping in Rajshahi, Rangpur: Holds Meetings in Char Areas of Teesta', *The Daily Star* (Internet edition), 31 August 2005.
27. Ibid.
28. Zayadul Ahsan, 'Jamaat Link to Militants Becomes Evident', *The Daily Star* (Internet edition), 22 September 2005.
29. News report, 'Khaleda Assures the US of Fair Polls Ahead', *The Daily Star* (Internet edition), 21 September 2005.
30. Hasan Jahid Tusher, 'Politicisation of EC: 150 JCD Men Made Election Officials', *The Daily Star* (Internet edition), 21 September 2005.

Index

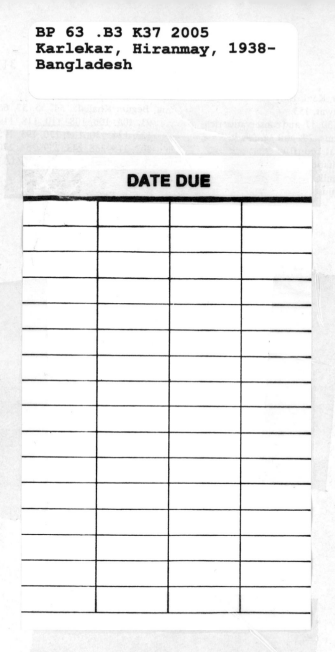

DATE DUE